FIRST EDITION

Handwritten Notes

ETHICS, INTEGRITY & APTITUDE (GS-4)

ARIHANT PUBLICATIONS (INDIA) LIMITED

卐 **Administrative & Production Offices**

Regd. Office

'Ramchhaya' 4577/15, Agarwal Road, Darya Ganj, New Delhi -110002
Tele: 011- 47630600, 43518550

卐 **Head Office**

Kalindi, TP Nagar, Meerut (UP) - 250002
Tel: 0121-7156203, 7156204

卐 **Sales & Support Offices**

Agra, Ahmedabad, Bengaluru, Bareilly, Chennai, Delhi, Guwahati, Hyderabad, Jaipur, Jhansi, Kolkata, Lucknow, Nagpur & Pune.

卐 **PRICE** ₹400.00

PO No. : TXT-59-T063888-03-25

Published by Arihant Publications (India) Ltd.

For further information about the books published by Arihant, log on to www.arihantbooks.com or e-mail at info@arihantbooks.com

Follow us on    

Few Words
to the Budding UPSC Aspirants

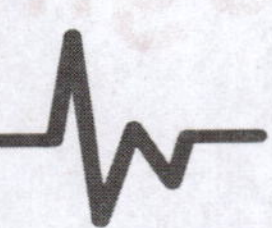

The UPSC Mains Exam is the most crucial stage on your path to becoming a civil servant. But conquering it isn't a walk in the park - it's a strategic game. You need the right arsenal (effective study materials) and honed tactics (answer writing skills) to succeed. **PULSE Mains Series** equips you for every challenge, a one-stop solution for your Mains preparation.

Forget about sifting through mountains of irrelevant information. **PULSE Mains books** are meticulously organized, packed with dynamic analysis and updated with the latest developments.

These books provide only exam-relevant content and removing the cluttered content available in the market, thus bringing time-optimised notes for the students.

Following are the salient features of Pulse Mains books:

- **Comprehensive and Exam-oriented content** covering all relevant topics in depth.
- **Content Enrichment with the help of current examples,** data & facts, case studies and supreme court judgements.
- **Innovative exam-ready frameworks** (PESTEL, Stakeholder, Life-cycle, etc) to meet evolving answer writing demands.
- **Visually appealing presentation by incorporating flowcharts,** timelines, mindmaps, hand-drawn diagrams, tables and maps.
- **Integration of PYQs** at the end of each chapter to align the content with the recent exam trends.
- **Easy for multiple revision of the syllabus** which can help in improving the Mains score.

On behalf of MentorsHut, I would like to express our deepest gratitude to each and every student for placing your trust in Pulse Books. **Thanks to your incredible support, Pulse Books have become best-sellers!**

We are also incredibly thankful to **Arihant Publications** for partnering with us and providing the opportunity to develop the PULSE series for the UPSC Mains examination.

The creation of these masterpiece Mains books wouldn't have been possible without the tireless, combined efforts of the entire MentorsHut family, who dedicated thousands of hours to the project. Our sincere thanks go to **Shadab Ahmad, Avinish Kumar, Ashutosh Bansal, CA Shalini Wadhwani, Vishal Singh, Tarun Sahu and Vishal Anand for their exceptional contributions.** Their creativity in content presentation, clear handwriting and unwavering support for each other were instrumental in this success.

I also want to express my **deepest gratitude to my daughter, Prisha Mangtani.** While I poured my heart into these books, I know the sacrifices this meant for you. You are truly special!

We at MentorsHut are dedicated to continuous improvement. While we believe Pulse Books represent our best effort, we recognize the possibility of human error. We welcome any suggestions for improvement to the content. Please feel free to share your thoughts at info@mentorshut.com

Amit Mangtani
Founder, MentorsHut
Economics Faculty

Let's Begin Our Journey

Part-A **Ethics Theory**

Part-B Applied Ethics and Case Studies

01 Ethics and Morality

66

"An unexamined life is not Worth living"
— Socrates

"Ethics is knowing the difference between what you have a right to do and what is right to do"
— Potter Stewart

"In law a man is guilty when he violates the rights of others. In ethics he is guilty if he only thinks of doing so"
— Immanuel Kant

"Ethics is the activity of man directed to secure the inner perfection of his own personality."
— Albert Schweitzer.

Mahatma Gandhi

"The best way to find yourself is to lose yourself in the service of others"

"Happiness is when what you think, what you say, and what you do are in harmony"

"Everyone thinks of changing the world, but no one thinks of changing himself".
— Leo Tolstoy

"The great secret of true success, of true happiness, is this: the man or woman who asks for no return, the perfectly unselfish person, is the most successful."
— Swami Vivekananda.

ETHICS

- The term "ethics" originates from the ancient Greek word "ethos" which translates to "Custom", "Character" or "disposition"
- It is also referred to as moral philosophy due to its focus on defining what constitutes "right conduct" and a "good life".
- Ethics studies human behaviour and actions aiming to identify the underlying moral principles that guide them.
- It grapples with fundamental questions such as:
  - **Right and Wrong**: What actions are considered right or wrong in specific situations?
  - **Moral Conduct**: How should people behave ethically?
  - **Rights and Responsibilities**: What are our fundamental rights and what responsibilities do we hold towards others and society?
  - **The Good life**: What constitutes a good life and how can we achieve it?

ETHICS IS ABOUT
- Principles of Right Conduct
- Moral Values
- Human behaviour
- Philosophy of Ideal/Good life
- Moral choices
- Rules and Regulations

Essence of Ethics

- Normative: Ethics is concerned with establishing norms or standards of behaviour. It seeks to determine what actions or behaviours are right or wrong, good or bad.
- Rational: Ethics encourages us to think critically about situations, consider the potential consequences of our actions and weigh them against our moral principles.
- Nature and Nurture: Ethics are shaped by both a person's genetic makeup (nature) and their environment (nurture)
- Social cultivation: Ethics are developed within Society through Social codes of conduct.
- Variability across cultures: Ethical standards can differ across cultures and ethnicities.
- Universal or relative: Some ethical principles like non-violence are universal while others like adultery laws can be culturally relative.
  - Ethics can be specific to a profession like medical ethics.

👉 Dynamic: Ethics is not a static state; it is a journey of continuous learning and growth which is influenced by changes in society, technology and cultures and must remain flexible and adaptable to remain relevant.

👉 Character Development: Ethics is not just about making isolated decisions; it is about cultivating a moral character.

👉 Accountability: Ethics involves a sense of responsibility beyond following external rules. **Example**: Addressing corruption requires not just legal compliance, but also honesty, integrity, courage to take tough decisions, etc.

Example

- Recent #MeToo movement and Black Lives Matter movement, highlights the importance of ethical values in addressing societal values.

Beliefs vs Values vs Principles vs Morals

Beliefs
- These are convictions we hold true often based on personal experiences, upbringing or cultural influences.
- Can range from strong convictions to tentative hunches. They can change based on new evidence or experiences.
- Eg- "I believe in aliens"; "I believe hard work is rewarded"

Values
- Values denote preference- good or bad, that we consider as important and desirable and has a major influence on person's behaviour and attitude.
- Values tend to be more stable than beliefs and form the bedrock of our ethical compass.
- Eg- Honesty, fairness, compassion, creativity, security.

Morals
- Desired values and beliefs about what is right and wrong, acceptable or unacceptable in a particular situation.
- It is a personal compass often based on cultural norms, religious teachings or personal values.

Eg- Stealing is wrong, helping others is good, lying is wrong

Principles
- These are moral values that are universal in nature regardless of culture or situation unlike values, beliefs and morals which vary from individual to individual.
- Principles are broader than morals and serve as a foundation for ethical decision-making.

Eg- Justice, fairness, respect for human rights.

DETERMINANTS OF ETHICS

- These are the factors that shape the ethical standards and behaviour of the people.
- These determinants are the basis on which people decide what is right or wrong.

Moral Development | Values and Beliefs | Character Traits | Culture | Family and Upbringing | Social groups and Peers | Education | Religion | Constitution and Law | Codes of Conduct | Leadership | Philosophies

1. Internal Compass

- **Moral Development**: Our evolving understanding of right or wrong. Ex - Purdah System, slavery, untouchability was once considered ethical practice but not in the present times.
- **Values and Beliefs**: Personal principle shaped by upbringing, religion and experiences. Ex - Ashoka adopted the policy of Dhamma after his experience in Kalinga war.
- **Character Traits**: Courage, empathy, justice etc, influencing ethical behaviour. Ex - Malala Yousafzai, demonstrated immense courage and perseverence in her fight for girls' right to education, even after being shot by Taliban.

2. Socio-Cultural influences

- **Culture**: Shared norms and expectations defining ethical behaviour within a Society. Ex - Western cultures tend to be more individualistic, while Indian culture emphasizes collectivism and tolerance.
- **Family and upbringing**: Values instil during our formative years.
- **Social groups and Peers**: Ex - Athletes boycotts of sporting events to protest social injustices highlight the power of social groups to influence ethical behaviour and push for change.

3. External Frameworks

- **Education**: Fostering critical thinking and ethical reasoning skills. Ex - Rise of bioethics as a field of study demonstrates the growing importance of ethical considerations in scientific advancements.

- **Religion**: Moral framework and ethical guidelines provided by religious teachings. Ex- Concept of Karma (Hinduism), Four noble Truths and Middle Path (Buddhism), Ahimsa (Jainism), Brotherhood and Langar (Sikhism), Zakat - Charity and generosity (Islam).
  Ex- Epics like Ramayana and Mahabharata provide guidance on ethical conduct and the importance of following Dharma.
- **Constitution and law**: Establish the baseline for ethical conduct and outline the consequences of unethical actions.
  Ex- Indian Constitution promotes values like justice, democracy, equality, fraternity etc.
- **Professional codes of conduct**: Ethical guidelines specific to different professions. Ex- The hippocratic oath for doctor emphasizes ethical obligations like patient confidentiality and the "do no harm" principle.

4. Other Determinants

- **Leadership**: Leaders can set ethical standards through their actions and pronouncements. India's democratic, liberal, and secular traditions have been shaped by its leaders. Ex- Lal Bahadur Shastri resignation taking a moral responsibility for the train accidents in 1956.
- **Philosophical Framework**: Different philosophical schools propose diverse ethical frameworks. Ex- Utilitarianism emphasizes maximising overall well-being, while deontology focuses on following moral duties.

Stages of Moral Development

- Kohlberg's theory proposes that individuals progress through six stages of moral development, which can be grouped into three levels.
- He suggested that people move through these stages in a fixed order and that moral understanding is linked to cognitive development.

1. Pre-Conventional Level:

- Focused on self interest and personal gain. The two stages within this level are:
  - **Stage 1**: Obedience and avoidance of punishment
  - **Stage 2**: Instrumental purpose and exchange - motivated by self-interest and may make decisions based on what they can gain for themselves.

2. Conventional Level:

- This level of moral development is focused on societal norms and expectations. The two stages within this level are
- Stage 3: Interpersonal relationship and conformity to maintain social norms and expectations.
- Stage 4: Maintenance of social order and adherence to laws and regulations.

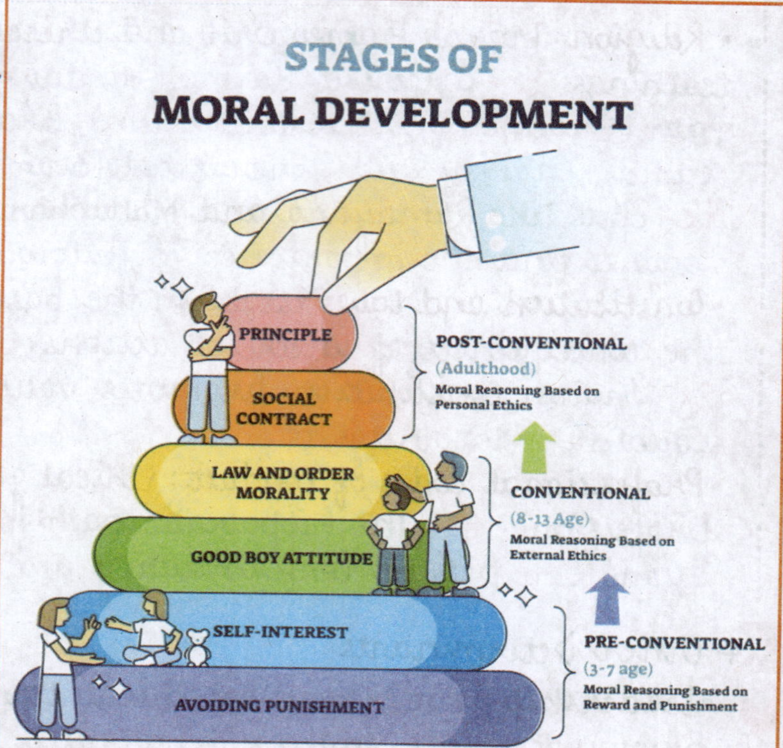

3. Post Conventional Level

This level of moral development is focused on universal ethical principles and values. The two stages within this level are:

Stage 5: Belief in social contract and the importance of individual rights
Stage 6: Universal principles and ethics such as justice, equality & human dignity.

Ethics and Law

*Please note - Detailed discussion of Ethics and Law is covered in chapter-9 (Sources of Ethical guidance)

- Ethics is a reasoned framework of moral principles, which is concerned with what is good for individuals and society. However law is structured system of rules and regulations enforced through certain authority to govern individual's behaviour, actions and social relations.
- Shared Goals: Both ethics and law aim to promote a just and well-functioned society. They establish guidelines for acceptable behaviour to maintain order and protect citizens' rights.
  - Law cannot address every ethical dilemma or social problem. It is just one tool among many for promoting a just and equitable society.

• Differences between Laws and Ethics

Aspect	Laws	Ethics
Origin	• Formal legislative Process	• Informal traditions, cultural norms or professional codes.
Focus	• Specific and enforceable laws	• Broader principle that guide decision-making.
Enforcement	• Enforced by government through sanctions and punishments	• Enforced through social pressures, professional consequences or an individual's conscience.
Relationship	• Laws often based on ethical principle (Not always)	• Ethics can inspire going beyond minimum legal requirements.

Laws Contrary to Ethics (laws might not encompass all ethical concerns): AFSPA, Sedition law, Anti-conversion laws, Rigid Censorship

Ethics not recognised by the laws as ethical principles might evolve faster than laws can adopt: New technologies such as deepfakes and facial recognition technology raising ethical issues of privacy concerns, women's rights. Marital rape raising ethical issues of women's consent, bodily autonomy etc

LAW — SIMILARITIES — ETHICS

Areas of Overlap (laws reinforcing the ethical principles)

Right to Equality (Article 14) = Fairness and equal treatment

Whistleblower Protection Act (2014) = Ethical conduct (Exposing corruption and wrongdoing within an organisation)

Right to Information Act (2005) = Transparency and Accountability.

Rights of Persons with Disabilities Act (2016) = Social Justice

Muslim women (Protection of Rights on Marriage) Act, 2019 = Women's Rights.

- Laws often codify core ethical principles, while ethical movements and concerns can inspire legal changes to create a more just society.
- It's important to note that legal frameworks might not always keep pace with evolving ethical considerations, but they serve as a crucial foundation for ethical behaviour within the country.
- Laws are the "rules of the road" enforced by the government, while ethics are the "moral compass" guiding our individual choices. They work together to create a framework for a just society.

Ethics and Religion

- Religion-based ethics, also known as divine command theory, is a moral philosophy that argues that God is the ultimate source of morality.
- Many religions have a moral code or set of ethical principles that guide their followers' behaviour.
  - Both religion and ethics generally value honesty as a core principle for building trust and fairness.
  - Religious teachings can influence a person's internal moral compass, shaping their sense of right and wrong.
- **Shared Goals**: Both ethics and religion aim to promote moral behaviour and a just society. They provide guidelines for right and wrong, encouraging compassion, honesty and respect for others.

- Difference between Ethics and Religion

Aspect	Religion	Ethics
Source of Morality	• Derives morality from a divine source (God or gods) or sacred texts. • Moral truths are considered absolute and divinely ordained	• Based on human reason, empathy, social norms or philosophical principles • Morality can be seen as evolving & adapting to changing context
Focus	• Emphasizes faith, rituals & spiritual connection to a higher power. Ethical principles might be embedded with religious teachings	• Focuses on principles for making good decisions and right actions, considering consequences and fairness.
Universality	Specific moral codes might be culturally specific and not universally applicable across all societies	Ideally strives for universal principles that can be applied in diverse contexts.

Conflict between Religion and Ethics

- **Interpretation:** Religious texts can be interpreted differently, leading to variations in how ethical principles are applied. Eg - Women are banned in certain temples during their menstrual cycle as differing religious interpretations consider this polluting the temple.
- **Secular vs. Religious Societies:** In Secular societies, ethical principles should apply to everyone, regardless of religion.

Ethics drawing values from Religion

Religion	Ethics draws values
Hinduism	Vasudhaiva Kutumbakam, Nishkam Karma, Satyameva Jayate
Islam	Equality, brotherhood, Tawhid (Oneness of God)
Jainism	Satya, Ahimsa, Asteya, Aparigraha, Brahmacharya
Buddhism	The middle path, Four noble truths, Compassion

Ethical actions inspired by religious values: India's Good Samaritan law (2019) inspired by the values of Dharma (Hinduism) and Karuna (Buddhism)

- Abolition of Triple Talaq reflects Gender Equality.
- Vaccine Maitri reflects Vasudhaiva Kutumbakam (Hinduism)

RELIGION ETHICS

Religion interpretation contrary to Ethics

- Animal Sacrifices (Hinduism) vs Right to life
- Caste System and untouchability (Hinduism) vs Equality, Justice & fairness
- Polygamy (Islam) vs Women's respect and Gender Equality.
- Aggressive conversion through material benefits (Christianity) vs Freedom of Religion.
- Sallekhana (Jainism) vs Right to life.

Religion and ethics are not mutually exclusive For many, religious beliefs inform their ethical compass. However, Secular ethical frameworks basing morality on human reason, empathy etc. are crucial for ensuring a just & equitable Society where everyone, regardless of religion, can participate and thrive.

Ethics vs Morality

Morality	Ethics
• Internal Compass: Morals are not personal and reflect an individual's sense of right or wrong.	• Systematic Framework: Ethics is a broader concept that refers to a structured framework for making moral decisions.
• They are often shaped by upbringing, cultural norms and religious beliefs.	• It involves philosophical theories, reasoning and principles that guide ethical behaviour.
• Focus on Action: Primarily concerned with specific actions and whether they are good or bad.	• Focus on Reasoning: Ethics delves deeper, considering the consequences of actions, applying ethical principles, and justifying moral choices. It is more about "why" behind our moral judgement
• Subjectivity: Vary from person to person depending on their background and experiences.	• Objectivity (to a degree): Certain ethical principles like fairness, justice strive for a degree of objectivity and aim to be applicable across cultures.
• Ex- Some people might find it difficult to eat meat, while others don't.	• Ex- the principle of "do no harm" is a core ethical principle found in many cultures and ethical frameworks.
• Morality is viewed from an individual's point of view.	• Ethics are relative to the perspective of those around us.
• Any shift in morality is directly proportional to any differences in an individual's outlook.	• The ethics may shift depending on the circumstances and therefore, have some room for flexibility.
• Mainly affects the behaviour of individuals	• Mainly affects the behaviour of individuals and organisations.
• Can change over time with personal growth and experiences.	• Can change over time and cultures.

Example - A person may have a personal moral belief that lying is always wrong, but as a lawyer, they may have an ethical duty to defend their client's case and present evidence that may not be entirely truthful.

• A healthcare professional may have a moral belief in preserving the sanctity of a life, but may also have an ethical duty to alleviate suffering & provide comfort to the terminally ill.

Ethical but not Moral — ETHICS — MORAL — Moral but not ethical

Euthanasia is ethical as it respect individual autonomy; and it is immoral as it is against the sanctity of life

Sabarimala Temple Entry Ban; Capital Punishment; Genetic Engineering & cloning Regulations.

Both can be same

Helping a stranger in need, Telling the truth.

Ethics vs Values

Justice, Gender Equality

VALUES: Patriarchy, Child Labour, Caste based System, Honour Killing

ETHICS

- **Meaning**: Ethics refers to the guidelines for conduct, that addresses question about morality. Values is defined as the principles and ideals, that help them in making judgement of what is more important.
- **Focus**: Values define what's important, while ethics provide a framework for acting on those values.
- **Specificity**: Values are broader principles while ethics involve applying those principles to specific situations.
- **Source**: Values are more personal while ethics draw on philosophical reasoning and principles.

All ethics are Values, but not all Values are ethics

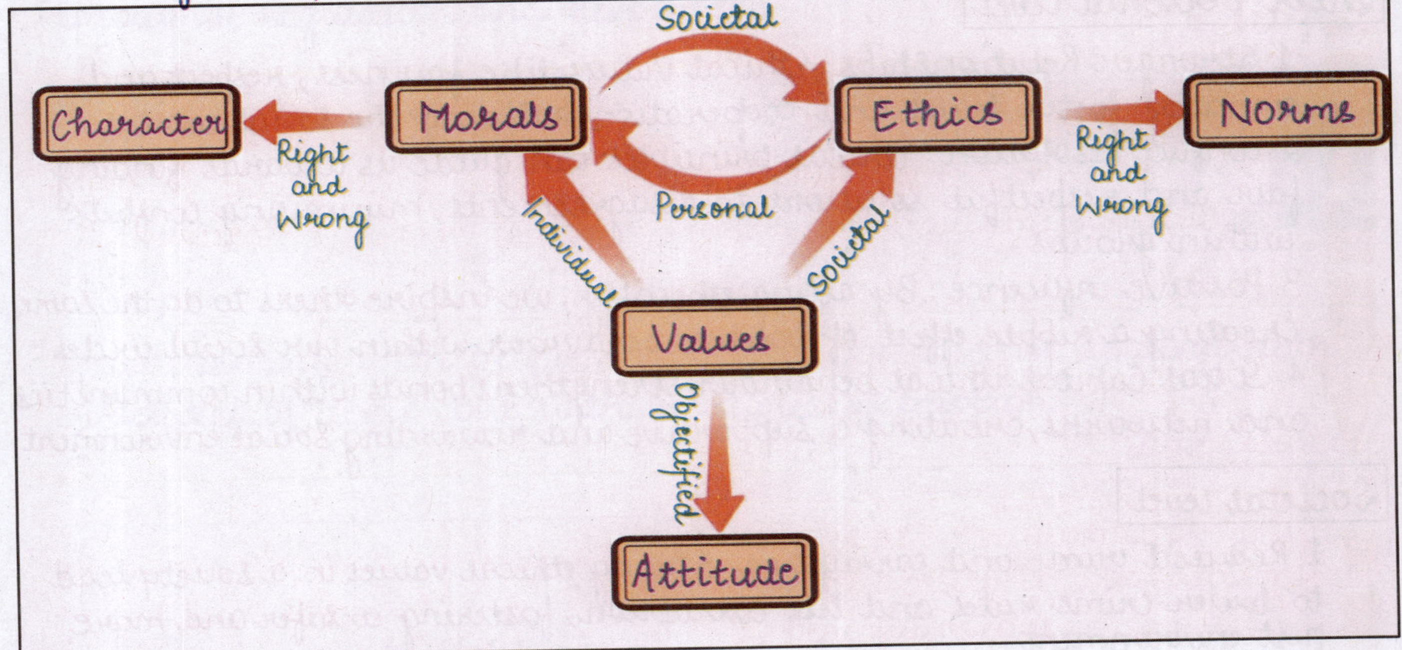

CONSEQUENCES OF ETHICS

- Refer to the outcomes of human actions guided by ethical principle. These Consequences play a role in determining how morally good or bad an action is judged to be.

Individual level

1. Trust and credibility: Ethical behaviour builds trust and a reputation for integrity especially in the current society plagued with widespread trust-deficit.
2. Greater happiness: Studies shows a correlation between ethical living and increased happiness and well-being. Such happiness leads to ultimate satisfaction.
3. Elevated sense of being beyond the lower order needs which leads to higher sense of fulfilment.
   - Absence of Ethics: Focused on the lower order needs such as wealth, fame, physical needs (Maslow's order of Hierarchy)
4. Practically beneficial and likely to achieve greater success in the long run. Eg- Kiran Bedi has held high positions in the government.
5. Empowered Decision making: A strong ethical framework allows for clear-headed and principled decision-making in ethical situations.
   - Absence of Ethics: Results into ambiguous and delayed decision making.

Inter-personal level

1. Stronger Relationships: Ethical values like fairness, respect and empathy foster trust and cooperation building the social capital.
2. Conflict Resolution: Ethical principles can guide us towards finding fair and respectful solutions to disagreements, minimising conflicts within groups.
3. Positive influence: By acting ethically, we inspire others to do the same, creating a ripple effect of positive behaviour within our social circles.
4. Social Capital: Ethical behaviour strengthens bonds within communities and networks, creating a supportive and rewarding social environment.

Societal level

1. Reduced crime and corruption: Strong ethical values in a society lead to lower crime rates and less corruption, fostering a safer and more just environment.

- **Absence of Ethics**: Results into higher crimes such as murder, gender based violence etc

2. Cooperation and Social harmony: Ethical behaviour promotes co-operation, trust and social harmony within communities

- **Absence of Ethics**: Results into communal riots, people's protest etc.

3. Greater equality and justice: A focus on ethics fosters a society that promotes equality, fairness and equal opportunities for all

- **Absence of Ethics**: leads to Untouchability, gender discrimination etc.

4. Environmental Sustainability: Ethical considerations encourage responsible environmental practices, leading to a more sustainable future.

- **Absence of Ethics**: Leads to overexploitation of natural resources, environmental degradation, global warming, etc.

5. Progressive societal change such as recognition of 3rd gender, decriminalisation of homosexuality, abrogation of adultery etc

- **Absence of Ethics**: Stagnation and regressive values hindering social progress.

6. Inclusive Development: Ethics ensure fair opportunity, fair distribution of resources, social mobility, etc.

- **Absence of Ethics**: Labour exploitation, increasing income inequalities etc.

Organisational Level

1. Strong Brand Reputation: Ethical practices foster brand loyalty and trust from consumers, investors, and partners. Eg- Tata Group of companies.
2. Positive employee relations: Ethical treatment of employees create a more positive, motivated and productive work environment.
3. Strong stakeholder relationships: Foster trust and positive relationships with all stakeholders, including customers, suppliers and communities.
4. Sustainability and long term growth: Promote responsible resource management and contribute to a company's long term success.
5. Attracting and retaining top talent: A culture of ethics attracts and retains high-calibre employees who value ethical conduct.

National Level

1. International respect and trust fostering positive diplomatic relations and attracting foreign investment.
2. Economic growth and prosperity: Ethical practices such as transparency, fair competition, corporate governance etc attracts higher investment and leads to a more stable and prosperous economy.

3. Global leadership: A nation that champions ethical behaviour on the world stage can inspire other countries to follow suit, contributing to a more just and peaceful global order.
4. Public Trust and participation: When citizens trust their government to act ethically, they are more likely to participate in civic life and hold leaders accountable.

Absence of Ethics

ABSENCE OF ETHICS

- Individual level: Selfishness, cheating, strained relationships, stress. Eg- Marital discord leading to divorce, neglecting work life balance etc.

- Political level: Criminalisation of politics, nepotism, power concentration, political instability. Eg- Buying of votes, political violence, communalisation, misuse of power, abuse of the constitution.

- International level: Border disputes, terrorism, human trafficking, environmental degradation, erosion of trust. Eg- Russia-Ukraine war, vaccine nationalism, trade wars, human rights violations.

- Societal level: Corruption, gender bias, commodification of life, moral decline, increased crime. Eg- Exploitation of women & marginalised groups, Social boycotts, stalking, drug abuse, poor law and order.

- Bureaucratic level: Conflict of interest, abuse of power, public neglect, poor implementation of policies. Eg- Bureaucratic delays, lack of due process of law.

- Environmental level: Deforestation, water pollution, wildlife exploitation, resource depletion. Eg- Poaching of endangered species, dam construction disrupting ecosystems.

ETHICS IN PRIVATE AND PUBLIC RELATIONSHIP

- Public relationships are those that exist by the virtue of Profession (Ex- Civil Services) or the position one holds in professional life (Ex- Prime Minister or President)
  - Ethics in public relationship guides one's behaviour, action and decision-making process which is vital to maintain the integrity of the profession.
- Private relationship refer to close connection between people, formed by emotional bonds and interactions.
- Ethics play a crucial role in both public and private relationships, influencing how we interact with others and build strong, trusting bonds.

Public vs Private Relationships

Aspect	Public Relationship	Private Relationship
Sphere	• These relationships occur in settings visible to the public eye. Eg- Professional collegues, classmates etc.	• Close, personal relationships with family, close friends or romantic partners, existing in private sphere (Confidentiality & intimacy are key aspects).
Focus	Fulfilling a specific role or achieving a common goal. Prioritisation of tasks, deadlines and following etablished procedures. • Transactional relationship in nature.	• Emphasis is on emotional connection, mutual support and fostering personal growth. • Sharing feelings, open communication and building trust are central.
Evolution	• Driven by external factors like job roles or public opinion. • Changes in the work envrionment or social trends can impact these relationships.	• Evolve more organically over time. • Personal growth, life transitions & shared experiences can naturally shape the nature of the bond.
Voluntary	• Mostly voluntary created relationships	• May be voluntary like friendship or may be involuntary like family.
Accountability	Held accountable for their actions to a wider audience by media, public opinion or supervisory bodies	• Accountability in close relationships is often more personal & informal

Emotional Attachment	• Involves a lower level of emotional investment	• Deeper level of emotional investment
Power dynamics	• Defined and hierarchical relationship	• Balanced and equitable as these relationships are based on mutual respect and Support.
Type of relationship	• Temporary, may get discontinued after mutual needs are fulfilled	• Relatively Permanent and not easily discontinued in times of discord.
Ethics	• Formal in nature, based on Societal and personal norms • Externally imposed and Controlled like office rules	• Informal in nature based on personal values, morality and family values. • Voluntary and Self-imposed.
Standards of Conduct	• Codified in laws, regulations or professional Codes of Conduct	• No formal Code but relies more on personal values & moral compass
Desired values	• Transparency, accountability, respecting diversity and many more Such values	• Honesty, love, care, respect, trust and responsibility are fundamental ethical values in private relationships

Common Ethical Principles

- Honesty and truthfulness
- Empathy and Compassion
- Respect and Appreciation
- Dedication
- Effective Communication.
- Responsibility

Principles in Public Relationship

- Rule of Law (Consumer Protection Act)
- Openness and Transparency (RTI Act)
- Accountability (CAG, Social Audit)
- Honesty and Integrity (Whistleblowing, Lokpal)
- Fairness and justice (Affirmative reservation policies
- Impartiality and Non-partisanship (Article 14)
- Spirit of Service

Principles in Private Relationship

- Love and Care
- Empathy & Compassion
- Respect & Appreciation
- Dedication
- Effective Communication

Separation of Public and Private Relationship

Need for Separation

- **Domain differences**: Public and private relationships operate in distinct spheres and maintaining this separation is crucial for the integrity of both relationships.
- **Involved efficiency**: A domestic argument shouldn't affect their performance at work, nor should workplace stress spill over into their personal interactions.
- **Conflict of Interest**: Entry of public relationships in private sphere can undermine the sanctity, privacy and intimacy of private life, while entry of private relationships in public sphere leads to nepotism & favouritism.
  Eg - the Mahabharata is a perfect example. King Dhritarashtra prioritized his family over his duty as a ruler, leading to a devastating war. This highlights the danger of blurring the lines between public and private obligations.
- **Divergence of values**: Public relationships demand transparency while private relationships often rely on confidentiality.
  Eg - This can be seen in the case of Dr. Shashi Tharoor, who faced false accusation after his wife's death.
- **Work-life Balance**: Separation allows a dedicated appropriate time & energy to both personal life and professional responsibilities without one bleeding into the other.
- **Privacy**: It allows one to keep its personal life confidential and protects sensitive information from public scrutiny.

Examples

- **Respecting privacy**: A doctor maintains patient confidentiality by not discussing their medical history on social media, even if they recognise them in public.
- **Reduced conflict of Interest**: A lawyer avoids representing friends or family members in court to prevent potential conflict of interest.
- **Professional reputation**: A social media manager avoids posting negative comments about their employer online, even if they are frustrated, to maintain professionalism.

Challenges in the Separation

- **Blurring of public and private relationships** especially with the rise of Social media.
- **Personal struggle:** Complete separation isn't always possible. Serious personal issues like grief or illness can inevitably affect your work performance to some extent.
- **Potential for mutual enrichment:** A rigid separation in between might be counter-productive and thus may not be always desirable.
  - Values learned in personal relationships, such as affection and care, can translate into a more humane approach in public service.
- **Shared core values:** Certain values like integrity and compassion, are essential in both public and private life.
  - A person who embodies these values in their personal life is more likely to uphold them in their professional values.
- **Feeling isolated:** Keeping a tight separation might make it difficult to connect with colleagues on a personal level, leading to feeling of isolation at work.

Conclusion

The separation of public and private relationships is a spectrum, not an on/off switch. The ideal level of separation will depend on your specific job, personality and comfort level.

PYQs Corner

(Write the Answer and Get Free Evaluation)

1. It is believed that adherence to ethics in human actions would ensure in smooth functioning of an organization/ system. If so, what does ethics seek to promote in human life? How do ethical values assist in the resolution of conflicts faced by him in his day-to-day functioning? (2022, 10 Marks)
2. Discuss the role of ethics and values in enhancing the following three major components of Comprehensive National Power (CNP) viz. human capital, soft power (culture and policies), and social harmony. (2020, 10 Marks)
3. Without commonly shared and widely entrenched moral values and obligations, neither the law, nor democratic government, nor even the market economy will function properly. What do you understand by this statement? Explain with illustration in the contemporary times. (2017, 10 Marks)
4. Explain how ethics contributes to social and human well-being. (2016, 10 Marks)
5. "A mere compliance with law is not enough, the public servant also have to have a well-developed sensibility to ethical issues for effective discharge of duties" Do you agree? Explain with the help of two examples where (i) an act is ethically right, but not legally and (ii) an act is legally right, but not ethically. (2015, 10 Marks)

02 Dimensions of Ethics

> "It is the greatest good to the greatest number of people which is the measure of right and wrong."
>
> —Jeremy Bentham

> "Act only according to that maxim whereby you can at the same time will that it should become a universal law".
>
> "Act in such a way that you treat humanity, whether in your own person or in the person of any other, never merely as a means to an end, but always at the same time as an end".
>
> Immanuel Kant

Aristotle

> Eudaimonia: "Happiness is the meaning and purpose of life, the whole aim and end of human existence"
>
> Golden Mean: "Virtue is a mean state between two vices, one lying in excess, the other in defect".

> "There are certain self-evident moral principles, such as the principles of keeping promises, that are known through intuition".
>
> — W.D. Ross

> "While an ethic of justice proceeds from the premise of equality - that everyone should be treated the same - an ethic of care rests on the premise of non-violence - that no one should be hurt"
>
> — Carol Gilligan

DIMENSIONS OF ETHICS

- The Concept of 'Dimensions of Ethics' refers to the various framework and approaches being used to understand and navigate moral questions
- These dimensions aren't mutually exclusive; they often work together to provide a comprehensive view of an ethical dilemma.

There are four main dimensions of ethics, each offering a different perspective on how we understand and make ethical decisions

NORMATIVE ETHICS

- Focuses on creating moral principles and guidelines for behaviour. It asks "What ought we to do?" and proposes framework for making ethical decisions.
  - There are several influential theories within this dimension:
    - Deontological Ethics
    - Teleological Ethics (Consequentialism)
    - Virtue Ethics
    - Feminist Ethics
- It is also called Prescriptive Ethics

META ETHICS

This dimension delves into the philosophical foundations of morality itself.

- These theories talk about fundamental abstract issues like what is meant by ethics, why should we be ethical, is ethics and absolute reality or a social construct and so on.
- Some key questions in Meta-ethics include:

Moral Subjectivism: Are moral truths objective or subjective? (e.g., Is lying always wrong, or can it be justified in some situations?)

Intuitionism: How do we justify our moral beliefs? (e.g., Is reason or intuition a better guide for moral decision making?)

DESCRIPTIVE ETHICS

This dimension focuses on understanding the moral beliefs and practices of different cultures and societies.

- It explores how ethical values vary across time and place
- It is value free approach to ethics
- It does not make judgements about morality of the practices and beliefs but simply describe the practices observed in different groups or cultures.
- Descriptive ethics helps us to:
  - Appreciate the diversity of moral viewpoints
  - Recognize the limitations of our own cultural biases
  - Identify potential areas of common ground for ethical dialogue across cultures.

APPLIED ETHICS	This dimension takes abstract ethical principles and applies them to specific situations and fields • It tackles real-world dilemmas by using normative framework Medical Ethics, Business Ethics, Animal Ethics, Media Ethics, Environmental Ethics

Please Note: Given below is the brief discussion on various ethical theories. Detailed discussion of corresponding thinkers is covered and chapter-17 &18.

CONSEQUENTIALISM

About: Teleological ethics, also known as consequentialism, is a branch of ethics that judges the morality of an action based solely on its consequences or outcomes.

Focus on Outcomes: The primary concern is the end result of an action, not the inherent rightness or wrongness of the act itself.

- An action is considered morally good if it leads to good outcome, and bad if it leads to a bad outcome.

Core Tenet: End justifies the Means. the emphasis is on the ends (goals, results) rather than the means (methods, action) used to achieve them.

Thinkers: Jeremy Bentham, J.S. Mill, Peter Singer

Example: Most people would agree that lying is wrong. But if telling a lie would help save a person's life, consequentialism says it's the right thing to do

Different types of consequentialism

1. Utilitarianism: Emphasizes maximising overall happiness or well-being for all involved. They weigh the potential happiness and suffering caused by each option and choose the one that leads to greatest net happiness.
   - Maximising human welfare: This could involve factors like health, security and education, not just happiness.
   - Minimising harm: This could involve avoiding actions that cause pain, suffering or environmental damage.
   - Example: Subsidies or welfare programs undertaken by the government is based on the principle of utilitarianism.
2. Egoism: Focuses on maximising one's own good or self-interest. The moral action is the one that brings about the best possible outcomes for the individual themself.

3. Rule Consequentialism. This theory Suggest that one should follow moral rules that are likely to lead to good consequences in the long run, even if breaking the rule might seem beneficial in a specific situation.

4. Act Centric vs Rule centric Consequentialism: Act consequentialism focuses on the consequences of each individual act, while rule consequentialism emphasizes following moral rules that generally lead to good outcomes

Advantages and Limitations of Consequentialism

Advantages	Limitations
• Practical framework for decision-making by focusing on achieving the best possible outcome in a given situation.	• Challenges of accurate prediction of consequences and therefore, action can lead to unintended efforts. Eg: Project Cheetah led to the relocation of cheetahs in India but resulted into the death of 10 cheetahs till date • Disregard for the minority rights or their well-being. Eg - Construction of big dams lead to displacement of communities.
Impartiality: Promotes fairness by considering the well-being of everyone affected by an action. • Avoid bias towards specific individuals or groups and strives to achieve the greatest good for the greatest number.	• Challenge in the measurement of 'Goodness' as happiness is subjective which is different from one person to the another. • Eg - Material goods vs Family fulfilment.
• Focus on Results: The emphasis on results can be seen as a strength, ensuring actions are judged based on their actual impact rather than abstract principle.	• Neglect in the importance of individual rights, duties or inherent wrongness of certain actions such as violence to justify the good outcomes. • Create a black and white construct of morality which is not possible in every real life situation.

DEONTOLOGICAL ETHICS

About: Deontology, also known as duty-based ethics, emphasizes on the inherent rightness or wrongness of an action itself rather than outcomes.

1. Emphasizes duty and following universal moral values as the foundation of right and wrong.
2. It argues that the morality of an action is determined by the inherent characteristics of the act itself, rather than the consequences it produces.

- Core Tenets

Core Tenets

1. Focus on Duty: Actions are Judged based on whether they fulfill a moral obligation or duty.

2. Universal moral Laws that apply to everyone, regardless of circumstances. These laws are seen as absolute and obligatory, not dependent on specific situations.

3. Respect for Persons: Deontology emphasizes the importance of respecting people as autonomous beings with inherent value. This translates to duties like treating others fairly and not using them merely as a means to an end.
   - Kant argued that every person has inherent dignity, deserving of respect.

4. Categorical Imperative: Kant proposed the categorical imperative as a guide for moral action which is the cornerstone of deontological ethics.
   - It essentially asks us to act only according to maxims (universal rules) that we could want to be universal laws

Thinker: German Philosopher Immanuel Kant.

Example: Mahatma Gandhi Suspended the Non-Cooperation Movement (NCM) after the Chauri-Chaura incident as the means of violence is inherently wrong even though it aims to make India free from the British Rule.

Why Deontology offers a good ethical framework??

- Clear moral guidance that can guide decision-making in complex situations and simplifies the ethical landscape Eg-Gandhiji's path of Satygraha & Non-violence
- Promotes Fairness and Justice through the emphasis on universal moral laws and treating everyone with respect. Eg- Eradication of manual scavenging in India.
- Protection of individual rights: Deontology safeguards fundamental rights by placing limitations on actions that could violate them, regardless of potential benefits.

Aspect	Deontology	Consequentialism
Focus	• Inherent rightness or wrongness of actions rather than their outcomes	• Focus on outcomes or consequences of actions.
Key Idea	• Actions are morally right/wrong based on rules, duties or obligations	• The rightness/wrongness is determined by goodness/badness of results
Philosophers	• Immanuel Kant	• Jeremy Bentham & John Stuart Mill.
Examples	• A doctor must keep patient confidentiality even if disclosing information could prevent harm to others, because the duty to respect privacy is paramount	• A doctor might breach patient confidentiality if it prevents a serious threat to public health, because the consequences justify the action.

VIRTUE ETHICS

About: Virtue ethics stands out from other ethical frameworks by focusing on character development rather than rules or outcomes.

- The goal is to become a virtuous person who consistently makes good choices, not just follow rules or aim for specific outcomes.

Central Principle: Emphasis is on developing good character through the nurture of virtues, which are excellent character traits that dispose us to act well in various situations.

- In virtue ethics, the core question becomes: "What would a virtuous person do in this situation?" This approach encourages us to internalize virtues and make ethical choices based on our character, rather than simply following external rules or calculating consequences.

Flexible list of Virtues: Virtues are not a rigid list but rather a collection of desirable traits that allow us to excel in different aspects of life.

- **Moral Virtues:** Honesty, courage, compassion, justice, temperance (self-control)
- **Intellectual Virtues:** Wisdom, curiosity, critical thinking.

> **Practical Wisdom (Phronesis):** An important virtue is phronesis which is the ability to discern the right course of action in a specific situation, considering all relevant factors

Golden Mean: Virtue Ethics often refers to the "Golden Mean", which suggests finding a balance between extremes.

Eg- Courage is the mean between cowardice and recklessness.

Thinkers: Aristotle, considered the father of virtue ethics, believed that happiness (eudaimonia) is achieved through living a virtuous life.

- **Confucianism** emphasized the importance of virtues like filial piety, respe for authority, and reciprocity.

Importance of Virtue Ethics

Promotes personal growth (character development) by encouraging individuals to cultivate desirable traits and become better version of ourselves

Can be applied to various situations, unlike rigid rules that might not always fit context

Holistic Approach by considering not just the actions but also the motivation behind them and the overall state of our character.

Focus on Good life: Virtue ethics aims to guide us towards living a flourishing and fulfilling life, where happiness is achieved through living virtuously

Challenges of Virtue Ethics

- **Subjectivity in defining and prioritising values** as cultures and individuals might place different values on certain traits.
- **Lack of clear-cut answers** Virtue ethics may not offer definitive solutions in complex situations
- **Difficulty in attainment of virtues** that requires consistent efforts, self-reflection and a willingness to learn from mistakes

Application of Virtue Ethics in Administration

Virtue ethics, with its focus on character development, offers a valuable framework to cultivate ethical conduct within the civil service.

Building Trust and Respect	Effective Governance	Ethical Leadership
• Satya (Truthfulness): Building a foundation of credibility • Dharma (Righteous Duty): Fulfilling one's duties with integrity and fairness strengthens public confidence	• Karuna (compassion) Empathy for the needs of citizens allow administrators to make sensitive & inclusive policies. • Kshama (forgiveness): Fosters a collaborative & learning-oriented environment which can lead to improved service delivery.	• Aparigraha (Non-possession): Discourages greed and corruption & focus on serving the public interest • Sahayog (cooperation): Create a more efficient and effective administration

INTUITIONISM

- About: Ethical Intuitionism, also known as moral intuitionism, offers a distinct perspeitive on how we grasp right or wrong.
  - This refers to the philosophical belief that there are objective moral truths existing independent of human opinion or cultural norms and that human beings can understand these truth intuitively.
- Core principle: Intuitionists argue that an individual have direct, non-inferential knowledge of moral truths through moral intuition.
  - This intuition is not based on reasoning, logic or experience, but rather a kind of immediate apprehension of what is right or wrong.
  - This intuition is a specific cognitive faculty dedicated to moral understanding
- Example: You see someone bullying a smaller child. You immediately know this is wrong, without needing to analyse a set of rules or think through the consequences. That's the kind of direct moral knowledge intuitionism emphasizes.
- Moral Intuition vs Moral Reasoning

Moral Intuition and reasoning aren't rivals but instead they complement each other. Intuition provides a starting point with gut feelings, while reasoning offers a deeper analysis.

Moral Intuition	Moral Reasoning.
• This is the immediate gut feeling we get when faced with a moral dilemma • It's a fast and automatic response driven by emotions, ingrained values, and past experiences. Eg- Feeling empathy and helping a homeless person without thinking. Historical Example - Mother Teresa's immediate response to suffering led her to help the poor without extensive analysis.	• This is the conscious and rational evaluation of ethical choices. • It involves applying logic, ethical principles and analysing potential consequences which leads to slow response Eg- Deciding to donate to a charity after researching its effectiveness Historical example - Dr. B.R. Ambedkar's fight for Dalit rights and his role in creating a just Indian Constitution stemmed from reasoned analysis of historical injustices.

Strengths and Limitations of Intuitionism

STRENGTHS	LIMITATIONS
Captures the immediacy of moral judgements.	Reliability of intuition: Intuition might not be a trustworthy guide for morality.
Universality of moral values: Everyone has access to this moral intuition, potentially explaining a sense of universal moral principles	Different people can have different moral intuitions (because of cultural differences leading to moral relativism where there are no universally right answers, just individual interpretations

MORAL RELATIVISM

- **About**: Refers to the idea that there are no universal or objective moral truths, and that what is considered right or wrong can vary based on the context - Culture, Society or historical period.
- **Examples**:
  - Food: In some cultures, eating cows is taboo (like Hinduism), while in others it is a common practice. This highlights how dietary restrictions can be based on cultural beliefs not universal morality.
  - Family structures: Monogamy is prevalent in many Societies while polygamous families exist in certain Societies (Islam, tribal Societies like Naga, Gond etc.)
- **Importance**: Moral relativism approach different cultures with an open mind and try to understand their moral values within their own Context. This can help us avoid cultural bias and ethnocentrism (believing our culture is Superior.

  Relativism promotes tolerance and acceptance of different practices which can be crucial in a globalized world with increased intercultural interactions.

Limitations:

- Problem of universal values: Moral relativism might seem to undermine the possibility of universal moral values. If everything is relative, how can one condemn atrocities like genocide or slavery, which most people find morally wrong?
- Difficulties in application: Moral relativism can be tricky to apply in real-world situations. When cultures with different moral codes clash, how do we decide which one takes precedence?
- Weaken the concept of universal Human Rights if harmful practices are justified solely on the basis of cultural norms.

FEMINIST ETHICS

• **About**: Feminist ethics challenges traditional ethical theories for neglecting women's experiences and perspectives. It aims to create a more inclusive approach to ethics by considering the social realities of gender.

• **Core Ideas**:

1. Exposing bias in traditional ethics such as gender bias or undervaluing of traditionally feminine acts like caregiving.
2. Emphasizes the importance of including women's voices and lived experiences in moral decision making
3. Gender analysis of moral issues.

Core Ideas

Critique of Traditional Ethics

- Pre-eminently focused on men's perspective with little regards to women's viewpoints (Eg- From Aristotle to Plato to Kant)
- Emphasizes masculine cultural traits like "Independence, autonomy, intellect, will, wariness, hierarchy, domination, culture, transcendence, product, asceticism, war and death"
- Gives less weight to culturally feminine traits like "interdependence, community, connection, sharing, emotion, body, trust, absence of hierarchy, nature, immanence, process, joy, peace and life".
- "Male" oriented convention in which moral reasoning is viewed through a framework of rules, rights, universality and impartiality and becomes the standard of a society.
- Caring and the moral issue of private life and family responsibilities were traditionally regarded as trivial matters.

Thinkers: Developed from Mary Wollstonecraft's 'Vindication of the Rights of women' published in 1972

• Carol Gilligan and Nel Noddings are exponents of a feminist care ethics which criticize traditional ethics as deficient to the degree they lack, disregard, trivialize or attack women's cultural values and virtues.

> 1. Gilligan's ethical theory is based on the "Communal nature of women." The theory is referred to as "ethics of care" as opposed to the more traditional male-oriented "ethics of justice".

Emphasis on terms like dependence and responsibility, as well as the need to develop ethical attitudes such as empathy and affection.

Importance of interpersonal relationship in moral decision making

Care in addition to (or in place of justice

Each moral decision is unique, Context dependent and specific

Importance of special ties when making moral decisions - people close to you may have different moral responsibilities than others.

2. Standpoint Theory: Emphasizes the importance of considering the perspectives of marginalised groups, arguing that their unique standpoint offers valuable insights for ethical analysis.

3. Justice-based approaches: These approaches prioritize achieving social justice and equality for women. They address specific issues that disproportionately affect women, such as reproductive rights, economic parity, and ending gender-based violence.

FOUR WAVES OF FEMINISM

- **About**: Feminism is a movement and ideology that advocates for equal rights and opportunities for people of all genders. It seeks to dismantle the social, political, and economic structures that perpetuate gender based discrimination and inequality.
- **Core ideas**

1. Political and economic equality: Fighting for equal right to vote, hold office and achieve economic parity through equal pay and opportunities

2. Reproductive Rights: Advocating for women's control over their bodies, including access to contraception and abortion

4. Ending violence against women: working to eliminate domestic violence, sexual assault and other forms of violence against women

3. Social justice: Challenging gender stereotypes and promoting equal opportunities in education employment and social participation

4 Waves of Feminism

1st wave (1848-1920)
- Women suffrage
- Property rights
- Political candidacy
- Introduction to voting rights and admissions to universities

2nd wave (1963-1980s)
- National agenda
- Equality (Equal pay)
- Reproductive Freedom
- Peace as a women's right.

3rd wave (1990-2012)
- Intersectionality
- Mainstreaming
- Gender awareness
- Participation in the workforce
- Addressing of Sexual harassment and rape culture
- Improvement in marriage and divorce rights

4th wave (2012-present)
- Women empowerment
- Internet movements
- '#MeToo', rise of Social media addressing Sexual abuse and misogyny
- Terms like "Mansplaining" (Rebecca Solnit) in public perception
- Higher public awareness for global equality development & ranking.

5th wave?
- Gender equity?
- Co-created future?
- Society of the future?
- Feminism as the driver for innovation?

Benefits of Feminism

1. Legal and political gains
   - The Sexual harassment of women at workplace (Prevention, Prohibition and Redressal Act, 2013.
2. Social and economic empowerment of women
   - Beti Bachao, Beti Padhao Andolan (2015)
   - Maternity Benefit Amendment Act (2017) increased the paid maternity leave from 12 weeks to 26 weeks for working mothers.
3. Increased awareness of gender issues
   - #MeToo Movement encouraged women to speak out against Sexual harassment and abuse by powerful figures in various industries

• Digital Activism: Social media campaigns like #IStandwithHer are raising awareness about gender-based violence and discrimination.

4. Increased Diversity: Feminism has become more inclusive and diverse over time, recognising the intersectionality of gender-based discrimination with other forms of discrimination, such as race, class and sexuality.

Supreme Court Cases relating to feminism

1. Vishakha vs. State of Rajasthan (1997): This case established guidelines for preventing sexual harassment in the workplace and recognised sexual harassment as a violation of fundamental rights under the Indian Constitution.
2. Suchita Srivastava vs. Chandigarh Administration (2009): This case dealt with the right to reproductive autonomy and upheld the right of a woman to terminate her pregnancy if it poses a risk to her mental or physical health.
3. Shayara Bano vs. Union of India (2017): This case declared the practice of Triple Talaq, a form of instant divorce in Islamic law, as unconstitutional and discriminatory against Muslim women.
4. Right to property for daughters: In 2020, a landmark Supreme Court decision granted daughters equal coparcenary rights in ancestral property, a significant step towards economic empowerment for women

PYQs Corner

(Write the Answer and Get Free Evaluation)

1. Differentiate 'moral intuition' from 'moral reasoning' with suitable examples. (2023, 10 Marks)
2. With regard to the morality of actions, one view is that means is of paramount importance and the other view is that the ends justify the means. Which view do you think is more appropriate? Justify your answer. (2018, 10 Marks)
3. "Human beings should always be treated as 'ends' in themselves and never as 'means'." Explain the meaning and significance of this statement, giving its implications in the modern techno-economic society. (2014, 10 Marks)

03 Human Values

"

"Hatred does not cease by Hatred, but only by love; this is the eternal law" (Emphasizes love and compassion as antidotes to negativity.

— Gautam Buddha

"To deny people their human rights is to challenge their very humanity." (This quote emphasizes the universality of human rights and the importance of respecting them as core human Values.

— Nelson Mandela

"liberty, equality and fraternity are not merely political ideals but the essence of civilization" (Emphasizes the importance of these core human values for a just and Civilised society.

— Dr. B. R. Ambedkar.

Mahatma Gandhi

"Non-violence is the greatest force at the disposal of mankind. It is mightier than the mightiest weapon of destruction". (Emphasizes non-violence, peace, and respect for all as fundamental ethical principles.)

"Education is the foundation of all progress. A Society that fails to educate its women lags behind" (Promotes education as a core human right and a foundation for societal advancement).

— Jyotirao Phule

"Service to other is the rent we pay for our room on Earth" (Promotes Selflessness and Service as core human values.

— Sister Nivedita.

VALUES

- Values refer to the belief or principles that individuals or societies hold to be important and worthwhile.
- They guide human-behaviour and decision making and help to shape one's worldview.
- Ethical decision-making often involves weighing values agai other and choosing which values to elevate.

Features of Values (Subjective)

1. **Subjectivity:** Differ from person to person based on their experiences, belief and culture
2. **Universality:** Some values are shared by most societies such as honesty, fairness and respect.
3. **Relativity:** Values can change over time and in different situations
4. **Hierarchical:** Some values are more important than others. Eg- A person may value honesty over loyalty.
5. **Emotional:** Values are often accompanied by emotional responses, such as feeling proud when living up to one's values
6. **Dynamic:** change over time with the change in person's experiences and beliefs
7. **Prescriptive:** Guide behavior and decision-making by telling individuals what they ought to do.

Thinker's definition of values

Max Weber

Defined values as beliefs and attitudes that people hold about the world around them. He believed that values are the driving force behind people's action and that they shape the way people see the world.

Values are foundation of social order. He argued that values create a shared understanding among members of a society and help to regulate behaviour.

Emile Durkheim

Abraham Maslow

Developed a hierarchy of human needs, which he believed were universal. At the top of this hierarchy were self-actualization needs, which he argued that people who are able to live in accordance with their values are more likely to achieve self-actualization.

Believed in the importance of values such as truth, Non-violence, and service to others. He believed that living in accordance with these values was essential for personal and societal transformation.

Mahatma Gandhi

Importance of Human values

Individual level

1. Provide Moral Compass: Guide an individual's decision and actions, promoting personal integrity and a sense of purpose.
Eg- Mahatma Gandhi's values of Satyagraha and Non-Violence.
2. Fosters self-respect and inner peace.
3. Ethical decision-making: Values provide a framework for navigating complex situations and making ethical choices.
Eg- Vinod Rai demonstrated the values of integrity, justice, etc. in his focus on exposing corruption.
4. Promotes moral responsibility: Values instil a sense of accountability for one's actions and their consequences.
Eg- Lal Bahadur Shastri resigned due to train accidents happened in his tenure.
5. Improves mental well-being: Positive values like gratitude and kindness contribute to happiness an overall well-being.
6. Living a meaningful life: Aligning with strong values allows individuals to live a life of purpose and contribute to a better world.
   - Malala Yousafzai displayed courage by defying the Taliban ban on girl's education and became a global advocate for education rights.

Societal level

1. Social Justice: Encourage individuals to consider well-being of others and act with compassion and empathy.

Eg- Mother Teresa dedicated her life to caring for the poorest and most vulnerable members of society.

2. Promotes Social order. Shared values create a foundation for cooperation, trust and respect within a Society resulting into the peaceful conflict resolution.

3. Reduced crimes in the Society especially against the vulnerable Section Such as women, SC/STs etc. Values like tolerance promotes Social harmony and reduced communal riots.

Eg- Iceland emphasizes Social equality, trust in institutions and a strong work ethic and therefore, ranks high in global peace and Security indexes.

4. Enhances relationships: Trust and respect, grounded in values, build stronger connections with friends and family.

5. Strengthens civic engagement: Values encourage individuals to participate in the democratic process and contribute to the common good.

Eg- Voting by the people in general election.

6. Equality and Justice: Ensures all members of Society have access to opportunities and are treated with dignity.

Eg- Minority rights under Article 29 and 30 of Indian constitution.

National and Global level

1. Sustainable Development: Environmental values guide responsible resource management and promote global sustainability.

Eg- Adoption of SDG Goals by 2030.

2. International Peace: Eg- India's Article 51 emphasises on promotion of international Peace.

3. Fight for universal human rights: Eg- India was first to bring the issue of Aparthied in the UN in 1946.

4. Global co-operation: Shared values on issues like Climate change, terrorism etc necessitate international collaboration for solutions.

Eg- Paris Agreement, FATF etc

5. Inter-cultural dialogue: Valuing diversity and understanding different cultures promotes global collaboration and progress.

TYPES OF VALUES

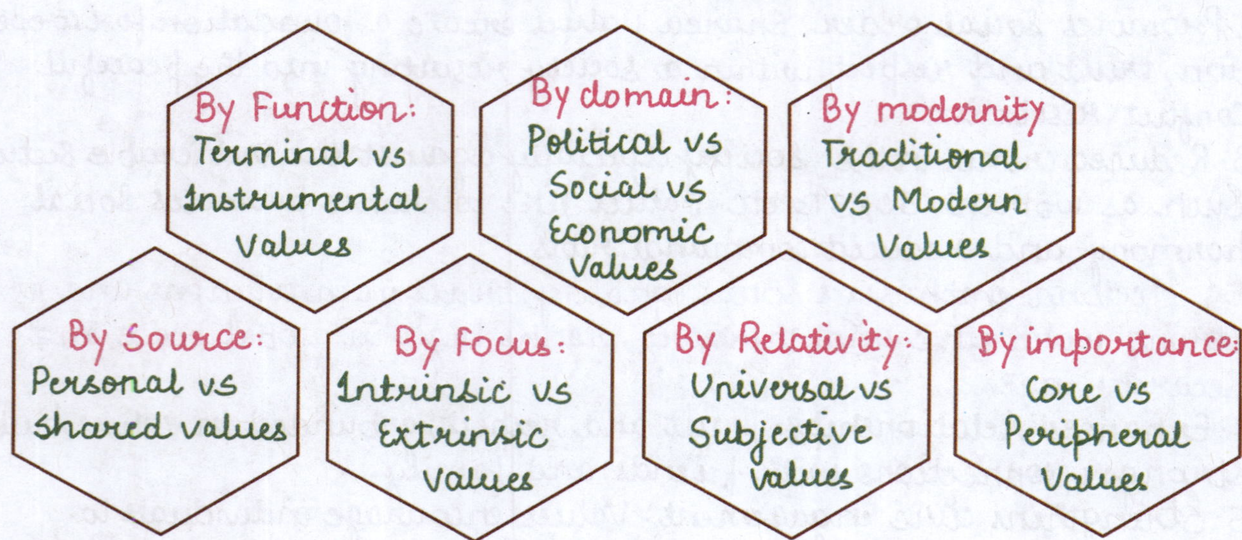

1. Personal Values vs Shared values

a) **Personal values**: These are the core beliefs that guide you as an individual. They shape your decisions, behaviours and how you view the world.
Ex- Honesty, kindness or ambition.

b) **Shared values**: They are the common beliefs that bind a group of people together, like a family, community or culture. They can be about what's right or wrong, or how people should behave.
Ex- Respect for elders, fairness or religious beliefs.

2. Terminal vs Instrumental values (Based on Rokeach Value Survey (RVS))

a) **Terminal values** refers to desirable end-states of existence. These are the goals that a person would like to achieve during his or her lifetime.

• True Friendship • Mature Love • Self-Respect • Happiness • Inner Harmony • Equality	• Freedom • Pleasure • Social Recognition • Wisdom • Salvation • Family Security	National Security A Sense of accomplishment A world of Beauty A world of Peace A comfortable life An Exciting life.

b. **Instrumental values** refers to preferable modes of behaviour. These are preferable modes of behaviour, or means of achieving the terminal values (ends in themselves)

• Cheerfulness • Ambition • Love • Cleanliness • Self control • Capability	• Courage • Politeness • Honesty • Imagination • Independence • Intellect	• Broad Mindedness • Logic • Obedience • Helpfulness • Responsibility • Forgiveness

3. Political vs Social vs Economic Values

Aspect	Political	Social	Economic
Definition	Political values are all about how a society is structured and governed	• Social values are the unwritten rules and shared beliefs that guide how people interact in a society.	• Economic values are concerned with how a society produces, distributes, and consume goods and services
Focus	They deal with the ideal way to distribute power, make decisions, and ensure the well-being of citizens	• They create a sense of order and predictability, and influence how people treat each other, form relationships, and function as a group.	They relate to ideal way to allocate resources, create wealth, and ensure economic well-being for all citizens.
Example	Democracy, freedom, equality, Justice, Security, Patriotism	Cooperation, respect, fairness, honesty, family, tradition, religion.	Efficiency, productivity, competition, wealth creation, economic security, Sustainability

4. Intrinsic vs Extrinsic Values

• Intrinsic Values: These are valued for their own sake, not as a means to something else. They are considered good in themselves.

Eg- Knowledge, creativity, love or beauty.

• Extrinsic values: These are valued because they lead to something else that is desirable. They are means to an end.

Eg- Wealth, fame or power might be extrinsic values because they can bring you happiness or security (Intrinsic values)

5. Core vs Peripheral values

• Core values are the fundamental and most important beliefs that guide one's life. They form the bedrock of one's character and significantly influence their decisions and behaviour.

- Core values are relatively stable and enduring, thus providing a direction in life.
- Eg-Honesty, Compassion, integrity, Creativity etc. depending on one's character.

- Peripheral values are less central to one's overall identity but still be important in specific situations.
  - They are more flexible and can change based on context or life experiences thus allowing for adaptation.
  - Eg- Punctuality (important for work meeting but less so with friends), Frugality (important for saving goals but less so on a special occasion).

6. Universal vs Subjective Values

- Universal values: These are the values that are believed to be important and desirable across cultures, societies and throughout history.
  - They are often seen as inherent to human nature or based on some form of objective truth.
  - Eg- Justice, Freedom, Honesty etc.
- Subjective Values: These are values that they are based on individual beliefs, preferences and experiences. They are relative and can vary greatly from person to person and culture to culture.
  - Eg- Collectivism in Indian Society while Individualism in western Societies. Fashion choices, food choices, religious beliefs, etc

7. Traditional vs Modern Values

Aspect	Traditional Values	Modern Values
Definition	They are long held beliefs, customs & practices passed down through generations	These are values that emerge alongside Social and technological advancements
Focus	• Maintaining stability & Social order • Preserving a culture's unique identity and traditions • Promote a sense of shared identity and belonging within a group.	• Importance of individual rights, autonomy & self-expression. • Progress and change: Innovation, Scientific advancement and adaptation to changing circumstances. • Promote equal opportunities and rights for all individuals, regardless of background

Source	They are often deeply rooted in a society's history, culture and religion.	They often challenge traditional norms and prioritize individual freedom, progress & equality.
Example	• Respect for elders • Importance of family and community ties. • Adherence to religious beliefs and rituals • Emphasis on specific gender roles • Strict social hierarchies	• Emphasis on gender equality and LGBTQ+ rights. • Focus on personal achievements and career success. • Concern for environmental sustainability and social justice issues.

Tension between the traditional and modern values

Some may see modernisation as a threat to cultural heritage and social stability. Others may feel that traditional norms are outdated and hinder progress.

This tension is the cause of various social crimes such as gender-based crimes, communal riots etc.

1. Technological Advancements

- Traditional view: Some cultures may view technology with suspicion, fearing it disrupts traditional way of life.
- Modern view: Modern values see technology as a tool for progress, improving communication, education and healthcare.

2. Gender Roles

- Traditional View: Defined strict roles for men and women - men as breadwinners and women as homemakers.
- Modern View: Challenged these rigid roles, promoting gender equality. Women are increasingly pursuing careers, and men are taking on more domestic responsibility.

VALUES INCULCATION

- Values inculcation refers to the process of instilling values in individuals
- It is about shaping their beliefs, attitudes, and behaviour according to certain ethical, moral or cultural standards
- The process of value inculcation is fast in early childhood and (throughout life, influenced by various factors.

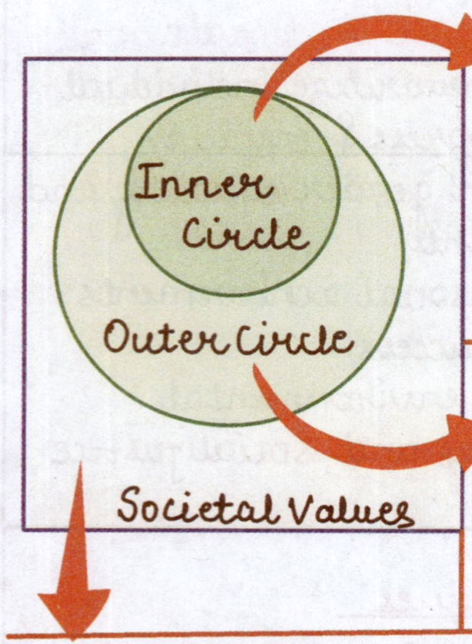

Includes family, close friends and primary caregivers. Most direct and powerful influence on values during a person's formative Years. Eg- Joint family structure is more likely to teach social cohesion, collectivism whereas nuclear family is more likely to teach individualism, independence and freedom.

Encompasses schools, religious groups, community organisations and social circles. Influences broaden as individuals interact with the wider world.

- Common values in almost all the religions- Abstinence, Generosity, Humility etc.

The broader cultural and societal values prevalent in a specific time and place also shape individual values. These can be transmitted through media, laws and social norms.

- Experiences of injustice, discrimination or hardship may lead to the adoption of values such as compassion, empathy and fairness.
- Constitutions are a source of values in a society such as Equality, liberty, Fraternity, Patriotism etc.

ROLE OF FAMILY

Methods of Value inculcation by the families

1. Early influence and observational learning: "Parents are the first teacher" as family is the first social environment a child encounters.
Eg- Families have a unique opportunity to shape a child's "blank slate" by introducing positive values early on.
2. Role Models: Children learn by observing and imitating the behaviour of parents and siblings. Parents who exhibit commitment, kindness and respect are more likely to raise children with those values.
Eg- Witnessing the honourable treatment of female family members can teach a child the value of gender equality.
3. Teachings: Sharing stories, fables, or historical accounts with moral lessons has a lasting impact.
Eg- Tales from epics like Mahabharata or Ramayana can teach valuable lessons about honesty, courage and justice.

4. Family Structure and Social influence: In Joint families, children observe interactions among extended family members. This fosters values like courtesy, respect, mutual care, tolerance, Sacrifice, cooperation etc.
• Family gatherings provide opportunities to learn social values through interactions with relatives.
5. Rewards and Punishments: Positive reinforcement goes a long way. Rewards for good behaviour, such as hugs or praise, motivate children and encourage them to maintain positive behaviour.
6. Discipline and Guidance: Families establish boundaries and expectations for behaviour. This helps children understand the consequences of their actions and teaches them Self-control.
7. Open Communication: Discussions with the children helps them to develop cognitive reasoning resulting into making responsible choices in the future.
8. Traditions and Customs: Families follow certain practices as a norm which are always adhered to by the children.
Eg- Touching elder's feet before leaving home develop respect for elders.

Critical Analysis in the role of family for value inculcation

• Foundational influence: The family is a child's "first school" where they learn basic social norms and values and therefore has a profound impact on their development.
Critique: Transmission of regressive values - Family values might be outdated or promote inequality (Ex- Casteism, patriarchy) which can hinder a child's understanding of fairness and respect.
Critique: Witnessing domestic violence, addiction or constant conflict within the family can negatively impact a child's sense of security or moral development.
Critique: Focus on materialistic values such as achievement and competition over humanistic values such as compassion, honesty and love. This creates a one-sided value system in children. (e.g. stressed students lacking coping skills

• Continuity in the reinforcement and development of values as families are a constant presence throughout a person's life.
Critique: limited autonomy - Families that don't allow children to explore and reflect on their own values may hinder internalisation. Children may simply accept values externally without truly understanding or believing in them.

- **Time allotment**: Children spend a significant amount of time with their families especially during their formative years and thereby creating a powerful influence on their value systems.

Critique: The rise of nuclear families and busy lifestyle can limit quality family time. This reduces opportunities for families to transmit values effectively.

Critique: Modern life with boarding schools, tuitions and exponential use of technology can create a disconnect between children and families, weakening their influence on moral development.

- **Diverse perspective from varied personalities** fosters a well-rounded value system.

Critique: Conflicting values among family members can confuse children Eg- Grandparents advocating stricter rules might clash with parents who allow more freedom, creating mixed message about acceptable behaviour.

- **Trust and respect** towards the family members help in the faster internalization of values.

Critique: Hypocrisy by the parents (Dissonance between words and actions) leads to the loss of faith by the children on the parents. Eg- A parent preaching honesty while engaging in dishonest behaviour undermines the importance of integrity.

- Families have a wider range of methods for value inculcation compared to other institutions. They can use a combination of positive reinforcement, guidance, discipline and tradition to shape a child's behaviour.

ROLE OF SOCIETY

- Socialization is the process by which individuals learn the norms, values and behaviours expected of them in their culture. Through interactions with family, peers, institutions and media, people internalize these values and understand how to function within society.
- Society act as a giant classroom, constantly shaping the values of its members through the following ways:

01 Religion: Religious teachings, rituals and stories often promote moral values like compassion, kindness and forgiveness. Religious leaders can serve as a role models and guides.

02 Traditions and customs: Cultural traditions and customs passed down through generations can instil values like respect for elders, community spirit and connection to history.

a. Exposure to various cultural and religious traditions can broaden a person's value perspective. This fosters tolerance and understanding of different viewpoints. Eg- Experiencing multicultural celebrations like Diwali (Hinduism) or Christmas (Christianity) can cultivate respect for diverse religious practices

03 Political Systems and ideologies promote certain values. Eg- Democracy emphasizes values like equality and participation, while an authoritarian regime might prioritize obedience and social order.

04 Economic System influences values. A market driven economy might emphasize competition and individualism, while a Socialist System might prioritize social welfare and collective responsibility.

05 Media: Media outlets (news, entertainment), shape values by portraying certain behaviours and lifestyle as desirable or unacceptable. They can influence public opinion on social issues and moral dilemmas.

06 Civil Society: Non-profit organisations, advocacy groups and Social movements promote specific values like Environmental protection, human rights or social justice.

Eg- The Black Lives matter movement advocates for racial equality and justice in policing.

07 Leadership (Role Models): Leaders, both political and social, are positive role models setting an example through their actions and words. Their integrity, compassion, and commitment to ethical behaviour can inspire others to uphold positive values.

Eg- Environmental activist Greta Thunberg inspire action on climate change.

08 Formal institutions: Laws and institutions can enforce certain values. Educational systems often promote critical thinking, respect for knowledge, and responsible citizenship. School rules against bullying reinforce values of respect and empathy.

09 Informal institutions. Social groups like sports teams or clubs can emphaize teamwork, leadership or sportsmanship.

- Community events and volunteer work can promote values such as civic engagement, empathy and social responsibility.

10. Stability and harmony: Shared values promote social cohesion and a social order within a society. Eg- Values like respecting laws contribute to smooth functioning society resulting into lower crimes and a peaceful society.

Weakness in the role of Society

1. Heterogenity (Cultural clashes) : Cultural and social differences can lead to conflicting values. Eg- Communal riots, Sons of the soil policy etc.
2. Orthodoxy (Outdated values) : Traditional values may become rigid and outdated, hindering societal progress.
   Eg- Discrimination against the LGBTQ+ community.
3. Corruption : Leaders or institutions who should have been the role models are engaged in the corruption which can undermine societal trust and moral authority. Eg- 2G scam, Misleading advertisement by influence for money etc.
4. Misdirected values (Materialism) : Emphasis on materialism and competition can create a culture of selfishness and disregard for others.
   Eg- Greed might overshadow values of environmental responsibility or Community service.
5. Boomerang Effect (Harsh punishment) : Harsh or forceful methods of imposing values can backfire. People may rebel against values they don't understand or feel forced to accept.
6. Media influence (Negative portrayals) : Media outlets (news, entertainment) can also shape values by portraying negative behaviours and lifestyle as desirable. Eg- Glorification of violence in movies can desensitivize people to real world violence.
7. Propaganda censorship : Societies that control information flow through propaganda and censorship can limit exposure to diverse viewpoints and hinder the development of critical thinking skills necessary for ethical decision making.
8. Social media algorithms can create echo chambers where users are primarily exposed to information that reinforces their existing beliefs, hindering exposure to diverse values and perspectives.
9. Rapid Societal change : Rapid Societal change can create confusion about values. Traditional values might be challenged by new ideas, leaving people unsure of what to believe in.
   Eg- Advancements in biotechnology raise ethical questions about genetic engineering.

ROLE OF EDUCATION

Educational institutions play a crucial role in shaping students' values beyond academics through the following ways:

1. Curriculum Design and Pedagogy

1. Integration of core values into Subjects: Eg- literature lessons can explore themes of Justice and compassion while science classes can emphasize the value of critical thinking and environmental responsibility.
2. Dedicated character education programs can explicitly teach values through discussions, activities and service learning.

2. School Environment and Policies

1. Inclusive environment that respects diversity exposes students to different culture, beliefs and perspectives which promote tolerance and understanding.
2. Safe and organised environment where values can be explicitly taught and consistently modelled.
3. Anti bullying policies and practices: Enforcing clear rules against bullying and promoting a culture of respect foster values like empathy, inclusion and courage.

3. Role modeling and classroom management

1. Teachers who embody positive values serve as role models for students. Eg- A teacher who treats all students with respect showcases the value of fairness
2. Positive Reinforcement: Acknowledging and rewarding positive behavior reinforces good values. Praising students for honesty, cooperation or helping others strengthen these values.
3. Open Dialogue: Class discussions about current events or literature can encourage students to analyse and defend their values (Eg- Discussing the ethics of media portrayal)
4. Democratic participation of students in decision making through class discussions allowing students to practice democratic values like fair responsibility, responsibility and compromise.

4. Experiential learning

1. Community Engagement (service learning) connect students with community needs instil values like social responsibility, empathy and giving back.

Eg- Volunteering at a local animal shelter can cultivate compassion for animals
2. Extracurricular Activities like sports or clubs provide opportunities to develop values like leadership, sportsmanship, teamwork and perseverance.

5. Peer Relationships (Positive Social interaction): Fosters values like Cooperation, communication, and teamwork. Eg- Group projects or collaborative activities.

6. Lifelong Learning: Education equip individuals with the critical thinking skills necessary to navigate complex moral situations throughout their lives. Eg- Applying ethical principles in their future careers)

Weakness in the Role of Education

1. Overemphasis on Testing: A focus on standardized tests may overshadow the importance of value development. Eg- Missing ethical implications of genetic engineering in biology curriculum.
2. Unconscious biases of teachers can unintentionally influence students' values. Eg- Favoring students from similar background.
3. Inconsistent implementation of values across schools or classrooms. Eg- One teacher emphasizes honesty while another emphasizes competitiveness
4. Inadequate training of teachers to integrate value-based education into their curriculum.
5. Socio-economic disparities: Students from disadvantaged backgrounds may have fewer opportunities to develop certain values due to resource limitations. Eg- Lack of access to community service programs.
6. Limited Scope: Formal education can't replace the role of families and communities in shaping values. Eg- Importance of family discussions on ethics.
7. Passive Learning: Traditional teaching method may not effectively engage students in active reflection of values. Eg- Rote memorization of ethical principles.
8. Focus on Knowledge, not Application: Students may learn about values but struggle to apply them in real life situations. Eg- Understanding fairness but not intervening in bullying.
9. Conflicts with family Values: There can be clashes between values taught in school and those at home. Eg- School promoting tolerance while family has prejudices.
10. Pressure for Grades: Students might prioritize getting good marks over developing strong ethical principles. Eg- Cheating in an exam to maintain high grades.
11. Limited Resources: Schools may lack resources like qualified teachers

or dedicated time for character development programe.

Eg- Overcrowded classrooms hindering personalised discussions on values.

DEGENERATION OF VALUES IN THE SOCIETY

Case Studies

- Decline in Societal values: "Bois locker Room case" refers to a controversial incident that occurred in Delhi, India in May 2020, where a group of teenage boys (class XI and XII students) allegedly created a private instagram group to share and discuss explicit photos of girls without their consent. The incident sparked outrage and raised concerns about the safety and privacy of women and girls online.
- Blue whale challenge is a social media phenomenon that originated in Russia in 2016. It is a dangerous online game that targets vulnerable individuals, particularly teenagers, and encourages them to complete a series of tasks over a 50-day period. These tasks escalate in severity and ultimate culminated in participant being instructed to commit suicide.
- Weakness in the educational system: A 7 year old student, Pradyuman Thakur was murdered at Ryan International school in Gurugram, India (September 2017). Investigations revealed a teenage classmate as the real suspect, with a reported motive of getting exams postponed.
- The incident of a student hitting a teacher with a slipper during a live class has sparked outrage and raised concerns about respect for others

Reasons for the degeneration of values

1. Shifting family structures from the traditional joint family system to the nuclear family system can lead to the erosion of values transmitted through generations.
2. Consumerism and Materialism can overshadow values like simplicity, frugality and delayed gratification.
3. Influence of westernisation might promote individualism, potentially leading to a decline in values like community service and sacrifice for the greater good.
4. Portrayal of violence, casual sex, and materialism in some media content can clash with traditional values of modesty, non-violence and spiritual pursuits.

5. Educational systems might prioritize rote learning and exam performance over inculcating ethical values and critical thinking skills.
6. Cyberbullying and online harassment eroding the values of empathy and respect. Eg- Bois locker Room.
7. Oversharing on social media can lead to a decline in privacy and a culture of instant gratification, potentially affecting values like patience and delayed gratification.
8. Excessive screen time can lead to social isolation and a decline in values like empathy and real world interaction.
9. The close knit communities of traditional India are often replaced by a sense of anonymity in urban environments.
10. Income inequality can breed resentment and a sense of unfairness, potentially leading to a decline in values like compassion and social justice
11. Increased religious polarization can lead to a decline in tolerance and respect for diverse beliefs, which were traditionally emphasized in Indian Society.

Value Education

- Value Education is the process of inculcating moral values, ethical principles, and social norms in an individual to help them develop into responsible and ethical citizens.
  - It helps individuals to develop a sense of empathy, respect for diversity, and concern for the environment.
  - It teaches individuals to uphold ethical principles and values like honesty, integrity and compassion.
- Value education should be an integral part of the education sytem from the elementary level to higher education.
  - It can be taught through various methods like story telling, role-playing discussion and debates.
  - It is essential that the teaching of values is not limited to the classroom but is reinforced in daily life through practice.
- Indian scholars have always recognised the importance of value education and its role in developing responsible and ethical citizens.

Swami Vivekananda: Emphasized the importance of character-building and moral education for the development of a strong and prosperous nation

Mahatma Gandhi: Believed that education without values is incomplete. He believed that education should focus on developing the character of individuals rather than just imparting knowledge

Rabindranath Tagore: Believed that education should aim at the holistic development of individuals. He emphasized the significance of value education in shaping an individual who is in harmony with nature and society. He believed that education should help individuals develop a sense of responsibility towards their community and the environment.

PYQs Corner

(Write the Answer and Get Free Evaluation)

1. "Education is not an injunction, it is an effective and pervasive tool for all round development of an individual and social transformation". Examine the New Education Policy, 2020 (NEP, 2020) in light of the above statement. (2020, 10 Marks)
2. 'Hatred is destructive of a person's wisdom and conscience that can poison a nation's spirit.' Do you agree with this view? Justify your answer. (2020, 10 Marks)
3. What are the main components of emotional intelligence (EI)? Can they be learned? Discuss. (2020, 10 Marks)
4. "The current internet expansion has instilled a different set of cultural values which are often in conflict with traditional values.' Discuss. (2020, 10 Marks)
5. The crisis of ethical values in modern times is traced to a narrow perception of the good life. Discuss. (2017, 10 Marks)
6. Increased national wealth did not result in equitable distribution of its benefits. It has created only some "enclaves of modernity and prosperity for a small minority at the cost of the majority." Justify. (2017, 10 Marks)
7. Social values are more important than economic values. Discuss the above statement with examples in the context of inclusive growth of a nation. (2015, 10 Marks)
8. The current society is plagued with widespread trust-deficit. What are the consequences of this situation for personal well-being and for societal well-being? What can you do at the personal level to make yourself trustworthy? (2014, 10 Marks)

04 Aptitude and Foundational Values for Civil Services

Views of Reformers / Thinkers on Aptitude

Caral Dweck

- Dweck's mindset theory suggest that individual's beliefs about their own abilities can influence their performance and growth
- Individuals with a growth mindset believe that their abilities can be developed through effort and practice, whereas those with a fixed mindset believe that their abilities are predetermined and unchangeable.

Swami Vivekananda

- Vivekananda emphasized the importance of self-discovery and self-realisation in developing one's aptitude.
- Every individual has a unique potential that can be realised through self-awareness and spiritual growth.

Mahatma Gandhi

- Gandhi believed in the principle of Nai Talim which emphasizes the integration of Intellectual, physical and moral education.
- Individuals should be educated in a way that aligns with aptitudes and interests, enabling them to contribute meaningfully to society.

Rabindranath Tagore

- Tagore emphasized the importance of creativity and imagination in developing one's aptitude.
- this will enable them to achieve personal fulfillment and contribute to society in meaningful ways.

APTITUDE

- Aptitude is the natural ability or innate potential to learn or acquire a skill.
- It is a natural tendency for successful learning of some specific set of skills, which can be further enhanced with adequate knowledge and training.
- It indicates aptness/suitability to succeed in particular field.
- Aptitude encompasses the capacity to learn and acquire new skills, as exemplified by individuals who become proficient in activities after receiving training, such as starting to swim after lessons.
  - Example: Virat Kohli's natural talent for excelling in cricket and become proficient after undertaking cricket training.
- Natural Aptitudes: These are inherent talent or abilities you possess from a young age. Example: A person with a natural aptitude for languages might find it easier to grasp grammar rules and pronunciation in a new language.
- Developed Aptitude: These aptitudes are acquired through experience, training and deliberate practice.

How Aptitude is different from Interest, skill or Intelligence?

Aspects	Interest	Skill	Intelligence
Meaning	Interest is something that attracts us without the need to have any particular skill for a thing.	Skill is the knowledge or ability to perform a given task with ease and precision	It is the capacity for learning, reasoning, understanding & similar forms of mental activity
Difference with Aptitude	A person may be interested in a particular activity, job or training, but may not have the potential/Aptitude to perform well in that particular area and achieve success.	Aptitude denotes the potential to get skilled if training is done.	It is the ability to learn and apply skills. On the other hand, aptitude is the specific ability of a person to master a skill.
Example	One may have intense interest in music, but not enough ability to succeed in a career as a performer	Carrying out the duties of Civil Servant after IBSNAA training	Chess Player requires intellectual prowess to analyse the opponent's move.

APTITUDE		PROFICIENCY		ACHIEVEMENT
Innate ability to learn skill Example: leadership skill		Ability to perform an activity with ease and precision Eg: Dhoni's ability to lead the team		Something achieved with ability and skill. Eg. Dhoni won ICC Trophy thrice

Aptitude for Civil Service: Two-pronged approach

Physical Aptitude

Refers to the physical and physiological fitness to efficiently perform your duties

1. Stamina and Endurance (long work hours)
2. Strength and Agility (Handle various situations)
3. Overall Health (Ensure peak performance)

Mental Aptitude

Refer to psychological and cognitive abilities

- General Mental Ability (GMA): Basic thinking capacity of an individual possessing analytical skills, problem solving skills, etc. Forms the bedrock of other mental aptitudes
- Appropriate Value System: Ethical compass that guides your actions as a civil servant. Includes empathy, objectivity, integrity, compassion etc.

Shifting landscape of Aptitude

- Traditionally, aptitude was looked from the narrow perspective by equating with technical knowledge, skills and intelligence- "Professional Competence in simpler terms.
- The evolving nature of society and governance demands a more holistic approach. This includes the following.

Ethical Acumen: Awareness of ethical issues and the ability to make sound ethical decisions.	Leadership Skills: The ability to inspire, motivate and guide others towards common goal
Emotional Intelligence: Recognising and managing your own emotions, and understanding the emotions of others	Analytical skills for modern challenges like climate change, technological advancements and social complexities

Common Aptitude for Civil Servant

General Mental Ability (GMA)

- Critical thinking: Analyse situations, identify core issues and consider diverse viewpoints to arrive at the most effective course of action
- Understanding of Indian Laws: A civil servant working under Environment Ministry needs to be familiar with EPA, 1986; NGT Act 2010.
- Adaptability: Technology adoption to keep pace with an ever-changing world. Example: SVAMITVA Scheme using drone surveying.

Value System

- Work Ethics: Dedicated to their tasks and strive for excellence. Example: Armstrong Pame (IAS Officer) who built a 100 km road connecting Manipur to Nagaland and Assam, opening access to two villages.
- Honesty and Integrity: Civil servants hold positions of power and must be trustworthy in their actions and decisions.
- Professionalism: Example: DM Cacher Initiative – 'Debo Na, Nebo Na' has simplified the procedure through which people can file their grievances with the administration.

Other Considerations

- Cultural Competency: An IAS officer posted to a state with a different dominant culture needs to be sensitive to local customs, religious beliefs and languages.
- Leadership: Harichandra DM Narayanpet (Telangana) exemplifies leadership through his "Toilet on Wheel" Initiative to achieve Open Defecation Free status.
- Inclusivity: Pawan Kadyan (DM Cooch Bihar) demonstrates inclusivity by focusing on women's menstrual health through his waste management program, Nirmal Cooch Bihar.

Importance of Aptitude for Civil Servants

1. High Administrative Excellence improving the government effectiveness of various policies and projects. Example- Ex-IAS officer Rohini Sindhuri, who spearheaded the "Kakinada Smart City" project, showcasing the importance of these skills in modern governance.
2. Effective governance and improved public service delivery: Communication and leadership aptitude ensures clear communication of government schemes

3. Handling Diverse Responsibilities: Aptitude for adaptability and learning new skills allows civil servants to address diverse challenges across different sectors from rural development and healthcare to infrastructure and taxation.

4. Adaptability to emerging challenges and implementation of innovative solutions: Eg- IAS officer Abhishek Singh, who implemented a block chain based land record management system in Andhra Pradesh is a prime example

5. Resolving ethical dilemmas: Eg. IAS officer Kannan Gopinathan, who resigned in protest against a highway project harming the environment, highlights the importance of a strong moral compass.

6. Collaboration for shared success: Eg- IAS officer Roopa Mishra, who successfully brought together stakeholders for a watershed management project, demonstrates her team work aptitude.

7. Inspiring positive change and motivating others to contribute to India's development.

8. The problem solving aptitude helps them find practical solutions to implement policies in diverse regional contexts.

Attitude vs Aptitude

Attitude	Aptitude
• Refers to a person's mindset or disposition towards a particular object, person or situation	• Refers to a person's inherent ability or potential to learn or excel in a particular skill or task.
• Can be influenced by a person's beliefs, values, emotions and past experiences	• Is largely innate and can be developed through practice and experience.
• Can be positive or negative, depending on the person's attitude towards the object, person or situation.	• Can be high or low, depending on the person's natural ability or potential in a particular skill or task.
• Can affect a person's behaviour, motivation, and decision making.	• Can influence a person's career choices, personal growth and success.
• Can be changed through intentional effort, self-reflection and learning.	• Can be developed through practice, training and experience
• Examples include positive attitude towards work, negative attitude towards change, and neutral attitude towards a new acquaintance	• Examples include aptitude for mathematics, aptitude for music, and aptitude for language learning.

FOUNDATIONAL VALUES

- Refers to the core set of principles and ethical standards that guide the conduct and decision-making of civil servants.
- These values serve as the bedrock of a well-functioning, ethical, and citizen centric bureaucracy.
- Indian Civil Services (ICS) shoulder immense responsibility as they are the architect of policy, the implementers of programs and the direct link between the government and the people. This immense power necessitates a strong foundation in core values to ensure it is used ethically and effectively.
- Foundational values for civil servants can be categorised into 2 main groups:

End Oriented Values
Values which civil servants aim to achieve while performing their duties. Eg: DPSP, FRs, etc

Means Oriented Values
Values in which civil servants behave or act while performing their duties. Eg: Transparency, Efficiency, Responsiveness etc

Importance of Foundational Values

1. Upholding the constitution, laws and underlying values
2. Promoting public trust and legitimacy of the government
3. Ensuring fairness and equality in treatment among citizens (Just society)
4. Prevent misuse of power (Reduced corruption)
5. Building a strong foundation for democracy
6. Moral compass for the Indian civil service.
7. Efficient and effective implementation of policies (Improved public service delivery
8. Fosters innovation and adaptability in fast changing world

Examples:

- **Darez Ahmad Shaikh, IPS officer:** Shaikh implemented a community policing program in Mumbai, involving citizens in crime prevention. This innovative approach led to a significant decrease in crime rates, demonstrating how efficiency can be achieved through collaboration.
- **Roopa Mukherji, IAS officer:** Mukherji, known as the "Lady Engineer of Bihar", worked tirelessly to improve infrastructure and irrigation systems in rural Bihar. Her empathy for the challenges faced by villagers motivated her to find solutions for water scarcity and poverty alleviation.

Sources of Foundational Values

Sources

1. Historical Precedents and Traditions (Kautilya's Arthashastra) - Good governance, Justice, Duty etc.

2. Indian Constitution (Preamble, FRs) - Equality, liberty, justice, Rule of law, Secularism, Democracy etc.

3. Reports of Commissions and Committees (2nd ARC, Nolan Committee) - Integrity, objectivity, Dedication to public service etc

4. Parliamentary Acts and Codes (Civil Services Act 1955; Central Service (Conduct) Rules, 1964; AIS Conduct Rules 1968) - Integrity, Neutrality, Efficiency, Accountability etc.

Nolan Committee - 7 principles of Public life.

- The Nolan committee was established at the United Kingdom in 1994 to examine and make recommendations on ethical standards in public life.
- The Committee produced a report called "Standards in public life", which sets out seven key principles of public life that has become known as the "Nolan principles".

Leadership, Integrity, Selflessness, Objectivity, Accountability, Openness, Honesty

Please note: Definition of each value is explained in chapter-8

Changing nature of foundational values

- The foundational values of civil service do evolve over time, but the core principles remain constant.
- Enduring core principles: Integrity, fairness, and dedication to public service from the bedrock of foundational values which are timeless, remaining relevant across generations.

Driving forces for change		Evolution of new values
1. Increased public participation	>>>	Responsiveness in service delivery.
2. Focus on social justice	>>>	Empathy and citizen-centricity.
3. Technological Advancements	>>>	Adaptability, creativity and innovation.
4. Evolving societal expectations	>>>	Transparency and Accountability.
5. Governmental reforms (such as LPG, Ease of Doing Business)	>>>	Efficiency and Transparency.

INTEGRITY

- The Word "Integrity" stems from the latin word "integer" meaning "Whole" or "Complete".
- Essentially, integrity refers to a state of wholeness where your internal world (beliefs, values) aligns with your external world (actions)

Nolan Commission defined integrity as : Holders of public office should not place themselves under any financial or other obligation to outside individuals or organisations that might seek to influence them in the performance of their official duties.

INTEGRITY
• A concept of consistency of actions, values, methods, measures, principles expectations and outcomes • The honesty and truthfulness or accuracy of one's actions. • The integration of ideals, conviction, standards, belief and behaviour.

Examples of Integrity

Historical	Emperor Ashoka (304BC - 232BC): After the kalinga war, Ashoka embraced non-violence and ethical governance focussing on public welfare, tolerance and justice setting a high standard for integrity in leadership.
Current	Greta Thunberg (Climate Activist): Despite her young age, she displayed remarkable integrity by challenging world leaders on climate inaction.
Administrator	IAS Officer Ashok Khemka: His unwavering stance against corruption (in land deals), despite facing challenges (transfers and threats), exemplifies the courage needed to uphold integrity within the civil service
Individual	Return of lost items: Imagine finding a lost wallet with a significant amount of money. Choosing to return to its rightful owner, even though there's no guarantee of reward, demonstrates personal integrity and honesty.

Types of Integrity

➡ Personal Integrity: Demonstrating consistency and adherence to one's own values, principles and beliefs Bridging the Gap between what you think, Say and do.

Example: Mahatma Gandhi's unwavering commitment to non-violence and truth led him to Suspend Non-cooperation movement.

➡ **Professional integrity**: Acting in accordance with professional ethics, standard and norms. Example: Doctors need to adhere to the Code of Medical Ethics Regulations, 2002 under the Indian Medical Councils Act, 1956.

➡ **Moral Integrity**: Upholding ethical principles and moral values in all aspects of life. Example: Kiran Bedi (first woman IPS) showcased ethical integrity by implementing various reforms and fighting against corruption during her tenure.

➡ **Intellectual Integrity**: Demonstrating consistency and honesty in one's thinking, reasoning, and pursuit of knowledge. Example: Dr. A.P.J Abdul kalam, the former President of India, exhibited intellectual integrity through his life-long dedication to Scientific research and inspiring the younger generation

➡ **Cultural Integrity**: Preserving and Promoting the cultural heritage, traditions and diversity of India. Example: Raja Ravi Varma, the renowned painter, contributed to cultural integrity by depicting Indian Mythological stories and capturing the essence of Indian beauty in his artwork.

➡ **Environmental Integrity**: Commitment to Sustainable practices, conservation and protection of the environment. Example: Jadav Payeng, Known as "Forest man of India," demonstrated environmental integrity by single-handedly planting and nurturing a vast forest ecosystem in Assam.

➡ **Social Integrity**: Upholding social justice, equality and inclusivity. Example: Dr. B.R. Ambedkar, the chief Architect of Indian Constitution, worked tirelessly for social integrity by advocating for the rights and empowerment of marginalised communities.

➡ **Technological Integrity**: Adhering to ethical practices in technology development and usage. Example: Nandan Nilekani, the cofounder of Infosys and the architect of Aadhar, played a crucial role in ensuring Technological Integrity by implementing a secure and inclusive digital identity system.

➡ **Political Integrity**: Consistent use of political power for the public interest independent of private interests. Demonstrating honesty, transparency and accountability in political leadership and governance. Example: Kailash Satyarthi, the Nobel Laureate and child rights activist, showcases political integrity by tirelessly advocating for the rights and well-being of children in India and globally.

Integrity in Civil Services

The 2nd ARC rightly emphasizes that integrity is the cornerstone of an effective civil service. It's about prioritizing the public interest above all else, ensuring decisions are made ethically and responsibly.

INTEGRITY AS A FOUNDATIONAL VALUE

- Building public trust: Civil Servants hold position of trust and thus intended to make morally right decisions even in the presence of external pressure.
- Responsible and transparent use of public services. Example: Former president A.P.J. Abdul Kalam's decision to personally pay for his family's visit during his presidency exemplifies unwavering commitment to public resources
- Effectiveness: fair and unbiased selection of beneficiaries for various welfare programs
- Public Interest: Civil Servants are involved in policy formulation and integrity ensures that these policies are created with public interest in mind and not for any private interest.
- Transparency and Accountability: Culture of Integrity can combat corruption and promote ethical conduct at the organisational level.
- Ethical foundation and administration: Trust and Transparency in the administration influence the overall culture of governance, allowing for more efficient processes and faster decision making.

Reason for low integrity in civil services

- Past instances created a culture of tolerance towards corruption
- Changes in Societal value and the desire for personal gain weaken the commitment to public Service.
- Economic factors Such as low Salaries and limited career prospects combined with increased cost of living.
- Lack of Strong public outcry and weak Social accountability
- Complicated procedures and red-tapism can create frustration and incentivize shortcuts that compromise Integrity.
- Poor implementation of anti-corruption laws and Constitutional protection to civil servants under Article 311.

↓

Leads to corruption in the Society - Bureaucratic corruption, Electoral corruption and moral corruption. (Separate chapter on corruption i.e. Chapter 14)

Measures to promote Integrity in civil Services

1. Policy/legislative changes

- Strong legal framework to protect whistleblowers. Eg- Whistleblower Protection Act (2014)
- Integrity pacts between government agencies and businesses promote ethical procurement practices.

2. Strengthening Institutions.

- Empowerment of anti-corruption agencies like CBI, CVC to ensure effective investigation & prosecution of corruption cases.
- Streamlining bureaucracy by simplifying procedures. (Eg- Single Window Clearance)
- Competitive salaries and benefits to reduce temptation in engaging in corrupt practices for personal gain. Eg: Singapore offers competitive salaries that attract highly qualified individuals to public Service.

3. Governance Reforms

- Mandatory public disclosure of asset for civil Servants (Mandated under Lokpal and Lokayukta Act, 2013)
- Establish online portals and grievance redressal system for citizens to report corruption and bureaucratic hurdles Example - South Korea's Online Anti-Corruption and Civil Wrongs commission, allows citizens to report corruption anonymously, promoting transparency and public participation.
- Develop clear performance metrics and conduct regular evaluations to hold civil servants accountable for their actions.
- Leveraging Technology for public service delivery that minimizes human interaction and reduce opportunities for corruption. Eg- UMANG App, Aadhar based DBT.
- Use of blockchain Technology to create secure and transparent record-keeping systems, minimising opportunities for manipulations. Example - Rwanda utilises blockchain technology in land registry systems, ensuring transparency.

4. Ethical Conduct

- Commitment by the senior officials to ethical conduct to set tone for organisation
- Ethical Dilemmas Training to help them take sound decisions. Example: New Zealand's State services commission provides comprehensive training on ethical leadership promoting culture of Integrity
- Public awareness campaigns to highlight the importance of integrity and encourage citizens to report corruption Example: India's "Satark Bharat, Samriddh Bharat" Campaign

Honesty

- It simply means holding the facts as they are i.e. upholding the truth.
- It is a facet of moral character that connotes positive and virtuous attributes such as integrity, truthfulness including straight-forwardness of conduct along with the absence of lying, cheating, theft etc.
- Nolan Commission defined Honesty as "Holders of public office have a duty to declare any private interests relating to their public duties and to take steps to resolve any conflicts arising in a way that protects the public interest"

Honesty vs Integrity.

- Honesty is about truthfulness: It's about telling the truth and being upfront
- Honesty is about moral character: It's about not only being honest but also adhering to a set of principles and values, even when it's difficult.
- Honesty is a subset of integrity: Integrity implies reliability, consistency in one's principles and values.
- Honesty is a necessary criteria but not a sufficient criteria for integrity.

Example: The Mahabharata example is a great way to illustrate this.

Arjuna honestly admitted his reservations about fighting his relatives, but that wouldn't necessarily show integrity. His integrity came from wrestling with his moral dilemma and ultimately choosing to follow his duty despite his personal feelings.

Examples of Honesty

Historical	Abraham Lincoln: Walking three miles to return an over-charge of 2 dollars exemplifies Lincoln's unwavering honesty and strong moral compass
Current	Mission Satyanishtha by Indian Railways: This initiative demonstrates the railways' commitment to promoting honesty and ethical conduct within their workforce.
Administrator	Satyendra Dubey: Exposing corruption in the Golden Quadrilateral project highlights the courage and integrity required to fight for ethical practices within powerful systems.
Individual	Noticing extra marks on your test and informing the teacher reflects your honesty and commitment to fairness.

Importance of Honesty for Civil Services.

IMPARTIALITY AND NON PARTISANSHIP

- Impartiality refers to a civil servant's ability to make decisions and deliver services based solely on merit, rules and the law, without any personal biases or influences.
- Civil servants must carry out their duties in a fair, unbiased and objective manner
- This principle is crucial for maintaining the trust of the public, as it assures them that services and decisions are administered fairly and without any discrimination.
- Example: A police officer investigating a crime scene focuses on collecting evidence objectively, without making assumptions based on suspect's religion or social status.
- Impartiality works at two different levels for civil servants:

Public Impartiality | Political Impartiality (Non-partisanship)

Criteria	Public Impartiality	Political Impartiality
Focus	Fairness and objectivity in public service delivery	Avoiding involvements in political matters in official capacity.
Scope	All interactions with citizens	Active political participation.
Considerations	Solely based on merit, rule or law	No promotion of specific political agenda
Example	A public health official over-seeing a vaccination drive ensures everyone has equal access to the vaccine, regardless of their background	A police officer maintains neutrality during an election, ensuring all political parties can hold rallies peacefully and citizens can exercise their right to vote freely.

Non-Partisanship refers to the principle that civil servants should not engage in political activities in a way that could compromise their ability to serve the government of the day in a neutral and objective manner.

- Infers that the officer is to do his task without any fear of, or favour to any political party, even if he has strong faith in any political thought

- **Neutrality** is with special reference to the relationship between civil servants and the government / Politician.

Politics - Administration dichotomy

Policy making is the prerogative of political executive	Policy implementation without any question is the task of civil servants.

Conduct Rules for Neutrality: The Central Civil Services Conduct Rules, 1964 and the All India Services Conduct Rules 1968 lays down the following provisions to ensure neutrality of public servants.

Conduct Rules:
- Public servants must not take part in politics.
- They must not give election fund/ assistance to any political party
- They can vote, but must not tell his preference to other people
- They must not display any election symbols on his person, vehicle or home
- They must not participate in rallies and demonstration etc, without government permission.

Committed Bureaucracy

Positive Connotation	Negative Connotation
↓	↓
Commitment to the objectives of state, Constitution and shows dedication to the public service.	Civil servants are loyal to the political party & functions only to serve the narrow interest of party in power.
↓	↓
Civil servants gives technical advice in accordance with the political philosophy of ruling party	Implies politicised bureaucracy. (Against the concept of political neutrality) Eg- Administrative System in Nazi Germany.

POLITICISATION OF BUREAUCRACY

About: It refers to the situation in which the bureaucracy is influenced by political considerations and is used to serve the interest of the ruling party or the political leadership.

- It undermine the foundational value of ruling party or the political leadership.

Recent News: In 2023, the Union government has asked all departments to nominate officers to act as Rath Prabharis or special officers, who will be expected to advertise and promote the achievements of the government over past nine years.

Possible Impact of Politicisation of Bureaucracy:

- Against the spirit of Indian Constitution's Separation of power among the three arms of the state - the executive, the judiciary and the legislature.
- Against the line of separation between the bureaucracy and the military from the political executive. These directives compel civil and military officials to assume partisan positions.
- Violation of Central Civil Services (Conduct) Rules, 1964: It bars government servants from participating in any political activity
- Undermines impartiality of Elections: It can undermine the election process in India, which has largely retained its credibility because of bureaucratic impartiality
- Irreversible damage to institutions: Disregarding norms in pursuit of electoral gains leading to underminining of institutions may lead to irreversible damage.
- Can lead to corrupt practices which ultimately leads to loss of public trust.

Steps to be taken to avoid politicisation of bureaucracy

- Merit based appointments and promotions in bureaucracy.
- Transparent transfer postings.
- Legal and institutional measures to strengthen the autonomy and independence of the bureaucracy. Eg- Whistleblower Protection Act.
- Adherence to code of conduct by civil servants.
- Strengthening ethics and values through training.
- Enforce a Code of Ethics for both the civil servants and the political executive.
- Civil Society organisations can play a crucial role in holding bureaucrats and politicians accountable.

Challenges in maintaining Impartiality and Non-Partisanship

- Political Pressure to favor a particular political agenda, making it difficult to maintain professional integrity.
- Social Pressures to favour members of their own community or caste.
- Historical practices of patronage systems where favors were granted based on personal connections, can leave behind a culture susceptible to bias.

- Resource constraints can make resource allocation decisions seen as favoring one group over another.
- Complex regulations can lead to unintentionally favoring certain interpretations.
- Lack of strong transparency and accountability mechanisms
- Lack of clear guidelines can leave civil servants without the necessary support for impartial decisions.
- Weak organisational culture of professionalism and ethical conduct.
- Ineffective training on overcoming the unconscious biases based on upbringing, social conditioning and personal experiences.

These challenges require a multipronged approach.

- Clear and well defined Code of conduct
- Effective system of transparency and accountability.
- Strong grievance redressal mechanisms.
- Training and capacity building.
- Public awareness campaigns
- Strengthening of institutions like judiciary, CAG, Election Commission etc

ANONYMITY

- The Principle of anonymity emphasises that permanent executive works from behind the screen and avoid media attention, public pronouncements or taking personal credit for achievements.
- India's civil service system is based on the British Westminster model, where anonymity is a core principle.

Benefits	Complete anonymity is not desirable
1. Maintain civil service neutrality 2. Provide frank advice to ministers 3. Promotes open and honest policy discussion. 4. Focus on long term development goals.	• Sense of detachment from the public and thus, lacking empathy. • Top down approach of policy formulation with "One size fits all". • Less accountable bureaucracy (Prevented from media scrunity or public questioning • Undesirable in the age of transparency and E-Governance

OBJECTIVITY

- Objectivity in governance means adherence to rationality, legality and proven standards, procedures and norms in institutions by the public authorities.
- It implies that the governance decision should be taken based on merit and after rigorous analysis of evidence.
- Evaluating a situation fairly, based on facts, without any biases, personal beliefs, feelings or external influence and thus antithetical to subjectivity.
- Nolan Commission defined objectivity as: 'Holders of public office should make decisions solely on the basis of merit and in the public interest.

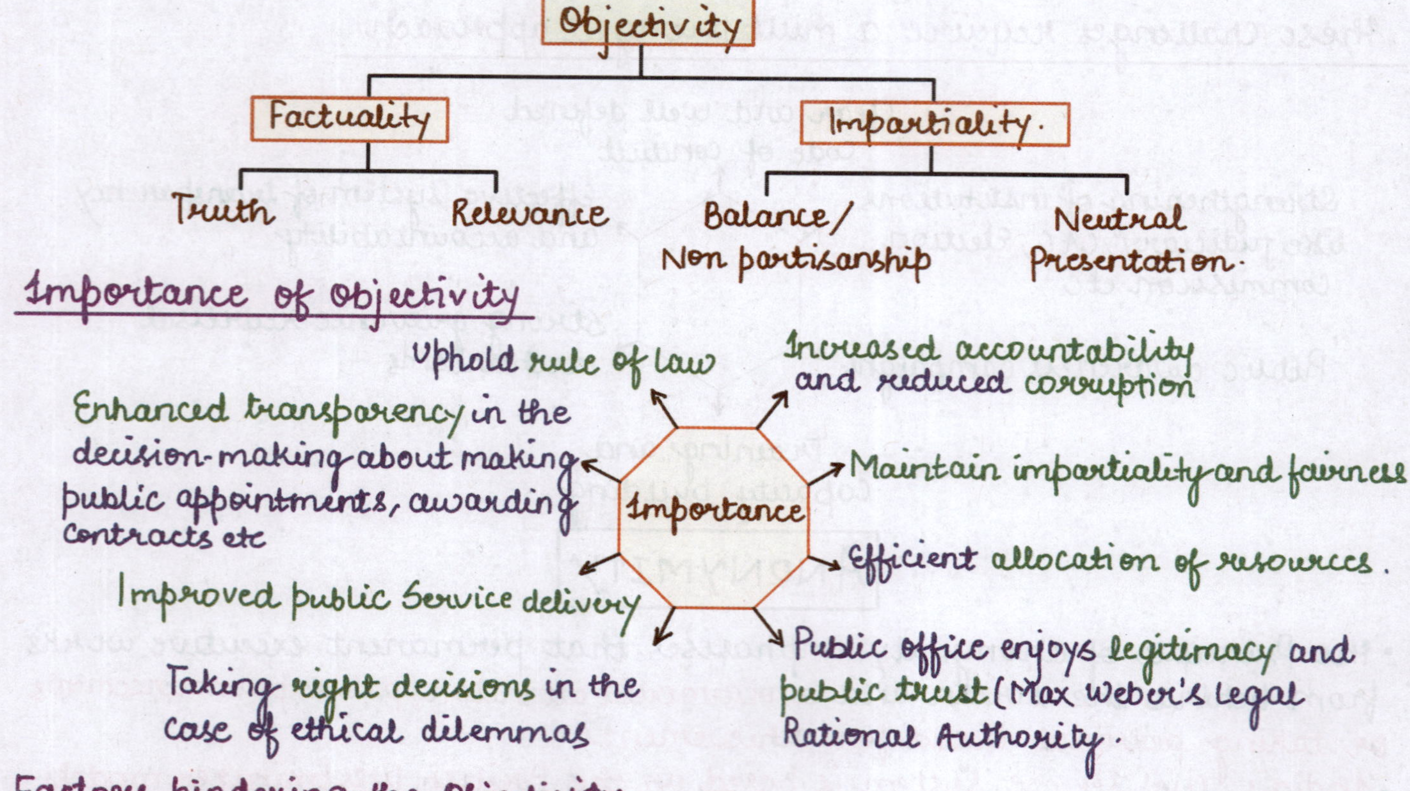

Factors hindering the Objectivity

- Stereotypes can lead to judging individuals based on those assumptions rather than any merit.
- Halo effect: Letting one positive trait overshadow other qualities, both positive and negative.
- Primary effect: Giving undue weight to first impressions, potentially overlooking later information.
- Recency effect: focussing too heavily on recent events or experiences, neglecting past contexts.
- Emotions: Strong emotions can cloud judgement and make it difficult to think rationally.

- Pressure from Superiors to make decisions even if that go against your objective assessment.
- Desire for personal gain or career advancements.

Complete objectivity is not desirable as it poses various challenges for the governance

- Indian constitution is not an objective document. Example: Positive discrimination towards SC, ST, women under Article 15.
- Executive decisions have inherent biases to achieve social good such as subsidies, reservation etc.
- Objectivity vs Empathy: Empathy is targeted towards the individuals while objectivity looks at the masses.
- Policy Paralysis: Absolute objectivity in governance could cause delays, inaction and inability to take policy decisions by the government.
  Example: India's defense procurement process is notorious for its lengthy bureaucratic procedures, impacting crucial acquisition such as Rafael deal.
- Elimination of administrative space for adjustment: India society being pluralistic, it is necessary to give scope for implementation of laws according to diverse socio-cultural and economic needs.
- Hinderance to efficient delivery of public services.
- Decrease administrative capacity to deal with extraordinary situations
  Example: Adopting violent methods is against the constitutional spirit of justice but in extraordinary situations like terrorist attack and riots, sometimes it becomes necessary to issue orders of shoot at sight.
- Objectivity is not an end in itself but a means to fulfill the constitutional values of equality, Justice etc

How to build enlightened objectivity among civil servants?

Although objectivity is a must in governance for maintaining accountability, transparency, neutrality and probity in governance but an enlightened objectivity rather than absolute objectivity is more appropriate to add fairness and caters to the needs of the changing social paradigms.

There are following measures that can be taken for building an enlightened objectivity:

- Enforcement of clear and robust ethical codes that govern civil servant conduct and decision making.
- Training of Civil Servants to make them aware of the procedures and updated with new changes. Eg: Training of Tax officers after the implementation of GST.
- Role modelling by highlighting exemplary leaders such as T.N. Seshan's dedication to fair elections.

• System like RTI, social audits, citizen charters and grievance redressal mechanisms regularly evaluate decisions for objectivity and fairness.
• Effective enforcement of anti-corruption laws like Lokpal and lokayukta to deter misconduct and reduced discretion.
• Embrace technology to reduce human intervention in decision making, minimising subjectivity in the process.
• Encourage citizen involvement in decision making to ensure government actions align with public needs.
• Evidence based policy making that aligns with the needs of people based on data & facts
• Information management system: Decision could not be taken in the lack of adequate information. Eg: the MGNREGA has said to have the best MIS, one that is aligned with the core idea of "proactive disclosure" of all information related to implementation of the schemes.

DEDICATION TO PUBLIC SERVICE

Dedication to public services is highest form of commitment to serve the public and their interests with diligence, sincerity and a focus on common good.

- Commitment suggests that one is bound or obligated because he/she has made a pledge or a promise through a formal agreement.

• Dedication is a commitment with inner motivation or passion for working in the larger public interest.

- A person is inspired by the sense of duty and his ideals or ideals of the society

• Dedication is the quality of being able to give or apply one's time, attention or self entirely to a particular activity cause or a person.

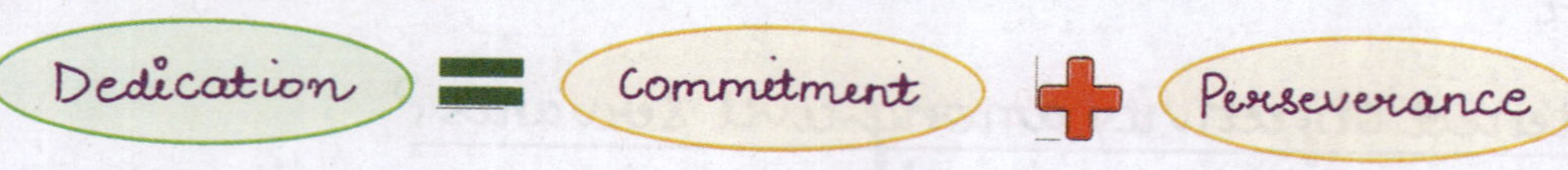

Perseverance is the steady persistence shown in achieving a particular goal despite difficulties & encouragement

Examples of Dedication to Public Services

Historical	Nelson Mandela: Devoted 27 years to prison for his fight against aparthied, showing unwavering dedication to justice and equality.
Current	Kailash Satyarthi is a prominent Indian social reformer who has dedicated his life to fight against child exploitation (Child labour)
Adminis-trator	• Aruna Sundarajan: Headed the Kudumbashree project, a poverty alleviation program in Kerala that empowered women through micro-credit and entrepreneurship.
Other	APJ Abdul Kalam (Scientist, Missile Man); Baba Amte (Social activist); Vikram Sarabhai (Space and Science); Homi Bhabha (Nuclear Energy); MS Swaminathan (Green Revolution in India); Dashrath Manjhi (Mountain Man)

Importance of Dedication in Public Services

- Prioritising Public interest: Eg: IAS officer MG Rajamanickam, during the kerala floods, carried rice sacks, putting public welfare above Personal Comfort
- Poverty alleviation requires a dedicated and responsive bureaucracy.
Eg: Implementation of DBT Scheme and linking with unique Aadhar ID.
- Infrastructure Development: Eg- E-Sreedharan, the "Metro Man", behind the success of metro rail projects in India.
- Realising the Constitutional ideals of justice, liberty, equality etc.
- Ensures probity in public life: Eg- Divya Dev Rajan exemplifies dedication by embracing the local language to serve effectively which fosters trust and transparency and reducing the scope for corruption.
- Handle stressful and difficult work situations especially in the backdrop of terrorist attacks and issue of Naxalism.
- Navigating social opposition faced during sensitive programs. Eg. Sonam Wangchuk's "Operation New hope" revolutionized education in Ladakh despite resistance.
- Driving Innovation: Eg- Dedication of thousands of Scientists and Civil Servants who worked tirelessly to develop indigenously COVID-19 vaccine and then undertaking World's largest vaccination drive.
- Increased efficiency and effectiveness of public Services.
- Enhances the credibility within administration and increases the trust of people in the government.

TOLERANCE

Tolerance refers to a permissive attitude towards those whose opinion, practices, race, religion, nationality, etc differ from one's own.

- It is an act or capacity to endure the diversity of views and practices in our environment.

Examples of Tolerance

Historical	• Ashoka's Dhamma Policy - People should be able to live in peace and harmony with one another. People should treat other religious faiths with respect and tolerance • Hinduism concept of 'Vasudhaiva kutumbakam' or Jainism concept of 'Anekantavada' preach the tolerance value.
Western Moral thinker	• Tolerance embraces the principle of 'Golden Mean' advocated by Aristotle
Indian Constitution	• Goal of Secularism that respect the religious views and beliefs of each religion. Article 25 - Article 28 of Indian Constitution provides for Freedom of religion.

	• Protection of linguistic and religious minorities (Article 29 & 30)
National level	• Adopted the 'Unity in Diversity' model that describes the unity and cohesiveness of India's diverse cultures, religions and languages.
International level	• Article 51 - Promote International peace and Security. • Principles of Non-Aligned movement (NAM) and Panchsheel.

Need of Tolerance in the Society

1. Peaceful Co-existence of diverse religious communities like Hindus, Muslims, Sikhs etc lead to reduced tensions and conflicts, fostering a more stable and harmonious society.
2. Strength in diversity that fuels innovation, creativity and problem solving, leading to a more dynamic and adaptable society.
3. Strengthening community bonds through the celebration of festivals like Diwali or Christmas that transcends religious boundaries.
4. Cultural enrichment through cross cultural exchange. Example - Indian classical music forms like carnatic music in the South and Hindustani music in the north have influenced each other over centuries.
5. Economic prosperity: Eg - India's IT industry thrives on its diverse workforce.
6. Foundation of Democracy: Tolerance allows for free speech, dissent and the peaceful exchange of ideas, which are cornerstones of democratic systems.
7. Global Peace: Eg - India's Foreign policy emphasizes peaceful coexistence and has played a mediatory role in international conflicts.
8. Personal Growth: Tolerance for diverse spiritual paths allowed individuals to explore their own faith.
9. Foundation of other values: Tolerance creates the space for empathy and compassion to flourish.

Importance of tolerance for civil services

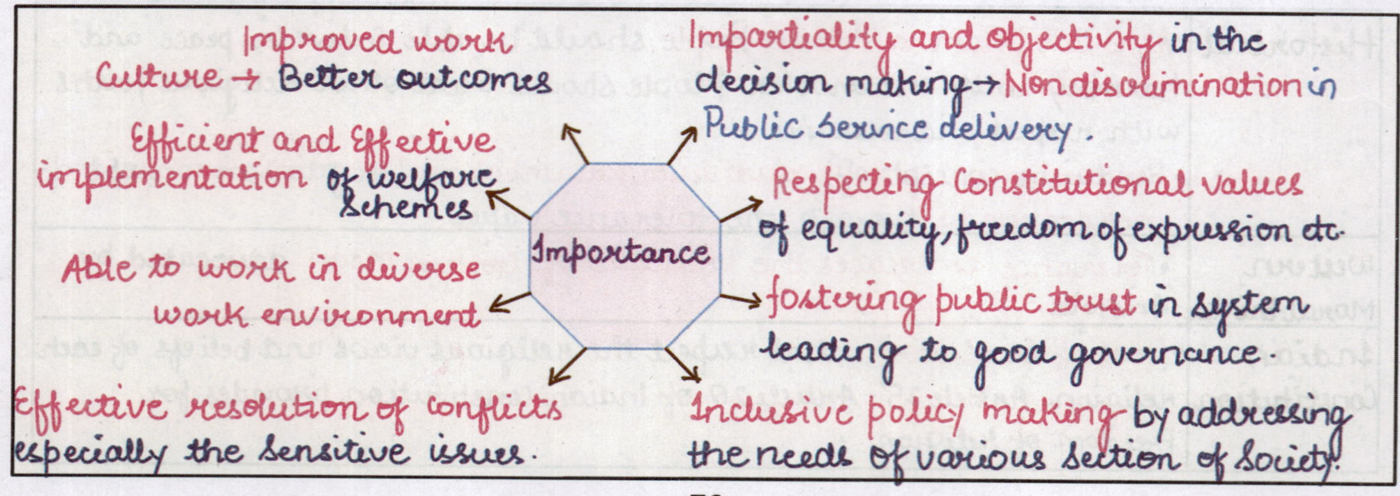

EMPATHY AND COMPASSION

Apathy → Sympathy → Empathy → Compassion

1. **Apathy**: Absence of any emotional response and being numb to someone else's struggles. Absence of Attachment.
2. **Sympathy**: Refers to acknowledging another person's emotional hardships and providing comfort and assurance. feeling of sorrow for someone else's misfortune. It involves a sense of distance or separation from the other person's experience.
3. **Empathy**: Involves putting yourself in another person's shoes and trying to understand their emotions. It's like feeling the other person's pain as if it were your own.
4. **Compassion**: This is the ultimate expression of care. It's not just understanding someone's suffering, but also taking action to alleviate it. Compassion motivates us to help those in need.

Example highlighting the difference

- A friend loses their job
  - Sympathy: You might say, "That's awful, I'm so sorry to hear that". (Acknowledges the situation but keeps distance).
  - Empathy: You might say, "I can imagine how stressed you must feel right now. Job hunting can be tough." (Understands the emotions)
  - Compassion: You might say, "I'm so sorry to hear that. Is there anything I can do to help? Maybe I can look over your resume or help you practice for interviews." (Combines understanding with a desire to help.)

Examples of Compassion

Historical	• Mother Teresa dedicated her life to caring for the poor, sick & dying, particularly those considered "untouchables" in Indian Society. Her work embodies selfless compassion.
Current	• Malala Yousafzai Shot by Taliban for advocating for girls' education in Pakistan, Malala Continues to fight for education equity globally, showing compassion for the future generation.
Administrator	• Operation Suleimani was introduced by Prasanth Nair(IAS), which guarantees a right to food without answering any question or long delays

Need for Empathy and Compassion in Bureaucracy.

1. Encourage citizen centric administration fostering trust and cooperation between citizens and the administration.
2. Effective delivery of public Services tailored to the needs of population.
3. Promotion of social justice by ensuring fair and equitable access to government Services for all citizens (Positive discrimination under Article 14, 15 and 16)
4. Fulfilling the goal of inclusive growth.
5. Humanistic Bureaucracy: Weberian bureaucracy is impersonal in nature but development require bureaucrats to imbibe these values and understand the suffering of citizens.
6. Change the colonial nature of bureaucracy which neglected the needs of Indians.
7. Encouraging public participation in the policy formulation, implementation and monitoring.
8. Improving emotional intelligence and better decision making.

Ways to Cultivate Empathy and Compassion

01 Provide sensitive training to inculcate empathetic attitude.

02 Exposure to the arts: Eg- Satyajit Ray's "Pather Panchali" portrays poverty and rural India, fostering empathy for those realities.

03 Self-Awareness: Practice mindfulness through yoga or meditation.

04 Perspective-Taking Exercises: Street plays (Nukkad Natak) depict citizen-bureaucracy interactions from the citizen's perspective.

05 Travel and cultural exchange broadens the perspective and fosters empathy for diverse ways of life. (Bharat Darshan for Civil Servants)

06 Active listening to others stories and experiences, without judgement, allows for deeper connection and fosters compassion.

07 Volunteering to slums or old age homes allows for first hand exposure to challenges faced by underprivileged communities.

08 Overcoming redtapism and making citizen- bureaucratic interactions more user friendly.

> This chapter is restricted only to the foundational values for civil Servants. There are other public Service values which one must go through in chapter-8.

PYQs Corner

(Write the Answer and Get Free Evaluation)

1. Apart from intellectual competency and moral qualities, empathy and compassion are some of the other vital attributes that facilitate the civil servants to be more competent in tackling the crucial issues or taking critical decisions. Explain with suitable illustrations. (2022, 10 Marks)
2. Should impartial and being non-partisan be considered as indispensable qualities to make a successful civil servant? Discuss with illustrations. (2021, 10 Marks)
3. "Integrity is a value that empowers the human being." Justify with suitable illustration. (2021, 10 Marks)
4. Identify five ethical traits on which one can plot the performance of a civil servant. Justify their inclusion in the matrix. (2021, 10 Marks)
5. State the three basic values, universal in nature, in the context of civil services and bring out their importance. (2018, 10 Marks)
6. One of the tests of integrity is complete refusal to be compromised. Explain with reference to a real life example. (2017, 10 Marks)
7. Why should impartiality and non-partisanship be considered as foundational values in public services, especially in the present day socio-political context? Illustrate your answer with examples. (2016, 10 Marks)
8. "Integrity without knowledge is weak and useless, but knowledge without integrity is dangerous and dreadful." What do you understand by this statement? Explain your stand with illustrations from modern day context. (2014, 10 Marks)

05 Attitude

"Attitude is a readiness of the psyche to act or react in a certain way"

— Carl Jung.

"A weak person never forgives. Forgiveness is the attitude of the strong." (This highlights a forgiving attitude as a sign of strength and wisdom).

"Be the change that you wish to see in the world". (This quote highlights the importance of a proactive and solution oriented attitude in creating positive change).

Mahatma Gandhi

"The only person you are destined to become is the person you decide to be." (Connects a growth mindset and positive attitude to self improvement)

—Ralph Waldo Emerson

"Words are the most powerful drug used by mankind"

(Highlights the power of language and persuasion in influencing thoughts and actions.

— Rudyard Kipling

" Yatha Raja, Tatha Praja (As is the King, so are the people)."

(Emphasizes the influence of leaders on society)

-Kautilya

ATTITUDE

- Attitude is a learned tendency to act, think and feel in particular ways towards a class of people, objects, place or event.
- Attitude refers to our feelings of preference, approval or disapproval towards different things, indicating our evaluations and reactions based on the information we receive.
- Attitude of an individual towards attitude object expresses the relationship (Positive or negative) with the attitude object.

EAGLY AND CHAIKEN - Attitude is "a psychological tendency expressed by evaluating a particular entity with some degree of favour or disfavour". In ethics, attitude refers to the moral stance an individual holds towards certain actions, behaviours, or beliefs. It involves evaluating whether something is right or wrong, good or bad, based on ethical principles or moral values.

Example

1. Attitude towards Environment:
   - Recycling reduces waste and benefits the environment.
   - Deforestation harms ecosystem and contribute to climate change.
2. Attitude towards Education:
   - lifelong learning enhances personal growth and career opportunities.
   - Illiteracy limits individuals' potential and hinders societal progress.

Belief + Value = Attitude

"Belief + Value = Attitude": Attitudes are formed based on our beliefs about something and the personal values we attach to it.

Belief	Value
• Belief refers to our thoughts or convictions about a particular object, person, situation or idea.	• Value refers to the importance or significance we assign to certain beliefs or principles.
• It's what we think or perceive to be true about something.	• Values represent our fundamental beliefs about what is good, desirable or important in life.
• these beliefs can be based on personal experiences, information we have received, or societal influences	• they guide our behaviour and decision making.

Values vs Attitude

- Values decide what we think is right or wrong or worth doing while Attitude determine our general likes and dislikes.
- Values are acquired after a substantial investment of time and energy; hence they are more or less permanent in nature. While Attitudes are difficult to change, but still change is possible.
- Values are derived from conscience, individual, family, education, religion, Society and cultural norms. While Attitudes are built upon beliefs, values, feelings and personal experiences.

Example: Animal welfare.
Belief: Someone believes that animals should be treated with kindness and compassion.
Value: they hold the value of empathy and respect for all living beings;
Attitude: As a result, their attitude towards animal welfare is positive
• They may advocate for animal rights, support organisations working towards animal welfare, or choose to follow a vegetarian or vegan lifestyle to align their actions with their beliefs and values.

Characteristics of Attitude

- Evaluation: Attitude involves making judgements about people, objects, events or ideas, whether positive, negative or neutral.
- Expressiveness: Attitude seeks expression through behaviour, words and emotions, reflecting our preferences and values.
- Influence: Attitude can influence how others perceive us and how we interact with them, attracting or repelling people based on shared or conflicting attitudes.
- Consistency: Our attitudes tend to be relatively stable over time and across different situations, providing a consistent lens through which we view the world.
- Predictiveness: Attitude can predict our future actions and behaviours, guiding our decisions and choices based on our preferences and beliefs.
- Multi-dimensional: Attitudes are multi-dimensional, composed of cognitive, affective and behavioural component.
- Learned: Attitudes are learned through a variety of processes, including direct experiences, socialisation, and exposure to pervasive messages.
- Reflect personality: It includes certain aspects of the personality as interest, appreciation, and social conduct. It indicates the total of a man's inclination and feelings.
- Mutable/Fluctuating: It can vary from time to time

ATTITUDE CLASSIFICATION

Positive Attitude	Negative Attitude
→ An optimistic way of thinking that leads to greater happiness and success in life.	→ Pessimistic mindset characterised by seeing the worst aspect of situations
→ Manifestations	→ Manifestations
• Creative and constructive thinking: Encourages innovative solutions and risk taking.	• Destructive thinking: Hinders creativity and problem solving.
• Motivation and Energy: Drives individuals towards acheiving their goals	• Lack of motivation: Drains energy and drive for action.
• Resilience: Provides strength to persevere through obstacles	• Unhappiness: leads to chronic sadness and dissatisfaction.
Example: Civil Servant 'X' remains optimistic despite setbacks in urban planning, viewing obstacles as opportunities for improvement.	Example: Industrialist 'A' views market challenges with pessimism, resisting innovation and growth opportunities due to fear of failure.

Bureaucratic Attitude	Democratic Attitude
• It is generally exhibited by public servants in government departments	• It is based on the principles of democracy, wherein public service is citizen centric.
• It follows a top-down, one size fits all approach and reflects hierarchical discipline.	• It follows a bottom-up, participatory & flexible approach to decision making.
• It is rules obsessed and there is implicit obedience to orders from above.	• It is people oriented and follows stake-holders approach while finding solutions to citizen's problems.
• It lacks accountability to the people & hold itself answerable only to the rules and regulations, hierarchy.	• It upholds accountability to the people making it responsive to the citizen's needs.
• It involves discretion in the hands of the select few who sit at the top of the organizational structure.	• Since citizens are included in the decision-making process, it is more transparent and inclusive.
• Adherence to rules, hierarchy makes it agonizingly slow and prone to Red Tapism	• Since it involves consensus building, it is also time consuming.

FUNCTIONAL APPROACH OF ATTITUDE

Attitude performs various functions for the individual as well as the Society. Katz (1960) proposed that the needs satisfied by attitudes, and consequently the functions they serve, can be classified into four main categories:

Knowledge (Understanding function)

- Attitudes provides a framework for understanding the world, making it more predictable and manageable.
- Enlightenment brought the shift in attitude to a focus on education and the pursuit of knowledge. (Importance of reason and critical thinking)

Value Expressive (Ego - Expressive)

- Attitudes serve as a way for individuals to express their core values and identity.
- Mother Teresa's attitude for poor represented to the world her value of serving the humanity.

Adaptive (Utilitarian function)

- Attitudes can help an individual to fit well in society by holding socially acceptable attitude.
- Example: A person develops a positive attitude towards a political viewpoint because it aligns with the views of their friends and family.

Ego - Defensive

- Attitudes act as a defense mechanism, protecting the individual's self-esteem or justifying actions that might be socially unacceptable.
- Example: An individual insecure about their intellectual abilities develops a negative attitude towards academic institutions, viewing them as elitist.

Social identity function: Shavitt added it as another function of attitudes

- This function focuses on how those attitudes reflect, express, and even create their social identities.
- We hold certain attitudes because they align with the values and beliefs of the groups we identify with.

Example: Purchase of an indian flag on Republic Day may be driven primarily by social identity goals rather than patriotic motivation.

Factors Influencing Attitude Development.

Attitude formation is the process through which we develop our opinions, feelings and beliefs towards various topics, actions or objects in our environment

Classical / Pavlonian conditioning:	Operant (Instrumental) conditioning:
• learns to respond in a desired manner to a previously neutral stimulus that has been presented repeatedly, in combination with an unconditioned stimulus that elicits the desired response • In this conditioning, the behaviour is involuntary. • Example – If a particular brand's commercial always features uplifting music and happy images, viewers may start associating positive feeling with that brand.	• learning from consequences of actions that reward or punish us. In this conditioning, the learner is active and is rewarded or punished. • Example – A child receiving praise and rewards for doing homework on time is more likely to repeat the behaviour, while a teenager getting grounded for breaking curfew may be less likely to do so again.
Observation learning:	**Social comparison**
• learning by watching and imitating others, especially role models. • Example – A young person adopting the fashion style of their favourite celebrity, influenced by someone they admire.	• forming attitudes by comparing ourselves to others or our peers. • Example – Someone adopting eco-friendly habits like recycling or reducing plastic usage after noticing their peers becoming more environmentally conscious to fit in with their social group's perceived norms

Example of Pavlov conditioning

• Pavlov taught dogs to respond to a ringing bell followed by food. Salivation was elicited by the food (Unsettled stimulus), and the bell elicited salivation after repeated bell-food pairings.

• The unconditional stimulus in this experiment is dog food, which produces an unconditioned response, saliva. The ringing bell is the conditional stimulus, and it causes the dogs to produce saliva as a conditioned response.

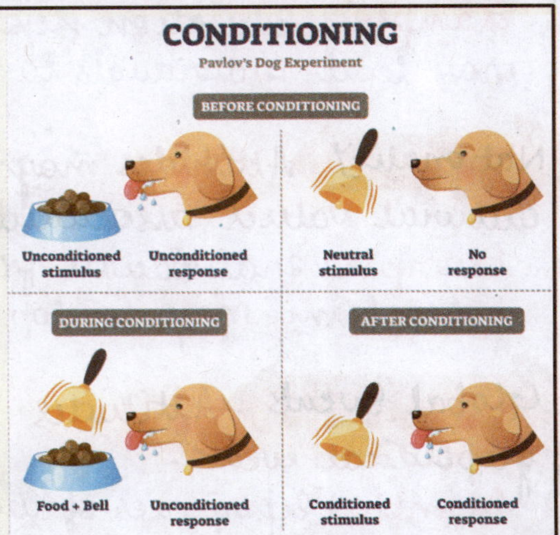

Key factors in Attitude formation

Personal Experiences Individual experiences shape attitudes.
Example: Someone who has had positive experiences with dogs may develop a favourable attitude towards them.

Family Values: Attitudes are often influenced by the value and beliefs instilled by one family.
Example: If a family places a high value on education, the individual may develop a positive attitude towards learning.

Peers As the individual develops, he comes in contact with the outer world and peers in the first place. Peers includes friends of same age, friends, neighbours, classmates etc.
Example: A child tries to internalize the attitudes of these peoples.

Community/Society Attitudes can be influenced by the cultural norms and expectations within a community or society.
Example: In a society that values collectivism, individuals may develop attitudes that prioritize group harmony over individual needs.

Religion: Religious beliefs and teachings can significantly impact attitudes
Example: A person following Buddhism may develop an attitude of compassion and non-violence.

Education: Attitudes can be shaped by formal education systems.
Example: Education system promoting environmental awareness may lead individuals to develop pro-environmental attitudes.

Nationality: Attitudes may be influenced by one's nationality and the cultural values associated with it.
Example: Individuals from a country with a strong tradition of patriotism may develop attitudes that prioritizes loyalty to the nation

Global Events: Attitudes can be shaped by international relations and geopolitical events.
Example: Experiences of war or conflict may lead individuals to develop attitudes of mistrust towards certain countries or cultures.

Prejudice : An Attitude could include prejudice, which occurs when we make assumptions about a situation before carefully considering all the available information.
Example: Media trials post suicide of Sushant Singh Rajput before court's verdict.

Media : It plays a major role in shaping people's opinions and beliefs.
Example: Opinion polls before the elections helps in shaping people's opinions

Conditioning : It occurs when we become accustomed or adjusted to certain people, situations or environments, influencing development of our attitudes
Example: when a patient's life is saved by a particular hospital during critical moments, they develop a favourable attitude towards the hospital and its staff.

Direct instructions : It refers to instances where information or guidance directly influences attitude formation.
Example: If someone provides detailed information about the benefits of a particular hair dye, it may lead us to develop a positive attitude towards it

Satisfaction of wants : Attitudes can be influenced by the extent to which our wants and needs are satisfied by people or objects.
Example: If a friend consistently helps us whenever in need, we are likely to develop a favourable attitude towards th

Attitude formation based on stages of Socialisation

Early childhood : Whatever child observes gets imprinted in his mind. Exposure to different object create different impression.
Example: Learning of mother tongue.

↓

Adolescent : Nature of attitude of a child is determined by nature of social environment the child is born and grows. Example- If a child sees his family stereotyping people, he also tends to develop it.

↓

Adulthood : Least effective stage as the adult has his own prejudices and knowledge. Example- the attitude of patriarchy which has been followed in family, has been observed in future also.

SOCIALISATION

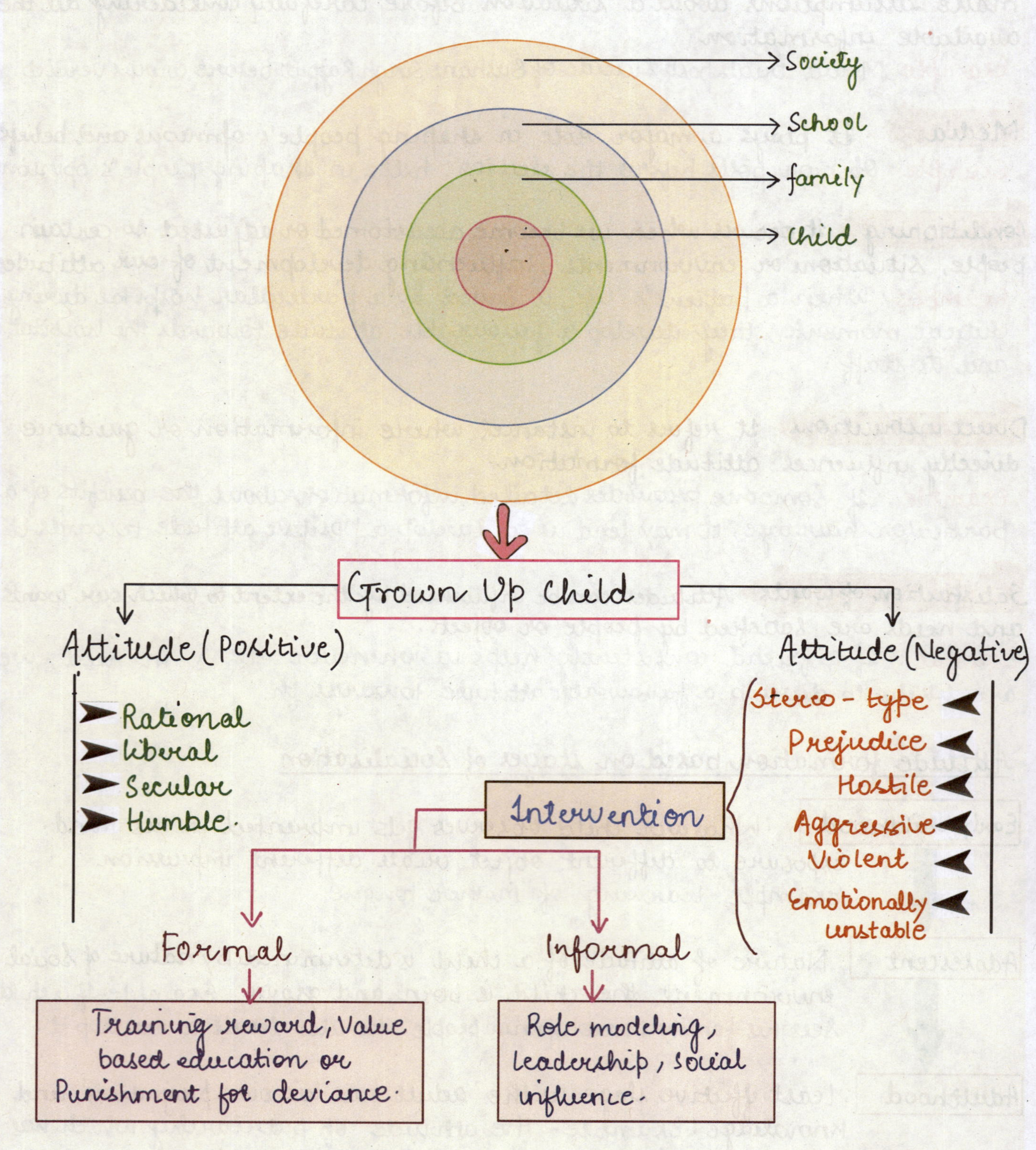

STRUCTURE OF ATTITUDE

1. ABC- Three layer Model of Attitude

- Three layer model of Attitude is a way to understand how we feel, think and act towards any attitude object in our life, like people, places, things etc
- Attitude is a complex construct comprising affective, behavioural and cognitive component, as described by social psychologist Donelson R. forsynth It's like breaking down our attitude into three main parts: What we feel, what we think and what we do.

1. Affective Component (Feeling)

- Emotional response: Our immediate emotional reaction to stimuli
- Example: You might feel anxious and scared around dogs

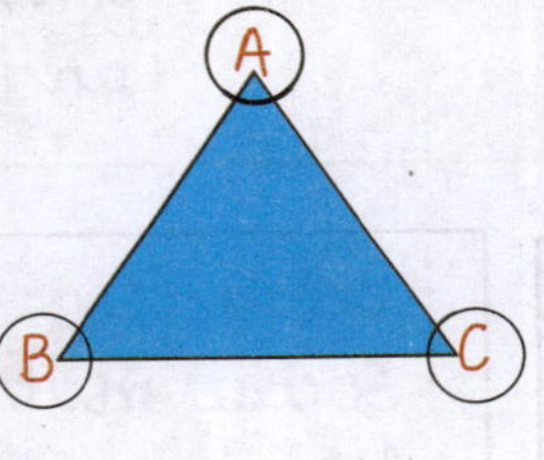

2. Behavioural Component (Acting)

- Actions and responses: Reflects our inclination to act based on attitudes
- Example: You might cross the street to avoid a dog because of your negative attitude towards them (Behavioural Component)

3) Cognitive component: (Thinking)

- Beliefs and perceptions: Involves our beliefs and understanding.
- Example - You might believe dogs are unpredictable and dangerous (Cognitive component of a negative attitude towards dog)

Synergy in ABC model

- All these components are strengthened and supported by each other.
  - Example: If an individual likes singing (affective component) and believes it helps in mental health management (cognitive element), then the individual is likely to join a singing class (behavioural component)
- ABC component are different but they are not completely independent but they are not completely independent of each other.

Cognitive

Behavioural

Affective

Expectancy Value Model of Attitude

Attitude towards issues are shaped by two main factors: our expectations of the outcomes of our actions, and the personal values we hold

Expectations	Values
• It focuses on what we anticipate will happen as a result of our actions. • Example: If we believe that behaving ethically will lead to positive outcomes, we are more likely to adopt ethical attitudes and behaviours. • Example: If we expect negative consequences from ethical actions, we may be less inclined to follow ethical principles.	• It emphasizes the importance of personal values in shaping our ethical attitudes. • Our attitudes towards ethical issues are influenced by the values we hold dear. • Example: If honesty is a core value for an individual, they are likely to adopt attitudes that promote honesty in their actions and decisions.

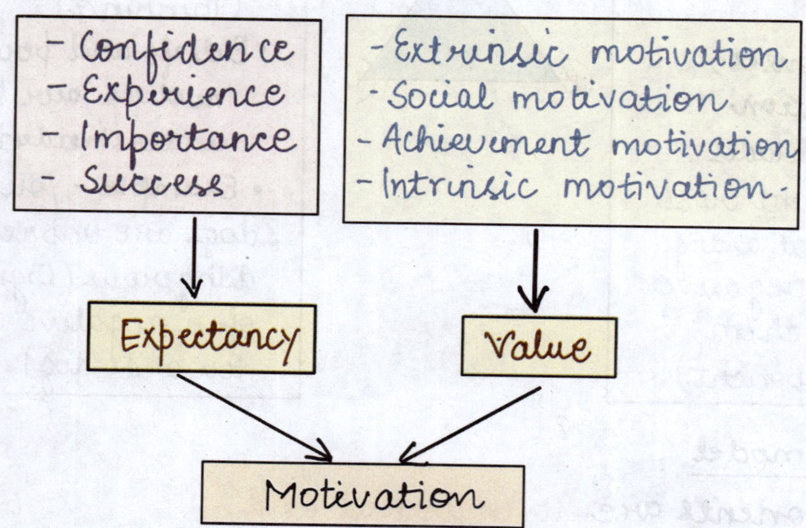

MODE Model: Theory of Attitude Evaluation.

- MODE Model: Motivation and opportunity as Determinants of the attitude-behaviour relation, is a theory that explains how attitude influences behaviour
- It suggest that two main factors determine whether attitudes will translate into behaviour: Motivation and Opportunity.

Motivation	Opportunity
• Motivation refers to the desire or willingness to act based on our attitudes. • If we are motivated to act in line with our attitudes, we are more likely to do so. • Source of motivation: Personal values, beliefs, external incentives etc.	• Opportunity refers to the external circumstances that enable or facilitate the expression of our attitude through behaviour. • Even if we are motivated to act in a certain way, if the opportunity to do is lacking, our behaviour may not align with our attitudes. • factors influencing opportunity: Social norms, resources or situational constraints

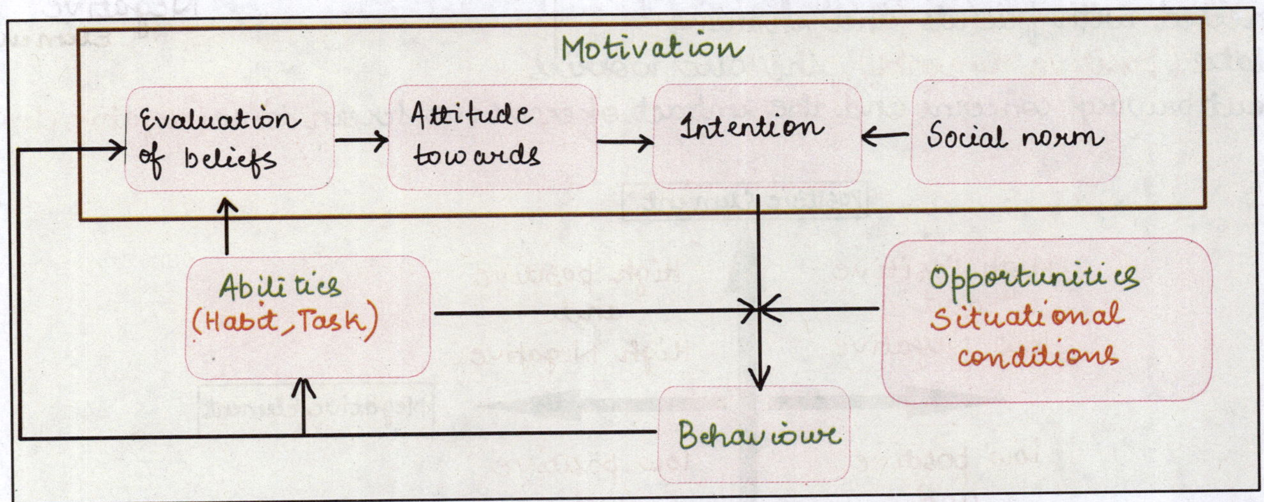

PERSPECTIVE IN ATTITUDE

Attitude structure encompasses the arrangement of positive and negative evaluations within the cognitive, affective and behavioural component (ABC).

Example: I have positive cognition (saving lives) towards blood donation, but when asked to donate blood (behavioural), I respond negatively because of negative emotions (affective), like fear of needles.

One dimensional perspective.

- Attitudes are envisioned along a single continuum, ranging from positive to negative
- It assumes that the presence of positive elements suppresses negative ones, resulting in a consistent stance towards an object or concept.

Example: John loves hiking. He always feels exhilerated when exploring new trails, admiries the beauty of nature, and eagerly plans his next outdoor adventure

- It points out that attitudes exist on two separate dimensions: One for positive elements and another for negative elements.
- It acknowledges the co-existence of positive and negative evaluations within attitudes, allowing for a mor nuanced understanding of human behavior

One Dimensional Perspective on Attitude

Positive elements

Strong Positive

Weak Positive

Neutral Elements

Weak Negative

Strong negative

Negative Elements

Example: Alia has mixed feelings about social media. While she enjoys staying connected with friends and sharing updates (positive elements), she also worries about privacy concerns and the impact of excessive screen time (negative elements)

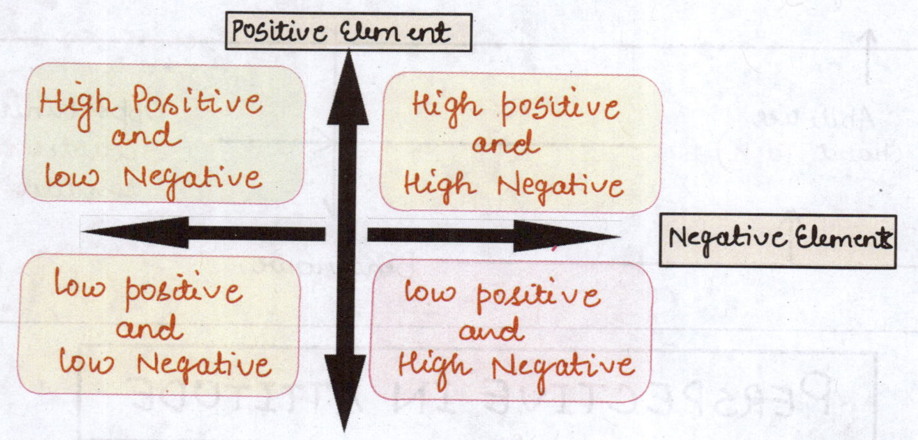

Attitudinal Ambivalence

- It arises when individuals harbor conflicting feelings or thoughts about a particular subject.
- It involves a simultaneous presence of positive and negative evaluations within the cognitive and affective components of attitudes.

Example: Alia feels conflicted about fast food. Although she enjoys the convenience and taste of fast foods (Positive thoughts), she is concerned about its negative effects on health (Negative feelings), leading her to indulge or resist temptation.

ATTITUDE AND BEHAVIOUR

- Behaviour refers to the potency of an individual (or group) to respond to external or internal stimuli.
- Attitude and behaviour also closely related but slightly distinct.

$$Behaviour\ (B) = Attitude\ (A) \times Environment\ (E)$$

Attitude	Behaviour
• Refers to an individual's overall evaluation or opinion about a particular object, person or situation. • It is a psychological construct, internal and subjective evaluation of an object. • Can be positive, negative or neutral. • May not always predict behaviour due to external factors such as social norms or situational factors. • Examples include liking or disliking a particular food or person.	• Refers to the action than an individual takes towards a particular object, person or situation. • It is an external, observable action towards an object. • Can be intentional or unintentional. • Is influenced by attitudes, but not always consistent with attitudes. • Examples include eating a particular food or interacting with a particular person.

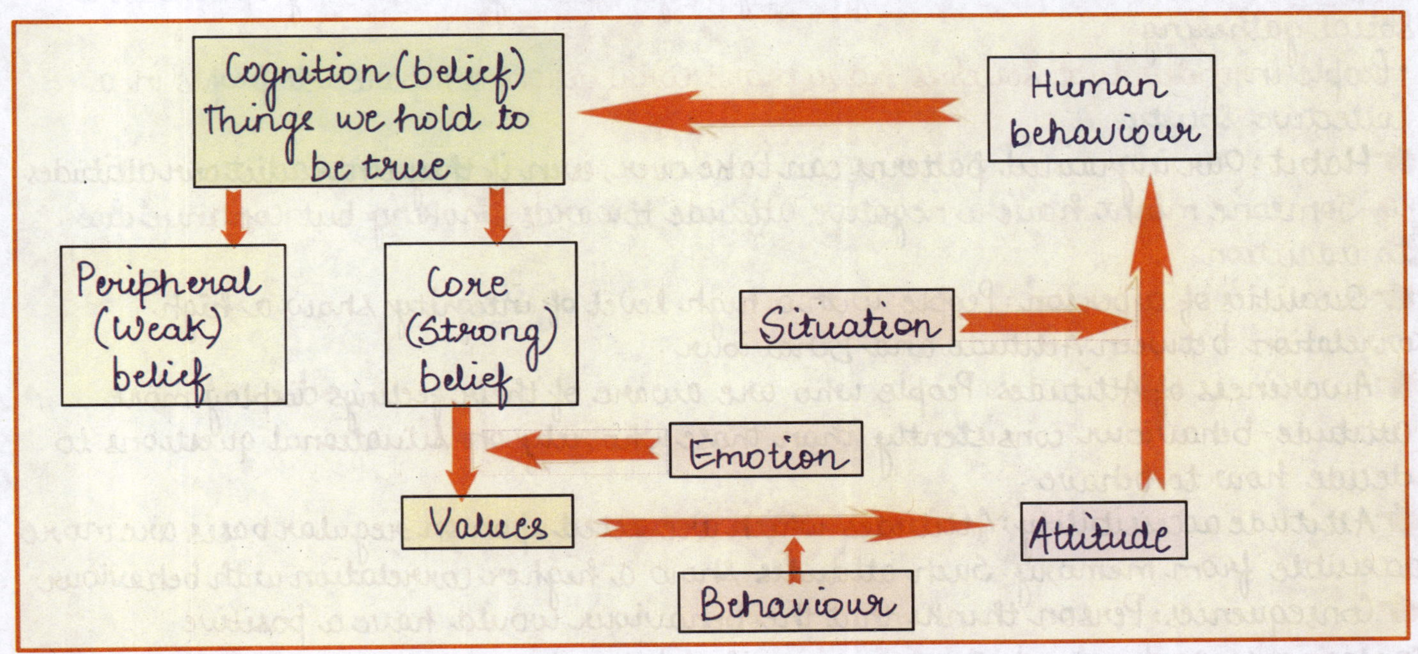

Relationship between Attitude and Behaviour

- Attitude is not the actual behaviour but a predisposition to behave in a particular way.

As such attitude is good predictor of behavior but prediction can't be a certainty.

- Example of Attitude translating to behaviour: Someone who strongly believes in environmental protection is more likely to take action, like recycling or volunteering, compared to someone with a more casual attitude.
- Example of Attitude not necessarily translating to behaviour (Inconsistency between the two:
  - We might value good health yet lack exercise and eat unhealthy (Desires conflict with actions)
  - Plenty of people may support a particular candidate, but they may not take the pain to go out and vote for him in this extreme heat (low voter turnout). Thus, attitudes may not always predict the actual pattern of one's behaviour.
  - LaPierre's study shows that the cognitive and affective components of attitudes do not necessarily coincide with behaviour.

Factors affecting the Attitude translating into Behaviour

- **Strength of attitude**: Deeply held, central attitudes are more likely to influence behaviour than weak or ambivalent ones.
- **Social Norms and Situational Pressures** can influence our behaviour even if they conflict with pre-existing attitudes.

Eg- Someone who values healthy eating might indulge in healthy options at a social gathering.

- People in individual societies have more correlation compared to people in a collective society.
- **Habit**: Our ingrained patterns can take over, even if they contradict our attitudes.

Eg- Someone might have a negative attitude towards smoking but continue due to addiction.

- **Qualities of a person**: People with a high level of integrity show a high correlation between Attitude and Behaviour.
- **Awareness of Attitudes**: People who are aware of their feelings display more attitude-behaviour consistently than those who rely on situational questions to decide how to behave.
- **Attitude accessibility**: Attitudes which are acted upon on regular basis are more accessible from memory. Such attitudes show a higher correlation with behaviour.
- **Consequences**: Person thinks that the behaviour would have a positive consequence and intends to engage in that behaviour.

Relationship of attitude and behaviour is actually a 2-Way street. Below are the ways through which behaviour affects the attitude:

Attitude ⇄ Behaviour — It's really a two-way street

• **Habits and values**: Repeated behaviours can become habits and eventually influence our values & attitudes.
Eg- Children repeatedly taught punctuality may develop attitude of valuing timeliness.

• **Social Norms**: Societal expectations can shape behaviour, which can then influence attitudes.
Eg- Women in a patriarchal society might internalize their subordinate position.

• **Symbolic behaviour**: Actions can be seen as symbolic and influence our attitudes.
Eg- A sports team's pre-game ritual might create a feeling of collective power.

• **Role-Playing**: Taking on a different role can lead to a change in perspective and attitude.
Eg- Smokers who act as cancer patients may develop a stronger anti-smoking attitude.

• **Law and enforcement**: Laws can mandate certain behaviours, which over time can influence attitudes. Eg- Strict anti-corruption laws might lead officials to develop a stronger aversion to corruption.

• **Leadership and Collective Action**: Leaders and social movements can influence behaviour, which can then lead to attitude shifts.
Eg- Gandhi's leadership inspired many to adopt non-violent resistance, eventually strengthening their commitment to the cause.

Cognitive Dissonance

• It is a psychological phenomenon that describe the mental discomfort one experiences when holding two conflicting beliefs, ideas, or values or when when our behaviours contradict our beliefs.

  • Eg- You might believe smoking is unhealthy (belief), yet continue to smoke (behaviour). This inconsistency creates cognitive dissonance, which might motivate you to quit smoking (changing behaviour) or justify your habit (changing belief)

Types of Dissonance

• **Belief-Behaviour inconsistency** when the actions contradict your beliefs. Eg- Eating unhealthy food despite valuing good health.

• **Belief-Belief inconsistency**: Holding two contradictory beliefs can create dissonance. Eg- Believing in both free will and destiny.

• **Dissonance after Decisions**: We might experience dissonance after making a difficult choice, even if it was the "right" one. Eg- Feeling some regret after buying an expensive phone, even if you need it.

• **Social Dissonance**: Conflict between our beliefs and societal expectations. (Eg- Disliking parties but feeling pressured to attend).

ATTITUDE CHANGE

- Attitude change refers to the process by which an individual's attitudes beliefs or behaviours are altered over time.
- Since attitudes are learned, they can be unlearned, relearned or changed too. Attitudes can be changed through various mechanisms and can be influenced by a multitude of factors.

Theories of Attitude change

Elaboration likelihood Model (ELM):
When people hear persuasive messages, they can take two routes to decide if they believe them.

- First Route: Central route where they carefully think about information and decide if it makes sense.
- Second Route (Peripheral route): When they focus on things like who's saying it or how attractive they are.

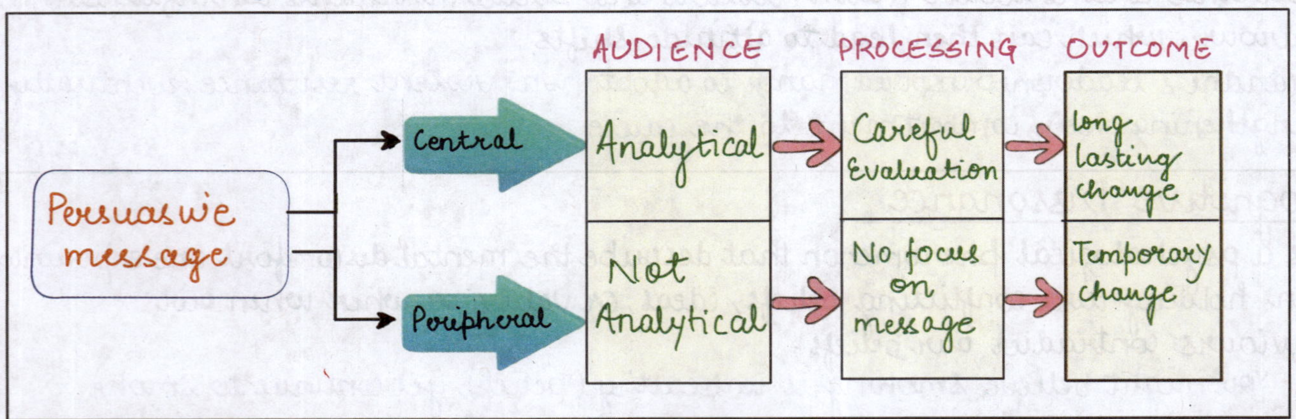

- Example: If a health supplement advt. shows lots of data and research, it might convince someone who pays attention to details.
  - But if a famous person endorses it, it might convince someone who doesn't pay much attention to the details but likes the celebrity.

Social Judgement Theory (Sherif and Hovland):
People have certain limits for accepting new ideas.

- Attitude change is more likely when new ideas fit well within these limits.

Example: Someone who likes renewable energy might agree with a message promoting solar panels, but might reject a message saying we should stop using all fossil fuels right away.

Theory of Planned Behaviour: How our intentions guide our actions, influenced by our attitudes, what we think others want us to do, and how much control we feel we have over our actions.

Example: Someone might recycle because they think its a good thing (attitude), they believe their friends support it (what others want), and they find recycling easy to do (Perceived control).

Self Perception theory: Watching our own behaviour can change our attitudes, especially if we think we are choosing our actions freely.

Example: If someone notices they keep picking vegetarian options, they might start thinking they actually like vegetarian food, even if they hadn't thought about it much before.

Reinforcement theories of attitude change: Our attitudes are shaped by our experiences.

Example: A child might start liking brushing their teeth because they get praised by their parents everytime they do it.

- This praise reinforces both the behaviour and the attitude.

Factors affecting Attitude change

Persuasive communication

- The effectiveness of persuasive messages, including the source, content and delivery, can influence attitude change.
- Factors such as credibility, attractiveness, and the emotional appeal of the messages play a role. Example: Swachh Bharat Abhiyan (Clean India Mission)

Social Influence

- Social norms, peer pressure and conformity can influence attitude change.
- Individuals may adjust their attitudes to align with those of their social groups or role models. Example: #MeTOO movement in India.

Cognitive Dissonance

- Cognitive Dissonance is a phenomenon in which a person experiences psychological distress due to conflicting thoughts, or beliefs.
- In order to reduce this tension, people may change their attitudes to reflect their other beliefs or actual behavior. Example - Farmer protest against Farm laws.

Education Information

- Access to accurate information and education about a topic can lead to attitude change
- Increased knowledge and understanding may challenge existing beliefs and attitudes, promoting individuals to adopt new perspectives

Example: LGBTQ+ Rights advocacy.

Emotional Appeals.

- Appeals to emotions, such as fear, empathy, or joy can influence attitude change.
- Emotional messages may evoke strong reactions that motivated individuals to reassess their attitudes and behaviours Example: COVID-19 Vaccination Drives

Cultural and Societal influences

- Attitude change may occur in response to cultural shifts, evolving social norms, or changing societal values.

Example: Women's empowerment Movement.

Self Perception and Identity

- Attitude change can be influenced by individuals' perceptions of themselves and their identity.
- Changes in self-concept or group affiliations may lead to corresponding shifts in attitudes to maintain a coherent sense of self.

Example: Dalit Empowerment movements.

Resistance to Attitude change

1. Avoidance – Occurs when individuals adhere to their existing beliefs and actively avoid information or experiences that challenge those beliefs

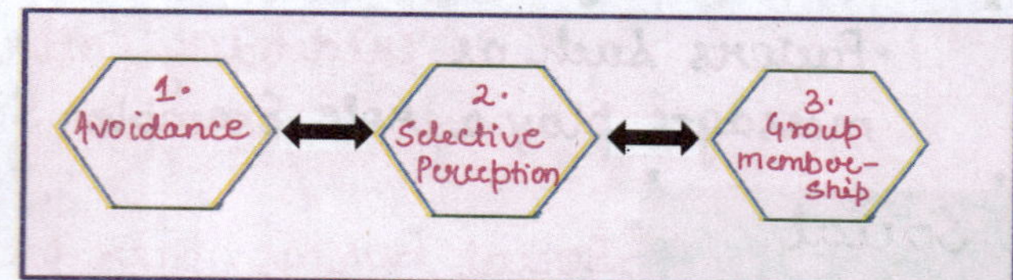

Example: A person avoid criticism or negative commentary about their favourite cricket team, despite potential evidence to the contrary.

2. Selective perception: People tend to selectively perceive information that align with their existing views while dismissing contradictory evidence.

Example: A person having encountered aggressive dogs, perceive all dogs as threat

3. Group Membership: Pressure to conform to group expectations can impede attitude change, particularly when deviation threatens social cohesion

Example: A person faces resistance from their family if pursuing a relationship outside their traditional social norms.

SOCIAL INFLUENCE

- Social influence encompasses the phenomenon where individuals within a Society are influenced by others' emotions, opinions and behaviours.
- Thus, Social influence can be Seen as a technique through which attitudes are formed as well as attitudes are changed.
- It is a Comprehensive Concept that can manifest at multiple levels: Values, Attitudes and Behaviour.

- **Levels of Social Influence**
- Compliance: Short-term change in behaviour due to external pressure.
- Identification: Change in behaviour and some attitude shift due to admiration (Eg- Buying a product endorsed by a celebrity).
- Internalisation: Deepest and most lasting change in both attitude and behaviour because it aligns with personal values.

	Behaviour	Attitude	Value
Compliance	✓	✗	✗
Identification	✓	✓	✗
Internalisation	✓	✓	✓

Types of Social influence

- **Conformity**: The tendency to adjust one's behaviour or beliefs to match those of a group in order to avoid social rejection or disapproval.
  Eg- Success of Swachh Bharat Mission relied on this principle.
- **Compliance**: Compliance is change in individual's behaviour which is result of direct request made to that individual. The compliance is generally change in behaviour only and not in attitude.
  Eg- You agree to help a Colleague with a Small task even though you are busy (avoid disapproval)
- **Obedience**: Following the orders of a figure in authority, even if we believe those orders are wrong. It is driven by a Sense of duty, respect for authority, or fear of punishment. Eg- Milgram experiment on obedience is a classic example.
- **Social Proof**: It is a powerful psychological phenomenon that influences our thoughts, behaviour & decision based on the actions or opinion of others.
  - We tend to believe things are true or actions are correct if we see others endorsing or performing them
  - This "herd mentality" can influences our choices, especially in uncertain Situations.
  - Eg-Trying a new restaurant because it has a long line of customers outside (Assuming popularity equals quality)
- **Reciprocity**: The feeling of obligation to return a favor or concession received from someone else. Eg- Often used in marketing Strategies, like offering free Samples or introductory discounts.

• **Persuasion**: It focuses on deliberately influencing the beliefs, attitudes, or behaviors of others through communication.
- It is a targeted effort to shift someone's perspective or motivates them to take a specific action.

PERSUASION

• **About**: Persuasion is the action or process of influencing someone's beliefs, attitudes, intentions or motivations, or behaviour towards a p rticular event, idea, object or individual.
- It involves conveying information, feelings or reasoning, either verbally or in writing, to change a person's attitude or behavior
- It is often utilised for personal gain, such as in election campaigns, sales pitches, or trial advocacy, where individuals use their personal or positional resources to alter others' attitudes or behaviors.
- Persuasion, however, is not always used for changing attitudes but also to prevent attitudes from changing.

Eg- A political candidate may use persuasive techniques during a campaign speech to convince voters to support their policies, leveraging emotional appeals and logi al arguments to sway their attitudes and behaviors.

Methods of Persuasion

- Understanding the methods with the help of an example: Pulse Polio Vaccination campaign.

ETHOS	• Ethos is the credibility that a speaker or writer brings to the subject that he or she is communicating about. Eg- Celebrity Endorsements: The campaign involved popular Indian celebrities such as Amitabh Bachchan as advocates, promoting the importance of vaccination and building trust among the public.
PATHOS	• Pathos is the use of emotion in debate or argument. Eg- Emotional Appeal: Public service announcements showcased the devastating effects of polio on children, evoking empathy and a sense of urgency.
LOGOS	• Logos is the appeal to reason, to the forcefulness of a well-thought-out and well-structured position. Eg- Logical Appeal: The campaign emphasized the effectiveness and safety of the polio vaccine, using data and statistics to dispel misconceptions.

Steps in the Persuasion Process

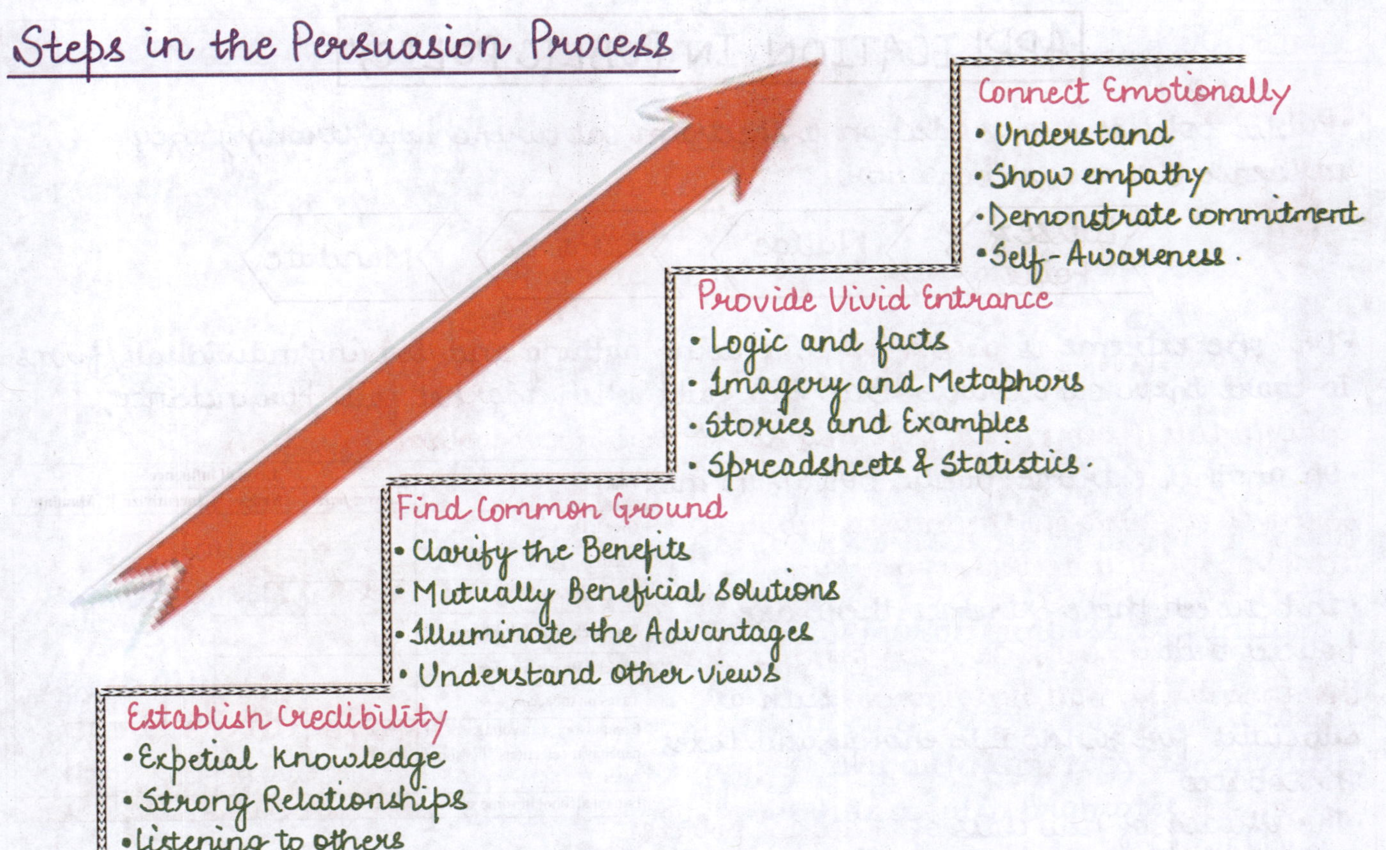

Persuasion and Social Influence

Aspects	Persuasion (Specific Form)	Social Influence (Broader concept)
Definition	• The act of attempting to change someone's beliefs, attitudes or behaviours through communication.	• The Overall effect that presence, actions, or characteristics of others have on us.
Focus	• Individual	• Group
Nature	• Always intentional, with a clear goal of influencing the recipient	• Can be intentional (Persuasion) or unintentional (Conformity due to peer pressure).
Source	• Typically comes from an external Source, Such as a persuasive message	• Can stem from anyone or anything in our Social environment.
Outcome	• Changes in attitudes or behaviours	• Conformity to group norms.
Motivation	• Motivated by a desire to change the target's attitudes or behaviours.	• Motivated by a desire for Social acceptance or a need to fit in.
Timing	• Can occur before or after the behavior or attitude is formed	• Occurs after the behavior or attitude is formed.
Examples	• Advertising, political campaigns, Sales pitches	• Peer pressure, Social norms, cultural traditions.

APPLICATION IN PUBLIC POLICY

- Public policies are graded on a spectrum capturing how strongly they influence (or coerce) behavior.

Laissez Faire → Nudge → Incentivize → Mandate

- On one extreme is laissez faire, i.e. doing nothing and leaving individuals/firms to chart their own course. But this fails when market fail. For instance, individuals/firms in a free market would not restrain pollution.
- On another extreme, public policy- in the form of regulation - mandates people to act in a socially desirable manner.
- In between these extremes, there are policies that incentivize good behaviour or dis-incentivize bad behaviour, such as subsidies for renewable energy and taxes on tobacco.

Policy	Level of influence			
	Laissez faire	Nudge	Incentivize	Mandate
Give It Up				
Aadhaar				
Jan DhanYojana				
Beti Bachao, Beti Padhao				
Swachh Bharat Mission				
Taxes on tobacco				
Compulsory voting in panchayat elections in some states				
Ban on alcohol in some states				

- The efficacy of new class of "Nudge" policies that lie between laissez faire and incentives have been recently discovered by behavioural economists.
- "Nudge" policies gently steer people towards desirable behaviour even while preserving their liberty to choose.

Successful Applications of Behavioural Insights in India

1. Swachh Bharat Mission (SBM)

- Launched on 2nd October, 2014 to leverage the values propagated by 'role model' Mahatma Gandhi and thereby create a mass movement on the lines of 'Satyagraha' for a cleaner India.
- Aim: To achieve universal sanitation coverage.
- Symbol: Invokes Gandhiji's values.
- Achievement: SBM is the first one to emphasize on behaviour change. Within five years of the launch of SBM, household access to toilet has increased to nearly 100% in all states.
- Learning: Toilet access and usage can be suitably increased with behavioural nudges that push female literacy rates up and discourage early marriage of girls.
- Use of Behavioural insights:
  - More than five lakh Swachhagrahis, foot soldiers of SBM, were recruited; the similarity with Satyagrahis is intentional to enforce the message.

- These Swachhagrahis, who were local, were able to leverage their social ties within their villages to effect change.
- SBM relies on community-based approaches to Sanitation through behaviour change techniques such as Participatory Rural Appraisal and Community-led Total Sanitation. Non Conformers, therefore, find their act more visible to their community.
- The fear of community scorn, or a desire to fit in, or both, have led many to renounce open defecation.

2. Beti Bachao, Beti Padhao (BBBP)

- **Background**: Between the 2001 and 2011 Census, 21 out of 29 states registered a decline in child sex ratio.
- **Launched**: On 22nd January, 2015 in 100 districts from Panipat, Haryana.
- **Symbol**: Choice of Panipat is symbolic through the association with the famous battles fought at Panipat in 1526, 1556 and 1761.
- **Use of Behavioural insight**:
- 'Selfie with Daughter' initiative: Started by one proud father in a village in Haryana, the campaign went viral and #SelfieWithDaughter became a Worldwide hit.
- Two elements enabled the campaign's Success: First, telling people what the norm is, and second, showcasing the thousands of other people who were acting in line with that norm.

Power of Clear Messaging

- Use of socially and culturally identifiable names gives a clear message of objectives of the programme - one of the principles of behavioural economics is that the messaging needs to be clear and simple.
- This is evident from the names used for various recent schemes, some of which are tabulated in table below:

Name of the Scheme	Literal Meaning of the Name	Objective of the Scheme Cultural/Societal aspect used
Namami Gange	Namami Gange means 'I pray to Ganga' as the river Ganga is revered in our culture.	To arrest the pollution of Ganga River and revive the river.
POSHAN Abhiyan	Poshan means holistic nutrition	Multi-ministerial convergence mission to ensure a malnutrition free India by 2022.
Ujjwala	Means 'bright, clear'	To safeguard the health of women by providing them with clean cooking fuel – LPG.
PM Mudra Yojana	Mudra means "currency, coins"	Provides loans upto 10 lakh to the non-corporate, non-farm small/ micro enterprises.
Jan DhanYojana	Jan Dhan implies "money of the people"	Financial inclusion program to expand access to financial services.
Ayushman Bharat	Ayushman means "Being Blessed with long life"	Universal and affordable access to good quality health care services.

Using Behavioural Economics to avoid 7 Social Sins (Economic Survey 2019-20)

Principles of Behavioral Economics	Social Sins of Gandhiji	Applications
Leverage loss aversion	Politics without principle	• **Design incentives to reward good behaviour** ex ante **with threat to revoke reward later if behaviour fails to match expectations.** • Policy makers and legislators exhibit loss-aversion in decision-making. • Behavioral insights to address the loss aversion of policymakers can improve policy and legislative outcomes and **uphold 'Politics with principle'.**
Disclose outcomes	Wealth without work	• The perception of **getting things for 'free' as an entitlement has to be reoriented** towards discharging our obligations towards society by rendering productive work and contributing to national growth. • The principles of behavioral economics, viz. **disclose the realized benefits of good behavior and the adverse outcomes of bad behaviour**, on the one hand, and emphasizing social norms, on the other hand, offer insights towards enhancing productivity and tax compliance.
Leverage default rules	Pleasure without conscience	• When less deserving people claim benefits of a development programme, it is an act of pleasure without conscience or a sense of responsibility. • The **behavioural principle of leveraging default rules** like making the default 'opt-out' for availing subsidy, etc. can be employed to nudge people towards confident displays and conduct of altruism. • The **"Give it up" campaign** can use this principle more effectively to broaden its adoption to surrendering all types of subsidies.
Match messages to mental models	Knowledge without character	• **Lack of moral element underlying the information explosion** bears the risk of desensitizing societies to ethics of harmony and brotherhood. • **Train people to shift to new rules of thumb**, for example, "fluids out – so fluids in" to increase fluid intake during diarrhoea.
Emphasizing social norms	Commerce without morality	• Highlighting **information regarding people who exhibit good behaviour and clarifying insignificant role of negative influencers** can help enhance conformity and deter unethical social behaviours. • Emphasize the number of people who vote, save regularly, file taxes on time, etc. – the enhancers of good behaviour. • The **National Corporate Social Responsibility Awards of Ministry of Corporate Affairs is an initiative in this direction**. These awards emphasize ethical behaviour and acknowledge companies that have positively impacted both business and society.
Making it easy to choose	Science without humanity	• Keep **options few in number and easy to comprehend.** • Using the behavioral principle of "Making it easy to choose", technology can make things simple to understand, cut through layers of processes and target the benefit to the actual beneficiary. • **Data in the present times can be created as a public good** within the legal framework of data privacy using technology.
Reinforce repeatedly	Worship without sacrifice	• **Remind people of past good behavior**. People tend to continue their past behaviour, especially when reminded about the same. • **Repeatedly reinforcing examples of people** following the positive sentiments of gender and caste equality as truly spiritual people can help establish the correct social norm that "serving man is serving God." • This may also be seen in the **MARD (Men Against Rape and Discrimination) campaign** underlying which is the sacrifice of the male ego in a patriarchal society for the larger good of gender equality.

PYQs Corner

(Write the Answer and Get Free Evaluation)

1. Attitude is an important component that goes as input in the elopement of humans How to build a suitable needed for a public servant? (2021, 10 Marks)

2. A positive attitude is considered to be an essential characteristic of a civil servant who is often required to function under extreme stress. What contributes to a positive attitude in a person? (2020, 10 Marks)

3. How could social influence and persuasion contribute to the success of Swachh Bharat Abhiyan? (2016, 10 Marks)

4. Our attitudes towards life, work, other people and society are generally shaped unconsciously by the family and the social surroundings in which we grow up. Some of these unconsciously acquired attitudes and values are often undesirable in the citizens of a modern democratic and egalitarian society. (a) Discuss such undesirable values prevalent in Today's educated Indians (b) How can such undesirable attitudes be changed and socio-ethical values considered necessary in public services be cultivated in the aspiring and serving civil servants? (2016, 10 Marks)

5. Two different kinds of attitudes exhibited by public servants towards their work have been identified as bureaucratic attitude and the democratic attitude.
   (a) Distinguish between these two terms and write their merits and demerits.
   (b) Is it possible to balance the two too create a better administration for the faster development of our country? (2015, 10 Marks)

06 Moral and Political Attitude

"To educate a person in mind and not in morals is to educate a menace to society".

— Theodore Roosevelt.

"Do not impose on others what you yourself do not desire" (The Golden Rule, emphasizing fairness and empathy in ethical decision-making.)

— Confucius

"One of the penalties for refusing to participate in politics is that you end up being governed by your inferiors".

-Plato

"Our lives begin to end the day we become silent about things that matter".

-Martin Luther King Jr.

MORAL ATTITUDE

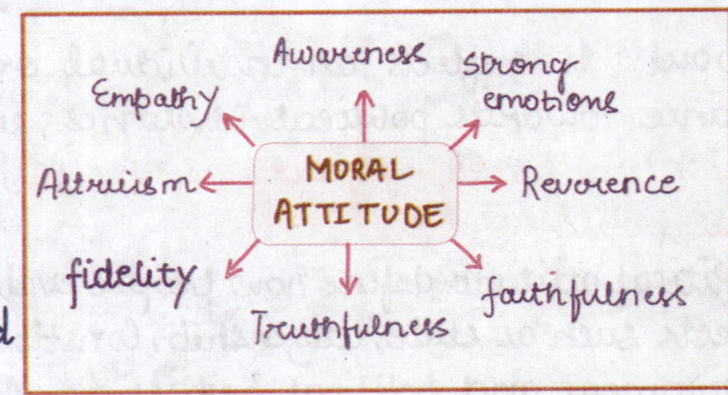

- Moral attitudes are deeply rooted in moral convictions, guiding individuals in distinguishing between right and wrong.
- These attitudes are strongly influenced by one's ultimate sense of morality and significantly impact how individuals act and judge social situations.
- Example - A person's disliking towards apple or oranges has no question of morality involved. But one may have moral considerations as far as being a vegetarian or a non-vegetarian is concerned.
- Environmental and social factors, including family, education, religion, profession and personal experiences, heavily shape moral attitudes.
- Moral attitude by nature is personal and vary from person to person.

Characteristics of Moral Attitude

- Resilience : Moral attitudes are highly resistant to change due to their deep-seated moral basis, which forms an integral part of an individual's character.
- Accessibility : These attitudes are readily accessible in memory and evoke strong physiological responses, indicating their importance.
- Quick judgement : Moral attitudes often lead to quick and intuitive judgements, accompanied by heightened emotional arousal when violated.

Implications of Moral Attitude

Positive Implications	Negative implications.
• Tied up with strong emotions. Hence, it prevents deviant behaviour due to fear of social ostracization e.g. child molestation • Example - Motivates a person towards Altruism, volunteerism and social service • Guides ethical decision-making. • fosters social coherence and trust. • Promotes a sense of justice and fairness. • Emphasises personal and social responsibility.	• People can use it to justify violent behaviour and lunacy, and still society will accept it because the moral attitude is based on strong emotions. • Example : Motivates a person towards riots, genocide etc to justify religious/regional issue • Can result in moral absolutism and inflexibility • May result to moral self-righteousness and superiority Can lead to moral policing, judgmental attitude • Can cause moral conflicts and dilemmas

POLITICAL ATTITUDE

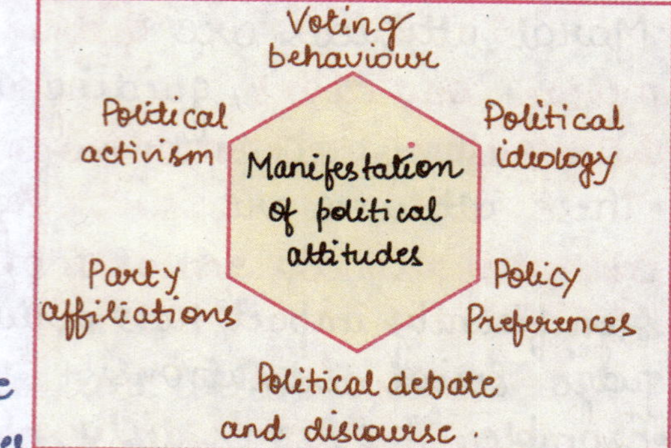

About : It reflects an individual or group's stance towards political ideologies, encompassing views on public figure, events, institutions, and policy issues.

- Political attitude define how people evaluate political objects such as state, citizenship, Constitution, laws, government and political parties. Eg- Attitude of people towards constitution is generally positive as it provides them rights and limits the authority of state.

Examples of political attitudes includes conservatism, liberalism, socialism, libertarianism and populism.

- These attitudes reflect different beliefs and values about the role of government, individual rights and freedoms, social justice and economic policy.

Factors influencing Political Attitude

Family influence : Exert enduring influence on political opinions through socialization, shaping preferences for parties, policies and political engagements

Example: In India, elders often dictate political allegiances.

- It also determines how likely a person is willing to join political activity.

Eg- Dynasty politics witnessed in various parties in India.

Generational difference : Older individuals tending towards conservatism and younger generations favouring liberalism.

Example : Indian freedom struggle exhibit conflicts between youth-led radical movements and moderate approach of elder leaders.

Social Identity : Socio-cultural factors such as religion, region and caste significantly shape political attitudes.

Example : Identity based politics in India underscores the influence of caste, language and regional affiliations on voting patterns.

Socio-Economic Status : Economic considerations influence political attitudes

Example : Industrial workers towards Socialist ideals, while business classes towards capitalist principles.

Education : Shapes political attitudes by providing knowledge of the political world and transmitting the values and attitude of the Society.

Example : Student politics in colleges led to early exposure to political ideologies and activism.

Religion: Religious affiliations can sway away political preferences.
Example: Religiously oriented parties like AIMIM, Akali Dal and candidates' religious leanings in mainstream politics in India.
Geographical factors: Regional disparities and local issues influence political attitudes such as Issues of North East (Inner line Permit, Separatist movement); Border states (Illegal immigrants, Organised crime, etc); Arid regions
Institutions and Governance structure: Example - Corruption in political institutions, bureaucracy, use of money and muscle power in political parties leads to negative and indifferent attitude among citizens.
Social media influence: Role in shaping political attitudes through debates, sensationalism, and the spread of misinformation.
Example: Cambridge Analytica's highlighted manipulation of citizen data for political gain.

Implications of Political Attitude

Implications:

- Guide decision making related to political activities and engagement.
- Shape public opinion on political matters and respond to political events and developments
- Contribute to political discourse and debates.
- Political polarization and division within the society
- Influence policy outcomes by promoting and implementing specific policies.

POLITICAL IDEOLOGIES

- A political ideology is a set of beliefs, principles and doctrines that explains how society should function and offer a blueprint for a particular social order
- It acts as a broad framework that shapes a person's or group's political views on various issues.

Core elements of Political Ideology

Values: Fundamental principles that guide the ideology, such as equality, liberty, justice or social order

Goals: The desired future state of Society, envisioned by the ideology (e.g., a classless Society or a strong welfare state

Methods: Preferred ways to achieve the desired goals. This could involve specific policies, forms of government or economic systems.

Different Types of Political Ideologies

Political Ideology	Description
Liberalism	• Core values: Individual liberty, equality of opportunity, Social justice, limited government intervention in the economy. • Goals: A society where everyone has the freedom to pursue their goals with a fair and just legal system protecting their rights. • Methods: Representative democracy, free markets with some regulations to prevent monopolies, social safety nets to ensure basic needs are met. • Example: Policies promoting free speech, universal education etc.
Socialism	• Core values: Social equality, economic justice, public ownership of key industries, strong role for government in regulating the economy and providing social welfare. • Goals: A Society where wealth is more evenly distributed, everyone has access to basic necessities like healthcare and education, and the government plays a significant role in ensuring social well-being. • Methods: Progressive taxation, government funded social programs (universal healthcare), public ownership of utilities and essential services, regulations to ensure fair labour practices.
Communism	• Core values: Classless Society, collective ownership of means of production, elimination of private property, central planning of the economy. • Goals: A Society without Social classes or economic inequality, where everyone contribute based on their abilities and receive benefits according to their needs.

	• Methods: State control of all major industries, collective farms, strict government planning of the economy. • Examples: Erstwhile Soviet Union aimed for complete government control of the economy and society
Feminism	• Core values: Gender equality, women's rights, dismantling the patriarchy. • Goals: A society where women have equal opportunities in all aspects of life, free from discrimination and violence based on gender. • Methods: Policies promoting equal pay for equal work, reproductive rights, access to education for girls etc • Examples: Campaigns against domestic violence and sexual harassment, legislations promoting equal parental leave policies, etc.
Environmentalism	• Core values: Environmental protection, Sustainability, ecological justice. • Goals: A future where human societies can thrive in harmony with the natural world, ensuring a healthy planet for future generations. • Methods: Regulations to curb pollution, promoting renewable energy sources, international cooperation on climate change (Paris Agreement)
Nationalism	• Core values: Devotion to one's nation, national identity, cultural preservation, strong national defense. • Goals: A strong and prosperous nation that prioritizes the interest of its citizens above all. • Methods: Policies promoting patriotism, restriction on immigration, economic protectionism (government subsidies) to safeguard domestic industries, increased military spending etc.
Fascism	• Ultra nationalism, authoritarian government, state control of the economy, often using violence and oppression to maintain order. Example:- Nazi Germany.
Anarchism	• Elimination of all forms of government, with individuals or small communities making their own decisions.

SOCIAL ATTITUDE

- Social attitude pertains to particular disposition towards social phenomena and members of society.
- Shaped by various factors: Family and community, personal experiences, Traditional cutoms or practices, societal expectations etc.
- Key characteristics of traditional social attitude in India:
- Collectivism: Priority to the community well-being over the individual desires.
- Respect for Hierarchy: Age, Authority figures, caste and class based interactions.
- Dominance of religious beliefs guiding an individual's attitude.
- Toxic masculinity attitude or patriarchal attitude or discriminatory attitude of the society against women.
- Shifting social attitude in recent times due to the following reasons:

☛ Rapid urbanisation and globalisation are leading to a shift towards more individualistic & egalitarian attitudes, especially among younger generations.
Eg- Nuclear family system, inter-faith marriages etc.

☛ Education and awareness: Increased access to education & exposure to different cultures can lead to a more progressive social attitudes on gender roles, career choices and social norms. Eg- Increased awareness about homosexuality, questioning child marriage, reduced caste discrimination.

☛ Role of social media and activism: Eg- #MeToo movement encouraged women to speak out against sexual harassment, leading to a public discourse & stricter legal measures.

☛ Economic growth and aspirations empower women who seek greater agency and challenge discriminatory practices.

☛ Government initiatives and legislations aim to create a more equitable society- Eg- Beti Bachao, Beti Padhao.

PYQs Corner

(Write the Answer and Get Free Evaluation)

1. Young people with ethical conduct are not willing to come forward to join active politics. Suggest steps to motivate them to come forward. (2017, 10 Marks)
2. What factors affect the formation of a person's attitude towards social problems? In our society, contrasting attitudes are prevalent about many social problems. What contrasting attitudes do you notice about the caste system in our society? How do you explain the existence of these contrasting attitudes? (2014, 10 Marks)

07 Emotional Intelligence

66

"What really matters for success, character, happiness and life-long achievement is a definite set of emotional skills- your EQ- not just purely cognitive abilities that are measured by conventional IQ tests"

—Daniel Goleman

"It is very important to understand that emotional intelligence is not the triumph of heart over land - it is the unique intersection of both"

— David Caruso

"It is not what happens to you, but how you react to it that matters" (Emotional Regulation and Response)

— Epictetus

"Holding on to anger is like grasping a hot coal with the intent of throwing it at someone else; you are the one who gets burned"

—Gautam Buddha

"When dealing with people, remember you are not dealing with creatures of logic, but with creatures of emotion"

—Dale Carnegie

"He who conquers himself is the mightiest warrior"

—Confucious

"Peace is not the absence of conflict, but the ability to cope with conflict by peaceful means."

—Ronald Reagan

EMOTIONS

Psychologist Robert S. Woodworth offered a definition of emotion as a "stirred up state of an organism" that manifests in two ways:

Internal Feelings: The Individual experiences a range of Subjective feelings

External Responses: Observers witness changes in the person's physical state, such as muscular tension

- Emotions are generally understood as intense feelings, favourable or unfavourable, that are directed at someone or something.
- Emotions are a conscious mental reaction (such as anger or fear) subjectively experienced as a strong feeling, usually directed towards a specific object and typically accompanied by physiological and behavioural changes in the body.
- All of us are born with capacity to experience emotions these are associated with different level of hormones in human body.
  - Example: Anxiety is associated with low level of dopamine while love is associated with high level of dopamine, serotonin and oxytocin.
- Emotions always emerge as a result to some stimulant.
  - The stimulant can be a physical object like fear on seeing a tiger or it can be a mental construct like though about uncertain future causing anxiety
- Emotions are one of the components of attitude, other being cognition and behaviour.
- Emotions influence our attitude towards the attitude objects and even overpower cognition sometimes.
- Such dominance of affective component may also lead to prejudice among individuals. As in acts of violence such as communalism, people have prejudiced notions about other community members.
- The ethical behaviour in daily events can witness decline when negative emotions such as rage, anger, greed etc. overpower reason.

How Emotion Operates?

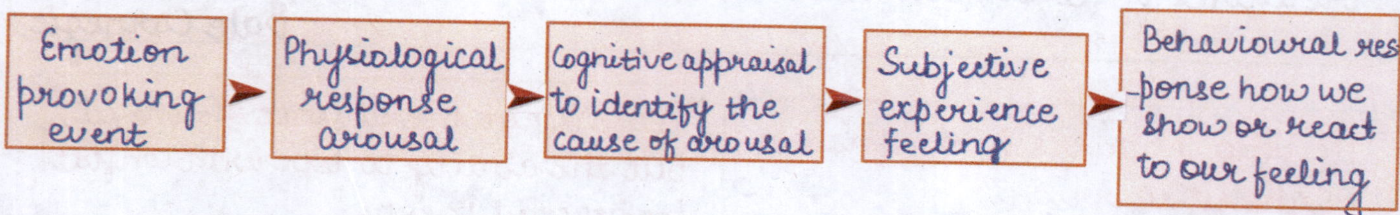

Elements of Emotions

1. Subjective Experience:	2. Physiological response:	3. Behavioural Response:
Refers to the unique emotional feeling a person experiences as these are subjective in nature. Eg: Anger can range from mild annoyance to blind rage	This encompasses the body's physiological changes in response to the emotion, such as increased heart rate, blood pressure, or sweating.	This refers to the outward expressions of the internal emotional state, such as facial expressions body language or actions.

Classification of Emotions

1. Primary vs Secondary emotions

Primary Emotions	Secondary Emotions
• Considered basic and universal • Automatic and experienced across all cultures and social contexts • Identified by Robert Plutchik as eight core emotions: Fear, Surprise, Sadness, Disgust, Anger, Anticipation, Joy, Trust.	• Arise from combination of Primary Emotion • More complex and nuanced than Primary Emotions. • Examples: Contempt – A blend of anger and disgust. Optimism: A combination of Serenity and interest.

2. Positive vs Negative Emotion

Positive Emotions	Negative Emotions
• Generally associated with pleasant feelings and a sense of well-being • Examples – Joy, Happiness, gratitude, love and hope • These emotions tend to be uplifting and energizing, motivating us to engage with the world around us. • They can promote creativity, social connection and resilience	• Generally associated with unpleasant feelings and a sense of distress • Examples – Anger, sadness, fear, anxiety and disgust. • These emotions can be demotivating and lead to avoidance behaviours. • They can trigger fight or flight responses, prompting us to address immediate challenges.

Functions of Emotions

1. **Communication** Emotions act as signals that convey our internal state to others. Example: Facial Expressions, body language etc. allowing us to communicate our feelings without words.*
2. **Motivation** Emotions can motivate us to take action.
Example: Positive emotions like Joy and excitement can motivate us to pursue goals, while negative emotions like fear or anger can mativate us to avoid danger or threats.
3. **Decision making** integrates the emotions and intelligence.
4. **Social Bonding** Positive emotions like love, compassion, and empathy help us connect with others and build strong relationships
5. **Good physical health** Chronic negative emotions like stress can weaken the immune system and increase the risk of illness, while positive emotions can promote overall Well-being.

Some Important Emotions

- **Happiness**: A feeling of joy, contentment, or satisfaction. Happiness is often associated with positive experiences or the fulfilment of desires.
  - **Bhagavad Gita**: True happiness doesn't come from external circumstances but from fulfilling one's dharma and performing actions without attachment to the outcome.
- **Grief and Sadness**: A feeling of sorrow, unhappiness or disappointment. Sadness is a natural response to loss or misfortune.
  - **Bhagavad Gita**: Lord Krishna advocates for detachment from worldly attachments, fostering a sense of acceptance during moments of grief.
- **Anger**: Anger is a hostile response to an event that a person detests. It can cloud our sense of judgement and decisions taken in impulse may often have undesirable outcomes.
  - Rational thought and reasoning should ideally prevent a civil servant from acting rapidly in anger.
  - **Bhagavad Gita**: Lord krishna emphasizes the destructive nature of anger.
  - He warns that anger leads to delusion, hinders judgement and ultimately causes one's downfall.
- **Fear**: A feeling of anxiety or apprehension caused by the presence or anticipation of danger.
  - Civil servants must be able to perform their duties in a legal and people centric manner without fear of retribution from the politicians.

- **Bhagavad Gita:** Lord Krishna encourages facing fear with courage and determination. He emphasizes that performing one's duty (dharma) is paramount, regardless of fear.

- **Hatred:** Strong emotion for disliking someone or an idea or any object. It is often associated with anger or disgust.
  - As a civil servant, an officer should ensure that his/her personal dislikes and hatred for someone is not acting as a bias in the decision making process

- **Greed:** It is the desire to accumulate more material wealth beyond one's actually needs.
  - The greed for money and power has resulted in a corrupt society and a culture of taking bribes by the public servants.
  - **Bhagavad Gita:** Lord Krishna identifies desires and attachments as the root cause of suffering. When desires remain unfulfilled, it leads to frustration and unhappiness.

- **Envy:** It is an emotion that arises when a person lacks a quality found in others and wishes that either he/she too possessed it or the other person did not have it.
  - Civil Servants must always take motivation from others and learn from the successful initiatives introduced by their colleagues, rather than putting them down and deliberately finding faults in their work.
  - In Ramayana, it was Queen Kaikeyi's envy that was the root cause of Lord Rama's exile.

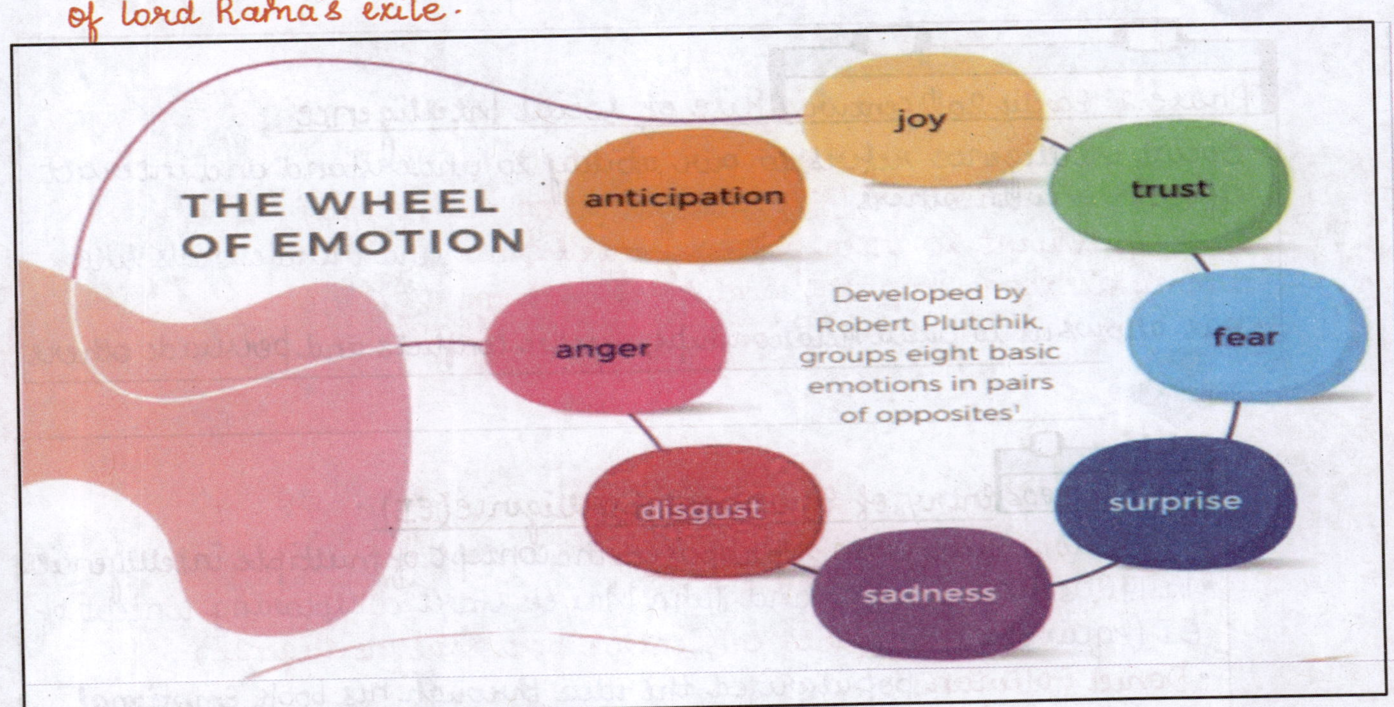

INTELLIGENCE

Intelligence is defined as the capacity of an individual to think rationally, act purposefully and deal effectively with his environment.

- It is the mental quality that consists of the abilities to learn from experience, adapt to new situations, understand and handle abstract concepts, and use knowledge to manipulate one's environment.

"The true sign of intelligence is not knowledge but imagination"
— Albert Einstein

"I know that I am intelligent, because I know that I know nothing"
— Socrates

- The Concept of intelligence has definitely evolved over time, expanding from a narrow focus on mental ability to encompass social & emotional intelligence

Phase 1: 19th century — Emphasis on Mental ability (MA)

- Focused on cognitive abilities like memory, reaction time, and logical reasoning
- These abilities could be measured through standardised tests like I.Q tests.
- Neglected the role of emotions in thinking and behaviour (Infact, it was believed that emotions were counter to cognitive tasks, because they are intense feelings)

Phase 2: Early 20th century — Rise of Social Intelligence

- Social intelligence refers to our ability to understand and interact effectively with others. (Ability to get along with people)
- It is equivalent to inter-personal intelligence and include skills like communication, empathy and co-operation.
- This allows us to build relationships, resolve conflicts and persuade others

Phase 3: 1980s — Entry of Emotional Intelligence (EI)

- 1983 – Howard Gardner proposed the concept of multiple intelligencies
- In 1980s Peter Salovey and John Mayer started exploring concept of EI (equivalent to Gardner's intra-personal intelligence).
- Daniel Goleman popularized the idea through his book "Emotional Intelligence" in 1995.

Good EI helps you manage stress, make sound decisions, build healthy relationships and achieve your goals

High MA can open doors to academic and professional opportunities.

Success Trinity

EI

MA

SI

Strong SI allows you to build strong networks, navigate social situations effectively, and collaborate with others

EMOTIONAL INTELLIGENCE

- Peter Salovey and Mayer define EI: 'The ability to monitor one's own and other people's emotions, to discriminate between emotions and label them appropriately, and to use emotional information to guide thinking and behaviour'
- EI refers to the ability to understand, use and manage your own emotions in positive ways to achieve your goals.
  - It also involves the ability to understand, empathise with and influence the emotion of others.
- It is not the triumph of heart over head, rather, the unique intersection of both.
- EI includes the intra-personal and interpersonal intelligence i.e. the ability to know oneself and others, in terms of abilities, current emotional state.

Models of Emotional Intelligence

1. Ability Model (Developed by Salovey and Mayer)

Perceiving emotions: Detecting and understanding emotions in oneself and others (Ability to specifically categorize current emotional state	Understanding emotions: Ability to understand the relationship between emotions, thoughts and behaviour.
Using emotions: Harnessing emotions to aid cognitive processes such as making or problem solving.	Managing emotions: Generating the desirable emotions in oneself and others which are conducive to the task (Emotions are energy for motions)

2. Mixed Model (Daniel Goleman)

• This definition was adopted by the Daniel Goleman and further categorized the emotional intelligence into 5 components.

- Self Awareness
- Empathy
- Motivation
- Self Regulation
- Social Skills

Five Components of Emotional Intelligence (Daniel Goleman)

	SELF	SOCIAL
WHO I AM — AWARENESS	Self-awareness: the ability to recognise and understand one's own emotions and how they impact thoughts and behaviour. Key Traits: Self Confidence and realistic self-assessment	Social awareness: the ability to understand and relate to the emotions of others, and to respond with sensitivity and care. Key Trait: Empathy.
WHAT I DO — REGULATION	Self-regulation: the ability to manage and control one's emotions & impulses in a healthy and productive way. Key Traits: Trustworthiness adaptability, innovativeness and openness to change.	Social skills: the ability to communicate effectively, build relationships and collaborate with others. Key Traits: Effective leadership, persuasiveness and team-building skills.
	HOW WE MANAGE OURSELVES	HOW WE HANDLE RELATIONSHIPS

Motivation: the ability to use emotions to achieve goals and stay motivated, even in the face of setbacks or obstacles.
Key Traits: Optimism, Resilience, Persistence.

Nature of EI according to Daniel Goleman

1. Emotional control of others: EI is not simply about controlling your own emotions, but also being able to understand and influence the emotions of others, including groups, individuals and even close relationships.
2. Emotional Awareness and Regulation: EI involves understanding how emotions work – what feels good and bad, and how to move from negative to positive states

3. Learned and Developed: Unlike cognitive intelligence (IQ), which is often considered fixed, EI is a skill that can be learned and developed throughout life through experiences.

4. Lifelong Development: EI typically increases with age and experience as a person progresses from childhood to adulthood.

5. Gender Differences: Men and women may have different strength and weaknesses in EQ. women often show greater empathy and social skills, while men might excel in self-regulation.

3. Trait Model

- Proposed by K.V. Petrides, it distinguishes between ability based and trait based
- The trait model suggests that Emotional Intelligence is a constellation of personality traits related to emotions (Trait emotional self-efficacy)
- Trait EI refers to individuals' self perceptions of their emotional abilities, measured through self-reports.

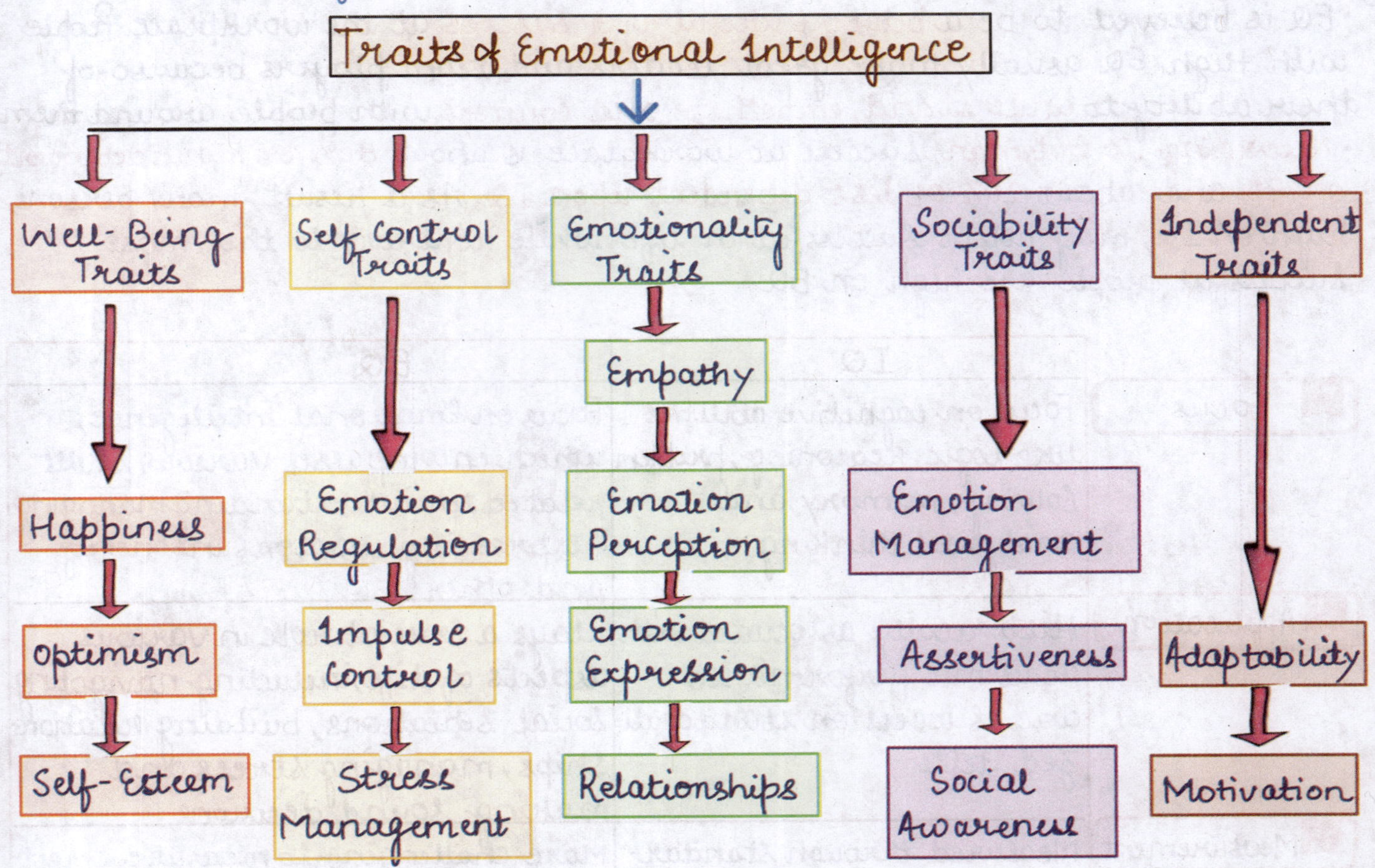

Traits – Low EI vs High EI

	Low EI	High EI
Leadership style	Aggressive, demanding, "bossy" egotistical, Confrontational.	Assertive, Ambitious, Determined, strong willed, Decisive.
Communication Style	Distractible, Selfish, poor listener, impulsive	Warm, enthusiastic, Sociable, charming, persuasive.
Management style	Resistance to change, passive unresponsive, slow, stubborn	Patient, stable, predictable, Consistent, good listener.
Working style	Critical, picky, "fussy", hard to please, perfectionistic.	Detailed, Careful, meticulous, Systematic, neat.

EMOTIONAL QUOTIENT (EQ) vs INTELLIGENCE QUOTIENT

- EQ is believed to be a better indicator of Success at the workplace. People with High EQ usually make great leaders and team players because of their ability to understand, empathize and connect with people around them.
- According to Goleman, Success at workplace is about 80% or more dependent on EQ and about 20% or less dependent upon IQ. As a result, many persons, high on IQ, may not be Successful in life, while contrary to this, most Successful people are high on EQ.

	IQ	EQ
Focus	Focus on cognitive abilities like Logic, reasoning, problem solving, memory and analytical thinking	Focus on Emotional Intelligence, which encompasses various skills related to understanding managing & expressing emotions in oneself and others.
Application	Historically associated with academic performance and Success on standardized tests.	Plays a crucial role in various aspects of life, including navigating Social Situations, building relationships, managing stress and making sound decisions
Measurement	Measured through standardised IQ tests administered by trained professionals	More challenging to measure objectivity. Self report questionnaires and behaviour-based assessments are used, but these can be Subjective

Nature vs Nurture	Generally considered to be a relatively stable trait, influenced by both genetics and early environment	Believed to be more malleable and can be developed through training and experience.

IQ is like the horsepower of a car which represents the raw power and potential of the engine while EQ is like the driver of the car that determines how skilfully the car is driven, how well it navigates different terrains and how safely it reaches its destination.

MULTI-LEVEL IMPORTANCE OF EI

Individual level

- Improved well-being: EI skills can help individuals to manage stress, cope with adversity and maintain emotional well-being
  Eg - Countries rank higher in World Happiness Index
- Informed and rational decisions: Can lead to better career choices, responsible financial management and healthier relationships.
- Higher motivation contribute to increased focus and productivity at work which benefits both individuals and organisations.
- Avoid taking impulse behaviour that could have negative consequences.
- Optimistic and resilient individuals who believe in their ability to overcome challenges and find solutions.

Community level

- Strong relationships: Effective collaboration and conflict resolution within communities can address various social issues.
- Reduced Social Conflicts: Contribute to a more peaceful and stable society. Eg-Addressing the issue of Naxalism
- Civic Engagement: Strengthens social fabric and promotes collective action for positive change.
- Women's Empowerment: Developing EI skills can equip women to navigate social challenges, advocate for their rights and become more effective leaders within their communities.

Organizational level

- Building Relationships: EQ fosters strong relationships with team members based on trust, empathy, and open communication.
- Improved work culture leading to higher productivity.

Eg- Google, Work Culture of new age startups such as MentorsHut.

- Effective leadership: EI allows leaders to inspire and motivate others, build trust with the public, and make sound decisions that considers th well-being of the nation.
- Performance Management: Utilising the 360 degree feedback that incorporates emotional intelligence can provide valuable insights for self-improvement and career development.

EMOTIONAL INTELLIGENCE IN GOVERNANCE

Need of EI in Governance

1. Citizen centric administration

- Fostering trust and strengthening of the relationship between the government and the people. Example: Community policing Initiatives.
- Greater engagement with diverse stakeholders, including marginalised communities and incorporating their perspectives into policymaking. Example: Community outreach programmes.
- Improved public service delivery by better understanding the needs and concerns of citizens and deliver public services with empathy and compassion.
- Building a vibrant democracy by empowering the citizens to be active participants. Example: Swachh Bharat Abhiyan (Clean India Mission), Gram Sabhas (Village Assemblies)

2. Capable and Empowered workforce

- Effective stress management which can unleash the full potential of the administrative workforce.
  Boost the motivation of civil servants, creating a work environment that fosters dedication, innovation, and a sense of purpose in public service
- Strong leadership: Leaders with high EI inspire and motivate their teams, leading to improved performance and a more positive organisational culture. Example - Building Social Capital.
- Effective conflict management especially in extra-ordinary situations such as communal riots.

3. National Development

- To promote social harmony and inclusivity within diverse Indian population.
- Addressing socio-economic disparities contributing to inclusive development.
- More productive, adaptable and collaborative workforce can contribute to faster economic growth

👉 Promoting India's position in the world's stage and fostering strong relations with the countries.

Some important traits of Emotionally Intelligent Administrator

1. Model the Way- Pankaj Jain, the District Collector of Katni district in Madhya Pradesh has set an example for others to emulate by sending her daughter to a rural childcare center or Anganwadi for pre-schooling instead of sending her to a high profile and costly play school in the city.
2. Inspire a shared vision- Mrs Indira Gandhi's slogan of "Garibi Hatao, Desh Bachao". Recent PM's slogan of "Sabka Sath, Sabka Vikas".
3. Challenge the existing status quo and bring radical reforms: Raja Ram Mohan Roy Crusaded against the cruel practice of Sati, which eventually led to the abolition of Sati.
4. Maintain balance in life.
5. Stay composed under pressure.
6. Recognising the contribution of others.

Challenges of developing EI in Bureaucracy

Bureaucratic attitude	• The bureaucracy has a long history of strict hierarchies, rule-based decision-making and resistant to change which hinders the development of empathy and social skills.
Work Pressure	• Bureaucrats face immense pressure, leading to a "do whatever it takes" mentality that prioritizes efficiency over empathy. Example. Police Working long hours might become insensitive to public needs.
Cultural Gap	• A disconnect exist between bureaucrats and the public they serve, hindering empathy and understanding. Example: Migrant workers struggling to communicate with local officials.
Use of Technology	• Increased reliance on technology in administration can create an emotional void. Example: A death due to bureaucratic red tape when a ration card wasn't linked to Aadhar.
Excessive Anonymity and Hierarchy	• Anonymity, a supposed strength, can lead to a lack of accountability and responsibility. Example: An official refusing aid to lack of paperwork instead of finding solutions.
Training Issues	• Traditional training programs primarily emphasize technical skills and administrative procedures leaving little room for soft skills development

Development of EI among the civil servants

01 Integration into Existing Training Programs such as modules on emotional awareness, communication skills etc at various levels.

02 Case studies and Role playing: Develop case studies based on real-world administrative scenarios where emotional intelligence plays a crucial role.

03 Mentoring and Coaching: Establish a mentorship program where senior administrators can provide guidance on navigating complex emotional situations

04 Organisation of Workshops on mindfulness, meditation and stress management techniques.

05 Incorporate citizen feedback surveys that assess an administrator's communication skills, empathy and problem solving abilities.

06 Leadership by example and creating a positive organisational work culture.

07 Utilising Technology: Develop online modules and e-learning courses on emotional intelligence that civil servants can access at their own pace, making training more accessible across the vast administrative network.

Instances of Public Servants displaying EI

Durga Shakti Nagpal

- Known for her crackdown on illegal sand mining in Uttar Pradesh.
- Her ability to handle political pressure and personal threats, maintaining her composure and emphathizing with the plight of affected communities demonstrated high EI.

Armstrong Pame

- Initiated and led the construction of a 100km road in a remote part of Manipur without any government funding, often referred to as the "People's Road."
- Pame's initiative involved understanding the community's needs, building trust, and mobilizing resources through crowdfunding.
- His empathy and social skills were pivotal in rallying the local population and external donors.

Dr. Kiran Bedi

- First woman to join the IPS and known for her prison reforms in Tihar Jail
- Bedi implemented various rehabilitation reforms such as education and vocational training programs, showcased her empathy and understanding of the inmates' needs.

Historical Case Studies displaying Emotional Intelligence

1. Ashoka the Great (304-232 BCE)

- After a brutal and bloody war with the Kalinga Kingdom, Ashoka witnessed the immense suffering caused by warfare. He grappled with feelings of remorse and guilt (Emotional awareness).
- Instead of succumbing to despair, Ashoka converted to Buddhism, a religion emphasizing non-violence and compassion (Empathy). He adopted a policy of Dharma, focusing on moral law and social welfare (decision making). He also sent out messengers of Peace to spread Buddhist teachings across Asia (Social skills)

2. Akbar the Great (1556-1605 CE)

- Akbar inherited a vast and diverse empire with religious tensions between Hindus and Muslims.
- Recognizing the need for social harmony (Empathy), Akbar implemented policies of religious tolerance (Din-i-ilahi). Akbar's implementation of Sulh-i-kul policies like abolishing the discriminatory Jizya tax on Non-muslims (decision making based on fairness). He established the "Institutes of Discussion" where scholars from various faiths debated religious ideal. (communication and promoting respect for diverse perspectives)

PYQs Corner

(Write the Answer and Get Free Evaluation)

1. ''What really matters for success, character, happiness and lifelong achievements is a definite set of emotional skills – your EQ – not just purely cognitive abilities that are measured by conventional IQ tests.'' Do you agree with this view? Give reasons in support of your answer. (2023, 10 Marks)
2. In case of crisis of conscience does emotional intelligence help to overcome the same without compromising the ethical or moral stand that you are likely to follow? Critically examine. (2021, 10 Marks)
3. "Emotional Intelligence is the ability to make your emotions work for you instead of against you." Do you agree with this view? Discuss. (2019, 10 Marks)
4. How will you apply emotional intelligence in administrative practices? (2017, 10 Marks)
5. Anger is a harmful negative emotion. It is injurious to both personal life and work life. (a) Discuss how it leads to negative emotions and undesirable behaviors. (b) How can hit be managed and controlled? (2016, 10 Marks)

08 Administrative Ethics

"Nearly all men can stand adversity, but if you want to test a man's character, give him power".

-Abraham Lincoln

"Righteousness is the foundation stone of peace and good governance"

-Confucius.

"Power tends to corrupt, and absolute power corrupts absolutely"

-Lord Acton

"The price good men pay for indifference to public affairs is to be ruled by evil men"

-Plato

Integrity without knowledge is weak and useless, and knowledge without integrity is dangerous and dreadful.

-Samuel Johnson.

"Ask not what your country can do for you - ask what you can do for your country" (Highlights the importance of public service and dedication to a greater good)

-John F. Kennedy

Ashoka - the Great: Inscriptions mention his focus on "Dharma-Rajya" (Rule of law) and equal justice for all. (Ashoka's reign highlights the importance of ethical governance that prioritizes fairness and justice).

ADMINISTRATIVE ETHICS

- Administrative ethics refer to the moral principles and standards that guide the conduct, behaviour and actions of civil servants in India
- These principles go beyond simply following rules and regulations with a commitment to serving the public good.
- Paul H Appleby argues that morality and administration cannot be separated. He remarked, "It is not merely bigger government that ultimately matters; what is significant is that morality in administration alone could ensure better government."
  - He delineated the following attributes of a moral administrator.

Attributes

- A sense of responsibility
- Skills in communication and personnel administration.
- Willingness to engage in problem solving and to work with others as a team
- Prefers to be influenced by public needs, interests and sensitivities rather than resorting to the use of raw bureaucratic power
- Personal confidence to initiate new ideas
- Ability to cultivate and utilize institutional resources

Need of Ethics in the Administration

- **Legacy of Colonial Rule:** India inherited a bureaucratic system that prioritized hierarchy, order and efficiency but administrative ethics ensure that the system the public effectively and ethically.
- **Position of public trust:** It is the duty of public official to act in the public interest.
- Public servants play a critical role in the implementation of the public policy and thus, expected to reflect the highest standards of morality.
- **Upholding of the democratic system:** Public servants need to ensure fair and equitable treatment for all citizens upholding the democratic principles.
- Perform the duties and functions efficiently, effectively and with integrity, in accordance with laws or administrative policies.
- **Developmental challenges:** Strong commitment to public service is required to address challenges like poverty, socio-economic inequalities, infrastructure deficiencies etc.

- Efficient and Effective utilisation of public resources.
- Increasing relevant in the modern times characterised by media vigilance, rising public awareness and culture of transparency in governance.

IMPORTANCE

- Citizen centric governance: Eg: Tilonia Model (Rajasthan), spearheaded by IAS officer Krishna Kumar, involved participatory budgeting
- Promote a culture of administrative accountability and responsibility
- Promote public welfare and social good: Eg- Akshaya Patra foundation, cofounded by IAS officer Madhavan Nair, provides mid-day meals to millions of underprivileged children across India.
- Upholding of the constitutional mandate.
- Curbing arbitrary actions and discretion of civil servants: Eg; RTI Act 2005 reduces the scope for officials to misuse their authority for personal gains
- Cultivating high standards of conduct in civil servants. Eg. PCA 1988 discourages unethical practices within the civil services.
- Strengthening legitimacy and public trust on administration.
- Providing direction in resolving ethical dilemmas especially when the law is silent on the issue.

The Santhanam Committee (1964) highlighted the importance of ethical civil servants. High moral standards are essential for India's progress, requiring a foundation of idealism and social responsibility instilled from a young age.

> "It is utmost important that the public administration should be efficient but it is even more important that it should be ethical. It is said of an individual that if character is lost, everything is lost. It could be stated about public administration, that if ethics is lost, everything is lost".
>
> —P. R. Dubhanshi

> "It is not merely bigger government that ultimately matters, what is significant is that morality in administration alone could ensure better government. One would not doubt that the morality in administration is sustained by patience, honesty, loyalty, cheerfulness, courtesy and like traits".
>
> —Paul H. Appleby

BUREAUCRACY

• Bureaucracy refers to a complex system of organisation that relies on established rules, procedures, and hierarchical structures.

Features of Weber's Ideal Bureaucracy

• **Hierarchy**: A clear chain of command ensures smooth decision-making, but can lead to rigidity. Eg- The IAS officer structure in district administration.

• **Division of Labour**: Specialisation improves efficiency, but might create communication silos. Eg-Separate departments for health, education and sanitation within a municipality.

• **Formal rules and procedures**: Standardised processes ensure consistency and impartiality but can stifle innovation. Eg- Standardised application procedures for government services.

• **Rational legal Authority**: Legitimacy comes from laws & regulations, not personal connections.

• **Meritocracy**: Selection and promotion based on qualifications, not favouritism. Eg- UPSC Civil Services exam for IAS recruitment.

• **Expertise**: Bureaucrats are trained specialists in their fields. Eg- Domain-specific training for doctors recruited into government hospitals.

• **Impersonality**: Decisions are objective and unbiased. Eg- Ideally, Service delivery should be based on need, not personal relationships.

• **Career Orientation**: Civil Servants have job security and long term career prospects. Eg- Permanent positions for government employees.

Aspect	Traditional Bureaucracy	Contemporary Bureaucracy
Based on	Weberian Model of Bureaucracy	Developmental Model of Bureaucracy
Features	• Rigid hierarchy, rules & regulations, specialisation, impersonality	• Collaborative governance, Public Service values, Performance-based management, client orientation.
Focus	Maximising efficiency & order	• Balancing efficiency with effectiveness in achieving development goals.
Strengths	Consistency, predictability and clear lines of accountability	• Emphasis on innovation, adaptation, and citizen participation.
Bureaucratic morality	• Adherence to rules & regulations, chain of command trump over personal conscience.	• Personal conscience, ethical values like empathy, compassion towards weaker section of people, integrity, honesty, accountability & transparency plays equal role along with rules & regulations
Power distribution	Centralisation of power	Decentralisation of power and delegated legislation

CATEGORISATION OF PUBLIC SERVICE VALUES

Ethical	Democratic	Professional	People
Integrity	Rule of law	Effectiveness	Caring
Fairness	Neutrality	Efficiency	Fairness
Accountability	Accountability	Service	Tolerance
Loyalty	Loyalty	Leadership	Decency
Excellence	Openness	Excellence	Compassion
Respect	Responsiveness	Innovation	Courage
Honesty	Representativeness	Quality	Benevolence
Probity	Legality	Creativity	Humanity

Nolan Committee - A cornerstone of Public Service Ethics

- The Nolan committee was established in the United Kingdom in 1994 to examine and make recommendations on ethical standards in public life.
- The Committee produced a report called "Standards in public life", which set out seven key principles of public life that has become known as "Nolan Principles".

SALIENT PRINCIPLES OF PROBITY BY NOLAN COMMITTEE

1. Selflessness: Holders of public office should take decisions solely in terms of public interest. They should not do so in order to gain financial or other material benefits for themselves, their family or their friends.

2. Integrity: Holders of public office should not place themselves under any financial or other obligation to outside individuals or organisation that might influence them in performance of their official duties.

3. Objectivity: In carrying out public business, including making public appointments, awarding contracts, or recommending individuals for rewards and benefits, holders of public office should make choices on merit.

4. Accountability: Holders of public office must be able to explain the rationale for their decisions taken or the way the duty has been performed and submit themselves to whatever scrutiny is appropriate to their office.

5. Openness: Holders of public office should be as open as possible about all the decisions and actions that they take. They should give reasons for their decisions and restrict information only when the wider public interest clearly demands.

6. Honesty: Holders of public office have a duty to declary any private interests relating to their public duties and to take steps to resolve any conflicts arising in a way that protects the public interest.

7. Leadership: Holders of public office should promote and support the above mentioned principles by leadership and set an example for others to emulate

Indian Public Service Values

The draft Public Service Bill outlines key values expected from civil servants in India:

- Allegiance to the constitution and laws of the nation: Upholding principles like justice, liberty and equality as enshrined in the Preamble.
- Apolitical functioning: Staying neutral and objective in decision making, not influenced by political parties. Example: The Election Commission of India, known for its neutrality in conducting fair and impartial election.
- Good governance for people's benefit: Prioritizing public service and welfare in all administrative actions. Example: RTI Act, 2005 ensuring transparency and empowering citizens.
- Objectivity and impartiality: Making decisions based on merits and facts, without bias or favouritism. Example: Justice Mahilamani Siridhar who upheld the law against her own son, demonstrating impartiality.
- Accountability and Transparency: Being answerable to the public and following open procedures. Example: Practice of Annual Performance Appraisal Reports (APARs) for evaluating civil servants work.
- Highest ethical standards: Maintaining integrity and avoiding corruption or conflict of interest

Example: Anna Hazare, a social activist who championed the Jan Lokpal Bill to promote ethical governance.

- **Meritbased Selection**: Recruiting Civil Servants based on qualifications and competence, considering diversity. **Example**: UPSC Civil Services Exam, a rigorous selection process aimed at identifying talented individuals for administrative roles.
- **Fiscal Prudence**: Ensuring efficient use of public funds and avoiding wasteful expenditure **Example**: Social audit mandated in various welfare schemes such as MGNREGA.
- **Healthy work Environment**: Promoting a positive and respectful workplace for all personnel. **Example**: The Sexual Harassment of Women at Workplace (Prevention, Prohibition and Redressal) Act ensuring a safe working environment.

Other Values include

- Patriotism and upholding national pride
- Discharge official duties with competence.
- Communication, consultation and cooperation: Encouraging participation and collaboration at all levels. **Example**: Gram Sabhas (village assemblies) fostering communication and communication in rural development initiatives.
- Ensure effective management, professional growth and leadership development
- Foster socio-economic development, with due regard to diversity of nations.

Status of Ethics in Administration

Given below are the various factors that influence Indian administration:

Factors	Indian provisions	Weakness in existing provisions
Legal and Regulatory Frameworks	• Constitutional Goals: Equality, Justice, liberty, Democracy etc. • Laws: RTI Act (2005), Whistleblower Protection Act (2014) etc	• Poor enforcement of laws • Weak investigative and judicial process • Backlog of cases in the judiciary • Exploitation of the loopholes • Political interference.
Institutional Design and Oversight	• CVC, CBI, ED • Public Service Commissions (UPSC and SPSCs)	• Resource constraints • Political influence • Bureaucratic hurdles • Lack of public awareness about their functions.
Ancient Texts and Traditions	• Dharmashastra emphasized virtues like Righteous rule (Dharma Rajya) that resonates to welfare state mentioned under Indian constitution. • Other values emphasized through Vedas, Upanishads are truthfulness, justice, compassion and duty.	• Designed for monarchical rule and may not translate directly to a democratic republic • The caste system and social inequalities prevalent in ancient India were reflected in the administration, with certain groups holding power and privileges.
Social and Cultural Values	• Indian society emphasizes values like Dharma (righteous duty) and social responsibility which can motivate ethical conduct.	• Historical legacies of Patronage systems • Tolerant attitude towards minor forms of corruption. • Discrimination in public service delivery.
Political Context	• Increasing discourse on anti-corruption led to the scrapping of electoral bonds. • Focus on hard work and ethical conduct by the PM imparts such culture in the administration • The government made changes	• Lax regulations on election finance • Political interference in bureaucratic process • Increased work pressure and consequent stress on the already over-burdened bureaucracy. • Non-objective performance

	to the rules of compulsory retirement for All India Service officers to remove non-performing bureaucrats earlier	appraisal System.
Training of Administration	• Foundation training at LBSNAA • Specialised training post LBSNAA Such as IPS officers go to SVP National Police Academy • Mission Karmayogi (Detailed explanation given below)	• Lack of uniform training standards across all levels. • Mainly focused on the core skills and the soft skills such as Empathy, compassion is neglected. • Implementing a large-scale reform program of Mission karmayogi across a diverse bureaucracy has its challenges.

Mission Karmayogi

- Launched in 2020 by the Indian government, Mission Karmayogi (Mission Capable Worker) is a major reform initiative aimed at revamping civil service training in India
- It aims to create a competent and future ready civil service, equipped with the skills and knowledge to effectively serve the public in a rapidly changing world.
- The focus is on
  - Shifting from Service Specific Silos to role based training.
  - Utilize online learning platforms for wider reach and accessibility.
  - Enhancing skills in areas like critical thinking, innovation, and citizen centric service delivery.
- A critical component of Mission Karmayogi is the online learning platform, iGOT Karmayogi (Integrated Government Online Training)
  - This platform allows for "anytime-anywhere-anydevice" learning, making it accessible to a vast number of civil servants across the country.
- Mission Karmayogi promotes a 70:20:10 model of lifelong journey.
  - This means 70% of learning happens on the job, 20% through coaching and mentoring, and 10% through formal training programs like those offered on iGOT karmayogi.

Technological Factors	• Egovernance initiatives (Digital India Mission) to improve transparency & streamline process potentially reducing opportunities for corruption	• Digital literacy gaps • Concerns about data privacy and Security.

IMPLEMENTATION OF ADMINISTRATIVE ETHICS IN INDIA

Sources

01 Historical Precedents and Traditions (Kautilya's Arthashastra, Scriptures like Vedas, Upanishads etc) - Good governance, Justice, Duty etc.

02 Indian Socio-Religious Reformers (Mahatma Gandhi, B.R. Ambedkar, Raja Ram Mohay Roy etc) - Truth, Non-violence, Inclusive Governance etc

03 Indian Constitution (Preamble, FRs, DPSPs, Fundamental Duties) - Equality, Liberty, Justice, Rule of law, Secularism, Democracy etc.

04 Parliamentary Acts and Codes (Central Service (Conduct) Rules, 1964, Prevention of Corruption Act 1988) Integrity, Neutrality, Efficiency, Accountability etc.

05 Weberian Bureaucracy - Rationality, Efficiency, Rules-Based, Impartiality.

06 Reports of Commissions and Committees (2nd ARC, Nolan Committee) - Integrity, objectivity, Dedication to public Service etc

Evolution of Administrative Ethics

- India doesn't have a single Code of Ethics for civil Servants like Some countries.
- Instead, ethical expectations are outlined in Various Conduct Rules such as Central Civil Services (Conduct) Rules, 1964, All India Services (Conduct) Rules, 1968 etc.
- These conduct rules codify long-standing ethical norms that were previously established through notifications and regulations. For example:
  - Discouraging excessive borrowing by civil Servants (Since 1869)
  - Banning the acceptance of gifts (Since 1876)
  - Restricting property transactions to avoid conflicts of interest (Since 1881).
- The Santhanam committee (1964) played a role in expanding the scope of the conduct Rules. Over time, the rules have been updated to address new issues like:
  - Maintaining courtesy towards the public.
  - Prohibiting dowry demands
  - Preventing Sexual harassment in the workplace.
- India's legal framework also includes provisions in the Indian Penal Code (IPC) that address Specific offenses:
  - Illegal gratification (bribery) - Section 161-165.
  - Criminal breach of trust by a public Servant - Section 409.
- The Prevention of Corruption Act (1988) - This Act created additional legal measures to combat corruption.
- 2nd ARC report on Ethics in Governance (2005): Recommended a 3-Tier Public Service Code.

CODE OF CONDUCT

- A focused document outlining expected behaviour for civil servants in specific situations.
- Defines acceptable and unacceptable practices within the organisation.
- Legally enforceable and sets ethical standards for public servants.
- Designed to prevent misconduct like conflict of interest, bribery and misuse of office.
- Violation of the code can lead to disciplinary actions and potential termination

All India Services (conduct) Rules, 1968

The Government of India has amended All India Services (Conduct) Rules, 1968, in rule 3(1) after sub rule (1) by inserting sub-rule (1A) and rule 3(2) after sub-rule (2A) by inserting sub-rule (2B) and these rules are called All India Services (Conduct) Amendment Rules, 2014

Under sub-rule (1A), every member of the Service shall maintain:

i. High ethical standards, integrity and honesty.
ii. Political integrity.
iii. Promotion of the principles of merit, fairness and impartiality in the discharge of duties.
iv. Accountability and transparency.
v. Responsiveness to the public, particularly to the weaker section.
vi. Courtesy and good behaviour with the public.

Under sub-rule (2B), every member of the service shall:

i. Commit himself to and uphold the supremacy of the constitution and democratic values.
ii. Defend and uphold the sovereignty and integrity of India, the security of state, public order, decency and morality.
iii. Maintain integrity in public service.
iv. Take decisions solely in public interest and use or cause to use public resources efficiently, effectively and economically.
v. Declare any private interests relating to his public duties and take steps to resolve any conflict in a way that protects the public interest.
vi. Not place himself under any financial or other obligations to any individual or organisation which may influence him in the performance of his official duties;
vii. Not use his position as civil servant and not take decisions in order to derive financial or material benefits for himself, his family or his friends.

viii. Make choices, take decisions and make recommendation on merit alone;

ix. Act with fairness and impartiality and not discriminate against anyone, particularly the poor and the under-privileged sections of society;

x. Refrain from doing anything which is or may be contrary to any law, rules, regulations and established practices.

xi. Maintain discipline in the discharge of his duties and be liable to implement the lawful orders duly communicated to him;

xii. Be liable to maintain confidentiality in the performance of his official duties.

xiii. Perform and discharge his duties with the highest degree of professionalism and dedication to the best of his abilities.

Critique of the Conduct Rules

CRITIQUE

Lack of values and Code of Ethics: The rules don't explicitly define the values or a code of ethics that civil servants should uphold

Focus on "Do's and Don'ts": The rules provide a list of restrictions rather than a framework for ethical decision making.

Overly restrictive nature: The rules are seen as highly restrictive, limiting freedom of expression and potentially impractical in some situations

Vague and specific rules: The code is a mix of both very specific rules (like gift restrictions) and broad, open ended ones ("conduct unbecoming of a member of the service"). This vagueness can lead to confusion and inconsistent enforcement

Outdated language: The code may not reflect the complexities of modern governance to address contemporary issues like conflict of interest

Weak Enforcement allowing potential violations to go unchecked.

Limited scope: Code of Conduct typically focus on professional behaviour, but might not address personal conduct that can impact Organisation's reputation

Strict compliance of laws can lead to situations where the "letter of the law" is followed but the spirit is not.

Code of Conduct for Legislators

The Committees on Ethics of the Rajya Sabha and the Lok Sabha have formulated guidelines for legislators in both Houses of Parliament. These guidelines encompass several key principles

1. Maintaining Parliament's reputation: Legislators must avoid actions that tarnish the reputation of Parliament and undermine their credibility.
2. Promoting Public welfare: MPs should leverage their position to advance the general welfare of the people.

3. Confidentiality: Legislators who possess confidential information by virtue of their parliamentary or Committee roles should refrain from using it for personal gain.

4. Upholding Fundamental Duties: Legislators should prioritize the fundamental Duties outlined in Part IV of the Indian Constitution.

5. High Standards of Morality: MPs are expected to uphold high standards of morality, dignity, decency, and values in public life.

Code of Conduct for Ministers

Ministers at both Union and State level are bound by ethical standards, which are delineated as follows:

01 Annual Asset Declaration: Ministers are required to annually declare their assets and liabilities to the Prime Minister or Chief Minister

02 Property Transactions: Ministers should refrain from buying or selling immovable property to the government except in cases of compulsory acquisition.

03 Business Restrictions: Ministers are prohibited from starting or joining any new business ventures.

04 Reporting Family Business: If a family member sets up or joins another business, the minister must report this to Prime Minister or Chief Minister.

05 Ministers are advised against accepting valuable gifts except from close relatives, and neither they nor their family members should accept any gifts from individuals with whom they have official dealings.

Code of Conduct for Judges

The Supreme Court of India, on May 7, 1997, unanimously adopted the 'Restatement of Values of Judicial Life', commonly known as 'Code of Conduct' for Judges. It includes the following provisions

Restriction on Family Use: Family Members who are Bar members are prohibited from using Judge's residence/facilities for professional purposes

Maintaining Dignity: Judges are expected to maintain an appropriate degree of aloofness befitting their office

Avoiding Conflicts: Judges should refrain from hearing cases involving family members, close relatives or friends.

Political Neutrality: Judges must abstain from engaging in public debates or expressing views on political matters or pending judicial cases

Media interaction: Judges should not give interviews to media, letting their judgements speak for themselves.

Gifts and Hospitality: Judges should only accept gifts or hospitality from family, close relation or friends

Financial speculation: Judges are prohibited from speculating in shares, stocks or similar investments

Disclosure of Interest: Judges must disclose any shares held in companies involved in cases before them, abstaining from hearing such cases if objections arise

CODE OF ETHICS

- Assembly of institutional guidelines used to reduce ethical vagueness and serve as a means of reinforcing ethical conduct within an organisation.
- Provides a framework for ethical decision making in all situations.
- Establishes a shared foundation for ethical conduct across civil service.
- Guides professionals on the steps needed to uphold ethical standards

- **Moral and Professional standards:** Sets expectations for honesty, dedication and performance. Example: IAS Officer Rajni Sekhri Sibal refusing a bribe to alter exam results.
- **Professional Behaviour:** Promotes tolerance, pride and responsibility within the Civil Service. Example: Atal Bihari Vajpayee's respectful treatment of all political leaders, even those in opposition)
- According to Robert Brown, Code of Ethics have two fundamental purpose:

They provide moral guidelines and professional standards of conduct. The professional codes hold people accountable for proper performance and devotion to honesty and obligation

The second purpose is to define professional behaviour to promote a sense of pride, tolerance and responsibility among professionals.

Code of Ethics VS Code of Conduct

Code of Ethics	Code of Conduct
It includes core ethical values, principles and ideals of the organisation	It is a directional document containing specific practices and behaviour, that are followed or restricted under the organisation

Code of ethics is a set of principles which influence the judgement	Code of conduct is a set of guidelines that influence employee's actions.
Code of ethics are wide; in nature as compared to code of conduct.	Code of conduct are narrow.
Ethical standards generally are non-specific and are designed to provide a set of values or decision making	Conduct standards generally provides a fairly clear set of expectations about which actions are required, accepted or prohibited.
It enable employees to make independent judgements about the most appropriate course of action	It enable employees to work in compliance with rules and actions are guided by the codes.
A particular rule in the code of Ethics might state that all employees will obey the law.	A code of conduct might list several specific laws relevant to specific areas of organisational operations, that employees need to obey.
May not be directly enforceable by law, but violations can have legal consequences depending on the severity	Usually enforced with the organisation with disciplinary actions for violations.

In essence

- A code of ethics sets the WHY behind ethical behaviour
- A code of conduct outlines the HOW to behave ethically

A well-defined code of conduct is often derived from the organisation's code of ethics. The code of ethics provides the overarching framework, while the code of conduct translates those principles into practical applications.

Limitations in the Code of Ethics

- Code of Ethics provide broad principles but lack specific instructions for navigating complex situations which can lead to confusion and differing interpretations of how to act ethically in a particular scenario.
- Code of Ethics cannot provide guidance for every individual in every situation.
- Internal vs External guidance: Balancing the code with individual and organisational ethics. Public Service should be guided by internal ethical principles, not just written rules.
- Upholding the code might hinder decision making in emergencies like riots or inter-communal conflicts.
- Lack of awareness and enforcement: limited awareness about the code and weak enforcement mechanism can render it ineffective

• Cultural Nuances: A One-size-fits-all code might not resonate with everyone, potentially creating conflicts between ethical principles and established cultural practices.

Key Considerations while designing a code

- **Desirable** It must meet the expectations and desires of an organisation and fit the Organisation theme
- **Clarity and Specificity** Use clear language that is easy for everyone to understand.
- **Logical Order** Present information in a way that flows logically.
- **Feasibility** Set realistic expectations that can be achieved
- **Enforceability** Ensure consequences are in place for violations. Without enforcement, the code loses its impact.
- **General Audience** Tailor the Code to a broad audience within Civil Service

2nd ARC RECOMMENDATIONS ON PUBLIC SERVICE CODE

The 2nd Administrative Reforms Commission (ARC) made significant recommendations regarding the Code of Ethics and Code of Conduct for civil servants in India.

- Statutory Backing: ARC advocated for a Public Service code with statutory backing which would provide a legal framework for ethical conduct.
- Three-level structure: The Commission proposed a comprehensive code with three levels:

- **Apex level**: Clean and concise statements outlining the core values and ethical standards expected of civil servants (Eg- Integrity, Impartiality, Public Service dedication)
- **Second level**: Broad principles guiding the behaviour of civil servants in various situations (Eg- Objectivity, Empathy)
- **Third level**: A specific code of conduct with a precise list of acceptable and unacceptable behaviour and actions (Eg- Conflict of interest rules, gift giving limitations)

- Leadership Role: The ARC highlighted the importance of leadership in promoting and inculcating these values within the organisation.
- ARC implicitly called for improved enforcement mechanism of code of conduct

• **Alignment with Code of Ethics**: The Commission emphasized the need for a strong alignment between the Code of Conduct and Code of Ethics. This would ensure consistency and clarity for civil servants.

Overall the 2nd ARC recommendations aimed to create comprehensive framework for ethical behaviour within the Indian civil Service. This framework combining a statutory Code of Ethics with a well-defined Code of Conduct, would help ensure that civil servants uphold the highest ethical standards in their service to the nation.

Hota Committee Report (2004)

• **Formalisation**: Recommended in developing a formal Code of Ethics for civil Servants which would provide a framework for ethical decision making in various situations.

• **Values**. This code would highlight core values like integrity, merit and excellence in public service.

• The Hota Committee believed that a combination of strong code of ethics and clear conduct rules would create more ethical civil service and enhance public trust

ETHICAL CONCERNS IN ADMINISTRATION

1. **Administrative corruption** in form of bribery and extortion, misusing public funds for personal gain or favoring friends, family or political allies based on personal connections. Eg: In 2022, Several forest officials in MP were arrested for allegedly colluding with timber mafias.
2. **Political interference**: Undue political pressure on civil servants to make decisions based on political interests can lead to nepotism and hinder fair implementation of policies.
3. **Neglect of Duty**: Eg. The 2017 Encephalitis Deaths in Uttar Pradesh was mainly because of shortage of doctors and inadequate medical supplies in the hospital.
4. **Patronage based appointments**: Eg- Post retirement assignments of senior officers to the constitutional posts like Governor or regulatory bodies.
5. **Caste System and Social Bias**: India's caste system can lead to discrimination in public service delivery.
6. **Complacency (Or Chalta hai Attitude) rather than diligence** leads to slow pace of public works project, resulting in cost overruns and public inconvenience along with safety concerns. Eg- The 2018 Delhi Metro collapse, attributed to faulty construction practices, could be consequence of such complacency
7. **Weak Accountability Mechanisms** such as ineffective RTI Act, poor protection to whistleblowers, inadequate focus on grievance redressal mechanisms etc.

Administrative Secrecy has become the norm and transparency or openness is the exception.

8. Bureaucratic red tapism trumps over the public interest (Lack of Compassion)
Eg: Denial of ration cards to eligible beneficiaries due to rigid verification procedures or documentation requirements.

9. Poor participation of citizens in the governance process.

10. Misuse of Resources: Squandering public funds due to mismanagement or wasteful practices.

11. Psychology of evasion when it comes to making difficult decisions such as loan waiver or loan write off.

BUILDING A STRONG ETHICAL FRAMEWORK

Eight Key components of OECD for an effective ethical infrastructure in public service

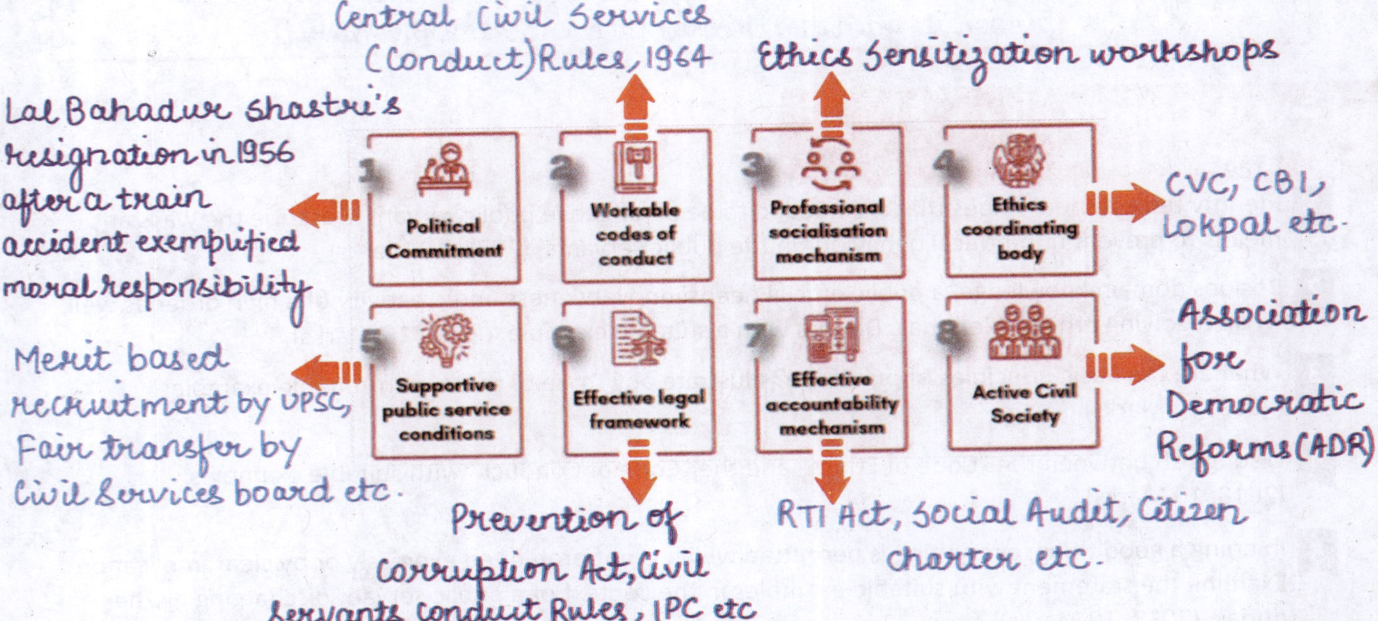

Maxims of Public Administration

Maxim	Description
1. Legality and Rationality	Adherence to laws and rules governing policies and decisions
2. Responsibility & Accountability	Acceptance of responsibility for decisions and actions, being accountable to higher authorities and the public.
3. Work Commitment	Performing duties with dedication, respecting time and commitments • Swami Vivekananda Observed: "Every duty is holy and devotion to duty is the highest form of Worship".

4. Excellence	Upholding high standards in decisions and actions, following Total Quality Management principles.
5. Fusion	Reconciling individual, organisational, and social goals, prioritizing ethical considerations in conflicts.
6. Responsiveness and Resilience	Adapting to challenges while maintaining ethical conduct and swiftly correcting deviations.
7. Utilitarianism	Policies aim to maximise benefit for greatest number of people
8. Compassion	Showing compassion within legal bounds, considering the needs of vulnerable.
9. National Interest	Prioritizing national interests while upholding universal principles and standards.
10. Justice	Adherence to principles of equality, fairness, and impartiality in policies and decisions, avoiding favouritism.
11. Transparency	Making and implementing decisions transparently, allowing stakeholders to understand the rationale behind decisions.
12. Integrity	Acting with honesty, refraining from using power for personal gain or illegitimate interests of others.

PYQs Corner

(Write the Answer and Get Free Evaluation)

1. Identify ten essential values that are needed to be an effective public servant. Describe the ways and means to prevent non-ethical behaviour in the public servants. (2021, 10 Marks)
2. Besides domain knowledge, a public official needs innovativeness and creativity of a high order as well, while resolving ethical dilemmas. Discuss with a suitable example. (2021, 10 Marks)
3. What are the basic principles of public life? Illustrate any three of these with suitable examples. (2019, 10 Marks)
4. Distinguish between the "Code of Ethics" and the "Code of Conduct" with suitable examples. (2018, 10 Marks)
5. In doing a good thing, everything is permitted which is not prohibited expressly or by clear implication". Examine the statement with suitable examples in the context of a public servant discharging his/her duties. (2018, 10 Marks)
6. Discuss the Public Services Code as recommended by the 2nd Administrative Refroms Commission. (2016, 10 Marks)
7. "Max Weber said that it is not wise to apply to public administration the sort of moral and ethical norms we apply to matters of personal conscience. It is important to realize that the state bureaucracy might possess its own independent bureaucratic morality." Critically analyse this statement. (2016, 10 Marks)
8. Today we find that in-spite of various measures of prescribing codes of conduct, setting up vigilance cells/commissions, RTI, active media and strengthening of legal mechanism, corrupt practices are not coming under control. (a) Evaluate the effectiveness of these measures with justifications (b) Suggest more effective strategies to tackle this menace. (2015, 10 Marks)

09 Sources of Ethical Guidance: Laws, Rules, Regulations and Conscience

66

"There is a higher court than courts of justice and that is the court of conscience. It supersedes all other courts"

— Mahatma Gandhi

"Never do anything against conscience even if the state demands it" (Emphasizes the importance of following one's conscience, even in difficult situations).

— Albert Einstein

"Where there is no law, there is no freedom." (Suggests that laws provide a framework for ethical conduct, protecting individual rights and freedoms)

— John Locke

Laws is "nothing else than an ordinance of reason for the common good, made by him who has care of the community, and promulgated".

— Thomas Aquinas.

"Morality cannot be legislated, but behavior can be regulated. Judicial decrees may not change heart, but they can restrain the heartless"

— Martin Luther King Jr.

SOURCES OF ETHICAL GUIDANCE

- Ethical Guidance refers to principles, frameworks or tools that help us make decisions that are morally right.
- It provides a structured approach to navigating complex moral dilemmas and making decisions that align with ethical values.
- Ethical guidance is needed for various reasons - Addressing corruption (2G spectrum), Promoting social responsibility (Plachimada case with Coca Cola), Ensuring fairness and equity (gender pay gaps), Navigating moral dilemmas, Strengthening public trust, Promoting responsible development & Use of new technologies etc.

INTERNAL SOURCES

- Moral Compass: Internal sense of right and wrong shaped by one's upbringing, values, and life experiences.
- Conscience: One's inner voice that guides you towards ethical behaviour and flags potential wrongdoings.
- Reasoning and Critical thinking: Based on various Ethical theories.

EXTERNAL SOURCES

- Laws and Regulations: Provide a baseline for ethical behaviour, outlining what is considered illegal and punishable.
- Professional Code of Ethics: Define ethical conduct and best practices within that field.
- Religious teachings: Offer Ethical guidance through scriptures, teachings and principles that promote good conduct and compassion.
- Cultural Norms: Social expectations and cultural values can influence what is considered ethical behaviour within a specific Society.

LAW AS A SOURCE OF ETHICAL GUIDANCE

- Law is a system of rules and principles that govern a behaviour within a Society.
- These rules can be formal and written down like Statutes enacted by a legislature or informal and unwritten like the customary practices.
- Laws are typically enforced by a Sovereign authority, Such as a government or a recognised Institution.
  - This enforcement can take various forms, including fines, imprisonment or other Sanctions for violating a law.
- Primary purpose: To maintain Order and Justice within a Society.
- The concept of legality is fundamental to the rule of law.

- It means that everyone, including the government, is Subject to the Law and no-one is above it. This ensures fairness, predictability and prevents arbitrary use of power.
- Law is not static; it evolves over time to reflect changing Societal needs and values.
- Law cannot address every ethical dilemma or Social problem. It is just one tool among many for promoting a just and equitable Society.

Thomas Aquinas' Four Types of Law

Types of Law

1. Eternal Law (Lex Aeterna)
- Reflection of God's reason and plan for the universe.
- Exists eternally, governing the natural order (Planetary motion, Energy flow)
- Not man made laws, but inherent principles.

2. Divine Law (Lex Divina)
- A Subset of Eternal law revealed through religious texts (Bible, Quran, Gita, Guru Granth Sahib)
- Complements the natural law by providing additional guidance and specific rules for human behaviour. Examples: Ten commandments, Teachings of Prophets

3. Natural Law (Lex Naturalis)
- Part of Eternal Law that humans can grasp through reason.
- Universal, objective principle for ethical and political life
- Examples: Do good, avoid evil, help those in need, do no harm.
- Applies to all rational beings, unlike Eternal law governing everything

4. Human Law (Lex Humana)
- Refers to the Law created by human beings, enacted by government or legislative bodies.
- Human laws should be based on natural law principles.
- Can change based on experience and practical needs
- Examples: CAA, RTE, Dowry prohibition etc

Thinker's views on Laws

Plato	• Believed in universal, ideal law based on reason and justice • He argued that man made laws should strive to reflect this ideal law.
John Locke	• Believed that individuals have natural rights such as life, liberty & property. • Laws should protect these rights and prevent the government from becoming tyrannical.
Thomas Hobbes	• Argued that people live in a "State of nature" lived in fear and chaos. • They entered into a Social contract to create laws & a Sovereign authority to enforce them, Sacrificing some freedoms for security.

Laws, Rules and Regulations

- Laws are enactments of legislature and enjoys the legitimacy of backing from the state.
  - Laws are Sacrosanct and their violation can be prosecuted in court of law.
- Rules are Sub-ordinate legislation and enjoy the Same enforceability as law.
  - Law by nature cannot be comprehensive and cover all possible Situations.
  - So, every law contains a provision for making rules necessary for its implementation.
- Regulations are directives that are formed in context of any particular Situations
  - The term 'Regulation' refers nowadays to regulations which regulatory authorities – like Central Electricity Regulatory commission – issue for regulating a particular Sector like power, insurance or telecom.

Criteria	Laws	Rules	Regulations.
Source	Enacted by the legislature	Made by the executive branch	Issued by Regulatory bodies.
Authority	Highest level of legal power	Subordinate to Laws, but can have force of law	Derived from enabling laws passed by legislature
Sanctions	Violation attracts State punishment	Violation may have penalties	Violations may have penalties.
Focus	Broad principles and Societal ethics	Specific details and procedures for laws	Specific details within a regulated Sector.
Examples	Right to Education Act, National Food Security Act	Traffic rules, waste management rules	TRAI regulations, CERC regulations.

- Laws are the foundation, Setting the overarching principles. Regulations build on the laws, providing details on how to comply. Rules can be established at various levels to guide behaviour within specific contexts.

Examples: Law: "It is illegal to steal". (Broad Principle).

Regulation: "Security cameras must be installed in all Jewellary stores". (Details how to Prevent theft).

Rule: "No running in hallways". (Specific action prohibited in a particular context)

- All the three (laws, rules and regulations) must adhere to Indian Constitution
- They are written to limit discretion and promote ethical standards.
- The judiciary can declare laws, rules and regulations unconstitutional if they violate the Constitution

How Laws and Rules Act as a Source of Ethical Guidance

Law as Source	Specific Examples.
1. Establishment of minimum standards Laws set a baseline for acceptable behaviour, ensuring people don't engage in harmful or unethical activities.	• Eg: Dowry Prohibition Act (1961) outlaws the practice of dowry, establishing a minimum ethical standard for marriage practices
2. Reflecting Societal norms: laws and rules reflecting the shared moral values of a Society and following them ensures adherence to accepted ethical standards	Eg: Stricter laws like the Criminal Law (Amendment) Act, 2013 against crimes against women reflect Society's growing disapproval of such violence
3. Protection of Fundamental rights which promote ethical principles of fairness, dignity and respect for all individuals.	Eg: RTI Act, 2005 fosters transparency and accountability, which are crucial ethical principles in democracy.
4. Fear of Punishment: Laws are enforced with sanctions, deterring unethical behaviour through the fear of punishment	Eg: Anti corruption laws like the Prevention of Corruption Act (1988) encourage ethical conduct among public officials by penalizing bribery
5. Promoting Social Justice: Laws can address historical injustices and promote equal opportunities for all	Eg: Protection of Civil Rights Act, 1955 promotes ethical treatment and inclusion
6. Legitimacy through representation: Laws enacted by representatives chosen through democratic elections hold legitimacy and public trust.	Eg: India's Constitution Serves as the ultimate ethical compass.

7. Consumer protection: Laws ensure fair market practices and protect consumers from explotation

Eg: Consumer Protection Act (2019) promotes ethical business conduct

8. Embracing best practices: Laws often incorporate best practices from around the world, promoting universal values like Right to life, dignity and Secularism.

Eg: Banning of Triple Talaq, discriminatory religious laws, etc.

9. Protection of the Environment: Environmental laws safeguard natural resources and promote sustainable practices

Eg: Environment Protection Act (1906) upholds the ethical principle environmental stewardship

10. Avoiding the slippery slope: Laws prevent a gradual decline into unethical behaviour by setting clear boundaries

Eg: Euthanasia law in India prevent the slippery slope of ending someone's life without proper safeguards.

Limitations of Law as a Source of Ethical Guidance

1. Incompleteness of law in the background of emerging technologies such as Artificial Intelligence, etc. Example: the growing use of facial recognition technology raises privacy concerns although there are no specific laws governing its use in India.
2. Coercive nature: Laws rely on punishment to deter unethical behaviour. This external pressure can be seen as less ethical than internal more convictions that guide good choices. Example: Following traffic laws might be driven by fear of fines rather than a genuine concern for safety.
3. Tool of the powerful: Laws can be manipulated by those in power to serve their own interests, undermining their ethical foundation.
Example: Historical instances of discriminatory laws like South Africa's Aparthied regime.
4. Collusive laws: Laws can be influenced by special interest or corruption, leading to unethical outcomes. Example: lobbying that weakens environmental regulations to benefit corporations.
5. Focus on legality rather than morality which is a broader concept.
Example: Many taxpayers use the loopholes in tax laws to avoid paying taxes. A person has acted legally but it is not an ethical action.

6. Unjust Laws: Sometimes, laws themselves are unethical, promoting discrimination or oppression. Example: Laws in Nazi Germany that legalised the persecution of Jews.
7. Neglecting Individual Rights: Laws may prioritize collective good over individual rights, creating ethical dilemmas. Example: Reasonable restrictions under Article 19(2) for freedom of Speech and expression were adopted to maintain social harmony.
8. Inconsistency and ambiguity: Conflicting or unclear laws can create confusion and difficulty in ethical decision making. Example: Right to Information Act and the official Secrets Act potentially contradicting each other.
9. Conflict with personal morality: Personal ethics might differ from the law, creating a struggle for individuals. Example: A doctor's moral code conflicting with laws prohibiting euthanasia.
10. Minimum standards: Laws set minimum acceptable behaviour, but ethical conduct may require going beyond the letter of the law.
Example: Following the "Spirit" of anti-corruption laws even if not explicitly required.

In conclusion, while law plays a crucial role in shaping ethical conduct, they are not a complete guide. Indians often navigate a complex landscape where legal frameworks, social norms, religious beliefs, and personal ethical principles all influence decision making.

CONSCIENCE AS A SOURCE OF ETHICAL GUIDANCE

- Conscience refers to the inner voice that guides one towards an ethical behaviour and right action.
- It is like an internal moral compass influenced by one's upbringing, values cultural background and religious beliefs.

Examples of Conscience in Action

- A Salesperson refuses to cheat a customer, even if it means losing a sale, because their conscience tells them it's wrong.
- A Student chooses to report cheating they witnessed in an exam, even though it might lead to social awkwardness, because their conscience compels them to uphold fairness.

- A well-developed conscience promotes ethical behaviour, fosters a sense of justice, an encourages individuals to be responsible members of society.

How Conscience act as a Source of Ethical Guidance

1. Immediate Source of information even in complex Situations where there is no time for extensive analysis.
2. Upholding of Dharma, promoting Social order and maintaining cosmic order.
3. Transcending legal boundaries as the laws only establish a baseline for acceptable behaviour.
4. Avoidance of Dissonance and consequently ethical actions. Example: Infosys whistleblower Ravi Srinivasan exposed accounting irregularities despite potential professional repercussions, highlighting conscience as a deterrence against unethical behaviour.
5. Constant Companion. Example: Environmentalist Saalumarada Thirumavalavan Continues to fight illegal Sand mining despite threats, demonstrating the unwavering nature of conscience.
6. Moral development. Example: Mahatma Gandhi's non-violent movement against British rule stemmed from his evolving conscience, urging ethical treatment and justice.
7. Interpretation of laws. Example: Justice Krishna Iyer's progressive judgements often prioritized the spirit of Indian constitution over a strict legalistic approach, reflecting the role of conscience in legal interpretation.
8. Challenging unjust System. Example: Dr. B. R. Ambedkar, a Dalit leader, fought against the caste system throughout his life, highlighting the role of conscience in challenging societal inequities.
9. Encourages critical thinking and consideration of potential consequences to deal with complex ethical dilemmas.

- Sanjeev Chaturvedi is a whistleblower who played a crucial role in exposing corruption at the AIIMS hospital

Limitations of Conscience as a Source of Ethical Guidance

LIMITATIONS

- Subjectivity in the ethical conclusion of right or wrong
- Differing cultural norms, upbringing and personal values bring subjectivity
- Social pressures and conform to Societal expectation can suppress inner voice
- Limited knowledge or awareness of ethical issues
- Self interest and ego can cloud one's judgement

CRISIS OF CONSCIENCE

A crisis of conscience occurs when a person experiences a significant internal conflict due to a perceived mismatch between their actions (for potential actions) and their moral priniiples.
It is a state of mental and emotional distress caused by a clash between what you believe is right and what you are doing, or what you might be pressured to do.

Key Aspects

1. Moral Conflict between what a person believes is right and what they are facing
2. Emotional Distress Such as guilt, shame, anxiety or fear
3. Difficulty in decision making (Ethical obligation vs Negative potential consequences.

Factors Contributing to the Crisis of Conscience in Indian Bureaucracy

- Pressure to conform: Bureaucracies have a hierarchical structure with established norms and expectations.
- Red Tape and inefficiency can lead to frustration and a sense of helplessness and thereby bending rules to achieve efficiency, creating a ethical dilemma
- Political interference can lead to bureaucrats overlooking ethical concerns or prioritizing political agendas over the public good
- Lack of transparency and accountability can create an environment where unethical practices go unchecked, fostering a sense of powerlessness and frustration for ethical officers.
- Limited resources can force bureaucrats to make difficult choices.

Consequences of Ignoring a Crisis

Whistleblowing against corruption

In 2003, Dinesh Mishra, an IPS officer in MP exposed a massive fake encounter case involving Senior Police officials

Prioritizing human rights over orders

In 2018, K. Gopinathan, a kerala IAS officer, refused to implement a government order to evict tribal families from their ancestral land with proper rehabilitation

Environmental Protection vs Development Projects

In 2019, an IAS officer Shivendra Singh Khandwi refused to approve a Sand mining project in ecologically sensitive Ganga riverbed

Strategies for mitigating crisis

1. Strengthening Ethical codes that outline acceptable behaviour and provide a framework for ethical conduct.

2. Promoting open communication to help officers navigate challenges and find solutions.

3. Stronger Whistleblower protection to encourage ethical conduct within the administration

4. Enhancing transparency within the administration fosters trust and empower officials to raise concerns without fear.

5. Leadership by example: Ethical leadership from senior officials sets a positive tone and motivates others to act with integrity

6. Ethical dilemmas training: Equipping officers with training to navigate ethical dilemmas and prioritize moral principles can guide decision making.

PYQs Corner

(Write the Answer and Get Free Evaluation)

1. Is conscience a more reliable guide when compared to laws, rules and regulations in the context of ethical decision-making? Discuss. (2023, 10 Marks)
2. The Rules and Regulations provided to all the civil servants are same, yet there is difference in the performance. Positive minded officers are able to interpret the Rules and Regulations in favour of the case and achieve success, whereas negative minded officers are unable to achieve goals by interpreting the same Rules and Regulations against the case. Discuss with illustrations. (2022, 10 Marks)
3. Distinguish between laws and rules. Discuss the role of ethics in formulating them. (2020, 10 Marks)
4. Law and ethics are considered to be the two tools for controlling human conduct so as to make it conducive to civilized social existence. (a) Discuss how they achieve this objective. (b) Giving examples, show how the two differ in their approaches. (2016, 10 Marks)

10 Ethics in International Relations

66

The phrase "Vasudhaiva Kutumbakam" translates to "The World is one Family". It is a powerful message that emphasizes the interconnectedness of all people and nations on Earth.

"An eye for an eye will only make the whole world blind." (Promotes international ethics based on forgiveness and non-violence to break cycles of conflict and foster respect for human dignity).

–Mahatma Gandhi

"there is some self-interest behind every friendship. There is no friendship without self-interests. This is a bitter Truth"

– Chanakya

"A country that demands moral perfection in its foreign policy will achieve neither perfection nor security"

–Henry Kissinger

"Injustice anywhere is a threat to justice everywhere."

-Marlin Luther King Jr

"The security of all lies in the mutual prosperity for all." (Focuses on shared security through global well-being)

–John F. Kennedy

"The Earth is but one country and mankind its citizens"

–Baha'u'llah (Founder of Baha'i faith)

INTERNATIONAL ETHICS

• International Ethics is about establishing a set of moral principles and guidelines for interactions between countries and other international actors in today's interconnected world. It strives to create a fairer and more just global order.

Importance of International Ethics

- Peaceful resolution of conflicts through dialogue and respect for sovereignty can lead to just and peaceful global order.
- Promote core values like peace, respect for all and equality within international organisations, declarations and forums
- Protection of Human Rights: International ethics provides a framework for defining rights and responsibilities on a global scale.
  - Eg- Universal Declaration of Human Rights, the UN charter, and the Geneva Conventions establish common ground on human rights and how nations should interact.
- Fair practices in a globalised economy: Eg- WTO ensures free and fair trade among countries; international courts and tribunals like ICJ, ICC etc establish justice
- Builds trust and legitimacy: Eg- Countries that prioritizes environmental protection and sustainability, gain international respect.
- Fosters a more compassionate global community and encourages a sense of shared responsibility, where countries assist each other during these events
  Eg- International aid provided during the Nepal Earthquake
- Coordinated global action in tackling international issues like Climate change, terrorism, etc. Eg- Common But Differentiated Responsibility - Respective Capability (CBDR-RC) principle enshrined in the Paris Agreement reflects this commitment.
- Preserves cultural heritage by encouraging respect for diverse cultures and traditions.

Development of International Ethics

• International ethics is not a static set of rules with guaranteed enforcement. It is an ongoing process of negotiation, debate, and adaptation as the world changes.

• However, the core principle of fairness, justice, cooperation and respect for human rights remain central to navigating the complexities of our globalised world.

- The Peace of Westphalia in 1648 is often seen as a significant turning point in the development of international ethics.

Before Westphalia

- **Limited Scope:** Prior to Westphalia, international relations were largely governed by religious authority (e.g. the Catholic church) and dynastic ties between monarchs.
- **Just war theory:** This framework developed in the Middle Ages, aimed to guide the use of military force through principles of just cause, proportionality and right intention.

Impact of Westphalia

- **Concept of Sovereign equality among states:** This meant that all independent states were seen as equal actors in the international system, regardless of their religion or size.
- **Focus on Secularism:** Religious justifications for war became less prominent, paving the way for a more pragmatic approach to international interactions.

20th Century: Rise of International Law and Institutions

- **Gradual Development:** The ideas of Sovereign equality and Secularism from Westphalia slowly led to the development of more formalised international law and ethics which included treaties, conventions & the establishment of international Institutions.
- **Post WWI:** Creation of the League of Nations, aiming to prevent future conflicts through collective Security and ethical considerations.
- **WWII and the Aftermath:** Emphasized the need for international co-operations and ethical frameworks.
  - This led to Creation of United Nations (UN) and the Universal Declaration of Human Rights (UDHR), establishing foundational principle for international Conduct.

Cold War and Beyond

- **Focus on Human Rights:** Increased focus on human rights, with activism and international instruments like the UN Covenants on Human Rights putting pressure on states to uphold these principles.

- **Global Economic Integration**: International trade agreements and institutions like the WTO aimed to promote fair trade practices and economic development, introducing ethical considerations into economic interactions.
- **New challenges**: Issues like environmental degradation, terrorism and pandemics have necessitated the development of new ethical frameworks for international cooperation in the 21st Century.

The Present and the future

- **Evolving landscape**: Technological advancements like artificial intelligence and Cyberwarfare raise new ethical challenges in international sphere.
- **Need for Continuous Dialogue**: As the world becomes more interconnected, ongoing dialogue and the development of new ethical frameworks are crucial for addressing global challenges.

Key Principles of International Ethics

- **Respect for Sovereignty**: Eg- UN recognised the right of Israel and Palestine to exist within secure and recognised borders.
- **Self-Determination**: Eg- Decolonisation movement in Africa and Asia in the mid 20th century were driven by the principle of self-determination.
- **Non-intervention**: Discourages one state from interfering in the internal affairs of another. Eg- India and Pakistan dispute over PoK is being resolved bilaterally without the intervention of any 3rd state.
- **Peaceful Settlement of Disputes**: Eg- World Bank brokered the Indus Water Treaty between India and Pakistan.
- **Protection of Human Rights**: Eg- Global campaign against aparthied in South Africa, grounded in human rights ethics, led to dismantling the system.
- **Responsibility to Protect (R2P)**: Every state has the R2P its populations from four mass atrocity crimes: genocide, war crimes, crimes against humanity and ethnic cleansing.
- **Global justice**: Eg- Adoption of the concept of CBDR (Common But Differentiated Responsibility) in addressing the climate change.
- **Environmental Protection**: Eg- Adoption of Paris Agreement (2015), Montreal Protocol (1987) etc.
- **Sustainable Development**: Eg- Adoption of Sustainable Development Goals (SDGs) till 2030.
- **Peace and Security**: Ethical principles guide the conduct of war (Jus in bello) and the justification for war (Jus ad bellum), while promoting peace

building and conflict resolution.
Eg- UN has also adopted the Declaration on the Right to peace, which stresses that peace is a vital requirement for the promotion and protection of all human rights.

- Transparency and Accountability: Eg- Automatic Exchange of Tax information between countries allows for the automatic annual exchange of Information on offshore financial accounts.

Theories of International Relations

Theory	Core Belief	Key Concepts	Example
Realism	Driven by self-interest and the pursuit of power in a competitive and anarchic (without a central authority) global system.	National Interest, power (military, economic), security dilemma.	China's assertiveness in the South China sea, prioritising economic interests and national security.
Idealism	Creating a more peaceful and just world order through cooperation, international law and ethical principles	International law, human rights, democracy, collective security.	India's Panchsheel principles, NAM movements etc.
Principled Realism	Acknowledge importance of power and national interest in international relations but they also believe in upholding certain ethical principles.	Balance of power, national interest, Selective intervention, just war theory.	International intervention in Rwanda to stop genocide.
liberalism	Emphasize inter-dependence, international institutions and democratic values	Mutual cooperation, international institutions (UN, WTO), democratic peace theory	European Union's co-operation based on shared democratic values

INDIA'S PRINCIPLES ON INTERNATIONAL RELATIONS

1. Constitutional Framework (Article 51)

- Friendly relation with other countries
- Respect for international law and international organisations like UN
- Peaceful settlement of international disputes through arbitration
- Promotion of international Peace and security.

2. Panchsheel

- The Panchsheel Agreement was a five point agreement between India and China signed in 1954 and it has become a guiding principle of India's bilateral relations with other countries also.
- These principles of Panchsheel were later incorporated in the Bandung Declaration, signed in the Afro-Asian conference held in 1955 in Indonesia.

PANCHSHEEL

1. Mutual respect for each other's territorial integrity and sovereignty.
2. Non-aggression against each other
3. Non-interference in each other's internal affairs.
4. Equality and mutual benefit
5. Peaceful co-existence

3. Principle of Enlightened National Interest.

Goes beyond simply maximising immediate gain for a country. It acknowledges the interconnectedness of the global community and emphasizes long term benefits for both the nation and the international order.

- Adheres to the Vasudhaiva Kutumbakam idea - The World is one family.
- Eg- theme of G20 Summit, 2023 in India - 'One Earth, One Family and One future'.

4. Policy of Resisting Colonialism, imperialism and Racism

- India was first to bring the issue of Aparthied in the UN in 1946
- Due to India's consistent efforts through NAM and other international forums, 14 African countries were liberated from the yoke of colonialism in 1964.

5. Regime change

India doesnot endorse the idea of regime change or violation of territorial integrity in a country by the use of force. Eg- US interventions in Iraq, Libya, Syria.

6. Sanctions

India doesnot endorse the idea of imposing Sanctions/military action against any individual country by another country.

7. Non-interference in the internal affairs of other countries but can intervene if an act - innocent or deliberate - by any country has the potential of impinging upon India's national interests. Eg- Bangladesh 1971, IPKF in Srilanka (1987-90), Maldives (1988)

8. Principle of strategic autonomy and believes in partnerships but shuns Alliances, particularly military alliances.

9. Advocates a global debate and global consensus on international issues such as world trade regime, climate change, terrorism, intellectual property rights, global governance

Underlying Principles of Jaishankar Doctrine

1. Greater realism in the contemporary foreign policy of India. Eg-India importing oil from Russia even after US Sanctions on Russia.
2. Shift from non-alignment to strategic need based alliances.
3. Stressed upon the historical, cultural and civilizational significance of India, by reinvigorating the civilisational consciousness of India and its cultural pride. Eg- India's vaccine diplomacy indicated the eternal Indian values of integral humanism.
4. From strategic ambiguity to strategic autonomy.
5. Growth of minilateral groupings. Eg- QUAD, Middle Eastern Quad (I2U2)
6. Multi-aligned and Multi-polar world.

ETHICAL ISSUES IN INTERNATIONAL RELATIONS

- Ethics of International Funding
- Ethics of Migration and Refugees
- Ethics of Just War
- Ethics of Humanitarian Intervention
- Ethics of Climate Change (Covered in Applied Ethics)

1. Foreign Aid and International funding

- Foreign aid encompasses voluntary resource transfers between countries, which can take various forms such as financial, military, technical or humanitarian assistance.
- It can be provided as grants, requiring no repayment or loans with concessional interest rates.
- While initially perceived as altruistic, foreign aid is often driven by strategic political interests rather than pure humanitarian motives.
- **Historical context**: Following world war II, foreign aid emerged as a strategic tool, with the USA initiating aid programs to rebuild western Europe under the Marshall Plan.
  - This approach extended into the Cold war era, with both US and USSR using aid to expand their spheres of influence.
  - This highlighted that foreign aid serves broader political and strategic objectives beyond mere charity.

Reasons for giving foreign aid

- Infrastructure creation especially in resource rich countries often to extract resource like minerals or oil from recipient country.
- Fostering positive diplomatic relations.
- Fulfilling moral and ethical responsibilities.
- Strengthening allies economically or militarily
- Exerting cultural influences and soft power projection.
- Enhancing international reputation and goodwill.
- Promoting peace and stability, especially in conflict affected regions
- Addressing historical injustices like Colonial exploitation.
- Endorsing recipient countries domestic policies.
- Influencing recipient countries behaviour.

Types of Foreign Aid

TYPES

1. Bilateral aid: Direct assistance from one country to another, often driven by strategic political considerations

2. Multilateral aid: Provided by international organisations like World Bank or IMF, focusing on human development

3. Tied Aid: Assistance with conditions attached, such as spending requirements in the donor country.

4. Project Aid: Resources allocated for specific projects like infrastructure or healthcare, limiting recipient autonomy.

5. Military Aid: Geared towards defense contracts or arms purchases, reflecting strategic interests

6. Voluntary Aid: Charitable contributions, exemplified by organisations like Doctors without Borders

India's Foreign Aid Strategy

- Government of India's approach to development partnership has been shaped by India's struggle for independence and solidarity with other colonised and developing countries.
- India's approach to development is mainly human-centric and is marked by Respect, Diversity, Care for the future, and Sustainable development
- **Most fundamental Principle**: Respecting development partners and be guided by their development priorities.

Other reasons behind giving a foreign aid

1. Fostering regional cooperation and stability by providing a significant amount of aid to its South Asian neighbours like Bhutan, Nepal and Bangladesh. Eg- India's grant assisted construction of the Tala Hydro-electric Project in Bhutan.
2. Strengthening political and economic ties: Lines of credit offered to resource-rich countries in Africa can secure access to critical raw materials for India's own industries. Eg- Indian government pledge of $1 billion credit to Zambia for various infrastructure development projects.
3. Projecting India's technological advancements and establishing itself as a leader in the developing world. Eg - One Sun, One World, One Grid (OSOWOG)
4. Humanitarian assistance in times of natural disasters or emergencies. Eg- India extend a USD 75 million for the reconstruction of infrastructure in Nepal Earthquake (2015)

5. Countering China's influence of Belt and Road Initiative (BRI) through the increased foreign aid to Indian Ocean countries and strengthening its ties.
6. Projection of Soft Power and enhancing its image as a responsible and benevolent global power. Eg- India's promotion of Yoga.
7. Directed towards countries with Significant Indian diaspora communities, fostering goodwill and strengthening cultural ties.

- Types of Foreign Aid: Grant in Aid, line of credit, capacity building, and technical assistance and trade concessions.

Ethical Issues in International Funding

1. Conditionalities

- Conditionality refers to policy changes which an aid donor agency stipulates a government must undertake in order to obtain, or retain access to the donor's financial support; it is an exchange of money for policy action. Eg- IMF imposed conditionalities when loan provided to India in 1991.

Issues associated with conditionalities

- Undermine the rights, choices and decisions of the people to determine their own demands and therefore, reduced ownership of developmental plans.
- Disregard of local societal diversities and local context in policies.
- Infringes on country's sovereignty and creates a power imbalance
- Undermines the basic principles of democratic ownership which implies mutual accountability, transparency, and participation in policies and programmes.
- Some policies can be highly controversial such as austerity or the privatisation of key public services which may provoke strong political opposition in the recepient country.

2. Risk of unsustainable debt burden

Risk of unsustainable debt burden by the countries preventing the countries to become self-sufficient economies and fosters a culture of aid dependency. Eg- Over the past two decades, the US provided Pakistan over $32 billion, increasing its economic reliance.

3. Cultural Imperialism

Cultural Imperialism: Cultural erosion by promoting specific cultural values of the donor country, potentially disregarding or undermining the recipient country's indigenous cultures and traditions.

4. Lack of transparency and accountability: Weak monitoring systems and corrupt practices in recipient countries can lead to aid money being diverted or misused, reducing the effectiveness of aid programmes.

- This undermines public trust in both donor and recipient countries.

5. Misdirected aid such as funding terrorism or extremism which can destabilise the region. Eg- Allegations of US aid to Afghanistan has benefitted Taliban or Pakistan's ISI using funding to support radical groups.
6. Funding to transnational NGOs which seeks to advance the interest of donor countries and carry forward their objectives like social disturbances, slowing down development works etc.
   a) Greenpeace serving western interest by protesting against coal power projects
   b) Foreign funding is undemocratic because it contradicts the principle of government "of the people, by the people, for the people"
7. Issue of Clinical trials: Many western countries have been accused of funding voluntary clinical trials in poor countries of Africa and Asia which is a clear violation of fundamental rights.
8. Inequality and Exploitation: Unequal distribution of resources can benefit the elite while neglecting the most vulnerable populations which can widen the gap between the rich and poor.
9. Acquisition of strategic assets in the recipient country: Eg- China's Belt and Road Initiative and Debt trap diplomacy resulted into the control of Sri Lanka's Hambantota port.

2. Ethical Concerns of Migration and Refugee

- Migration refers to the movement of people from one place to another, with the intention of settling, either permanently or temporarily, in a new location.
- Migration is both seen as an asset and a liability by the world. In order to utilise asset and shun away liability, countries around the world devise policies and laws as per their suitability.

Refugees

- Refugees are persons who are outside their country of origin for reasons of feared persecution, conflict, generalised violence, or other circumstances that have seriously disturbed public order and as a result, require international protection.

• The refugee definition can be found in the 1951 UN Refugee convention and regional refugee instruments, as well as UNHCR's statute.

Legal Framework Present in India

• India is neither a signatory to the 1951 UN Refugee Convention relating to refugee status nor of its 1967 protocol.
• It does not currently have a national law on refugees.
• The refugees and asylum seekers were entitled to the rights in Article 14, 20 and 21 of the Constitution.
• Governed by Acts: Foreigners Act 1946, Citizenship Act 1955.

International Organisation for Migration (IOM) launched the world Migration Report 2024.

• The report reveals significant shift in global migration patterns, including a record number of displaced people and a major increase in international remittances
• With an estimated 281 million international migrants worldwide, the number of displaced individuals due to conflict, violence, disaster and other reasons has surged to the highest levels in modern-day records, reaching 117 million, underscoring the urgency of addressing displacement crisis.
• India host the world's largest number of international migrants (18 million) residing in UAE, USA and Saudi Arabia.

Key Stakeholders and their interests

Individual	People leave their homes in search of a more decent life.
Origin Country	It brings remittances and on the other hand, it causes brain drain (migration of talented people)
Destination Country	It wants to receive only productive migrants and refugees. Also, they are not open to migration above a certain limit as it may impact demographic change and resource utilisation patterns
International Organisation	Organisations such as International Organisation for Migration (IOM) oversee that migrants' rights are well protected wherever they live.

Ethical Issues for different stakeholders

Stakeholder	Ethical Issues
Individual	• Loss of Security, experiencing immense trauma and loss. • Unable to access protection due to lack of legal status, inadequate legal frameworks or other administrative barriers. • Challenges in accessing basic needs such as food, water, shelter and healthcare, which can lead to poor living conditions and health outcomes • Difficulties in the cultural integration and inclusion within the host community.
Origin Country	• Loss of skilled workforce through migration which can hinder their economic development. • Conflicts, violence or Persecution in refugee producing countries • Violation of human rights and dignity, including exploitation, abuse, discrimination and social exclusion.
Destination Country	• Lack of fairness: Give priority to the migration of skilled work-force and discourage distress migration and refugees. • Funding and resource requirement to support the needs of refugees, including funding for humanitarian assistance, infrastructure and education programs. • Competition for jobs and housing can create tensions and resentment among some members of the host community. • Contribute to political instability and can exacerbate existing conflicts • National security vs moral obligation to provide asylum: Raise security concerns in host countries, particularly if they are vulnerable to exploitation by criminal or terrorist groups.
International Organisations	• Non recognition of climate refugees. • Advocate for fairer burden-sharing among wealthier nations as the responsibility of resetting refugees often falls disproportionately on neighbouring countries • Focused on providing the immediate humanitarian aid

Recent Refugee Crisis

1. Syrian Civil war (Since 2011): This remains the world's largest protracted refugee crisis. Over 12.1 million people are displaced within Syria, and more than 6.7 million Syrians have become refugees in neighbouring countries like Turkey, Lebanon, Jordan and Iraq.

2. Russian Invasion of Ukraine: The February 2022 invasion triggered a mass exodus. The UN Refugee Agency (UNHCR) estimates over 9.2 million Ukrainians have fled the country as refugees to neighbouring, Poland, Romania, Moldova, and other European nations.

3. Afghan Displacement: The withdrawal of US troops in 2021 and the Taliban takeover of Afghanistan led to a surge in displacement. An estimated 5.8 million Afghans are internally displaced within the country, while over 2.3 million are refugees in neighbouring Pakistan and Iran.

Conclusion

- The UNHRC recognises that refugees are among the most vulnerable people in the world, and that they have a right to protection and assistance.
- The UNHRC has called on governments around the world to uphold their obligations under international law to protect the rights of refugees, including the right to seek asylum and the right to non-refoulement (the principle that refugees should not be returned to a country where they face persecution.
- It has called for greater international cooperation and solidarity to address the refugee crisis, including increased support for host countries and communities that are hosting large number of refugees.

3. Ethics of Humanitarian Intervention

- Humanitarian intervention refers to the use of force (military or otherwise) in another country, undertaken to provide or stop widespread human rights abuses.

1. Motivation	2. External Intervention	3. Sovereignty vs Responsibility
To protect civilians from violence or atrocities committed by their own government or another armed group.	Often involves the use of military force but it can also encompass economic sanctions or diplomatic pressure	Challenges the principle of national sovereignty based on the idea that the international community has a responsibility to protect civilians from grave harm, even if it means violating sovereignty.

Responsibility to Protect (R2P)

The Principle was unanimously adopted in 2005 at the UN World Summit consisting of 3 pillars:

- Pillar 1- Every state has the Responsibility to Protect its population from four mass atrocity crimes-genocide, war crimes, ethnic cleansing, crimes against humanity
- Pillar 2: The wider international community has the responsibility to encourage and assist individual states in meeting that responsibility.
- Pillar 3: If a state is manifestly failing to protect its populations, International community must be prepared to take appropriate collective action, in a timely and decisive manner and in accordance with UN charter.

• Examples of humanitarian intervention

- Iraq war (2003): US-led invasions of Iraq.
- Libya (2011): NATO led intervention supported rebels fighting to overthrow Muammar Gaddafi's regime.
- Bangladesh liberation war (1971): India's intervention in the Bangladesh resulted in the protection of millions of Bengali civilians.

Ethical Issues in humanitarian intervention

1. Just cause and Right intentions: What constitutes a "just cause" can be subjective and open to interpretation.
   a) Humanitarian intervention may be motivated by strategic interests or national security concerns alongside humanitarian goals.
2. Deciding Authority - UN vs Unilateral Action: Should only the UN Security council authorize interventions, or can individual countries act alone?
   a) Unilateral action violate the principles of collective decisions-making and international law.
   b) 2003 invasion of Iraq lacked explicit UNSC authorization, leading to debates about the intervention's legitimacy and adherence to international norms.
3. Effectiveness of the Intervention: Military intervention can have unpredictable and destablizing effects which might surpass the positive impacts.
   Eg- US intervention in Afghanistan contributed to the rise of ISIS and overall insecurity in the region.

4. Respect for human Rights: The intervention itself should avoid violating human rights through civilian casualties or abuses by intervening forces.

5. Proportionality: The use of force should be proportionate to the threat and the potential benefits. Unrestrained military actions may lead to unintended civilian casualties and long lasting damage to infrastructure.
   Eg- U.S. led intervention in Iraq in 2003 faced criticism for its disproportionate use of force and the subsequent destabilization of region

6. Last resort option: Military intervention should be the last resort after exploring diplomatic or economic alternatives.

7. Long term consequences and post-intervention responsibility: Ethical considerations extend beyond the immediate intervention and have the responsibility of the intervening states in rebuilding and stabilizing the affected region.
   a. Inadequate planning for the post-intervention phase can lead to prolonged instability and worsen humanitarian conditions.
   b. The aftermath of the NATO intervention in Kosovo in 1999 highlighted the challenges of post-conflict reconstruction and the need for sustained international involvement.

8. Cultural Sensitivity: Interventions should be conducted with respect for the intervened nation's culture and traditions.

Conclusion

States use military force for humanitarian interventions but they face ethical challenges involving Sovereignty, just cause, proportionality, accountability and impartiality. While these interventions aim to protect vulnerable populations, it's crucial to navigate these dilemmas to uphold human rights and minimize harm.

4. Ethics of War

• **Background**: Long drawn Russia-Ukraine conflict, Israel-Palestine conflict.
• **About**: War Ethics is the study of the extent and scope of morality of going to war and maintaining a moral conduct during the war. It is basically a code of conduct for armed conflict. It is about trying to:
• Minimize the human cost of war by focusing on how to fight with some degree of decency.
• Hold warring parties accountable for actions that violate ethical principles.
• Encourage peaceful resolution to conflicts whenever possible, because war should always be a last resort.

Ethical issues associated with war

- Loss of Human life: The indiscriminate targeting of civilians, intentional or not, is considered a grave violation of ethical principles.
- Degradation of moral equality: War often involves dehumanizing the enemy, creating an ethical challenge in how combatants perceive & treat each other.
- Many times, Prisoners of War (PoW) get humiliated and abused by detainees.

Eg - The Abu Gharib Scandal during the Iraq war exposed widespread torture and abuse of detainees by US forces.

- Negative Long term consequences: Wars can have far reaching consequences in the long term such as displacement, environmental damage and economic instability.

Eg - 1. The Syrian civil war has displaced millions of people internally and as refugees.

2. The use of Agent Orange, a defoliant by the US military during the Vietnam war caused widespread environmental damage and health problems for Vietnamese civilians.

- War crimes and Atrocities: The commission of war crimes, such as torture, rape, summary execution and genocide, is a grave ethical concern.
- Repercussions of using weapon of mass destruction: The development, possession, and use of weapons of mass destruction raise significant ethical concerns due to their potential for massive destruction and loss of innocent lives.
  - For example: 1. Bio-chemical weapons like chlorine, phosgene (a choking agent) and mustard gas (which inflicts painful burns on the skin) caused indiscriminate damage to people and regions.

    2. Atomic Bombings in Hiroshima and Nagasaki in World war II.
- Damage to civilian infrastructure: The destruction of civilian infrastructure, such as hospitals, schools, and essential facilities, can have severe humanitarian consequences.
- Arms Race: War can lead to global arms race that can contribute to perpetuating conflicts.
- Limitations of international organisations such as International Criminal Court (ICC), International Criminal Justice (ICJ), etc in holding the warring penalties accountable for their actions.

JUST WAR THEORY

- Just War Theory outlines principles for when war is considered morally justified and how it should be conducted.

1. Jus ad Bellum (Just cause): This principle focuses on the justification for going to war in the first place.

a) Just cause include- Self-defense, stop aggression, genocide or oppression.
b) Last Resort: All peaceful options to resolve the conflict must be exhausted before resorting to war.

2. Jus in Bello (Just Conduct): This principle deals with how to fight a war ethically. Key aspects include:

a) Proportionality: The force used should be proportionate to the goal and avoid unnecessary civilian casualties and destruction.

b) Discrimination: Only combatants and legitimate targets can be attacked. Innocent civilians and civilian property should be protected.

c) Right Intention: The war should be waged with the goal of achieving a just outcome, not for personal gain or conquest.

3. Jus Post Bellum (Just Peace): This principle focuses on achieving a just peace after the war. It emphasizes elements like fair terms in peace treaty and reconstruction efforts to rebuild war-torn societies.

Example

- The 'Just war' doctrine was followed by India in the Bangladesh liberation war. The intentions of Indian government were noble and did not annex or exercise control over the new country - Bangladesh.
- Iraq invasion by the US armed forces was not a 'Just war', rather it was just a war. US forced failed to find any WMDs, that was cited as one of the reason for an invasion + US invaded and occupied Iraq territory and made post war Iraq no better than the pre-war Iraq.

PYQs Corner

(Write the Answer and Get Free Evaluation)

1. International aid' is an accepted form of helping 'resource-challenged' nations. Comment on 'ethics in contemporary international aid; Support your answer with suitable examples. (2023, 10 Marks)
2. Russia and Ukraine war has been going on for the last seven months. Different countries have taken independent stands and actions keeping in view their own national interests. We are all aware that war has its own impact on the different aspects of society, including human tragedy. What are those ethical issues that are crucial to be considered while launching the war and its continuation so far? Illustrate with justification the ethical issues involved in the given state of affair. (2022, 10 Marks)
3. "Refugees should not be turned back to the country where they would face persecution or human rights violation." Examine the statement with reference to the ethical dimension being violated by the nation claiming to be democratic with an open society. (2021, 10 Marks)
4. 'The will to power exists, but it can be tamed and be guided by rationality and principles of moral duty.' Examine this statement in the context of international relations. (2020, 10 Marks)
5. Strength, peace and security are considered to be the pillars of international relations. Elucidate. (2017, 10 Marks)
6. At the international level, bilateral relations between most nations are governed on the policy of promoting one's own national interest without any regard for the interest of other nations. This lead to conflicts and tension between the nations. How can ethical consideration help resolve such tensions? Discuss with specific examples. (2015, 10 Marks)

11 Corporate Governance

66

"The Social Responsibility of Business is to increase its profits."

– Milton Friedman

"Business need to go beyond the interest of their companies to the communities they serve"

– Ratan Tata

Warren Buffett

"It takes 20 years to build a reputation and five minutes to ruin it. If you think about that, you will do things differently".
(Emphasize the importance of long-term reputation management)

"The real threat to business is from within, from poor ethical standards and lack of integrity that can do incalculable harm."

– Azim Premji

"Corporate governance is concerned with holding the balance between economic and social goals and between individual and communal goals."

– Sir Adrian Cadbury.

"Corporate Social Responsibility is not philanthropy. It is not a charity. It is an investment in our collective future".

– Dr. Manmohan Singh

Business Ethics

- Business ethics is a field of study that focuses on the moral principles that guide businesses in their decision making.
- It encompasses how companies act in all aspects of their operations, from how they treat employees and customers to how they source materials and interact with the environment.
- It examine how businesses can balance the pursuit of profit with social responsibility and fair practices.

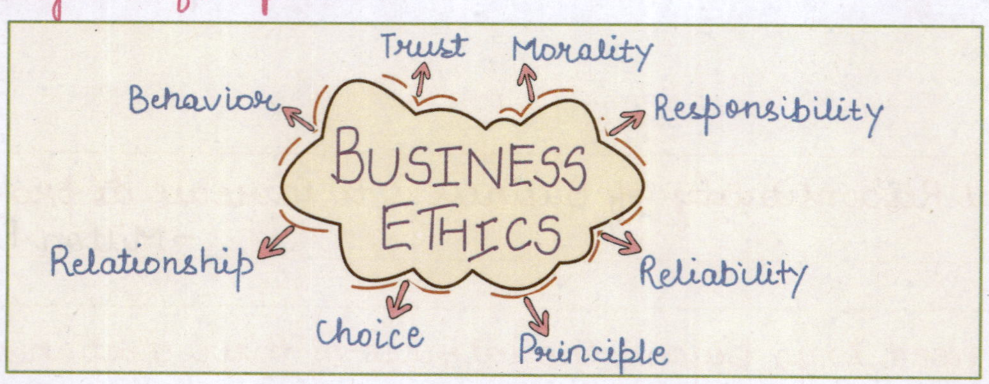

Evolution to the concept of Business Ethics

Trade off (Self Interest vs Societal Benefit): The World of business operates on a tightrope balancing the natural human drive for self-interest with the need of contributing to the greater good for society.

- This delicate balance has fuelled economic progress for centuries, but it also carries the risk of self-interest morphing into harmful practices.

Natural Driver: Self-interest, the desire to secure one's own well-being, is a fundamental human motivator. In business, this translates to pursuing profits, growth and market dominance.

- Adam Smith famously proposed the "Invisible hand" theory. He argued that individuals acting in their own self-interest, driven by competition, would ultimately create a more prosperous society through the market.
- Businesses, seeking profit, would produce goods and services people desire, leading to efficient allocation of resources and economic growth.
- While Smith emphasized the importance of moral foundation for the market to funtion effectively, the theory has its limitations.

Unchecked self-interest can morph into harmful practices, leading to

- Crony Capitalism: Businesses may seek to influence governments for personal gain, creating an unfair advantage and stifling competition.

- Exploitation of natural and human resources: The pursuit of profit may prioritize cheap Labor, create poor working condition for labour, violate environmental regulations leading to environmental degradation.

The potential for Self-interest to turn into Societal harm led to the development of Business Ethics

Importance of Business Ethics

1. Building public trust: Ethical practices lead to a positive public image, attracting customers and investors. Eg - TATA group (operates with integrity)
2. Mitigates risk such as legal trouble, reputational damage and financial losses by acting ethically. Eg - The Plachimada case (2002) of Coca-Cola: Reputation damage
3. Compliance with various environmental and labour laws reduces the burden on regulatory bodies. Eg - HUL - Leader in integrating ESG factors in Business.
4. Protection of consumers by avoiding misleading advertising and product alteration (Eg: Addressing the issue of spurious drugs)
5. Reduced corruption: Ethical practices ensure fair competition, preventing scams like the 2G spectrum case, which ultimately hurt consumers through higher prices and lower quality.
6. Fosters a positive work environment, leading to higher employee satisfaction and lower turnover rates. Eg - Google.
7. Fair business dealings such as fair contracts, transparent pricing, and avoids exploiting Suppliers. This fosters long term, mutually beneficial partnerships
8. Going beyond the profits by fulfilling the Social and environmental responsibility.

Thus, a company acting ethically attracts top talent through positive work Culture, strengthen its brand by complying with various laws and build trust with stakeholders translating to long term Success and profitability

Principles of Business Ethics

1. Honesty and Integrity: Eg - ITC openly acknowledge the Health risks associated with tobacco use while continuing to operate in the legal cigarette market.

2. Transparency and Disclosure Eg: Satyam Computer Services' accounting Scandal highlighted the need for transparency

3. Compliance with Laws and Regulations Example: Companies Act, 2013

4. Fairness: Eg - Amul Cooperative operates on fair trade principles, ensuring fair prices for its farmer members.

5. Accountability and Responsibility
Example- The Bhopal Gas Tragedy where Union carbide India failed to take responsibility for the disaster, serves as a stark reminder of corporate accountability.

6. Building an Ethical Culture: Eg Tata Group's longstanding reputation for ethical business practices has earned them immense respect and loyalty from stakeholders.

7. Sustainability and Environmental Responsibility. Eg: ITC's "Sunita" brand encourages farmers to adopt organic methods.

8. Respect for stakeholders: Eg. Fair trade movement in India ensures fair wages and working conditions for farmers and artisans.

CORPORATE GOVERNANCE

- Corporate governance encompasses the rules and processes guiding the management and oversight of a company, crucial for ensuring ethical operations and prioritising the interests of all stakeholders.
  - It aims to prevent corporate misconduct and uphold responsible and transparent business practices.
- It determines the relationship that exist between board, corporate, managers, shareholders, employees, auditors, consumers, government and society at large.
- Corporate Governance is acceptable of the fact that shareholders are the real masters and management has a role of trustee on behalf of stakeholders

Core objective: To maximise profit for shareholders in a sustainable manner, ensure society gets their due share in development while operating within bounds of law.

Naresh Chandra committee on corporate governance (2002) remarked "Good corporate governance involves a commitment of a company to run its businesses in a legal, ethical and transparent manner- a dedication that must come from the very top and permeate through organisation. That being so, much of what constitutes good corporate governance has to be voluntary. Law and regulations can at best, define the basic framework-boundary conditions that cannot be crossed"

According to Cadbury committee on the Financial Aspects of Corporate Governance,(1992) "Corporate governance is the system by which companies are directed and Controlled. Corporate governance is concerned with holding the balance between economic and Social goals and between individual and communal goals. The governance framework is there to encourage the efficient use of resources and equally to require accountability for the stewardship of those resources. The aim is to align as nearly as possible the interest of individuals, corporations and society.

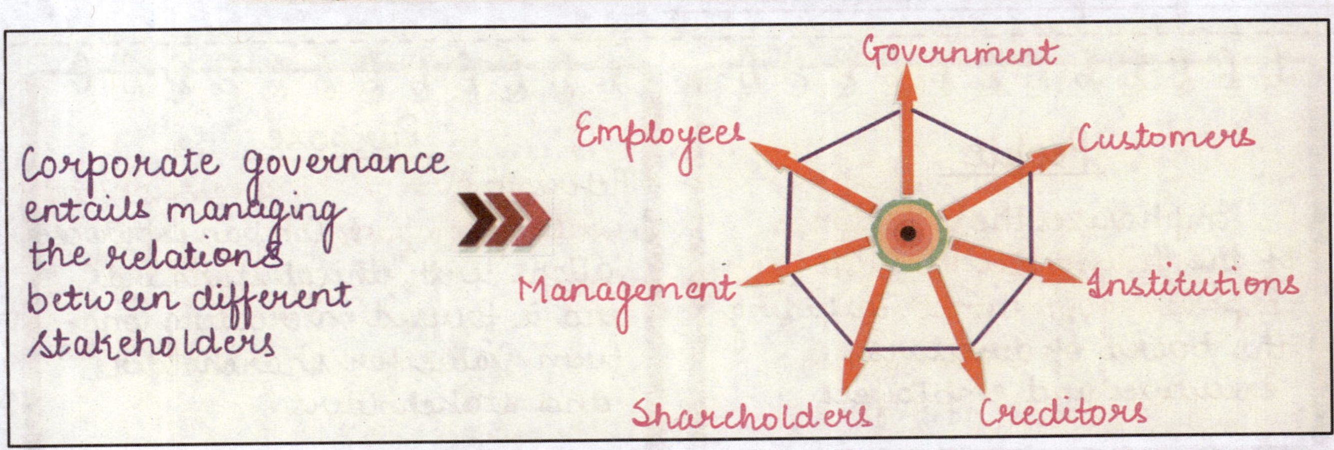

Principles of Corporate Governance

Rooted in two ethical ideals - "Spirit of Cooperation" and "human dignity".

Spirit of Cooperation	Human dignity
Working together for common good enabling mutual prosperity with healthy and fair competition.	Value of each person as an end, not as a means to fulfill the purpose of others

1. Transparency and Disclosure: Providing clear, accurate and timely information regarding financial performance, conflict of interest and risks to all stakeholders.

2. Accountability and Fiduciary Duty: Boards of directors and management hold a position of trust (Fiduciary Duty) towards shareholders and other stakeholders

3. Fair treatment to all stakeholders in areas like compensation, decision making, and access to information

4. Avoid illicit activities such as corrupt practices, bribery, money laundering or other illicit activities

5. Compliance with the spirit and intent as well as letter of the laws and regulations

6. Commitment to the values and ethical conduct by corporations as well as corporate leaders.

7. Contribution to the economic, social and environmental development of the communities

8. Respect stakeholders beyond the shareholders.

4P's of Corporate Governance

People

Emphasizes the importance of the individuals involved in corporate governance, including the board of directors, executives and employees

Purpose

Refers to overarching mission and goals of company. Company's purpose aligns with ethical standards and is focused on creating long-term value for shareholders and stakeholders.

Processes

Involves the systems and procedures established to oversee and manage the company. Includes how decisions are made, how risk is assessed and managed, and how accountability is maintained

Practices

The governance framework monitors and evaluates the performance of the company against established benchmarks

Importance of Good Corporate Governance

- Transparency fosters confidence: Strong corporate governance establish trust with investors which is essential for attracting capital and long term investment.
    - In 2023, net Foreign Institutional Investor (FII) inflows into the Indian stock market reached a record high of $10 billion.

- Enhanced brand reputation by building stronger relationships with customers and partners and thereby, resulting into higher profits for the shareholders.
- Minimize risks associated with corruption, fraud or mismanagement which can protect investors from financial losses.
    - Eg- RBI has implemented various regulations to strengthen risk management practices in banks, following the financial crisis of 2008.
- Innovation and Efficiency: Encourages responsible management practices and strategic planning, leading to innovation and operational efficiency within Indian companies.
- Global Competitiveness: Indian companies like TCS are adhering to international corporate governance standards to compete effectively on the global stage.
- Contribution to overall economic stability.
- Long term sustainability of the company through higher profits, respecting the local traditions and by building loyalty among the customers.
- Social Responsibility: Strong governance frameworks promote CSR practices, creating a positive social impact.
    - Eg- Mahindra Foundation run programs like "Nanhi Kali" for girls' education and "Pride Schools" for vocational training.
- Important determinant of the work culture can lead to higher retention than morale of the employees.
- A well-regulated corporate sector with strong governance attracts foreign investments and fosters entrepreneurship, contributing significantly to India's economic growth.

Failure of Corporate Governance in India.

- Satyam Computer Services Scandal (2009): This major accounting fraud highlighted weakness in internal controls and importance of independent oversight.
- Kingfisher Airlines Collapse (2012): It raises questions about responsible financial management and board oversight.
- Mehul Choksi case (2018): Highlighted potential weaknesses in loan disbursement practices and credit assessment by financial institutions.
- Infrastructure failures: Point to issues with quality control, adherence to safety standards and potential corruption during construction process these incidents raise questions about corporate governance in infrastructure sector.

Evolution of Corporate Governance in India

- **1956**: Companies Act 1956 contains the first reference to corporate Governance in India.
- **1990s**: liberalisation of Indian Economy
  - Economic Reforms: Led to increased foreign investment and a growing capital market which highlighted the need for stronger corporate governanance to attract investors and ensure market stability.
  - Regulatory Push: The government enacted new regulations and established institutions like SEBI to oversee corporate governance practices.
- **1997-98**: CII (Confederation of Indian Industries) introduces a voluntary 'Code of corporate governance' based on UK Model
- **2000**: SEBI-appointed KM Birla committee introduces clause 49 in the Listing Agreement detailing governance norms for listed companies in India.
- **2003**: Motivated by foreign interest in Indian IPOs and a desire to attract foreign investment in secondary markets, SEBI-appointed Narayan Murthy Committee introduces new and tighter rules w.e.f. 2006.
- **2013**: Companies Act 2013 introduces mandatory concept of 'board independence', class action suits, CSR, gender diversity on the board of directors, extensive regulation of related party transaction etc.
- **Present Context**:
  - Rise of CSR initiatives: Many Indian companies adopted CSR initiatives, aligning business goals with social and environmental well-being.
  - Continuous improvement: The regulatory framework and best practices are constantly evolving, with a focus on areas like Cyber Security, data privacy and good corporate citizenship.
  - Ensuring effective implementation: The focus has shifted beyond just having governance structures in place to ensuring their effectiveness in promoting ethical behaviour and sound decision making

Clause 49 of the Listing Agreement

Clause 49 of the listing agreement between a company and stock exchanges in India (NSE, BSE) is a crucial document outlining corporate governance requirements for listed companies.

1. Board of Directors:

- Number of Directors: Varies based on company size (Minimum: 1 for one person companies, 2 for private companies, 3 for public companies; Maximum-15)

- Gender Diversity: At least one woman director is mandatory on all boards of listed companies.
- Independent Directors: Mandates a minimum percentage of independent directors on the board, ensuring unbiased decision making.
  - Executive Chairman: Minimum 50% of the board should be independent directors
  - Non-Executive chairman: Minimum one third of the board should be independent directors.
- A Director shall not be a member in more than 10 committees.
- Code of Conduct: The Board shall lay down a code of conduct for all board members and Senior management of the company.
- Board Committees: The Sub-groups of the board focus on specific areas:

Audit Committee	Compensation Committee	Nominating committee
Oversee financial reporting, internal controls and risk management	Recommends executive compensation package	Identifies and nominates qualified candidates for the Board.

2. Shareholders and Stakeholders

- Shareholder Rights and Responsibilities: Vote on key decisions (Eg. Board elections, mergers/acquisitions etc); Receive dividends; Inspect company books and records etc
- Minority shareholder protection: Minority shareholders (Owning less than 50% of shares) still have voting rights and can hold directors/officers accountable, promoting efficiency and financial returns.

3. Disclosure and Transparency:

- Related Party Transactions: Requires companies to disclose any transactions with related parties, ensuring transparency and mitigating potential conflicts of interests.
- Remuneration of Directors: Disclosure of directors' remuneration packages is mandated, promoting accountability and fair compensation practices.
- Financial Reporting: Companies disclose financial information to stakeholders through financial statements (balance sheets, income statements, cash flow statements). Reporting adheres to accounting standards (GAAP, IFRS)
- Non-Financial Disclosure: Companies disclose information beyond financial performance, including Environmental, Social and Governance (ESG) practices.

CII launched Corporate Governance Charter for Start-ups

- CII in April 2024 has come up with a Corporate Government charter for start-ups to serve as a self-governing code for them in their compliance journey
- The charter is intended to be used by start-ups as a "ready reckoner" as they glide along the path of good governance.
- The Early adoption of good governance practices helps start-ups gain tangible and intangible benefits including long term value creation, stakeholders' trust, better access to finance from investors and banks, reduced reliance on promoters, effective organisational structures and improved chances of long term survival of the business.
- The charter has been curated to provide guidance to start ups during their lifecycle segregated into four stages: Inception, Progression, growth and going public.

At the 'Inception' stage Start up governance may be focussed on board formation, setting the tone at the top, compliance monitoring, accounting, finance, external audit, policies for related party transactions and conflict resolution mechanism.

At the 'Progression' stage Start up may additionally focus on expansion of board oversight, monitoring key business metrics, maintaining internal controls, define hierarchy of decision making, focussed overview of finance, accounts and external audit, setting up audit committee and risk and crisis management

At the 'growth' stage It may also focus to build stakeholder awareness towards vision, mission, code of conduct, culture, ethics of organisation, functional policies & procedures, form board committee and ensure Diversity, Equity and Inclusion (DE&I) on Board.

- They should fulfill statutory requirements as per Companies Act 2013 and comply with CSR and ESG norms.

At the 'Going public' stage Start ups may expand its governance in terms of monitoring of functioning of various committees, focus on fraud prevention and detection, grievance redressal mechanism, minimise information asymmetry etc.

Issues of Corporate Governance in India

1. Conflict of Interest - Risk of managers prioritizing personal gain over shareholder interests. Example: In 2018, ICICI Bank's former CEO, Chanda Kochhar, was accused of approving a loan to Videocon for a quid pro quo deal benefitting her husband.

2. Weak Boards - Lack of diverse experience and independent oversight. Example: The Infrastructure Leasing and Financial Services (IL&FS) crisis in 2018 exposed the ineffectiveness of some boards.

3. Family-Owned Businesses: this can lead to decisions prioritizing family interest over professional management. As of 2021, family-owned businesses contribute to over 70% of India's GDP.

- As family businesses grow, internal conflicts and inefficiencies can threaten their sustainability.
- Lack of transparency and independent oversight can hinder good governance practices.
- Promoter's emotional attachment to the company acts as a blinder and thus, cannot take right decisions at the right time in the company.

Example: Naresh Goyal's reluctance to relinquish control of Jet airways.

4. Excessive Executive Compensation: Shareholder disputes have arisen regarding high executive compensation packages, raising questions about accountability and alignment with company performance.

5. Accountability and Risk Management: Many companies have poor risk management, poor internal audit, statutory audit and whistleblowing policies. Example: Reebok India case in 2012-13.

6. Poor transparency and disclosure lapses by various companies. Example - Franklin Templeton India case.

7. Lack of awareness and structure: Many companies, especially smaller ones, lack a proper framework for corporate governance which includes limited awareness about regulations, board responsibilities and shareholder rights.

8. Insider Trading: Lack of thorough investigations by SEBI and difficulty of securing convictions in court. Eg- SEBI slapped a fine of ₹1 crore on Aptech Ltd for violating insider trading norms back in 2016.

9. Lack of succession planning. Eg- Big corporations like Infosys have failed to find a replacement of Mr Narayan Murthy

10. Lack of gender diversity. Eg- France and Norway have mandatory 40% board representation for women, while, in India, they only accounted for 17% of the board seats for Nifty 500.

11. Inadequate monitoring and response failure by the regulatory authorities lead to weak oversight by the regulators.

12. Ineffective Independent Directors: Concerns remain about the independence and effectiveness of these directors in checking unethical practices by promoters (controlling shareholders)
- Favouritism and Nepotism (ignoring the capability) in the induction of independent directors.
- Concerns persist about their passivity and frequent removal by promoters.

Independent Directors.

1. An independent director is defined as a non-executive director of a company who does not have any fiduciary relationship with the company, and/or has not been an executive with the company in three preceding financial years.
2. Independent directors are the "Conscience" of the board

Role and Importance of Independent Directors

- Fraud Prevention and detection
- Protecting interest of minority stakeholders
- Mediating in Situations like Conflict between Management and shareholder's interest.
- Improving corporate credibility.
- Risk management of the company.
- Prime role in naming and removing Executive directors of a company.
- As a regulatory authority they are vested with Sole responsibility to monitor proper conduct and impartial judgement owing to the interest of investors.
- To act as a strong instrument to check intended corporate Scandals.
- Playing a supervisory role in the company.

Strengthening Corporate Governance in India

1. Implementation of Uday Kotak Panel Recommendations
2. Promote diversity on boards in terms of gender, ethnicity, skills, and experience. This can lead to a wider range of perspectives and more informed decision making. Eg- Infosys, which has been recognised for its diverse board composition.
3. Companies should adopt effective risk management practices to assess potential risks and make informed decisions.

4. Establish clear policies and procedures that guide behaviour at all levels of the organisations. Eg. Companies like Tata Steel are known for their commitment to ethical conduct.
5. Ensure a clear separation of responsibilities between the board of directors and management which prevents conflicts of interest and promote accountability.
6. Conduct regular board evaluations to identify weaknesses and areas for improvement which can strengthen overall governance processes
7. Enhance shareholder communication: Establish clear channels for communication between shareholders and the board
8. Strengthen Board Accountability: This includes overseeing financial performance and risk management strategies.
9. Promote Ethical Conduct: Implement a code of conduct and a code of corporate governance to guide ethical behaviour within the organisation. Eg. Companies like Mahindra & Mahindra have established strong codes to promote ethical practices.
10. The board should ensure fair treatment of all shareholders, including minority and foreign shareholders which will foster trust and confidence in the company's governance.
11. Prevent Insider Trading: Maintain a robust internal audit function to deter insider trading. SEBI can also play a role in strengthening its investigative and enforcement mechanisms to address insider trading effectively.
12. Timely disclosure of all material information regarding the company, including financials, performance, ownership and governance practices.

By implementing these measures and learning from successful examples within India, companies can create a strong foundation for good corporate governance, leading to sustainable growth and increased investor confidence.

Committee Recommendations on improving Corporate Governance

1. Kotak Panel Report (2017):

Focus: Strengthening board composition and independence.

Key Recommendations: Separate Chairman and CEO roles

- Minimum Number of Directors: Enforce a minimum of 6 directors on board with at least one being an independent woman director.
- Transparency in the appointment of independent directors and they should play a more active role in board discussions and decision making.
- Public Sector companies governed by listing regulations, not ministries

- Penalties for auditor with lapses
- Disclosure of medium to long term business strategy in annual reports.

2. TK Vishwanathan Committee Report (2018)
- Focus: Combating insider trading and improving fair market conduct.
- Key Recommendations.
  - Two separate code of conduct for insider trading.
  - Minimum standard for handling insider information by companies
  - Standards for intermediaries handling sensitive information.
  - Maintaining details of relatives and financially linked individuals to those handling sensitive information
  - Direct power to SEBI to tap electronic communication for investigations (currently limited to call records)

CORPORATE SOCIAL RESPONSIBILITY

Organised business | Dealing with people | Accountability between the two

CSR refers to a company's commitment to assess and take responsibility for its impact on society and the environment.

- Implementation of CSR in India: India is a global leader in CSR, with the companies Act, 2013 (Article 135) mandating CSR spending for certain companies.

Features of CSR

Applicable to the companies with an annual turnover exceeding ₹1000 crore, net worth exceeding 500 crore, or net profit exceeding ₹ 5 crore must comply

CSR Committee: Companies must establish a CSR committee to recommend a CSR policy and monitor its implementation

CSR spending: Companies are encouraged to spend 2% of their average net profit from the previous three years on CSR activities

Approved CSR Activities: Schedule VII of Companies Act outlines approved CSR activities, including: Poverty & hunger alleviation, Education and gender equality promotion etc

Examples of CSR Initiatives in India: ITC's 'e-Choupal' Initiative, Mahindra and Mahindra's 'Nanhi Kali' Initiative, Wipro's 'Wipro cares' program; etc

Benefits of CSR

- Providing the required resources by the organisations (public or private) that can complement the limited resources of the government
- ESG Compliance: Strong CSR practices contribute to a company's ESG compliance, a growing focus for investors.
- Addressing social & economic disparities: CSR initiatives can address issues like poverty, illiteracy and lack of access to healthcare, promoting inclusive growth
- Favouring public image: Responsible CSR initiatives can enhance a company's brand image and reputation among stakeholders who value social responsibility.
- Companies with strong CSR initiatives can attract and retain top talent and socially responsible investors.
- Collaboration and Innovation: Partnership with NGOs foster knowledge sharing and innovative solutions for social problems.
- Plays a vital role in supporting the government in India's development process
- Improved employee morale and engagement.

Challenges in CSR Compliance

- Preference to profit motive over social responsibility by the companies
- Compliance vs Impact: Some companies focus solely on meeting the spending quota, neglecting the social impact of their initiatives (Disadvantage of making CSR mandatory.
  - Companies spending heavily on advertising their CSR initiatives rather than on the actual project themselves.
- Lack of transparency and monitoring: Inadequate tracking mechanisms make it difficult to measure the effectiveness of CSR projects and identify fraudulent practices.
  - A FICCI report revealed that only 60% of companies mandated under CSR law file their CSR reports within the stipulated timeframe
- Imbalance in CSR spending as most of CSR funds goes to education and health sectors while other sectors like sanitation, infrastructure etc get very limited share.

- Regional disparity in the deployment of CSR funds.
    - In FY 21, 10 states including Maharashtra, Gujarat, Karnataka and Andhra Pradesh accounted for over 44% of the CSR funds while eight north eastern States received a meagre 0.91% share
- Many CSR projects are short lived, hindering long term sustainability and community empowerment.
- Limited Expertise: Companies sometimes lack the internal expertise to design and implement impactful CSR programs effectively.
- Limited local community engagement and awareness about CSR hinder project effectiveness.
- Shortage of well-Organised NGOs in rural areas limits their ability to assess community needs and Collaborate effectively on projects.

Improving CSR Effectiveness

Company's Role	Government's Role
• Focus on outcomes: Shift the focus from spending to achieving measurable Social and Environmental outcomes. • Strengthen monitoring: Conduct regular progress reviews on CSR initiatives • Accountability regime: Implement a professional approach to CSR with clear objectives and align all the stakeholders with them • Collaboration with NGOs: Communicate business needs to NGO partners to ensure transparency and commitment • Establish standard Operating Procedures (SOPs) for fund utilisation, impact assessment, and project planning Companies should go from CSR to CSV i.e. Creating shared value	• Ensure companies implement their CSR policies effectively. • Implementing standardised CSR reporting formats that would improve transparency and comparability of CSR activities across Companies • Introducing a CSR performance grading system can incentivize companies to go beyond compliance and strive for excellence in CSR practices. • Empowerment of NGOs: Address the issue of non-availability of qualified NGOs in rural areas. • Explore using technology (AI, machine learning) to monitor CSR spending and improve policy. • Consumer Awareness: Raise Societal awareness about the importance of CSR activities

PYQs Corner

(Write the Answer and Get Free Evaluation)

1. What do you understand by 'moral integrity' and 'professional efficiency' in the context of corporate governance in India? Illustrate with suitable examples. (2023, 10 Marks)

2. In contemporary world, corporate sector's contribution in generating wealth and employment is increasing. In doing so, they are bringing in unprecedented onslaught on the climate, environmental sustainability and living conditions of human beings. In this background, do you find that Corporate Social Responsibility (CSR) is efficient and sufficient enough to fulfil the social roles and responsibilities needed in the corporate world for which the CSR is mandated? Critically examine. (2022, 10 Marks)

3. Corporate social responsibility makes companies more profitable and sustainable. Analyse. (2017, 10 Marks)

12 Probity in Public Life

66

PHILOSOPHICAL BASIS OF GOVERNANCE

Kautilya's views (Traits of the King/Ruler of a well governed state)

"In the happiness of his subjects lies his happiness, in their welfare, his welfare, whatever pleases himself, he doesnot consider as good, but whatever pleases his subjects he considers as good"

According to him, "Yogakshema" or welfare of the people is the ultimate goal of the ruler. Kautilya in his treatise 'Arthashastra' laid out a comprehensive vision for governance:

- **King as Servant, not ruler:** Kautilya believed the king existed to serve the people, not the other way around. The king's happiness was tied to the welfare of his subjects.
- **Welfare State:** The Arthashastra outlines a system where the state plays a role in public welfare. This includes providing for the vulnerable sections of the society and ensuring infrastructure development
- **Strong, Skilled leadership:** For good governance, Kautilya emphasized the need for a capable king with qualities like leadership, intellect and morality. He also advocated for a competent and well-chosen administrative team.
- **Accountability and Responsibility:** To prevent corruption and ensure responsiveness, Kautilya believed in a system where rulers were accountable and officials could be removed for misconduct.
- **Balance and Order:** Kautilya stressed the importance of maintaining order and stability within the kingdom. This involved a strong legal system and a well-trained military.

Social Contract as a basis of Governance

- The Social Contract theory is a prominent philosophical concept that explores the legitimacy of government and relationship between governed and the governing.
- It proposes that individuals in a state of nature, voluntarily enter into an agreement to create a society and establish a governing body known as the state (or government). This agreement outlines the rights and obligations of both citizens and the government
- Through social contract, people yield some personal control and rights to the ruler. In exchange, ruler takes up the responsibility of ensuring that rights of the people are protected from others who would seek to trample upon them

Views of different thinkers on Social Contract

Dimension	Thomas Hobbes (1588-1679)	John Locke (1632-1704)	Rousseau (1712-1778)
State of Nature: Thinkers like Thomas Hobbes, John Locke, and Jean Jacques Rousseau all envisioned a hypothetical "State of nature" where humans existed before organised society.			
State of Nature	Brutal and chaotic place characterised by "war of all against all". • Life was solitary, poor, nasty, brutish and short	• State of liberty and equality where individuals have natural rights to life, liberty and property. • However there was a lack of an impartial authority to enforce these rights.	• State of peace and equality, but people eventually corrupted it with private property and social inequality.
Social Contract: Flawed by the limitations of the state of nature, individuals came together through a Social contract to establish a state (government) to secure their rights and promote common good.			
Reason of Social Contract	• To escape the violence of the State of nature in exchange for security and order.	• To form a government deriving its legitimacy from the consent of the governed with the limited purpose of protecting their natural rights.	• To create a society based on reason and the 'general will' of the people. This collective will aims at the common good of all citizens.
Power of the sovereign	• Primary responsibility is to protect the lives and property of its citizens. • Absolute authority to enforce the social contract and maintain order	• The government's power was limited by social contract and could be overthrown if it failed to protect those rights.	• Sovereignty resided with the people and the government derived its legitimacy from serving the general will.
Individual Rights.	• Limited in return for protection and security	• Natural and inalienable	• Natural and inalienable

GOOD GOVERNANCE

Governance is defined as "the exercise of economic, political and administrative authority to manage a country's affairs at all levels. It comprises the mechanisms, processes and institutions, through which citizens and groups articulate their interests, exercise their legal rights, meet their obligations and mediate their differences".

— United Nations Development Programme (1997)

World Bank defines good governance as "The manner in which the power is exercised for the management of a country's economic and social resources for development"

Characteristics of Good Governance

- Multi-stakeholder: Governance is not only carried out by the government but there are multiple actors involved - Government, Market and Civil Society.
- Shift from traditional top-down government only model to a more collaborative approach that leverages the strengths of various stakeholders.
- Right-based governance (leading to active citizenry): Emphasizes the importance of protecting and fulfilling human rights for all by moving away from the traditional approach that considered citizens as passive beneficiaries.
- Bottom-up approach: Citizen's participation in the policy formulation, implementation and monitoring stage.
- Multi-dimensional: Focuses on the range of multiple issues such as ease of doing business, social services and not just focused on promoting economic growth.

Civil Society: Act as watchdogs, advocating for citizen rights, promoting social justice and also provide essential social services

State: Creating a favourable political, legal and economic environment. Formulation of policies and its effective implementation.

Market: Contribute to economic growth, creation of jobs and invest in communities

Four Pillars of Good Governance

Ethos - Exhibits citizen centricity and inclusiveness, special care for the marginalised and disadvantaged, commitment to the organisation, promotes public good and leading others as a role model	**Ethics** - Demonstrates integrity, transparency, openness, self confidence, fairness and accountability for its own actions.
Equity - Treating all citizens alike, ensures justice to all, with empathy for the weaker sections	**Efficiency** - Promotes operational excellence and value for money, result oriented mindset, innovative thinking, speedy and effective delivery of service without harassment

8 Components of Good Governance along with Initiatives taken in India

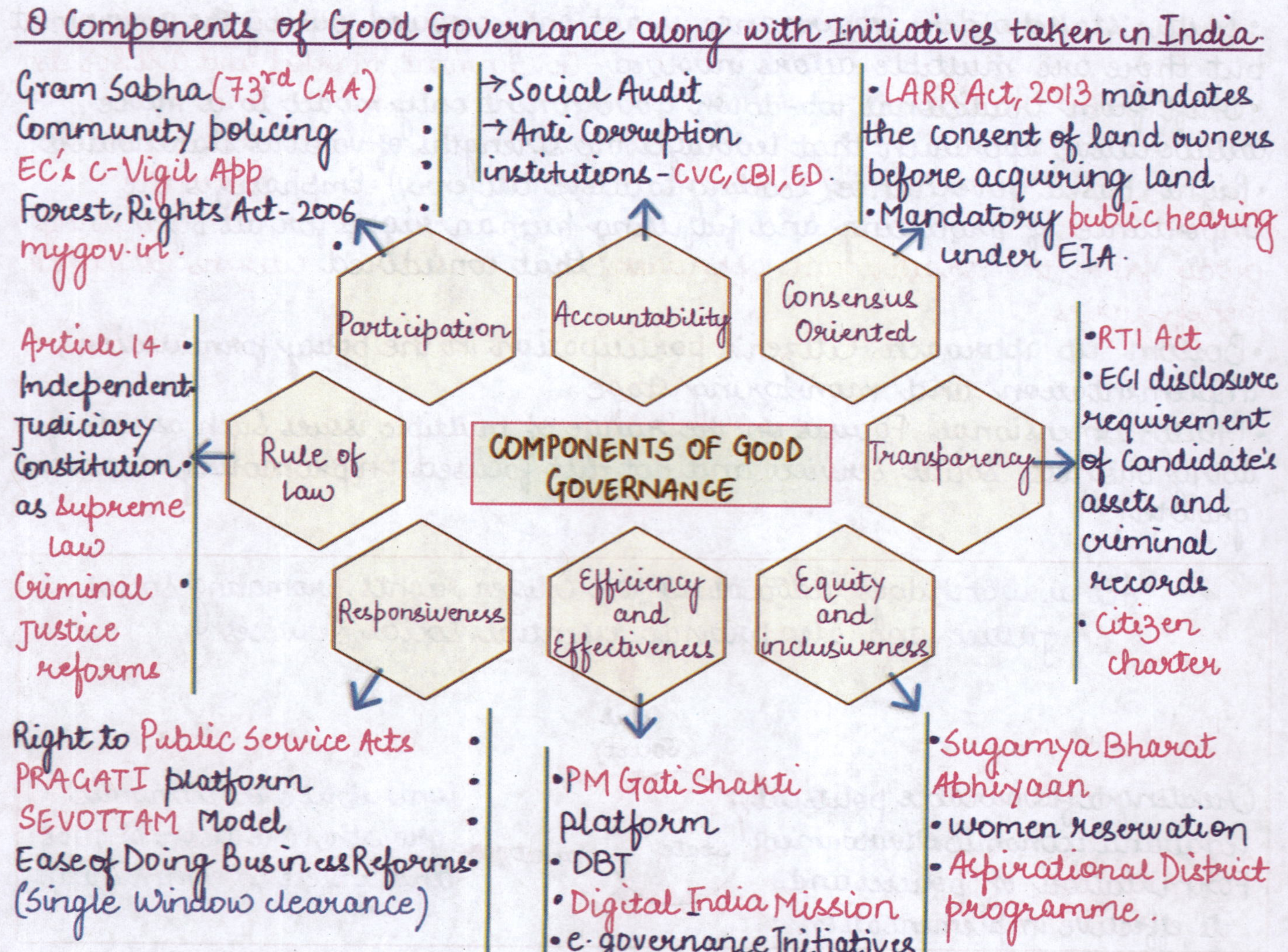

Mahatma Gandhi's Concept of Ram Rajya and Good Governance

Mahatma Gandhi's vision of Ram Rajya aligns closely with the principles of good governance in several key aspects:

- Equality and Justice: Both emphasize equal rights and access to opportunities for all citizens, regardless of caste, religion or gender.
- People's Sovereignty: Both place power ultimately in the hands of the people. This can be achieved through democratic systems and citizen participation in decision making processes.
- Rule of Law: Both rely on a strong legal framework which ensures predictability, protects rights and prevents arbitrary use of power.
- Moral foundation: While Ram Rajya incorporates the concept of "dharma" (righteousness), good governance emphasizes ethical conduct, transparency and accountability. Both require a strong moral compass to function effectively.
- Decentralisation and Participation: Ram Rajya envisions power residing with self-governing villages (panchayats), empowering local communities to manage their own affairs. Good governance also promotes decentralization, where appropriate, allowing local governments to be more responsive to the needs of their citizens

Necessary pre-conditions for ensuring Good Governance

1. Sound Legal Framework
   a) Strong Constitution
   b) Sound laws and regulations

2. Robust Institutional mechanism for Implementation of laws
   a) Independent and strong Judiciary
   b) Competent bureaucracy
   c) Robust anti-corruption institution

3) Citizen's participation
   a) Free and Independent media.
   b) Vibrant civil Society with NGOs and Social watchdogs.
   c) Public awareness about their rights and duties as citizens

4) Citizen centric and Accountable Governance
   a) Principle of Subsidiarity
   b) Policies for decentralization and delegation.
   c) Information sharing and Transparency.
   d) Effective citizen's charter
   e) Strong grievance redressal mechanism
   f) Independent evaluation of Services
   g) Adoption of E-Governance initiatives.
   h) Re-engineering governance processes

Dimensions of Governance in India

Dimension	Key features	Issues
Political	1. Effective Democracy 2. Exercise of Adult Franchise 3. Functioning of Legislature 4. Federalism and Decentralisation	1. Criminalisation of politics 2. Electoral Corruption 3. Ineffective devolution of functions, functionaries and finances to local bodies
Legal and Judicial	1. Rule of law (Law & Order) 2. Judicial Independence 3. Access to Justice and judicial accountability 4. Safeguarding of human rights	1. Ineffective implementation of Laws. 2. Weak Judicial accountability mechanisms 3. Huge Pendency of cases (Delayed Justice)
Administrative	1. Citizen Centric administration 2. Bureaucratic inefficiency 3. Improved Service delivery 4. E- Governance	1. Lack of Sensitivity, transparency and accountability. 2. Bureaucratic redtapism and delays 3. Resistance to change 4. Bureaucratic corruption.
Economic	1. Sustainable Economic growth 2. Fiscal management 3. Business environment	1. Challenges like income inequality, job creation and ensuring inclusive growth. 2. High debt - GDP ratio.
Social and Environment	1. Human development 2. Social Cohesion 3. Environmental management	1. Gender inequality, caste based discrimination or lack of basic Services for marginalised groups. 2. Dumping of Solid waste, environmental pollution etc

MINIMUM GOVERNMENT, MAXIMUM GOVERNANCE

- It is a concept popularised by Indian Prime Minister Narendra Modi which aims to strike a balance between the roles of the government and the private Sector in achieving efficient and effective public Service delivery.

Minimize unnecessary government intervention resulting intostreamlining bureaucracy, reducing red-tapism and simplifying regulations.

Empowerment of citizens and businesses by creating an enabling environment with least restrictions.

Maximise efficiency & effectiveness in public service delivery with minimal waste or corruption.

Implementation in India

- Digitalisation: Online platforms for government services like applications, grievance redressal and bill payments can reduce bureaucratic hurdles and improve accessibility.
  Eg- Aadhar card registration, Online passport applications.
- Reduced role of government from certain sectors: Eg- Starting June 1, 2024, private driving schools can conduct driving tests and issue certificates required for obtaining a driver's license which eliminates the need for applicants to visit RTO for the test.
- Single window clearance system.

PROBITY IN GOVERNANCE

- The term "Probity" has its roots in the Latin word "Probitas", which means "good".
- It represents a set of moral principles that individuals strictly adhere to, including honesty, uprightness, transparency and incorruptibility.
- Probity in governance refers to ethical and principled conduct by those in power.

Principles of Probity

- It is concerned with the propriety and character of various organs of the government as to whether these uphold the procedural uprightness, regardless of the individuals manning these institutions.
- Upholding probity in governance involves more than just refraining from corrupt or dishonest actions.

- Absence of corruption is a fundamental need for guaranteeing probity in governance.
    - It refers to moral behaviour that upholds community ideals and ensures justice, accountability, and transparency, all of which foster public trust and promote civic engagement.

Need for Probity in Governance

From ancient texts like Arthashastra (emphasizing kingly duties) to leaders like Mahatma Gandhi (championing truth and non-violence), probity has been seen as a cornerstone of good governance.

- Upholding Democracy: Maintain the democratic values of equality before the law, justice and fairness.
- Promoting trust between the government and its citizens and increasing the citizen's confidence on government's ability to govern effectively.
- Prevention of corruption by creating a strong deterrent against corrupt behaviour.
- Maintaining public order and promote social harmony.
- Enhancing public participation in government affairs which leads to more informed decision-making and greater citizen engagement in public affairs.
- Ensuring Transparency which promotes accountability and consequently, effective and efficient public service delivery.
- Optimal utilisation of public resources
- Promoting fairness by creating a level playing field and no discrimination in the decision making.
- Strengthening the rule of law which promotes stability and certainty in the legal system, essential for economic growth and social development.

Inculcating Probity in Governance

National Commission to Review the working of Constitution (NCRWC) made several recommendations to improve the probity in Governance:

- Ethics Committees should be established in Parliament and State legislatures to look into complaints against members and to promote ethical conduct among them.
- Code of Ethics should be formulated for all elected representatives, including Ministers, to ensure that they maintain high standards of ethical conduct.
- Strengthening of investigative agencies along with greater autonomy to carry out their functions effectively.

• Judicial reforms to improve the efficiency and effectiveness of the Judicial System in dealing with corruption cases.

Other measures include:

1. Ethics training should be made a part of the initial and ongoing training for public servants which should focus on values such as integrity, honesty and respect for the law.
2. Strengthening accountability mechanisms: This can include measures such as independent audits, regular reporting and monitoring of public officials' activities.
3. Encourage whistleblowing in exposing unethical practices in public administration. This requires amendments in the Whistleblower's Protection Act (2014) to report any wrongdoings without fear of retaliation.

PYQs Corner

(Write the Answer and Get Free Evaluation)

1. 'Probity is essential for an effective system of government and socio-economic development.' Discuss. (2023, 10 Marks)
2. Explain the term social capital. How does it enhance good governance? (2023, 10 Marks)
3. What do you understand by the term 'good governance'? How far recent initiatives in terms of e-Governance steps taken by the State have helped the beneficiaries? Discuss with suitable examples. (2022, 10 Marks)
4. What do you understand by probity in governance? Based on your understanding of the term, suggest measures for ensuring probity in government. (2019, 10 Marks)
5. What do you understand by the terms - 'governance', 'good governance' and 'ethical governance'? (2016, 10 Marks)

13 Accountability and Ethical Governance

66

Accountability Framework

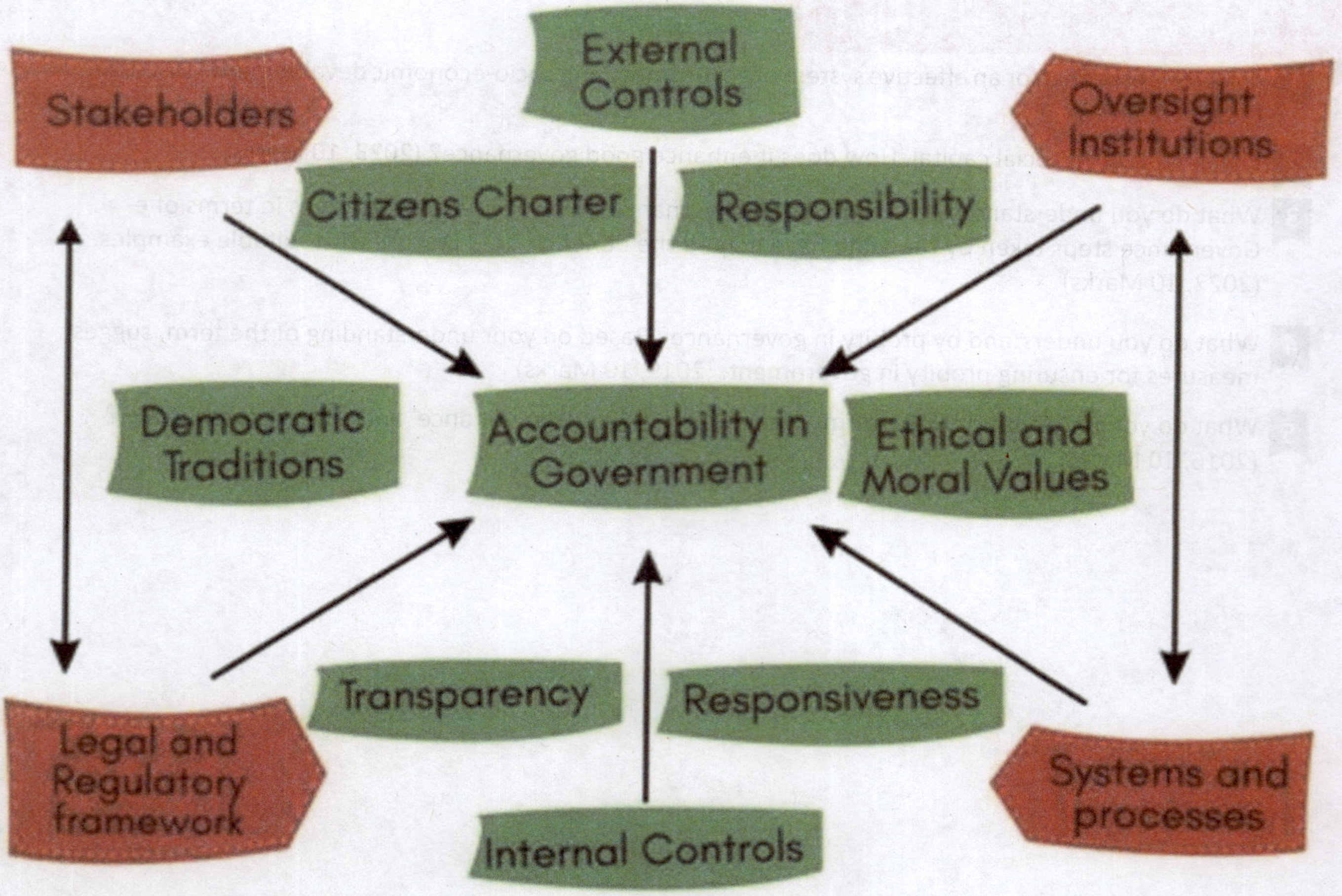

External Controls

Stakeholders

Oversight Institutions

Citizens Charter

Responsibility

Democratic Traditions

Accountability in Government

Ethical and Moral Values

Transparency

Responsiveness

Legal and Regulatory framework

Systems and processes

Internal Controls

TRANSPARENCY

- 2nd ARC defines transparency as the "availability of information to the general public and clarity about the functioning of governmental Institutions."
- According to Vishwanathan and Kaufmann (1999), transparency involves the "increased flow of timely and reliable information accessible to all relevant stakeholders".
  - This perspective emphasizes not only the availability of information but also its reliability and accessibility.
- Transparency and information sharing from the two most important pillars of the good governance in a mature democracy.

Transparency as a key pillar of Good Governance

- Protection of individual Rights
- Ensures Participative Governance
- Necessary for Accountable and Responsible Government
- Effective and Objective Public Service delivery
- Check rates of political Corruption
- Builds trust and legitimacy to government actions
- Not just a means but an end in itself.
- Empowerment of citizens ("Voice Power")
- Promotes Democratic Decision making
- Citizen-Friendly Governance (4 E's in Governance)

Voice power is defined as the Capacity of citizens to pressurize the frontline officials in ensuring effective delivery of public Services. This voice power results in greater accountability.

4 E's in Governance:
- Efficient
- Effective
- Ethical
- Equitable

- Informating sharing refers to the exchange of data among various governing bodies, organisations and the general public.
- It is Sine-qua-non for transparency which can be achieved through various means like:

- Open meetings and public forums - Direct engagement of citizens with the policymaker. Eg- mygov.in.
- Freedom of information (FoI Laws) - Legal right to the Citizens fostering a culture of openness
- Government websites - Information available to a wider audience to easily access relevant information.
- Social Media engagement - Leverage platforms like Twitter and Facebook to disseminate information directly to the Public Eg-Twitter Samvad
- National open data platform: Providing citizens with access to a vast amount of government data on various topics like agriculture, health and education Eg- India Open Data Platform: https://data.gov.in/.

Concerns of increasing transparency for the administration

- Slowdown in the policy making due to the involvement of too many parties in policy making.
- Frivolous requests leads to the diversion of resources from handling genuine requests.
- Privacy concerns of those who hold public offices
- Can lead to political action as the focus will shift more on managing perception of the public rather than taking tough decisions
- Increased administrative burden for making vast amount of data publicly available.
- Chilling effect on innovation due to the fears of public Scrutiny over internal deliberations.
- Misinformation and misinterpretation of data among citizens, with greater access to information.
- Sensitive information might be strategically leaked to damage reputations or manipulate public opinion

Philosophers/Reformers views on Transparency

Montesquieu

- A champion of limited government and Separation of powers, Montesquieu believed transparency was crucial to prevent abuse of power.

• A proponent of individual liberty, Mill believed transparency was essential for a healthy democracy	John stuart Mill

 John Rawls	• He proposed the concept of "Justice as fairness". • He argued that a just society would be one where citizens, under a "veil of ignorance" (not knowing their social position), would agree to the principles governing their Society. • Transparency in government actions would be necessary for citizens to assess this fairness

• He championed transparency throughout his life who believed in Satyagraha (truth force) and non-violent resistance, principles that relied on openness and honesty	 Mahatma Gandhi

DR. B. R. Ambedkar	• He believed that an open and accountable government was vital for protecting the rights of all citizens, especially marginalised communities.

• He recognised the value of transparency in preventing tyranny. • However, he also cautioned against the dangers of "factionalism" – the formation of groups pursuing their own interests at the expense of common good.	 James Madison

Hannah Arendt	• She argued that absolute transparency could hinder effective government action. • She believed some level of secrecy might be necessary in certain situations.

• He led the Total Revolution Movement in 1970s against corruption and authoritarianism. • He emphasized the need for citizen participation and transparency in governance to hold leaders accountable and ensure a more democratic system	 Jayaprakash Narayan

Challenges and Solutions to bring transparency in administration

Challenges	Solutions
Institutional Challenges 1. Fragmented information systems across departments makes information retrieval difficult and time consuming. Eg - 42% of RTI requests in India faced delays (Transparency International) 2. Lack of skilled personnel. Eg - 38% of public officials in a developing nation felt unprepared to handle RTI requests (Commonwealth Ombudsman) 3. Bureaucratic Red tapism and complex procedures	1. Standardised data formats and invest in centralized information management systems. 2. Streamline RTI procedures, simplify application forms, and promote a service-oriented mindset within the administration.
Technological Challenges 1. limited IT infrastructure and Lack of digitalisation (World Bank 2021 report. 2. Concerns of cyber-Security and data protection especially related to critical infrastructure	1. Invest in modern IT infrastructure and promote e-governance initiatives (Digital India Mission and BharatNet) 2. Implement robust cybersecurity measures to safeguard sensitive information (Cyber Security Policy, 2013) 3. Establish clear data classification policies to balance transparency and data protection (Digital Data Protection Act, 2023)
Cultural & Behavioural Challenges 1. Bureaucratic inertia and a culture of secrecy create resistance to transparency initiatives. 2. Low public awareness about their rights and RTI procedures can limit citizen engagement. Eg - Only 30% of the Citizens were aware of their RTI rights	1. Promote a culture of openness and accountability within the administration. Eg - Jan Soochna Portal (Rajasthan) and E-governance initiatives. 2. Educate citizen about their rights and procedures through public awareness campaigns (IEC Campaigns)

Political challenges	
1. Lack of political will especially related to campaign finance of policies such as PM CARES fund	1. Strong political leadership committed to transparency is essential 2. Public Pressure from citizens and advocacy groups can hold politicians accountable. Eg. ADR, Transparency International

Evolution of Transparency Laws in India

1766: Sweden enacts the first Freedom of Information (FOI) law.

1923: India adopts the official Secrets Act, a legacy of British rule, which restricts public access to government information.

1970s and 1980s: A global trend towards greater transparency in governance emerges. Many countries enact FOI laws during this period, including Norway (1970), France (1978), and Canada (1982)

1990s: The movement for Right to Information (RTI) gains momentum in India

- Grassroot Campaign: The Mazdoor Kisan Shakti Sangathan (MKSS), a farmer's rights group, launches the first national campaign for RTI in India (1994)
- Drafting the RTI law: The National campaign for People's Right to Information (NCPRI) is formed in 1996 and drafts an initial RTI law proposal for the government.
- Tamil Nadu leads the way: TN becomes the first Indian state to enact a Right to Information Act in 1997.

2002: The Freedom of Information (FoI) Act is passed by the Indian Parliament but is not effectively implemented.

2005: Right to Information (RTI) Act is passed, replacing the FOI Act. This landmark legislation establishes a framework for citizens to request information from public authorities.

RIGHT TO INFORMATION

If liberty and equality, as is thought by some are chiefly to be found in democracy, they will be best attained when all persons alike share in the government to the utmost.

– Aristotle

- A cornerstone of a functioning democracy is an informed public, and transparency is essential to holding governments accountable and combating corruption.
- In recognition of the need for transparency in public affairs, the Indian parliament enacted the Right to Information Act (referred to as the RTI Act) in 2005.

Objectives of the RTI Act

- To empower Citizens
- To promote transparency and accountability
- To enhance people's participation in the democratic process.
- To contain corruption

- It is a path breaking legislation that signals a radical shift in the governance culture.
  - From a culture of Secrecy to a new culture of openness
  - From personalised despotism to authority coupled with accountability.
  - From unilateral decision making to participative governance

Judicial pronouncements on the evolution of RTI

1. Bennett Coleman & Co. vs. Union of India (1958). SC recognised the right to freedom of the press (Article 19(1)(a)) as encompassing the right of citizens to access information. Court stated that freedom of press also implies the right of the people to read and be informed.
2. State of Uttar Pradesh vs. Raj Narain & Ors (1975): SC while upholding the right to freedom of speech and expression, directed the government to disclose information about security arrangements and expenditure

incurred on the visit of then Prime Minister. This case highlighted the importance of transparency in government functioning.

3. Union of India vs Association for Democratic Reforms (ADR) (2002): SC held that electors have a right to know about the antecedents of candidates. This right was seen as flowing from the fundamental right to freedom of speech and expression (Article 19(1)(a)) as it allows voters to make informed choices.

These pronouncements, along with others, have established a strong foundation for the right to be informed in India. While not explicitly mentioned as a separate fundamental right, it is seen as integral to the exercise of other fundamental rights and essential for a healthy democracy.

Provisions of the RTI Act, 2005

Identifying Public Authorities (Section 2(h))	• Broadly defines public authorities to include all organisations, bodies and authorities under the control of the central government, or local bodies. • NGOs and civil society organisations that receive significant funding (directly or indirectly) from public funds are also classified as public authorities
Right to Information (Section 3)	• Guarantees every Indian citizen the right to information subject to the provisions of the Act. (Disclosure is the norm, Secrecy is the exception)
Proactive Disclosure (Section 4)	• Encourages public authorities to proactively disclose certain categories of information through various means like websites and publications.
Obligation of Public authorities (Section 5)	• The Act designates Public Information officers (PIOs) within each public authority responsible for receiving and responding to RTI requests within a stipulated timeframe of 30 days.
Sample RTI filing process (Section 6)	• Straightforward procedures for citizens to request information under RTI Act.
Time limits for Response (Section 7)	• Within which the government must respond to RTI requests and provide the requested information to the citizen.

Exemptions and limitations (Section 8)	• Recognizes certain exemptions from disclosure, including information affecting national security, foreign relations, commercial confidentiality, personal information (with some exceptions), and information relating to ongoing investigations. • These exceptions ensure a balance between transparency and legitimate concerns. • Section 8(2) clarifies exemptions related to the Official Secrets Act, 1923, where disclosure could potentially harm national Security or public interest.
Appellate Mechanism (Section 19)	• The Act establishes a two tier appellate mechanism: • Applicants dissatisfied with response from the PIO can appeal to the First Appellate Authority (FAA) within public authority. • If further dissatisfied, they can appeal to State Information Commission (SIC) or the Central Information Commissioner (CIC) depending on the nature of public authority.
Penalties for non-compliance (Section 20)	• The Act prescribes penalties for PIOs who fail to comply with its provisions without reasonable cause. These penalties can include disciplinary action and even fines.
Public agencies exempted from purview of the Act.	• Specifically exempts organisations listed in the Second Schedule which include intelligence agencies like the CBI, RAW and IB. • RTI doesn't apply to the judiciary.

Official Secrets Act, 1923

- It is an act enacted during the British Raj to safeguard classified information related to national Security.
- It discourages espionage and unauthorized access to government Secrets.
- The Act categorizes information into different secrecy levels, including "Secret", "top Secret", and "confidential".
- OSA created a culture of Secrecy under which confidentiality became the norm and Disclosure is the exception.
- The Official Secrets Act can potentially act as a barrier to transparency mandated by the Right to Information Act (RTI) of 2005

RTI- Master Key to Good Governance (2nd ARC)

• Fosters trust between the public and government (Improved transparency)	Empowerment of Citizens (Active Citizenry fighting for their rights)
• Reduced corruption within the government bodies (Fear of exposure acts as a deterrent for public officials)	Citizen Centric Administration (Sensitivity, Responsibility to the development process.
• Strengthen grassroot democracy (Demand better implementation of the schemes)	Facilitates fairness and objectivity (Reduced discretion and open decision making).
• Better Public Private relationships (Improved citizens monitoring of the projects)	Improved public Service delivery (Responsive and Accountable Administration)
• Participatory Democracy (Constructive criticism by citizens)	Rights based approach to development.

Success stories of RTI

1. Combating corruption: 2G Spectrum scam, Coal Block Allocation Scam, Commonwealth Games Scam etc.
2. Improving public Services: Villagers in Karnataka used RTI to highlight the issue of inadequate food supplies under Right to Food Scheme, prompting corrective action.
3. Minimum wages for Workers: Brick kiln workers in Tamil Nadu, facing exploitation and denied minimum wages used RTI to access government records, file legal cases and secure rightful compensation.
4. Proper utilisation of public funds: RTI applications have exposed instances of ghost workers, inflated wages and misuse of funds under the implementation of MGNREGA in various states.

Challenges in the Successful implementation of RTI

Supply-Side (Government Side)

- Passive approach by public authorities to fulfill their obligation under Section 4 in proactive disclosure of information, leading to a surge in RTI requests.
- Overburdened and understaffed Information commissions (ICs) leads to delays in resolving cases → Mounting backlog of cases

Eg- A total 3.2 Lakh appeals and complaints are pending in 27 State Information Commissions across the country. Maharashtra (1.15 Lakh) followed by Karnataka (41,047)

- Workforce shortages: Several Information commissions, including the CIC, operate with less than the sanctioned number of members, hindering efficiency.

Eg- Four State Information Commissions (Jharkhand, Telangana, Mizoram, and Tripura) are completely defunct due to retirement of serving commissioners and lack of new appointments.

- Six Information commissions are currently headless - The Central Information Commission, and the State Information Commissions of Manipur, Chhattisgarh, Maharashtra, Bihar and Punjab.

- Absence of a national database to track RTI applications at the state or central level making it difficult to track the volume of RTI applications received
- Lack of penalties for appellate authorities who fail to meet the specific timelines in providing information
- RTI Amendment Act, 2019 diluting the autonomy of ICs and therefore, hampering its independence.
- Absence of contempt provisions weakens the ability to ensure compliance with the Act.
- Whistle-blower Protection: RTI Act does not provide adequate protection for whistle-blower which can deter individuals from reporting wrongdoing or exposing corruption.
- Poor record keeping as most of the old records are not available in the digital format.

Demand - side (Citizen Side)

- Intimidation and death of various RTI activists discourages citizens from filing RTI applications
- Low public awareness particularly among marginalised communities like women, disadvantaged social groups etc., about their rights and use of RTI Act.
- Most ICs are being located in state capitals has limited accessibility for citizens in remote areas.
- Frivolous request or misuse of RTI for personal vendettas or irrelevant queries placing an unnecessary burden on already strained administrative resources
- Cumbersome appeal procedures and thus, unsuitable for RTI appeals.

• Based on the findings of the 'Report card on the Performance of Information Commissions in India, 2022-23' by the Satark Nagrik Sangathan (SNS) there is an urgent need for addressing the dysfunctionality of information commissions, ensuring proper appointments, and addressing the rising backlog of appeals and complaints. Failure to do so undermines the effectiveness of the RTI Act and the public's right to access information.
• In February 2019, the Supreme court addressed the non-appointment of information commissioners in a PIL case and underlined that it was vital for ICs to function effectively with adequate commissioners to ensure a proper implementation of the RTI Act. The court said not having enough commissioners would defeat the purpose of the RTI law.

Strengthening the RTI Act: 2nd ARC Recommendations

1. Improved Record Management: Proposed exploring technologies like blockchain to enhance record management.
2. Expanding the Scope of "Public Authority": 2nd ARC proposes a broader definition of "public authority" which could include the lowest office with decision making power or record keeping responsibilities within an organisation.
3. More entities under RTI: Organisations performing public functions traditionally carried out by the government or its agencies, along with those enjoying a natural monopoly, might be brought under RTI ambit.
4. Mandatory RTI training for all government officials. It Suggested organising training programs in a decentralised manner at the block level to ensure wider coverage.
5. Strengthening Oversight Mechanisms: Entrust the CIC and SICs with the task of monitoring the effective implementation of the RTI Act across all public authorities.
6. Establishing Regional offices: Proposes the setting up four regional offices of the CIC, each Headed by a Commissioner. Similarly, it recommend establishing regional offices of SICs in larger states.
7. National Coordination Committee: Proposes establishing a National Coordination committee (NCC) chaired by the Chief Information Commissioner.
   • This committee would serve as a national platform to review the Act's implementation, analyze rules and executive orders issued by governments, and recommend improvements.

ACCOUNTABILITY

- Accountability refers to the obligation of individuals or organisations to take responsibility for their actions and decisions and to be answerable to their stakeholders for the outcomes of their actions.

Responsibility	Answerability	Enforcement
• Refers to the obligation or duty, an individual or organisation has to perform a task or fulfill a role. • It entails carrying out assigned duties effectively, adhering to ethical codes, and using public resource wisely.	• Emphasizes the requirement to explain, justify and provide information about actions, decisions or performance • It involves being accessible and responsive to feedback, complaints and questions raised by citizens.	• Refers to mechanisms in place to ensure consequences for failing to meet responsibilities or fulfill answerability obligations. • It involves disciplinary actions within the civil service, legal repurcussion, or even public censure.

Importance of Accountability in Governance

POLITICAL
- Realisation of true democracy by making government answerable to the people for its actions and decisions.
- Empowerment of citizens and participative democracy.

BUREAUCRATIC
- Improved and timely service delivery.
- Responsive, efficient and empathetic bureaucracy.
- Increases public trust and confidence on government institutions.
- Prevention of corruption and misuse of power.

SOCIO-ECONOMIC
- Promotes fiscal responsibility through efficient utilisation of public funds and minimises wasteful spending.
- Attractive foreign investment which fuels economic growth.
- Fosters a fairer and more equitable system

Types of Accountability Mechanisms

- Public service accountability involves the methods by which a public agency or a public official fulfils its duty and obligations. It includes the process by which that agency or the public official is required to account for such actions.

Ends	Means (Tools)
legitimacy	• Constitutions and electoral systems for establishing government and decision-making bodies; Bureaucratic system of representation; Royal prerogative; legislations; Letter of appointments; Standing orders and formal delegations of authority.
Moral Conduct	• Upholding social values, concept of social justice & public interest; professional values; training/induction programs.
Responsiveness	• Public participation and consultation; debates; advisory bodies; Public meetings, freedom of speech.
Openness	• Parliamentary questions time; Public information services, freedom of information laws; public hearings; green and white papers; annual reports.
Optimal resource utilisation	• Budgets; financial procedures; rules of vehement; parliamentary public accounts committees; auditing; public enquiries & participation; formal planning systems.
Efficiency & effectiveness	• Information communication systems, Setting objectives and standards; programme guidelines; approval; feedback from public.

Horizontal vs Vertical Accountability

Horizontal Accountability (Within the State)	Vertical Accountability (Outside the state)
• Refers to the system of checks and balances among different branches or levels of govt.	• Refers to accountability of govt. officials to citizens & Civil Society organisations.
• Involves creating mechanisms to prevent any one branch or level of governments from becoming too powerful and abusing its authority.	• Involves creating mechanisms for citizens to hold public officials accountable for their actions or inactions, including use of electoral processes, public participation in policy-making etc.
Examples: Internal (Within the executive) - Superior officers through rewards & punishments, disciplinary procedures, performance management system; Internal Audit; Grievance Redressal Mechanisms. External (Outside the executive) - Separation of powers, independent oversight bodies like parliamentary committees, CAG, anti-corruption institutions - Lokpal, CBI, CVC, etc.	Example: General elections, RTI Act (2005), Social Audit, Citizen's charter, Civil Society Activism, media Scrutiny etc.

- Horizontal Accountability helps ensure that the different branches of govt. are held in check, while vertical accountability ensures that public officials remain responsive to the needs and interest of citizens.
- Together, these two approaches create a system of checks and balances that promote transparency, accountability and democratic governance.

Five Types of Accountability

Organisational Accountability	• Traditional hierarchical accountability within an Organisation (classical weberian bureaucratic form of administration)
Political Accountability	• Administrators are 'duty bound to recognise the power of political authority to regulate, set priorities, redistribute resources and to ensure compliance with orders.
Legal Accountability	• Public officials are hold accountable for not following legislative norms or legal delegations by a judicial review.
Professional Accountability	• Obligations of civil servants to be responsible & answerable for their actions, decisions and performance in their official capacity.
Moral Accountability	• It is more than obedience of laws and bureaucratic norms. A moral public official is the one who "strives for a moral government

CITIZEN CHARTER

- According to 2nd ARC, Citizen charter is public statement that defines the entitlements of citizens to a specific service, the standards of the service, the conditions to be met by users, and the remedies available to the latter in case of non-compliance of standards.
- The Charter concept empowers the citizens in demanding committed standards of service. Thus, the basic thrust of Citizens' Charter is to make public services citizen centric by ensuring that these services are demand driven rather than supply driven.
- A strong citizen charter acts as a promise between an organisation and the people it serves.

Following are the key components that make it effective.

- **Vision and Mission Statement**: A clear statement of the organisation's purpose and what it aims to achieve for the citizens it serves.
- **Details of the organisation**: A brief introduction about the organisation its function and the kind of services it provides.
- **Services offered**: A comprehensive list of the services provided by the organisation, outlining the specific details of each service. This might include eligibility criteria, application processes and expected timelines.
- **Quality standards**: Clearly defined benchmarks for service delivery. This include aspects like turnaround time, accuracy etc.
- **Grievance Redressal Mechanism**: A well-defined process for citizens to register complaints and get them addressed.
- **Citizens' Responsibilities**: This could involve providing necessary documentation, adhering to guidelines and maintaining respectful communication.
- **Additional commitments** in situations where service delivery falls short. This could involve compensation for delays or a mechanism for service improvement.

Philosophical basis of Citizen Charter

 Mahatma Gandhi	"A customer is the most important visitor on our premises. He is not dependent on us; we are dependent on him. He is not an interruption on our work; he is the purpose of it. He is not an outsider on our business; he is part of it. We are not doing him a favour by serving him; he is doing a favour by giving us an opportunity to do so".
Social Contract Theory.	• Articulated by thinkers like John locke and Thomas Hobbes • Suggest a reciprocal agreement between citizen and government • Citizens cede some power to the government in exchange for the protection of their rights and the provision of essential services • Citizen charters act as a concrete representation of this agreement, outlining the services citizens can expect and the standards they deserve.
Public Service Ethics	• Public servants hold a position of trust, obligated to serve the public good. • Citizen charters reflect this ethical principle by promoting transparency and accountability. • By clearly stating service standards, the government becomes more accountable for its performance.

Evolution of citizen Charter

Beginning in 1991

The credit for initiating Citizen Charter goes to United Kingdom

- Introduced by then PM John Major, it aimed to enhance the quality of public services and build trust with citizens.

Global Adoption (Late 1990s)

The concept resonated with countries like Australia, Canada and India. In India, the idea was adopted in 1997 at a Conference of CMs with a focus on key service like railways, telephones etc

Core Principles (Late 1990s)

UK established core principles for Citizen charters which became a framework for charters adopted around the world.

Six Principles of Citizen's charter movement

Quality: Improving the service quality

Choice: for the users whenever possible

Accountability: of service provider (individual and organisation)

Transparency: in rules, procedures, scheme and grievance redressal

Standards: specifying what to expect within a time frame

Value: for the taxpayers' money

2002

DARPG, recognising the need for a standardised approach, launched a website specifically for citizen charters providing a central repository for charters from different ministries and departments.

Since 2000s

The Initiative of citizen charters wasn't limited to central government.

- Many state governments also adopted the concept and formulated Citizen charters for their own departments, aiming to improve service delivery at state level

Importance of Citizen Charter

1. Empowerment of citizens with clear understanding of Service delivery methods.
2. Enhances accountability of the public Service providers
   - Citizen Report card in Karnataka allows citizens to assess public Services like Schools and health clinics, empowering them to hold institutions accountable
3. Efficient and time bound delivery of public Services which is reflected in welfare of citizens.
4. Increased citizen participation in evaluation as well as policy implementation.
5. Means for promoting good governance through citizen's participation in administration making the government more responsive, accountable and transparent. Eg- Jan Sewa Kendras in Ahmedabad
6. Can Seek Compensation for undue Service delivery. Eg- Sakala Service Act in Karnataka mandates time-bound delivery of Services with penalties for delays, ensuring accountability.
7. Increases the organisation performance and effectiveness by making a public commitment. Eg- Sangram Program in Maharashtra Sets specific timelines for resolving land record disputes, ensuring consistent and efficient Service delivery.
8. Cultivates compassionate and inclusive Service delivery.
   - A police department's charter with women's help desks and Sensitivity training fosters a respectful and inclusive environment for all citizens seeking assistance
9. Decreases the opportunity for corruption by increasing transparency and fairness.
10. Effective implementation of citizen's charter fosters trust between citizen and the service providers.
11. From bureaucratic attitude to Service-oriented attitude.

Challenges in Citizen Charter

Charter Formulation

- Limited participation of the civil Society or local stakeholders lead to charters that are impractical or irrelevant to daily operations.
- Lack clarity and specificity, making is difficult for citizens to understand their rights.
- Absence of clearly defined Service standards makes it difficult to assess if an organisation is meeting its commitments.

- One-Size-Fits-All Approach: Uniform charters across all offices within an organisation often fail to address local issues and service delivery variations
- Rarely updated to reflect changing circumstances or service delivery methods. This lack of dynamism can render them outdated and ineffective over time.
- Limited scope in the coverage of services offered by a department
- Non inclusive as it does not include the interests of the vulnerable sections of the society - women, disabled, elderly etc.

Charter Implementation

- Absence of legal backing to charters.
- Lack of public awareness about the existence of citizen charters, hindering the ability to hold organisations accountable.
- Poor publicity about the charters
- Absence of grievance redressal mechanisms can render charter ineffective
- Lack of training for staff on adhering to the charter's guidelines
- Resistance to attitude change within bureaucratic structures
- Resource constraints for training, publicity and grievance redressal systems
- Redtapism stands as a barrier between the citizen and effective public service delivery.

Making Citizens Charter more Effective

- Stakeholder consultation: Both citizens and staff should be consulted at every stage of formulating a citizen charter. (IIPA Recommendation)
- Participation of the civil society should be actively involved in the process to help refine the charter's content, promote adherence and educate citizens about its importance (2nd ARC).
- One size does not fit all by allowing local units to tailor charters to their specific needs (2nd ARC).
- Quantifiable commitments: Charters need to be clear and make specific, measurable service delivery commitments to citizens/consumers. (2nd ARC)
- Staff training and orientation on the key features, goals and objectives of the Citizen's charter along with the attitude change (IIPA)
- Budget Allocation: Earmarking specific budgetary resources is

necessary for effective awareness of generation activities. (IIPA)

- Wider publicity of the charter through print media and electronic media.
- Grievance Redressal Mechanism: The charter should clearly outline the relief an organisation is obligated to provide if it fails to meet its promised service standards. (2nd ARC)
- Periodic updates: Citizen charter should be updated regularly, preferably by an external agency, to ensure they remain relevant and effective (2nd ARC)
- Accountability Framework: Specific responsibility should be assigned to officers for adhering to the citizen's charter. This ensures someone is held accountable if defaults occur (2nd ARC)
- End user feedback can be timely aid to assess the progress and outcomes of an agency that has implemented a citizen's charter (Standard practice for charters implemented in UK)

Successful Citizen's Charters in Action

- Passport Seva (India): The Ministry of External Affairs transformed the passport application process. Online tracking, faster turnaround times, and clear information on fees and documents empowered citizens. Additionally, robust grievance redressal mechanisms minimised corruption.
- Jan Seva Kendra (Ahmedabad, India): This one stop shop for government services revolutionised accessibility. Citizens can access various services under one roof with assistance from trained staff, simplifying procedures and boosting satisfaction.
- Sakala Mission (Karnataka, India): This time-bound service delivery act tackles delays. It guarantees specific timelines for crucial services like land records and birth certificates, enhancing predictability and accountability. Penalties for non-compliance ensure adherence

SEVOTTAM MODEL

About: Sevottam is a Service Delivery Excellence Model which provides an assessment-improvement framework to bring about excellence in public service delivery.

- Sevottam, derived from Hindi words "Seva" (Service) and "Uttam" (Excellent), translates to "Service excellence". It emphasizes a citizen centric approach to public service delivery.

Need for Sevottam: It introduced by Department of Administrative Reforms and Public Grievances (DARPG) to address shortcomings identified in previous initiatives:

- Citizens' Charter by themselves could not achieve the desired results in improving quality of services.
- Absence of a credible grievance redressal mechanism within organisations
- It was felt that unless there is a mechanism to assess the outcomes of various measures, the reform initiatives would not yield the desired results.

Evaluation: The model works as an evaluation mechanism to assess the quality of internal processes and their impact on the quality of service delivery.

Implementation: Introduced in ten government departments with broad public interfaces from April 2009 to June 2010.

- Later the IS 15700: 2005 standard was developed by the BIS, which allows public service organisations to be awarded the Sevottam symbol of excellence if they adopt and can demonstrate compliance with a collection of management systems.

Components of Sevottam Model

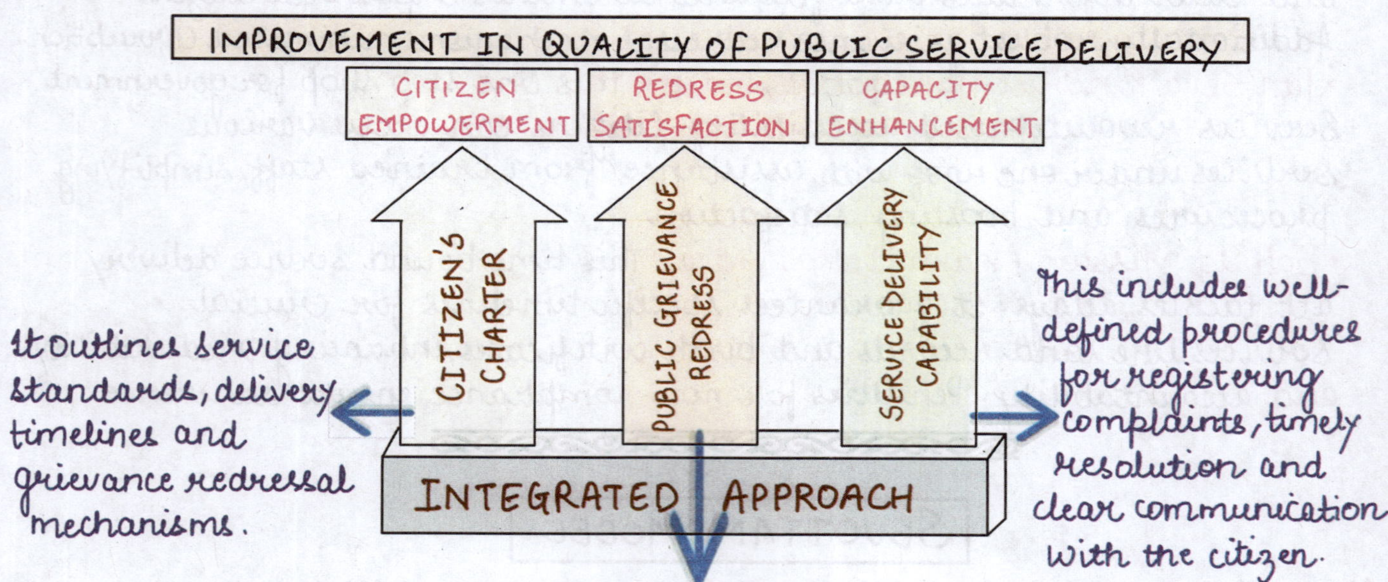

Success of SEVOTTAM depends on

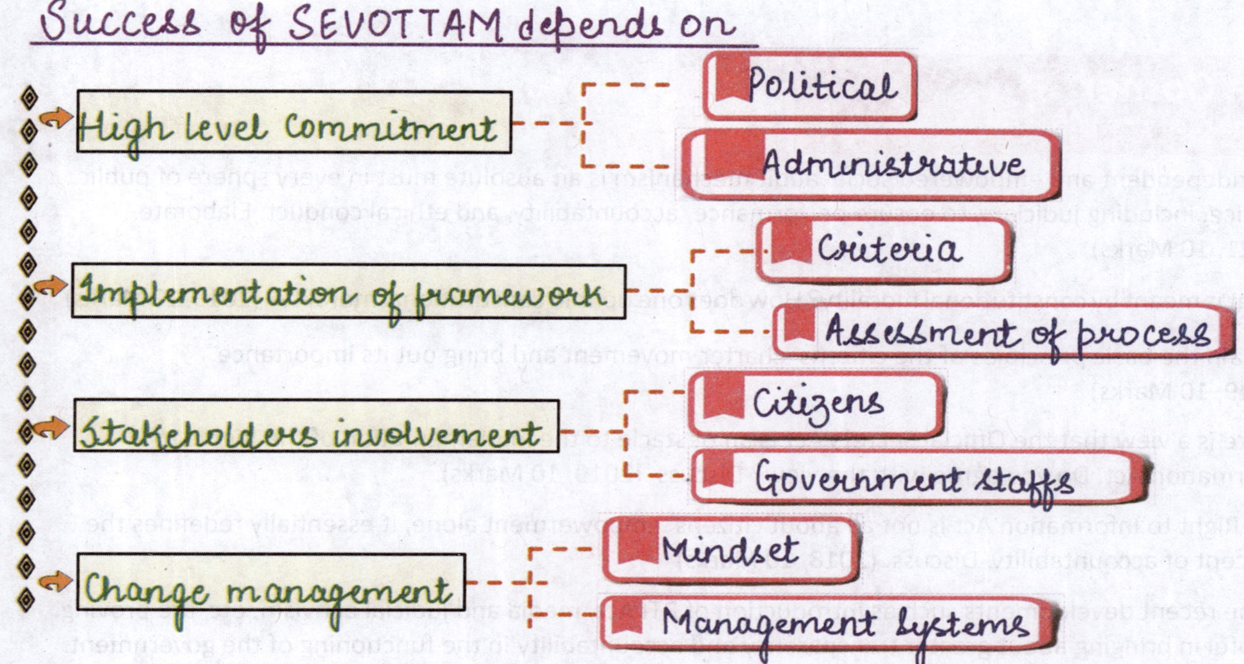

ARC 7-Step model for citizen centricity

- The 2nd ARC recommended that Union and State Governments should make the seven-step model mandatory for all organisations having public interface.
- 7 step model is a simplified version of the Sevottam Model which outlines a clear and easy-to-follow process for organisations, particularly those in public sector, to become more citizen-centric.

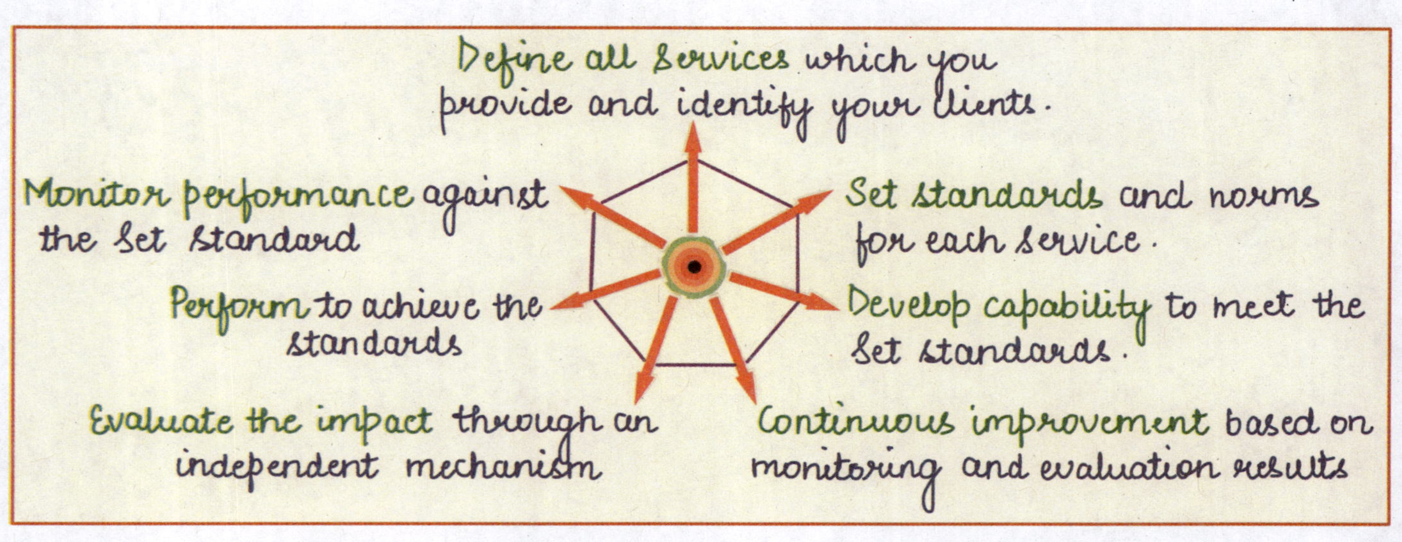

PYQs Corner

(Write the Answer and Get Free Evaluation)

1. An independent and empowered social audit mechanism is an absolute must in every sphere of public service, including judiciary, to ensure performance, accountability, and ethical conduct. Elaborate. (2021, 10 Marks)

2. What is meant by constitutional morality? How does one uphold constitutional morality? (2019, 10 Marks)

3. Explain the basic principles of the citizens' charter movement and bring out its importance. (2019, 10 Marks)

4. There is a view that the Official Secrets Act is an obstacle to the implementation of the Rights to Information Act. Do you agree with the view? Discuss. (2019, 10 Marks)

5. The Right to Information Act is not all about citizens' empowerment alone, it essentially redefines the concept of accountability. Discuss. (2018, 10 Marks)

6. Some recent developments such as introduction of RTI Act, media and judicial activism, etc. are proving helpful in bringing about greater transparency and accountability in the functioning of the government. However, it is also being observed that at times the mechanisms are misused. Another negative effect is that the officers are now afraid to take prompt decisions. Analyse the situation in detail and suggest how the dichotomy can be resolved. Suggest how these negative impacts can be minimized. (2015, 10 Marks)

7. What does 'accountability' mean in the context of public service? What measures can be adopted to ensure individual and collective accountability of public servants? (2014, 10 Marks)

14 Corruption in India

66

"The Corruption of the best things gives rise to the worst."

—David Hume

"If corruption is a disease, transparency is a central part of its treatment."

—Kofi Annan

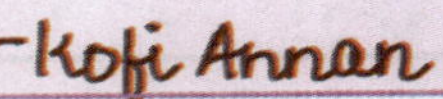

"Without strong watchdog institutions, impunity becomes the very foundation upon which systems of corruption are built. And if impunity is not demolished, all efforts to bring an end to corruption are in vain."

—Rigoberta Menchu (Nobel Prize Laureate)

"Corruption comes from the never-ending greed. The fight for corruption-free ethical society will have to be fought against this greed and replace with 'What can I give' spirit."

—Dr. A.P.J. Abdul Kalam

"People's indifference is the best breeding ground for corruption to grow"

—Delia Ferreira, Chair of Transparency International

CORRUPTION

Corruption is defined as the abuse of entrustred power for private gain. It can take many forms and can include behaviours like:

- Public Servants demanding or taking money or favours in exchange of services
- Politicians misusing public money or granting public jobs or contracts to their sponsers, friends and families
- Corporations bribing officials to get lucrative ideas.
- There are different forms of corruption including bribery, embezzlement, extortion, networking, under-the-table transactions, manipulation of election result, money laundering and more.

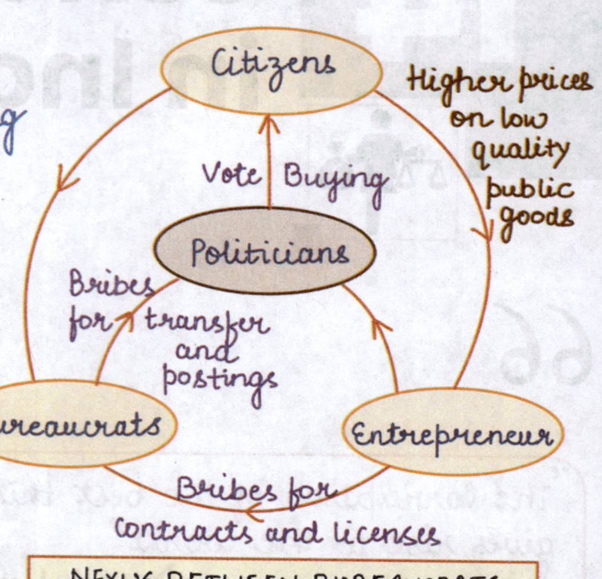

NEXUS BETWEEN BUREAUCRATS, POLITICIANS AND BUSINESS OWNERS

COST OF CORRUPTION

- Corruption incurs the financial cost which reaches into the trillions of dollars annually at the global level.
- Beyond the financial burden; corruption erodes trust, weakens democracy hampers economic development and further exacerbates inequality, social division and environmental crisis.

ECONOMIC COST	• Deterrence of Investment by the businesses to invest in environment riddled with corruption due to the risk of bribery and unfair corruption. This stifles economic growth and job creation • lost revenue: World Bank estimates corruption reduces global GDP by upto 5% which translates to staggering loss of trillions of dollars • Reduced economic growth: Corruption promotes inefficiencies in utilisation of resources, distorts the markets, compromise equality which adversely affect the country's economic development. • Estimates show that in India, government loses about Rs. 2 Lakh crore annually due to tax evasion while about Rs 40,000 crore is lost due to delay in cost.

SOCIAL COST	• Diversion of resources from the essential sectors such as healthcare, education etc to the pockets of corrupt officials. Example: A 2023 study by Transparency International revealed that in countries with high corruption levels, education spending is often 20% lower than in corruption free countries • Human Rights Abuses: Corruption creates an environment where human rights violations are more likely to occur. **Example:** Human Rights violations are often seen in countries like Syria, South Sudan which are highly corrupted. • Widening of social inequality which leads to perpetuation of poverty. • Gender inequality: Corruption restricts women's access to opportunities and public resources.

POLITICAL COST	• Erosion of public trust in government and undermines the credibility of government institutions. Eg- 2G Spectrum Scam (2007), Colgate Scam (2012) • Undermine the Rule of law (RoL): Corruption can lead to selective enforcement of laws and a lack of accountability for those in power. • It can lead to social unrest, political instability and weakening of democratic processes • **Example:** Voter turnout generally tends to be lower in countries with high corruption, indicating a sense of disillusionment with the political system.

OTHER COSTS	• Implications for National Security: Criminal, bureaucrats and political nexus can support illegal activities such as money laundering, drug trafficking, etc. • Environmental Damage: Corruption facilitates illegal activities - deforestation, pollution and wildlife trafficking which harm ecosystem and endanger public health. • **Example:** A 2022 report by World Wildlife Fund linked a rise in illegal logging activities due to increased corruption in certain regions.

Corruption Scenario in India

- India ranked 93rd out of 180 countries in 2023 Corruption Perception Index.
- Transparency International reports that over 62% of Indians have paid bribes to secure jobs in both public and private sectors and expedite bureaucratic processes.
- According to Transparency International's Global Corruption Barometer Asia, India has the highest bribery rate in Asia at 39% along with the highest proportion of citizens using personal connections to gain advantages at 46%

FACTORS CAUSING CORRUPTION IN PUBLIC SECTOR

Corruption = (Monopoly + Discretion) - (Accountability + Integrity + Transparency)

Administrative Factors

- Weak enforcement of laws: India has a number of anti-corruption laws, including the Prevention of Corruption Act (1988). However a 2022 report by Transparency International found that India's conviction rate for corruption cases is mere 6.4%.
- Procedural complexities create delays and frustrations, incentivising people to bypass them through bribes.
- A 2021 survey by the ASSOCHAM found that 72% of businesses in India perceive obtaining government permits as a major hurdle due to complex procedures.
- Red tapism: Excessive regulations and unnecessary paperworks create opportunities to exploit loopholes and extract bribes.
  - A 2019 World Bank report estimated that Indian businesses spend an average of 30% more time complying with regulations compared to OECD average
- Weak grievance redressal machinery led people to resort to bribes in getting things done. A 2020 RTI (Right To Information) query revealed that over 2,00,000 corruption cases were pending investigation with the CVC.
- Bureaucratic resistance to reforms: Attempts to digitalize government services in India have faced pushbacks from some officials who fear a loss of control or increased transparency.
- Secrecy in Bureaucracy: A lack of transparency in decision making creates fertile grounds for corrupt practices.
- According to World Bank estimate, the average bribe to obtain a public contract in India is estimated at 15% of the contract value.

Political Factors

- Criminalisation of Politics can distort the system for personal gain
  - A 2019 report by ADR found that over 34% of Members of Parliament (MPs) in 17th Lok Sabha have criminal charges against them
- Lack of Political will weakens anti corruption efforts.
  Example - Slow progress on enacting comprehensive electoral funding reforms in India raises concerns in addressing the issue of money power in elections.
- Politicization of civil service through political influence on appointments and promotion in the civil service. **Example** - Frequent transfers of civil servants in India often based on political considerations can disrupt continuity and weaken institutional memory.

- Excessive use of Money Power in India: Heavy reliance on financial resources for campaigning can create pressure on politicians to recoup their investments through corrupt means.
- Lack of Voter maturity: Apathy or a short term focus among voters can perpetuate the cycle of electing corrupt officials.

Miscellaneous Factors

- Large number of functionaries: India has a vast bureaucracy with multiple levels of approval required for government processes. This diffuses the accountability and increases the risk of corruption.
- Colonial Legacy of unchallenged Authority: Residual Attributes from colonial times where officials enjoyed unchecked power can contribute to a sense of entitlement and abuse of authority.
- Lack of values: Focus on rote learning and lack of emphasis on value education can breed dishonesty & corruption.
- Social acceptance: Over the years, Social stigma attached to corruption has reduced and there is now growing social acceptance & tolerance for corruption.

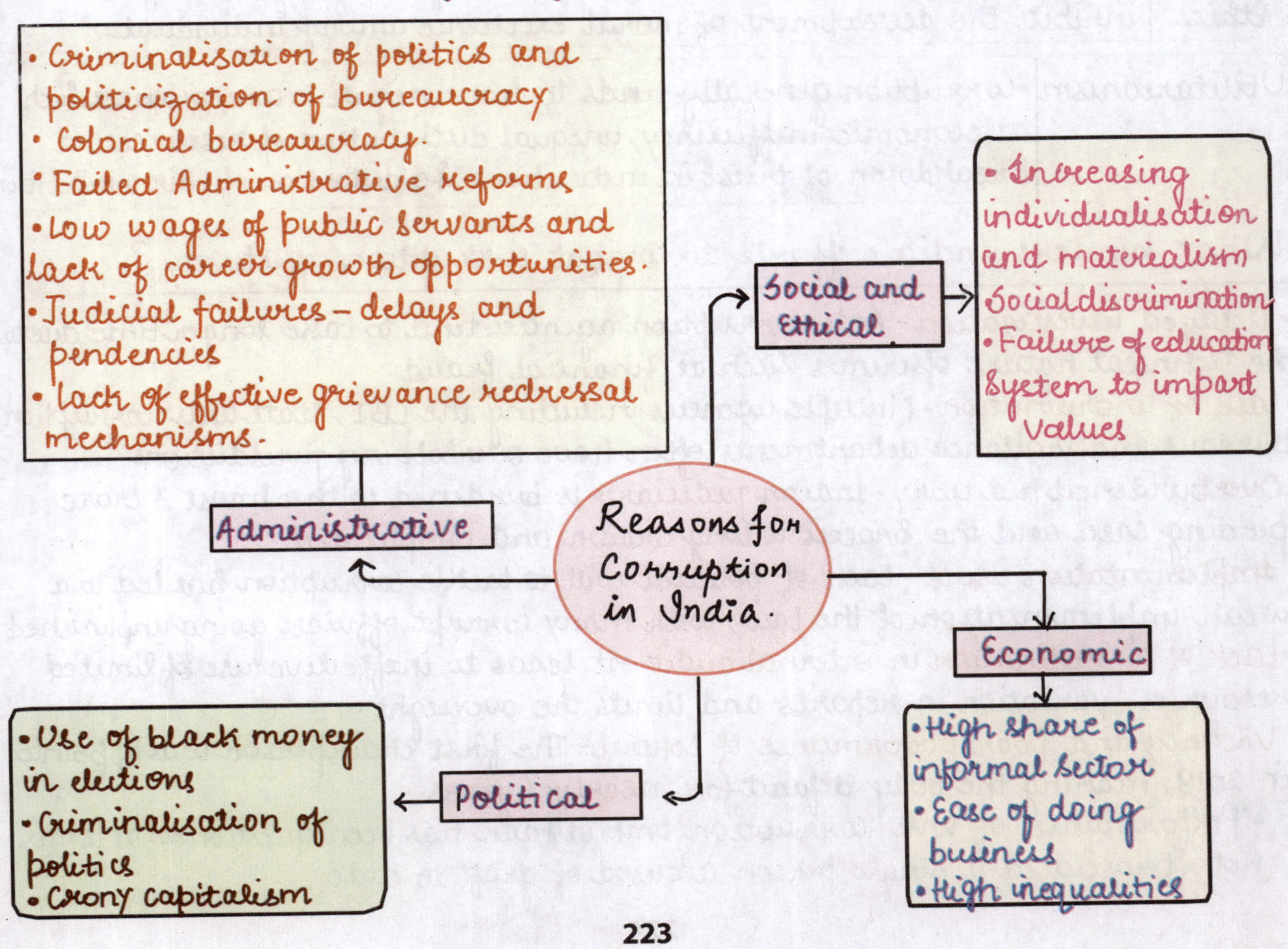

Kautilya's views on Corruption

- The Arthashastra mentions various corrupt practices employed by government officials.
- Kautilya compared government officials handling public money to fish swimming in water.
  - Just as it's difficult to tell if a fish is drinking water or not, it might be hard to detect when officials embezzle small amount of money.
- Kautilya also used the honey analogy to describe the temptation of corruption.
- Just as honey is sweet and alluring, the opportunity to take public money can be very tempting for officials.
- The analogy emphasizes the need for strong deterrents and ethical values to resist this temptation.
- The Arthashastra outlines elaborate methods to prevent corruption - Strong leadership, effective spy system, strict punishment, fair compensation to officials.

Philosopher's Analysis on Corruption

Virtue Ethics	• Corruption condradicts the virtue of honesty, integrity, trust fairness & inhibits the development of moral excellence among individuals.

Utilitarianism	• Corruption generally tends to have negative consequences such as economic inefficiency, unequal distribution of resources, a breakdown of trust in institutions, & a distortion of fair competition.

What hinders India's efforts to combat corruption effectively?

- Delayed investigation - Anti-corruption agencies tend to take longer time due to the technical nature of crimes such as financial fraud.
- Lack of co-ordination - Multiple agencies including the CBI, state anti-corruption bureaus and vigilance departments often have overlapping jurisdictions.
- Overburdened judiciary - Indian judiciary is burdened with almost 3 crore pending cases and the process is long drawn and complicated.
- Implementation issues - Lack of political will to tackle corruption has led to a weak implementation of the law, with many corrupt officials going unpunished.
- Lack of co-ordination in internal audit - It leads to ineffective use of limited resources, variation in reports and limits the oversight.
- Vacancy and poor performance of Lokpal - The first chairperson was appointed in 2019, making the body defunct for nearly 6 years.
  - Performance of anti-corruption ombudsman has been questioned as it has not prosecuted a single person accused of graft to date.

MEASURES TAKEN TO CURB CORRUPTION

Measures to Curb Corruption

Legislative Measures

1. Section 169 and 409 of IPC, 1860
2. Prevention of corruption Act (PCA), 1988: Provides for penalties in relation to corruption by public servants and for those who are involved in the abetment of an act of corruption.
3. Prevention of Money Laundering Act, 2002
4. Companies Act 2013: Provides for corporate governance and prevention of corruption and fraud in the corporate sector.
5. Whistleblower Protection Act, 2013: Provides a mechanism to investigate alleged corruption and misuse of power by civil servants.

Governance Reforms

1. E governance Reforms such as Direct Benefit Transfers, Faceless Assessment schemes, e-auction of government resources etc.
2. Grievance Redressal Mechanism (GRM): Centralised platforms such as CPGRAMS have allowed citizens to lodge grievances.
3. Enactment of Right to Public Service Delivery Acts: Set of statutory laws that guarantee the timely delivery of public services to citizens and provide a mechanism for punishing public servants who fail to provide the service. Example: Rajasthan enacted the act in 2011.
4. Technology driven solutions: 'One Nation One Ration Card' and the 'Digital India Land Record Modernization Program' have leveraged technology to enhance public service delivery, reduce corruption and empower citizens.

International Cooperation

1. UN Convention Against corruption: Signatory countries are obligated to implement anti corruption measures and cooperate in investigation and prosecutions.
2. Financial Action Task Force (FATF): An intergovernmental body that sets international standards for combating money laundering and terror financing.
3. World Bank and International Monetary Fund (IMF): These institutions provide financial and technical assistance to developing countries to implement anti corruption reforms and strengthen governance.

Institutional Measures

1. Lokpal and Lokayukta Act, 2013: Establishment of an "ombudsman" to inquire into allegations of corruption against certain public functionaries.
2. Central Bureau of Investigation (CBI): Investigates cases related to corruption under PCA, 1988.
3. Enforcement Directorate (ED): Law enforcement agency responsible for enforcing economic law and fighting economic crime in India.
4. Central Vigilance Commission (CVC): Statutory body that supervises corruption cases in government departments.

2nd ARC RECOMMENDATIONS TO TACKLE CORRUPTION

Strengthening Anti-Corruption Measures

- Whistleblower Protection Act 2014: Amendments to enhance protection and incentives for whistleblowers which includes safeguarding them from harassment and providing financial rewards.
- Anti-corruption agencies: Strengthening the CVC and CBI in preventing and combating corruption by giving it more independence, resource and authority.

Reducing Discretion:

- Standard Operation Procedure (SOPs): Development of clear SOPs for government processes and services to minimize the discretionary powers of officials which reduces the scope for corruption and arbitrary decision making.
- Use of Technology: Leveraging technology and e-governance can reduce human interface and discretion in government transactions.

Police Reforms

- Police Accountability: Highlighted the need for comprehensive police reforms to enhance the integrity and effectiveness of law enforcement agencies.
- Community Policing: Promoting community policing can build trust between the police and the public, reducing oppurtunities for corruption and abuse of power.

Promoting Ethical Governance:

- Code of Ethics: Development of a code of ethics for public officials and employees to promote ethical behaviour.
- Citizen Charters: Encouraging government departments to adopt citizen charters can enhance accountability and improve public service delivery.

Public Awareness Campaigns:

- Media and Education: The commission suggested using media and educational institutions to create awareness about the detrimental effects of corruption and the importance of ethical conduct.

Strengthening Parliamentary Oversight.

- Parliamentary Committees: Strengthening the role of parliamentary committees in scrutinising government operations and expenditures can help in detecting and preventing corruption.

E governance and Digitalization

- **Digital Transformation:** Comprehensive digital transformation of government processes to reduce human intervention and oppurtunities for corruption.

Governance Reforms

- **Simplification of processes:** Adoption of 'single window system', minimizing hierarchial tiers, time limits for disposal etc.
- **Audit:** External periodic mechanism of 'audit' of complaints in offices having a large public interface.

PYQs Corner

(Write the Answer and Get Free Evaluation)

1. ''Corruption is the manifestation of the failure of core values in the society.'' In Your opinion what measures can be adopted to uplift the core values in the society? (2023, 10 Marks)
2. Whistle-blower, who reports corruption and illegal activities, wrongdoing and misconduct to the concerned authorities, runs the risk of being exposed to grave danger, physical harm and victimization by the vested interests, accused persons and his team. What Policy measures would you suggest to strengthen protection mechanism to safeguard the whistle-blower? (2022, 10 Marks)
3. "Non-performance of duty by a public servant is a form of corruption" Do you agree with this view? Justify your answer. (2019, 10 Marks)
4. "Corruption causes misuse of government treasury, administrative inefficiency and obstruction in the path of national development." Discuss Kautilya's views. (2016, 10 Marks)
5. It is often said that poverty leads to corruption. However, there is no dearth of instances where affluent and powerful people indulge in corruption in a big way. What are the basic causes of corruption among people? Support your answer with examples. (2014, 10 Marks)

15 Public Service Delivery

66

"Efficient public service delivery is the cornerstone of a strong democracy. When citizens can easily access essential services, they feel empowered and contribute more effectively to society."

CITIZEN EMPOWERMENT | REDRESS SATISFACTION | CAPACITY ENHANCEMENT

CITIZEN'S CHARTER | PUBLIC GRIEVANCE REDRESS | SERVICE DELIVERY CAPABILITY

INTEGRATED APPROACH

CONCEPT OF PUBLIC SERVICE

- Public Services are essential services provided by the government or a designated body for the benefits of all citizens.
  - They address the basic needs and well-being of a Society and are crucial for a functioning democracy.

Example:

- Essential infrastructure such as roads, bridges, public transportation system, etc.
- Social services such as education, healthcare, public housing etc.
- Safety and Security: Police, fire departments, national defense etc.

Key attributes of Public Service

- Providing essential services to the citizens (Citizen-centricity)
- Intangible benefits by improving the quality of life for all citizens
- Multi-stakeholder public service delivery but largely government led.
- Funded through taxes, user fees combination of both.
- Operate within a complex legal & administrative framework.
- Monopolies i.e. provided by a single entity to ensure efficiency (Eg-Indian Railways).
- Building a thriving welfare state (Eg-DPSPs)
- Guided by principles and a commitment to the public good
- Obligatory (not voluntary) for the government and other actors.
- Accessible and affordable for all citizens, regardless of income or social status.
- Vital for the effective functioning of the society.
- Not primarily driven by profit.

Philosophical Foundation of public Service

Social Contract theory (T. Hobbes, John locke	• A Social contract exists between the government and the people under which citizens surrender some individual liberties in exchange for the government providing Security, law & order and essential services. • Public service delivery becomes a manifestation of this social contract

•Public Services play a crucial role in maximising happiness and well-being for the greatest number of people by providing essential services like education, healthcare & infrastructure leading to a better quality of life for all.	Utilitarianism (Jeremy Bentham, J.S. Mill)

Social Justice	• Public Services serve as a tool for promoting social justice by ensuring access to basic necessities and minimizing inequalities.
Rights Based Approach	• Emphasizes fundamental human rights such as access to education, healthcare and a decent standard of living. • Public Service delivery becomes an obligation of the state to uphold these rights and ensure all citizens can fulfil their potential.

Public Servant → • Dedication to serving the needs of others
→ • Works for the benefit of the people, not private interests.

• A public servant is a person who works for the government or a designated body to deliver public services.

• They are entrusted with the responsibility of using their skills and expertise to serve the public good, not for personal gain.

PUBLIC SERVANTS

POLITICIANS	CIVIL SERVANTS	CIVIL SOCIETY	OTHERS
Public representatives who make policies and law	Appointed by govt. to implement its policies & laws	Voluntary groups that cobilize & work for common cause	Judiciary, Media Military, Technocrats

How are civil servants different from public servants

1. Profession: Civil service is a profession & not a voluntary initiative like civil society or movement like that of politicians.
 • Civil servants are supposed to adhere to the norms of professionalism like specialisation, objectivity, efficiency etc which is not mandatory for other public servants.

2. Appointment: Civil servants are appointed through a merit based exam process such as UPSC conducts examination to select IAS/IFS/IPS officers in a free and fair manner, whereas other public servants such as politicians are mostly elected through the electoral process.

3. Career-Oriented Job profile: Civil servants enjoy assured career advancements and job security which is not available for other public servants such as politicians.

4. Code of Conduct: There is a prescribed code of conduct that civil servants must follow while discharging his duty which is not generally applicable to public servants.
 Eg- Civil servants should adhere to strict political neutrality whereas other public servants such as civil society organisations can take political sides.

QUALITY OF SERVICE DELIVERY

Public service delivery in the present times is not just the responsibility of the government. Instead, a network of multiple actors (government, market and civil society) collaborates and actively participate to ensure 5E's in public service delivery.

NGOs + Self Help Groups

Civil Society

State

Market

- Govt Schools;
- Water Supply
- Govt Schools
- Sanitation
- National Defense
- PDS System

- Private Schools,
- Private hospitals,
- Private DISCOMs
- Telecom
- PPP projects

- Effective: Service must address the intended purpose and achieve positive outcomes (Focus on measurable results).
- Efficient: Services should be delivered with minimal complexity, delays or bureaucratic hurdles.
- Equitable (Inclusive): Ensuring fairness and equal access to services for all citizens, regardless of background or socio-economic status.
- Economy: Optimum utilisation of the resources - human, financial and technological resources to achieve the best possible outcomes
- Ethical: Client-Centric, transparent and responsive public service delivery.

- Quality of service delivery is a holistic concept which essentially means that right services are provided to the right people in the right manner.
- Government often acts as the dominant service provider and Citizen is the highest client that is to be served with the highest possible quality in return for their contribution to the government in the form of taxes, fees or other user charges.

- Changing nature of service delivery

Aspect	From	To
Approach	Top-down	Multi-directional
Actors	Only Government	Multi-stakeholders
Local needs	One size fits all	Tailored approach
Role of Citizens	Passive Beneficiaries	Active participants
Example	PDS System, Mid Day Meal, etc	NFSA Act, RTE Act

Why Quality Service Delivery matters?

1. Right based approach and Civil Society activism led to the increased demand of quality service delivery. Eg- Certain public services like education, food, healthcare are increasingly recognised as rights of the citizens and not as welfare procedures. — RTE Act 2009; NFSA Act, 2013.

2. Social upliftment: Reliable access to public services like education, healthcare and Social welfare programs is essential for improving lives and creating opportunities.

3. Fosters public trust and enhanced legitimacy of the state.

4. Failure of quality service delivery can lead to discontent and Social unrest. Eg- Protests erupted in several Indian cities like Chennai and Bangalore in 2019 and 2023 due to water shortages.

5. Value for Taxpayer Money: Citizens contribute financially through taxes and expect a reasonable return on their investment in form of quality services. Eg- DBT has reduced the corruption and leakages in various welfare schemes along with increased effectiveness of Service delivery.

6. Faster economic growth: India needs a robust infrastructure with reliable electricity, connectivity (roads, internet) and other services for a sustainable high economic growth. Eg- India's logistics cost is around 14% of India's GDP which is affecting export competitiveness and thereby hampering India's economic growth.

7. Globalisation. In a globalised world, India needs to compete for investments and talent which necessitates meeting international standards of good governance. Eg- Improving service delivery, like streamlining business registration processes can lead to ease of doing business in India which can attract investments.

Hallmarks of Good Quality Service Delivery in Government

- Effective Grievance Redressal: Eg-3 Tier Grievance redressal mechanism under Consumer Protection Act, 2019
- Timeliness: Response to RTI requests within 30 days.
- Transparency: RTI Acts
- Responsiveness: Passport Seva Program
- Participation: Gram Sabha, mygov.in
- Quality standard: Eg- National Health Mission has defined Service delivery standard.
- Convenience: Doorstep delivery of Service initiative in Delhi.
- Accountability - Mandatory social audit in MGNREGA
- Efficiency & Economy - DBT scheme etc
- Equality & Equity - Sugamya Bharat Abhiyan

Challenges in Quality Service Delivery in India

Policy Formulation

- Top down approach by the government without the involvement of other actors involved in governance process
- One-Size-Fits-all policy without incorporating the local needs.
- Lack of realistic and objective targets prevents the effective accountability of public officials.
- Policy paralysis especially at the times of coalition government
- Sustainability concerns: Ensuring long term financial and operational sustainability of service delivery programs remains a challenge.

Policy Implementation

- Human Resource constraints: Shortage of qualified and motivated personnel can lead to service delays and inefficiencies
  - A 2022 report by CAG highlighted staff shortages in various government departments.
- Lack of proper training (including sensitivity training) and skill development results into incapable workforce with an insensitive attitude.
- Bureaucratic Red tapism lead to long wait times, delay and frustration for citizens trying to access services.
- Corruption and leakages: Bribery and misuse of funds can divert resources away from service delivery, impacting quality and reach.
- Fragmented Governance: With multiple levels of government involved in service delivery, coordination issues can arise, leading to duplication of efforts and inefficiencies.
- Infrastructure Deficit: Poor infrastructure, like roads and electricity, creates logistical barriers to service delivery, especially in remote locations.
  - Lack of reliable electricity disrupts healthcare services in rural hospitals
- Digital Divide: limited internet access and digital literacy skills hinder access to online services, particularly in rural areas.
- Social Biases: Prejudices based on caste, gender, or religion can lead to discriminatory treatment in service delivery by officials.
- Poor implementation of Conduct Rules and Code of Ethics

Policy monitoring

- Poor accountability mechanisms within the bureaucracy can lead to a lack of motivation to improve service delivery.

- **Ineffective grievance redressal mechanisms** can discourage citizens from reporting poor Service quality or Corruption.
- **Non-incorporation of the policy feedback** from the Jan Sunwais (Public hearing) or audit reports resulting into the continuation of poor service delivery.
- **limited public awareness** about available Services and entitlements can prevent citizens from claiming their rights.

The 5 Gap framework, also known as the Service Quality gap Model, can be a Valuable tool for understanding and improving public Service delivery in India.

Gap 1: The Citizen Expectation Gap: This exists between what citizens expect from public Services and what the government perceives those expectations to be:
Eg- Authorities focus on building new schools (government's perception) with addressing teacher shortages or curriculum relevance (Citizen expectation), hindering learning outcomes.

Gap 2: The Service Design and Standards Gap: This happens when there is a disconnect between the Service standards government sets and the actual design of the Service delivery System.
Eg- RTI Act mandates a response within 30 days (Service quality standards). However, delays due to bureaucratic hurdles (Service delivery design) creates a gap.

Gap 3: The Service Performance Gap: This arises when the designed Service delivery System fails to meet the established Service standards.

Gap 4: The Communication Gap: This Occurs when there is a mismatch between what the government communicates about its Services and the actual Service delivery. Eg- Government campaigns advertise Speedy Passport renewal (Communication). However, outdated online Systems (Service delivery) create delays, causing frustration.

Gap 5: The Citizen perception Gap: This is the most crucial gap, representing the difference between citizen expectations and their perceptions of the actual Service delivery. Eg: A citizen has had a negative experience in a public hospital, facing long wait times and limited communication from doctors. Even with improvements in staffing and infrastructure, this Citizen might Still perceive public healthcare as unreliable due to past experiences.

Reforms taken to improve public Service delivery

REFORMS

Policy and Institutional Reforms

- Multistakeholder approach: PPP model, NGO participation (GONGOs)
- Transformational approach: JAM Trinity, DBT scheme
- Anti-corruption Institutions: Lokpal and Lokayuktas.
- Rights-based approach: Right to public Service Acts (MP was 1st state)

Governance Reforms

- Transparency and Accountability: Citizen charter, RTI Acts, Social Audits
- Training and capacity building: Mission Karmayogi.
- Excellence in public service delivery: Sevottam Model
- E-governance Initiatives: Digital India, E-Kranti
- Decentralisation & Delegation: PRI System
- Performance Measurement: 360° Appraisal System

Citizen-Centric Reforms

- Citizen's participation at all levels: Gram Sabha, Swachh Bharat Abhiyaan, Jan Sunwai
- Use of Social media: Twitter Seva, Twitter Samvad.

Other reforms to be taken

- Inculcation of Public Service Ethos in the institutions and individuals such as empathy and compassion.
- Social accountability must complement the Traditional Accountability Process.
- Periodic review of procedures, methods, rules and regulations by removing barriers and reformulation of acceptable practices for expeditious service delivery.
- Privatisation and outsourcing for better service delivery which is likely to improve efficiency and quality of government services.

UTILISATION OF PUBLIC FUNDS

- Public fund is a money that the government generates to provide goods and services to the general public.
- It is held by the government as a custodian and not as an owner.
- Judicial and effective utilisation of public funds is very crucial for development as well as providing minimal essential services in a developing democracy like India.
- Budget 2024-25 estimate of revenue and expenditure is given below:

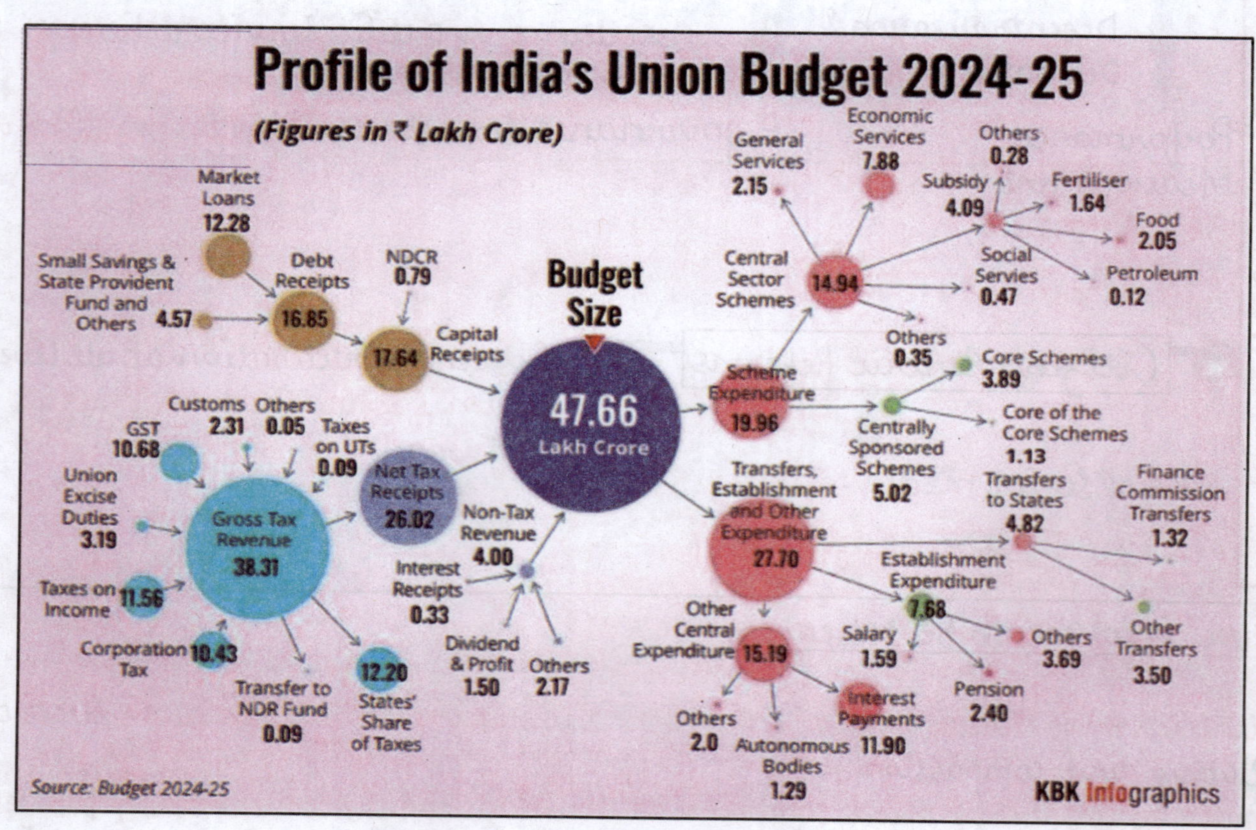

Principles of Public fund utilisation

- Lawfulness (Budgetary approvals)
- 4Es (Efficiency, Effectiveness, Economy and Equity)
- Fairness (Interest of marginalised Sections of Society)
- Predictability (Long term Planning such as FYPs)
- Sustainable use Eg-Free power leads to overuse of water
- Openness and Transparency (Pre-Budget consultations)
- Accountability (CAG Audit, Parliamentary committees, RTI Act)
- Interest (Code of conduct and Code of Ethics)
- Optimal utilisation (PM Gati Shakti Platform)
- Public Participation (MGNREGA)

Ethical Issues in Public fund utilisation

Ethical Issues

1. Fairness and Resource Allocation:

- **Business Bailouts:** Do bailouts encourage inefficient businesses or protect vital economic functions?
- **Taxation:** Do tax structures burden lower income earner disproportionately?

2. Transparency and Accountability:

- **Government promotion:** Do government publicity campaigns serve the public interest, or political agendas? Are public funds allocated based on genuine needs, not political expediency?
- **Loss making PSUs:** Are publicly funded enterprises evaluated for efficiency and restructuring? Can resources be diverted from PSUs to support more productive investments

3. Prioritization and Social Welfare:

- **Resource Distribution:** How do investments in health, defense, and research balance each other?
- **International aid:** How does international aid address domestic poverty & inequality? Are transparent mechanisms in place to monitor and ensure the effectiveness of aid?

4. Combating Corruption: Erosion of Trust and Development: How does corruption in public fund management undermine public trust? How can a culture of integrity & accountability be fostered within the government

Existing Framework for Effective utilisation of public Funds

- To maintain transparency in utilisation of public funds several procedures exist, such as the provision of presenting and passing the budget each year in the Loksabha
- Further enhanced institutional mechanisms like CAG financial audits which assess the economy, efficiency and effectiveness of funds spent.
- To institutionalise financial discipline, FRBM Act has been passed. Direct Benefit Transfer, use of Aadhar for welfare schemes etc. are also an effort towards ensuring efficiency in utilisation of public funds.
- For transparency in Direct Benefit Transfer, a comprehensive payment, receipt and accounting network is maintained through the Public fund management Systems. (PFMS).

Reasons for under-utilisation / mis-utilisation of public funds

POLITICAL REASONS	• **Inefficient Planning and Budgeting**: Delays in finalising budgets or poorly designed programs with unrealistic goals can lead to unspent funds. • **Policy paralysis**: Delays, inaction and an inability to make clear decisions by government waste time and resources. • **Political rivalry**: Competition between politicians can lead to a lack of cooperation and hinder development efforts. • **Political interference** to allocate funds to projects based on political favors or personal connections, rather than on objective criteria and public need • **Politicised projects**: Disruptive protests can delay projects and increased costs. • **Lack of political will** can lead to programs like MPLADS being underutilised. • **Ineffective procurement practices**: Lax regulations or biased bidding processes can lead to inflated contracts or awarding projects to unqualified companies, resulting in a waste of public resources.
SOCIAL REASONS	• **Corruption apathy**: A societal acceptance of corruption can lead to a lack of public pressure to hold officials accountable. • **Ineffective education**: Educational systems may not adequately emphasize values like honesty and integrity. • **Inequality**: Social and economic disparities can create incentives for individuals to prioritize personal gain over public good.

ADMINISTRATIVE REASONS	• Bureaucratic Red-tapism: Unnecessary regulations, paperwork, and slow procedures slow down project implementation. • Lack of effective transparency and inadequate auditing mechanisms prevent the accountability of public officials. • Lack of Co-ordination: Disjointed communication and collaboration between government departments can hinder project implementation and slow down spending. • Weak monitoring mechanisms to track progress and identify underutilized funds or areas for improvements. • Corruption: Embezzlement, bribery and misuse of funds for personal gain divert resources away from legitimate projects and hinder development. • Shortage of trained staff or inadequate infrastructure at the local level can make it difficult to absorb and utilise allocated funds effectively. • Fear of Scrutiny or lack of clear guidelines lead to a risk-averse approach and underutilisation of funds.

Recommendations for efficient use of Public Funds

1. Empowering citizens through the integration of Social audits into governance frameworks.
2. Strengthening the CAG's capacity to conduct comprehensive audits and equip parliamentary committees with the resources to effectively scrutinize flagged irregularities.
3. Shift from input based evaluations (focussing on resource allocated) to outcome based evaluations (assessing program effectiveness)
4. Cultivating an informed citizenry by strengthening RTI Act.
5. Leveraging e-Governance tools to provide real-time data on fund movement, enhancing transparency and enabling citizens to track progress on critical projects.
6. Enforcing cannons of financial propriety: Hold public officials accountable for adhering to ethical financial principles.
    - This includes exercising prudence with public funds, avoiding wasteful spending and prohibiting Self-Serving or discriminatory allocation of resources.
7. Enhancing Bureaucratic efficiency through capacity building and introducing the performance based management.
    - Shifting the focus from just following procedures to measuring outcomes and citizen satisfaction with service delivery.

8. Decentralisation: Empowering local governments to better understand and address the specific needs of their communities.
9. PPP: Collaboration with the private sector combining the strengths of both sectors leading to the optimal utilisation of resources.

Public Financial Management Systems (PFMS)

- India's Public Financial Management System (PFMS) is a web-based platform designed to improve transparency, efficiency and accountability in government spending.
- Developed and managed by the Controller General of Accounts (CGA), Ministry of Finance, Government of India.

Core Functions

- Track Funds: Monitors the release of funds for all government schemes, providing real time data on expenditure at various levels.
- Direct Benefit Transfers: Acts as a channel for electronically transferring payments directly to beneficiaries under various government schemes, reducing leakages and delays.
- Accounting and Reporting: Facilitates a comprehensive accounting and reporting system for government receipts, expenditures and financial health.
- Integration: Interfaces with financial management system of states, banks, and other external system to ensure seamless data exchange.

Benefits of PFMS

Transparency: Increased visibility into government spending promotes public trust and reduces opportunities for corruption.

Accountability: Provides a clear audit trail for tracking funds and holding officials accountable for their use

Targeted Delivery: Enables Direct Benefit Transfer. ensuring funds reach intended Beneficiaries directly.

Efficiency: Streamlined processes minimize bureaucratic hurdles and expedite the execution of government programs.

Informed Decision making: Real time data empowers officials to make informed decisions regarding resource allocation and program effectiveness

PYQs Corner

(Write the Answer and Get Free Evaluation)

1. Wisdom lies in knowing what to reckon with and what to overlook. An officer being engrossed with the periphery, ignoring the core issues before him, is not rare in the bureaucracy. Do you agree that such preoccupation of an administrator leads to travesty of justice to the cause of effective service delivery and good governance? Critically evaluate. (2022, 10 Marks)

2. What do you understand by the term 'public servant'? Reflect on the expected role of a public servant. (2019, 10 Marks)

3. Effective utilization of public funds is crucial to meet development goals. Critically examine the reasons for under-utilization and mis-utilization of public funds and their implications. (2019, 10 Marks)

4. What is meant by public interest? What are the principles and procedures to be followed by civil servants in the public interest? (2018, 10 Marks)

16 Work Culture

66

WORK CULTURE

- Work Culture refers to the way in which rules/regulations, policies, traditions/rituals, shared values, beliefs and practices contribute to the unique social and psychological environment in an organisation.
- It not only guides the way employees interact with each other and the organisation but also directs the functioning of an organisation.

Shared values and attitudes - what the company believes in and how employees are expected to approach their work
Eg- A company might value creativity over teamwork

Behaviours - How employees are expected to communicate, collaborate and dress. Eg- Formal or casual dressing.

Expectations - Unspoken rules about what's expected. Eg- working hours, taking breaks etc.

Factors influencing Work Culture

HISTORY

- Legacy of Colonial rule: The hierarchical structures and emphasis on following established procedures prevalent during the British rule continue to influence work culture in some sectors especially the public sector.
- Family-owned Business: Foster a paternalistic work environment where loyalty and respect for elders are valued highly. Eg-TATA group exemplifies this culture

NATURE OF SECTOR

- Industry standards: Work cultures can be influenced by industry norms and expectations.
- Certain sectors such as IT or Finance demands a fast paced, deadline driven work culture with a focus on innovation and collaboration.
- Civil Services responsible for public service delivery, prioritizes adherence to rules and regulations, resulting in a more cautious & detail oriented work style.

LEADERSHIP STYLE

- Authoritarian, democratic or collaborative leadership styles all influence company culture.
- The values and ethical principles upheld by leadership set the tone for the entire organisation.
- Decision making: Top down decision-making can lead to a culture of fear & disengagement while collaborative approaches can foster ownership & motivation

SOCIETY'S CULTURE

- Collectivism: Indian Society emphasizes group harmony and cooperation which can translate into a strong sense of teamwork & collaboration within Organisation.
- Power Distance: India scores high on power distance index, indicating acceptance of hierarchical structures and less questioning of authority.

Public vs Private Work Culture

Dimension	Public Sector	Private Sector
Goal Orientation	• Focuses on public good and service delivery. • Efficiency is important, but not the primary driver	• To generate profit for the company's owners. Efficiency and meeting financial targets are crucial.
Work Style	• Bureaucratic and process-oriented (compliance of rules and regulations). • Hierarchy can be more rigid, leading to slower decision making • There might be a stronger emphasis on work life balance	• Result Oriented work environments can be more competitive and demanding. • long hours and tight deadlines might be more common.
Innovation	• Slow Innovation due to risk aversion and bureaucratic hurdles	• open to innovation and calculated risk to stay ahead in market.
Job Security and Advancement	• Offer greater job security with well-defined career paths and benefits. • Promotions might be based on Seniority.	• lower job security and advancement often depend on performance and achieving specific goals.
Compensation	• Salaries might be lower than in private sector	• Compensation packages can be more competitive, with higher base salaries and bonuses tied to performance.
Demerits	• Leads to complacency, non-Performance, redtapism, risk averse behaviour, insensitive to the client's demands	• Priority to productivity over the principles and therefore, lacks ethical foundation. Often leads to the exploitation of workers and poor working conditions.

Indian vs Western Work Culture

Aspect	Indian Culture	Western culture
Hierarchy and Respect	• Emphasis on hierarchy and respect. Clear hierarchical structure with well-established authority. Titles and formalities play a significant role. Decision making often involves consultation with higher-ups.	• Emphasis on open communication and a flatter hierarchy. Decision-making processes may be more decentralised.
Relationship building and Teamwork	Strong emphasis on building personal connections. Collaborative and friendly atmosphere. Teamwork is highly valued. Decisions made collectively. Success attributed to the entire team's efforts.	• Emphasis on individual achievements. Recognition of personal accomplishments. Success attributed to individual efforts rather than the collective team.
Work-life Balance	• Shift towards recognising the importance of work-life balance. Growing awareness of employee well-being. Desire to establish a healthier equilibrium between professional and personal life	• Emphasis on structured work hours. Clear distinction between professional and personal time. Time management is crucial.
Regional Diversity	• Significant influence of regional variations. Each region contribute unique flavors and practices. Fosters an environment of inclusivity and adaptability. Professionals encouraged to appreciate and learn from different customs and traditions.	• May exhibit more standardised practices influenced by broader cultural context. less influenced by regional differences.
Efficiency and Management	• Shift towards recognising the importance of efficiency and productivity	• Emphasis on efficiency and productivity. Work hours structured. Time management is crucial
Cultural Homogeneity	• Diverse regional variations contribute to cultural diversity	• May exhibit more standardised practices influenced by broader cultural context

Features of good work culture

A positive work culture fosters a productive and satisfying work environment for employees, leading to higher morale, better performance, and ultimately organisational success.

Social/Emotional Well-being	• Mutual respect and Collaboration: Requires values of tolerance, teamwork, respectfulness etc. Eg- Chennai-based zoho corporation is known for its flat hierarchy and collaborative culture. • Fairness and objectivity: Merit-based compensation and advancement (not personal biases). Eg- Performance evaluation and improvement programs by many companies. • Open and transparent communication across all levels: Top down, Bottom up, and peer to peer fosters trust, allows for better decision making and helps identify and address grievances. • Recognition and appreciation of the employee's work motivates them and boost their morale.
Mental Well-being	• Commitment to efficiency: Timely completion of the work (More important in the public administration). • Punctuality: Reflects a professional attitude and commitment to one's role which enhances the productivity of an organisation. • Client responsiveness: Providing prompt, courteous service to clients builds trust and loyalty. Eg- The Taj Group of Hotels prioritizes exceptional customer service. • Empowerment of employees to take ownership of their work fosters a sense of accountability and fuels creativity and innovation.

Supportive workplace	• Participative decision-making: Creates a sense of ownership and increases their commitment to achieving organisational goals. Eg- HUL encourages employee participation through suggestion boxes and feedback mechanisms. • Diversity, Equity and Inclusion (DE&I): Embraces diversity and create a welcoming environment which includes fair treatment, equal opportunities, and a sense of belonging for all employees regardless of background or identity. • A clean, well equipped and safe work environment with comfortable workplaces enhances employee well being and productivity.
Work-life Balance	• Acknowledges the importance of personal life and encourages employees to maintain a healthy balance. This reduces stress and burnout, leading to engagement and productivity Eg: Flexible work arrangements, parental leave etc.
Physical Well-being	Promoting physical well-being can lead to improved health and reduced absenteeism. Eg: CEO of Zerodha prioritizes physical well-being and is open about his fitness routines, including early morning workouts

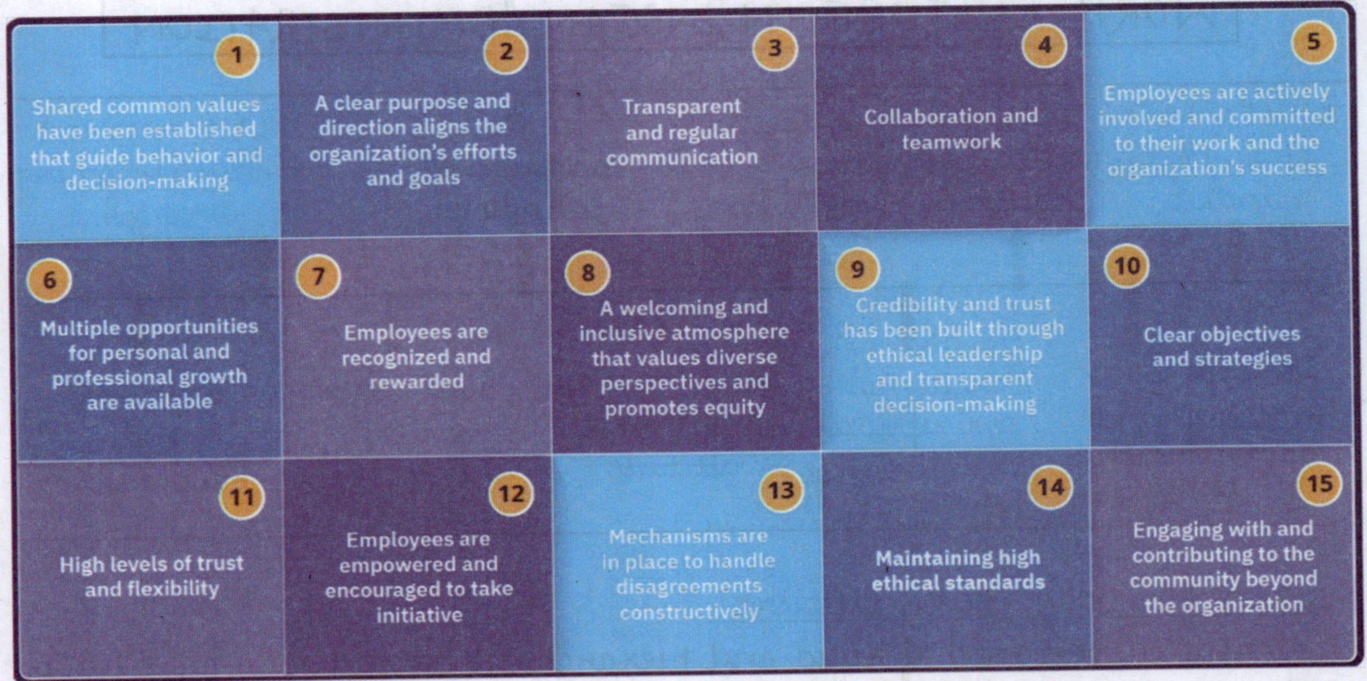

Significance of Ethical Work Culture

- Builds trust in a competitive market resulting into customer loyalty.
Eg: Dabur, known for its commitment to using natural ingredients and traditional practices.
- Minimises risk associated with scandals or corruption
- Boosts investor confidence and investors are more likely to back companies with a strong ethical reputation.
- Sound decision making aligned with company's ethical values.
- Boosting employee satisfaction and loyalty which translates into enhanced productivity of an organisation.
- Attracts the top talent in today's competitive job market. This also leads to lower turnover and a more stable workforce.
- Enhanced brand image and higher customer acquisition which directly contributes to the business financial profit.
- Setting a good example of a just and responsible business environment which can ripple outwards, encouraging other organisations to adopt ethical conduct
- Lowers the regulatory risks due to increased compliance of laws & rules.
- Unethical work culture can lead to corporate bankruptcies and frauds.
Eg- Lehmann Brothers crisis, Satyam crisis etc

WORK CULTURE IN INDIAN ADMINISTRATION

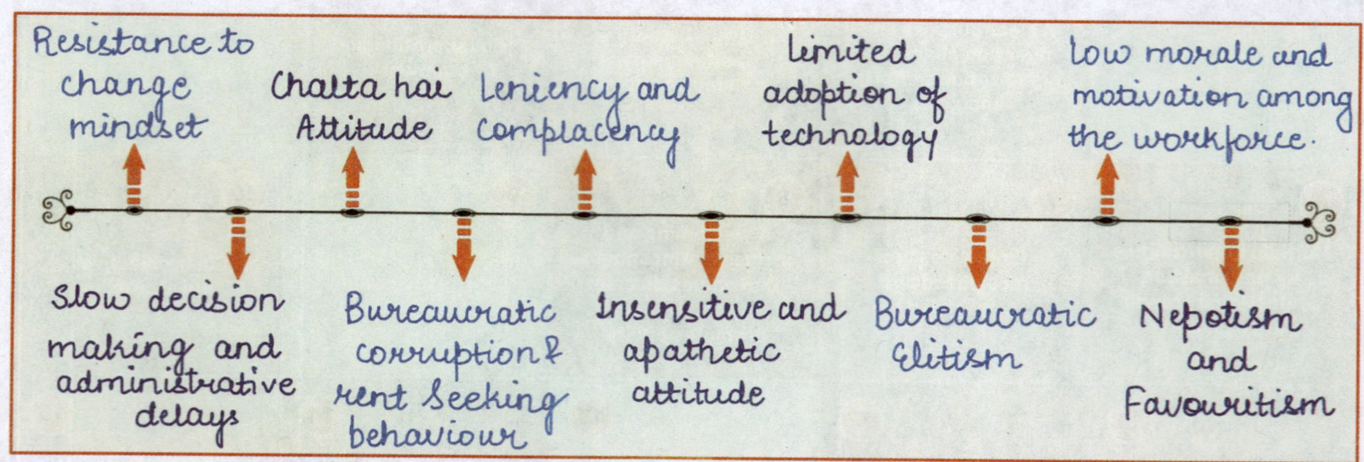

Reason for poor work culture

1. Colonial inheritance of rigid and hierarchical bureaucracy have led to a slow and combersome work environment.

2. Lack of objective performance evaluation sytem demotivates high performers as there are no clear rewards or recognition for good work.
3. Strong Job security can lead to employees taking their positions for granted, regardless of performance.
4. Multiple bureaucratic approvals to get any project approved by the government resulted into delayed decision making.
5. Risk aversion with a culture of playing it safe and avoiding blame. This discourages innovative solutions and can lead to a "Check-the-box" mentality where employees focus on completing tasks without considering improvements.
6. Focus on rules over outcomes: Strict adherence to rules can sometimes hinder the achievement of desired outcomes.
7. Limited resources for training, technology and infrastructure upgrades.
8. Bureaucratic disconnect between the administration and the people it serves, with a lack of responsiveness to citizen concerns.
9. Uninformed Public: A public unaware of their rights and how to hold the government accountable creates an environment where employees are less pressured to perform well.
10. Seniority over merit: Promotions based solely on experience can lead to less qualified individuals in leadership roles, reducing overall effectiveness.
11. Slow promotion and stagnation with limited opportunities for advancement based on performance can lead to a sense of demotivation and lack of drive to excel.
12. Poor accountability mechanisms such as inadequate implementation of Citizen charters, ineffective grievance redressal mechanism, weak institutional mechanism etc
13. Conflict between managers and sub-ordinates can lead to logjams, stagnation and loss of productivity.
14. Inadequate focus on sensitivity training hinders the development of foundational values such as empathy and compassion.

Ways to Improve Work culture in Indian Bureaucracy

Citizen-Centric Reforms	• Improving communication and feedback mechanisms. Eg - CM Helpline, Twitter Samvad etc. • Flexible arrangements for work life balance. Eg. Paternity leaves • Public awareness about the rights and duties of the citizens • Enhance people's participation to hold public authorities accountable.

Policy Reforms	• Right to Public Service Acts: Madhya Pradesh Public Services Guarantee Act, 2010 Sets time limit for service delivery. Similar acts across India can hold employees accountable and improve service quality. • Simplifying procedures and approvals can reduce redtape and expedite decision making. Eg - Single window clearance system such as India Customs Single window. • Adoption of private sector practices which can include performance targets, managerial autonomy, performance linked pay etc.
Institutional Reforms	• Implementation of performance feedback with clear benchmark can drive improvement: A 2017 study by the World Bank found that performance based incentive in Indian bureaucracy led to a 21% increase in tax collection. • Performance based promotions and incentives can motivate employees to excel and reward high performers. Eg - Performance Related Incentive Schemes (PRIS) adopted for Department of Space. • Promote Empathy. Equipping civil servants with these skills can enhance public interaction and build trust. • Skill Development and Training Programs for the civil servants with special focus on sensitivity training. Eg - Mission Karmayogi. • Encouraging innovation and risk taking - Eg - National Award for Excellence in Public Administration. • Transformational leadership to promote collaborative and result-oriented leadership styles
Governance Reforms	• Expansion of E-governance initiatives can improve efficiency, transparency and accessibility. Eg - DigiLocker, Government e-Marketplace. • Adopting the excellence in Service delivery model. Eg - ARC-7 Step model along the lines of Sevottam Model • Public Hearing: Expanding on RTI's Success, regular public hearings like Jan Sunwai program can address grievances effectively. • Strengthen the accountability mechanisms such as infusing greater powers and autonomy as 5C's - Courts, CVC, CBI, CIC, CAG.

Administrative reforms taken to improve work Culture

- 360 Degree Performance Evaluation (also known as Multi-Source Feedback) This approach gathers feedback from multiple stakeholders (Supervisers, clients, colleagues, etc.) to create a well-rounded assessment of individual performance. Eg- Indian Navy is implementing a new 360-degree appraisal mechanism for officers being considered for promotion.
- Compulsory retirement: This policy aims to enforce accountability and promote a culture of high performance by targeting underperforming and unethical employee.
- Biometric attendance implemented in Indian government offices to ensure punctuality and discipline among employees, fostering a more productive work environment
- Gender empowerment: Measures like maternity benefits, creches and anti-harassment committees aim to create a safe and supportive workplace for women, fostering a more diverse and inclusive culture.
- Adoption of citizen Charter by various departments of the government.
- Digital India Mission spearheads the adoption of e-governance across departments.
- Lateral entry scheme (2018): Fresh perspectives and best practices are brought in by recruiting experienced professionals from the private sector to government positions.
- PM's Awards for Excellence in Public Administration to recognize and honour outstanding civil servants for their exceptional work.
- Mandatory Social audits for MGNREGA program
- Performance Monitoring Platforms such as PRAGATI to enable leaders to oversee projects, identify issues, and ensure accountability across government organisations.

Success Stories

- Resourceful and Innovation (Indian value of Jugaad): ISRO's work culture is admired globally for its focus on productivity, cost-effectiveness, team-work and quality. (A culture of "frugal innovation")
- Employee well-being: Google India prioritizes employee well-being with a focus on a healthy work environment, freedom in workplace design etc
- Remote work champions: Automattic (US), the company behind WordPress, thrives on a fully remote work model, trusting employees and promoting global talent.

NEW TRENDS IN WORK CULTURE

FIRE Movement | 70Hr/week Debate | Hustle Culture | Moonlighting.

1. FIRE Movement

FIRE stands for Financial Independence, Retire Early. It is a movement popularised in the United States that focuses on achieving financial independence at a much younger age than traditional retirement (typically around 65).

Financial Independence

This means having enough passive income (from investments, rental properties, etc.) to cover your living expenses without needing a job

Retire Early.

Once you achieve financial independence, you can choose to retire from your traditional job and pursue other passion or interest.

Reasons for FIRE Movement Catching up in India	Challenges of FIRE Movement in India
1. Shifting priorities of millenials and GenZ to personal experiences and financial Security over owing a big house or car.	1. Societal expectations to support extended families which make achieving FIRE goals difficult.
2. Remote work opportunities allows professional to achieve location independence	2. Average salaries is lower in India than western countries.
3. Increased financial literacy among the young professionals to save and invest aggressively early	3. Concerns of job Security or huge informal workforce.
4. Dis-satisfaction with the inflexible traditional work culture	4. High cost of education can impact savings potential.

3-Pronged approach for Indians to adapt FIRE

1. Focus on early savings and invest early
2. Prioritizing needs over wants for mindful spending and higher saving rates
3. Side Hustles and creating multiple income streams

2. 70 Hr/Week Debate

Infosys founder Narayan Murthy sparked a debate by proposing a 70-hour workweek for young Indians to boost national productivity.

Hustle Culture

- Hustle culture is a pervasive mindset that emphasizes constant work, striving, and busyness as the key to success.
- It glorifies long hours, prioritizing work over personal life and the relentless pursuit of achievement.
- It often emphasizes self-reliance and individual achievement, placing the onus of success solely on the person and the willingness to hustle

Arguments for 70Hr/Week Debate	Argument against 70Hr/Week Debate
1. Increased productivity: India's productivity lags behind China and Japan and a longer week can address this gap. 2. Historical Examples: Murthy cited examples of countries like Japan and Germany that emphasized extended working hours after World War II to achieve rapid economic recovery. 3. Leveraging India's demographic dividend which offers a competitive workforce advantage and accelerate national development. 4. Skill development of employees to develop job-related skills and achieve mastery which consequently results into higher output	1. Decreased productivity: Studies show a significant decline in productivity after 50+work hour/week (Unsustainable 2. Countries moving towards 4-day week culture for producing optimal output. Eg- Germany, Belgium etc 3. Contemporary work landscape prioritises efficiency, output and innovation rather than the number of hours clocked in. 4. Work-life balance: Extremely long work hours can lead to burnout, decreased job satisfaction, and a neglected personal life. 5. Health issues: Can lead to sleep disturbances, increased risk of heart disease, obesity, stress, anxiety etc 6. More concerning for working mothers which can hinder career advancement

Note: The average young Indian works 7.2 to 8.5 hours daily, which is already substantial. Uttrakhand has the highest average of 9.6 hours, still far below the proposed 70 hours.

WHO study on long working hours

- 745,000 people died from a stroke and heart disease associated with long working hours in 2016
- Working 55 hours or more per week is a serious health hazard
- Capping hours would be beneficial for employers since that has been shown to increase worker productivity.

Striving work-life balance in India

1. Leveraging Technology

- Utilize digital tools and AI to automate repetitive tasks
- Encourage employees to learn new skills relevant to emerging technologies.

2. Focus on output rather than the number of hours.

- Move away from a culture of presenteeism and evaluate performance based on results achieved.
- Provide employees with the necessary tools and resources to be efficient.

3. Growth and Career advancement

- Offer challenging opportunities by assigning tasks that promote growth and motivates young professionals
- Create a work environment built on trust and transparency and promote employees based on their skills and Contribution.

4. Prioritising well-being

- Encourage employees to take breaks and engage in activities that promote relaxation and well-being.
- Promote healthy sleep habits by encouraging employees to maintain a regular sleep schedules which is crucial for both physical and mental health.

3. Moonlighting

- Refers to the practice of holding a second job or running a side business while still employed at a primary job, typically done outside of the regular working hours.
- Debate: Premji (Wipro) in 2023 sparked a national debate by calling moonlighting "cheating" and firing 300 employees suspected for working for competitors while employed at Wipro.
  - Following Wipro's actions, other IT companies like Infosys and IBM India expressed similar concern about moonlighting and the potential impact on employee performance and data security.
- Prevalence: The rise of the gig economy, remote work opportunities and the growing need for supplemental income have all contributed to the increase in moonlighting in India.
- Legality: There's no specific law in India that explicitly prohibits moonlighting for most private-sector employees.
  - Employment contracts often have clauses on exclusivity or conflict of interest that can restrict moonlighting activities.
  - The Factories Act, 1948 restricts dual employment for factory workers

Ethical Issues regarding Moonlighting

Focus and Productivity: Higher fatigue and decreased focus on primary job can impact the performance raising ethical concerns about fulfilling employment obligations	Fairness and Flexibility: Strict limitations on moonlighting might be unfair to employees seeking additional income or skill development opportunities.
Potential conflict of interest which can lead to using company's resources for side hustle.	Issue of ensuring employees well-being along with maintaining higher productivity
Dishonesty with the employer about moonlighting activities	Issue of data security and confidential information

Open communication, clear policies of moonlighting and a focus on both employee well-being and company interests are essential for navigating this evolving workplace trend

PYQs Corner

(Write the Answer and Get Free Evaluation)

1. In the context of work environment, differentiate between 'coercion' and 'undue influence' with suitable examples. (2023, 10 Marks)

17 Western Moral Thinkers and Philosophers

66

Socrates

- **Classical Greek philosopher**, famous for his **Socratic method of questioning**, a technique which uses a series of questions to lead to a deeper understanding of the subject.
- **Teaching:** Seeking knowledge and living a virtuous life is the ultimate goal of life.
    - **Wisdom comes** from understanding one's own ignorance.

Ideas	Description	Relevance in India
Questioning Everything	• Socrates disrupted norms by critically examining prevalent ideas and fostering a scientific approach through rational inquiry.	• Indian jnana yoga and rigorous philosophical debates (shastras).
The world of Ideas	• He proposed two realms: the world of senses and the world of ideas, emphasizing knowledge over sensory experiences.	• Advaita Vedanta's view of ultimate reality (Brahman) beyond perception.
Practical Philosophy	• Philosophy should yield practical results for society's well-being, aiming for an ethical system based on reason rather than religion.	• Concept of dharma and righteous action (karma).
Self-examination	• Constant reflection on actions and their impact is crucial for strong moral reasoning.	• Self-study (svadhyaya) and introspection (vichara) for moral clarity and growth.
Knowledge as Virtue	• Knowledge, especially self-knowledge, is the most important virtue, leading to wisdom and happiness through the process of accepting ignorance, gaining knowledge, developing virtues, and achieving wisdom.	• Vidya (knowledge) as a virtue leading to wisdom (prajna) and liberation (moksha).
Moral Intellectualism	• No one knowingly acts immorally; true knowledge of good leads to good behavior.	• Ahimsa (non-violence) and satya (truthfulness).
Happiness through Action	• Everyone desires happiness. • Happiness depends not on external goods but how we use these external goods. • Happiness is pursued actively through virtuous behavior guided by knowledge, leading to a good life.	• Happiness (ananda) through virtuous actions guided by knowledge.
Leadership by the wise	• Wise individuals with exceptional knowledge and self-awareness should be leaders.	• Indian rishis and gurus, revered for their knowledge and self-awareness.

Speaking truth to Power	• Socrates questioned authority relentlessly, exemplifying intellectual integrity and courage in challenging the status quo.	• Gandhi and Vivekananda opposed oppression.

Socrates vs the State

- **Socrates' Challenge**: He encouraged his students to **question authority** in pursuit of knowledge.
- **Threat to Order**: State relies on **tradition**, **religion**, and **rule of law** for stability.
  - They saw Socrates as a threat to the established order.
- **Charges and Execution**: Accused of **impiety** and corrupting the youth, Socrates was sentenced to death.
  - He refused to compromise his beliefs and died by drinking hemlock.
- **Ethical Implications**:
  - **Individual vs. State**: The balance between individual freedom and state authority.
  - **Reason vs. Tradition**: The value of reason in questioning established traditions.
  - **Free Speech vs. Censorship**: The importance of free speech versus limitations imposed by the state.

Plato

- Plato student of Socrates and teacher of Aristotle, wrote a book named **'Republic.'**
- Plato was more of a theoretical thinker, recording his ideas in influential writings.

Plato Four Cardinal Virtues: Essential for individual happiness and a well-functioning society.

Virtue	Description	Relevance in India
Prudence (Practical Wisdom)	• **Reason as the Helm:** The ability to use clear thinking and sound judgment to navigate life's challenges. • It's like the captain steering the ship of your actions towards a virtuous destination.	• **Bhagavad Gita** emphasize making wise choices based on knowledge and understanding.
Temperance (Moderation)	• **Finding the Golden Mean:** Practicing self-control and avoiding extremes. • It's about finding the balance between indulgence and deprivation for a well-harmonized life.	• **Arthashastra** emphasizes just governance.
Courage (Fortitude)	• **Moral Bravery:** The strength to do what is right, even when it's difficult or unpopular. • It's standing up for your values and convictions, not fearing challenges in the pursuit of justice.	• **Soldier on the border** displays courage while defending the nation against external threats
Justice	• **Harmony Within and Without:** On an individual level, it's about aligning your internal desires with your sense of right and wrong. • Socially, it's about creating a fair and just society where everyone plays their part and receives their due.	• India emphasizes **yama (restraint) in spiritual practices: Yoga.**

Tripartite Soul and Virtues:

- Plato believed the human soul is composed of **three parts: reason, emotion and desire**.
- **Unity of Virtues:** Virtues are interconnected, and true virtue requires having all four in balance. A person lacking in one area would be deficient in all.
- Each virtue has a specific connection to one of these parts:

Soul Part	Description	Virtue
Reason	• The reasoning and intellectual part, striving for knowledge and truth.	**Prudence**
Emotion	• The emotional and passionate part, responsible for courage, ambition and anger.	**Courage (Fortitude)**
Desire	• The base desires and bodily needs, focused on pleasure and gratification.	**Temperance (Moderation)**
Justice is the ultimate virtue, achieved when all three parts of the soul work together in harmony.		

Justice in Society

Class		Description	Virtue
Guardians (Rulers)	• Philosopher-kings who govern the state, possessing wisdom and understanding of the forms	• Virtuous, selfless, committed to the common good, motivated by justice and wisdom	• Swami Vivekananda, who combined spiritual insight with social reform
Auxiliaries (Warriors)	• Warrior class responsible for defense, law enforcement, and maintaining order.	• Courage, discipline, loyalty, willing to sacrifice for the greater good	• Arjuna from the Mahabharata, epitomizing the virtues of this class
Producers (Artisans and Farmers)	• Engage in practical tasks like farming, craftsmanship, trade, and commerce	• Hard work, productivity, resourcefulness	• Vaishya caste in India, contributing to economic stability and prosperity

- **Harmonious Balance:** Plato believed a just society arises when the Guardians, Auxiliaries, and Producers work harmoniously, each fulfilling their unique roles.
- **India:** Concept of dharma emphasizes a similar balance.

Plato's vision of Governance

- It is based on a **meritocratic system** where the most qualified individuals lead based on their intellectual and moral virtues.
- It reflects Plato's belief in the importance of **rationality, virtue, and the pursuit of the common good** in creating an ideal society.

Aristotle

Virtue	Description	Relevance in India
Source of Knowledge	• **Empiricism**: Knowledge comes from experience and observation.	• **Education:** India's emphasis on practical learning (e.g., Skill India)
Ethics	• **Practical Science**: Apply knowledge for virtuous action, leading to true happiness (eudaimonia).	• **Concept of Dharma** (righteous duty)
Virtue	• **Habit and Practice**: Cultivate good habits to become a virtuous person.	• **Practice of yoga** disciplines the mind and body,
Moral Development	• **Practice**: Moral virtues are learned through repeated ethical choices.	• Guru-Shishya Parampara **(teacher-student tradition)**
Happiness (Eudemonia)	• **Reason and Virtue**: True happiness comes from living a virtuous life using reason, not just external factors.	• **Concept of moksha (liberation)** emphasizing self-knowledge, ethical living, and fulfilling one's potential for true happiness.

Doctrine of the Mean: Finding Balance in Virtue

- **Theme:** Virtue lies in a **balanced state** between two extremes → **excess and deficiency.**
- **Virtue as a Mean:** Imagine a continuum with an excess (vice) on one end and a deficiency (vice) on the other. The sweet spot in the middle represents virtue.
- **Examples:**
  - **Courage:** The mean between cowardice (deficiency) and recklessness (excess). A courageous person acts bravely but avoids foolishness.
  - **Temperance:** The mean between self-indulgence (excess) and insensibility (deficiency). A temperate person enjoys pleasures in moderation.
- **Not a Rigid Formula:** Mean is not a precise mathematical formula, it ay vary depending on the situation and the individual.

- **Practical Wisdom Matters:** Application of doctrine requires practical wisdom (phronesis) - the ability to make sound judgments in specific situations.
- **Similar philosophies:** Plato's Cardinal Virtues + Buddha's Middle Way + Dharma and Leadership

The Golden Rule (Doctrine of the Mean)

Deficiency (Vice)	Mean (Virtue)	Excess (Vice)
Sloth	Ambition	Greed
Cowardice	Courage	Rashness
Apathy	Composure	Irritability
Insensibility	Temperance	Self-indulgence
Stinginess	Generosity	Extravagance
Negligence	Prudence	Inconstancy
Envy	Righteousness	Malicious

Application of Doctrine of the Mean

1. Public Service:

- **Empathy vs. Duty:** Civil servants need empathy, but too much can hinder their ability to fulfil their duties, like land acquisition.
- **Transparency Dilemma:** Transparency is crucial, but excessive disclosure can breach confidentiality and lead to inaction.
- **Temperance and Tolerance allows** for flexibility, rationality, and inclusivity in decision-making.

2. Justice: Aristotle defined justice as giving people what they deserve. This avoids extremes - not giving someone enough or giving them more than is merited.

Aristotle Framework of Justice

Political Justice	Individual Justice	Distributive Justice	Corrective Justice
• Leaders should be **virtuous (wise and good)**. • He saw laws as **essential for a just society.** • **Ex:** Anti-discrimination laws promote fairness.	• This is a personal quality – consistently acting fairly. • **Ex:** A person who returns a lost wallet even if it has a lot of cash.	• Fair distribution of resources • **Ex: Progressive taxation.**	• Restores balance when someone is wronged. • **Ex: A cyberbullying lawsuit seeking to compensate** the victim and deter future bullying.

Aristotle divided Justice into two parts:

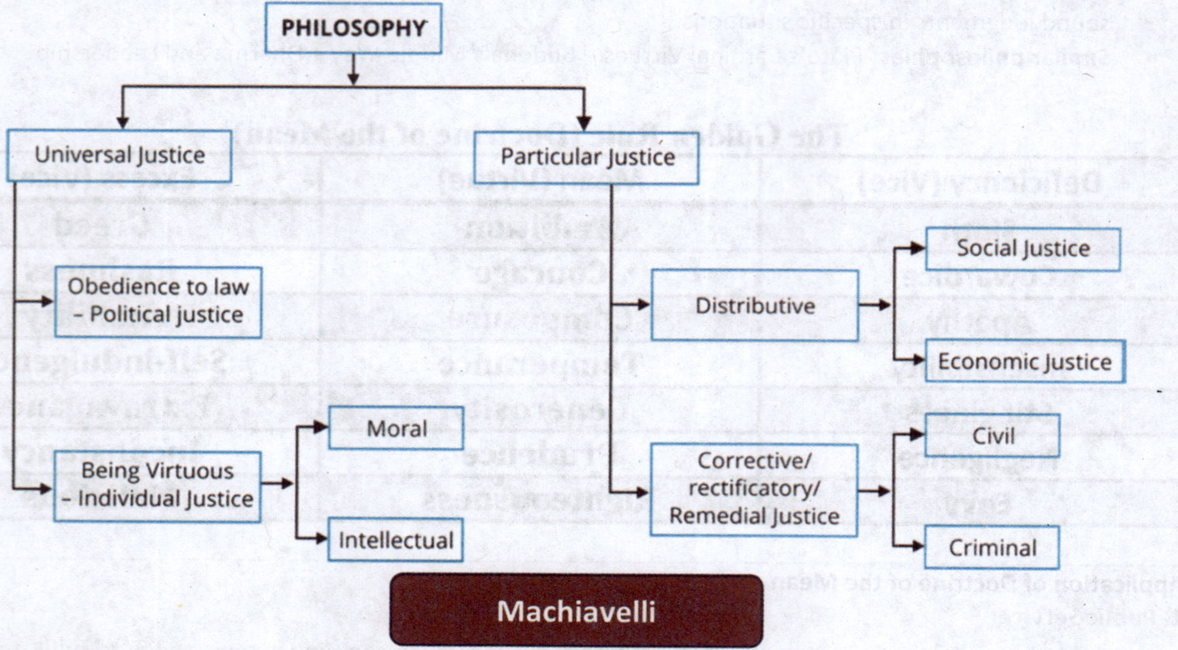

Machiavelli

Niccolò Machiavelli's key ideas challenging traditional views on ethics and politics:

- **Separating Ethics from Politics:** Rulers should prioritize maintaining power and stability, even if it means using traditionally immoral tactics.
  - **Ex:** Emergency (1975-1977), **Prime Minister Indira Gandhi suspended civil liberties** and suppressed dissent to consolidate power.
- **Moral Relativism:** The "ends justify the means" captures Machiavelli's perspective. Morality depends on context and consequences, not inherent rightness or wrongness.
  - **Ex:** Chanakya advised King Chandragupta Maurya to eliminate rivals for stability.
- **Pragmatism (realpolitik):** Leaders must focus on practical effectiveness rather than abstract ideals.
  - **Ex:** Sardar Patel used realpolitik to integrate princely states
- **Virtuous Prince:** He valued virtues in leaders—courage, decisiveness, and cunning—for effective governance.
  - **Ex:** Shivaji Maharaj exemplified courage, cunning, and strategic thinking in building an empire.

Machiavelli's The Prince (1513)

- **Power Above All**: Moral principles are tools, not absolutes. Actions are justified if they secure power.
- **Pragmatic Contracts**: Keeping agreements depends on their benefit to the ruler.
- **Fear Over Love:** A ruler inspires loyalty through fear, not love, for better control.
- **Outcomes Matter**: A ruler's worth is judged by results, not intentions.

Rousseau

- Rousseau's ***Discourse on Inequality*** and ***The Social Contract*** are cornerstones in contemporary political thought.
- **Impact:** Influence **western Europe**, including aspects of the **French revolution** and the development of modern political thought.
- **Philosophical Ideas:**

Ideas	Description
State of Nature	• He proposed people in the State were **self-sufficient, fairly solitary by choice,** sympathetic to others, and **peaceful.** • People are innocent and incapable of being **malicious (Morality not invented yet).** • When people move into society, human nature becomes **corrupted with growth of social interdependence**.

Private property	• It promotes greed and egotism.
Social Contract	• To **secure their liberty and well-being**, individuals enter into a hypothetical social contract. • This agreement establishes a **society and a legitimate government.**
General Will	• Social contract expresses the general will, which represents the **collective good of all citizens, not just special interests.** • It's the **foundation for just laws.**
Sovereignty of the People	• Ultimate power resides with the people as a whole, not with any individual ruler. • The government acts on behalf of the general will.
Individual Freedom and Obedience	• **Individuals surrender some freedoms** to the social contract but gain a different kind of freedom – civil liberty protected by law. • **By obeying just laws**, they are ultimately obeying themselves (the general will).
Right to Revolution	• If the **government fails to uphold the social contract** and the general will, the people have the **right to revolution and establish a new government.**

John Locke

- **Natural Law and Rights:** Locke believed in a universal moral law (**natural law**), discoverable through reason, that predates human governments.
    - Locke introduced the concept of inherent rights (life, liberty, property) existing before society.
    - This law grants inherent rights, like life, liberty, and property, to all individuals.
- **Empiricism:** Knowledge comes from experience and sensory observation, not just innate ideas or religious dogma.
    - We learn and understand the world through reason applied to our experiences.
- **Social Contract:** Similar to Hobbes and Rousseau, Locke saw government as arising from a **social contract**.
    - People agree to give up some freedoms to a government whose purpose is to protect their natural rights.
    - However, unlike Hobbes, Locke believed this **power is not absolute.**
- **Limited Government:** The government's authority is limited to protecting natural rights. If it fails to do so or violates these rights, the people have the right to overthrow it (**right to revolution**).
- **Consent to Govern:** Legitimate government requires the consent of the governed. People give up some rights to protect others.
- **Three Fundamental Rights:** Life, liberty, and property are core natural rights governments must protect.
- **Influence on America:** The U.S. Declaration of Independence reflects Locke's rights, with "pursuit of happiness" replacing "property."
- **Separation of Powers:** To prevent abuse of power, dividing legislative, executive, and judicial functions.
- **Religious Tolerance:** Government shouldn't impose a particular religion, and individuals should be free to practice their faith as long as it doesn't harm others.

J S Mill

***Utilitarianism* (1861):** Actions are morally right insofar as they promote the greatest happiness for the greatest number of people.

- **Moving Beyond Quantity:** Mill disagreed with Bentham's view that all pleasures are equal. He argued for **qualitative utilitarianism**, where pleasures differ in value.
- **Higher vs. Lower Pleasures:** Mill categorized pleasures as **higher** (intellectual pursuits) and **lower** (bodily pleasures).
    - He believed higher pleasures are more valuable.
- **Pain for the Greater Good:** Pain or sacrificing pleasure could be justified if it directly benefits the greater good.

- **Rules for Happiness:** It outlines basic principles to guide maximizing pleasure and minimizing pain.
- **Principle of Harm:** This primary rule states that only actions causing harm are wrong. People are free to act as long as they don't harm others.
- **Foundation for Environmental Ethics:** Humans are part of nature, and all species have a right to exist
- **Altruistic Hedonism:** Individual actions shouldn't harm society, advocating for a system where everyone benefits from each other's pursuit of pleasure (**universalistic hedonism**).
- **Defense of Free Expression:** Free expression allows for discovering truth and personal growth.
    - Even wrong ideas can help us refine our understanding through debate.

Immanuel Kant

- The most famous **deontological thinker**, emphasizing **duty-based ethics over consequences**.
- Focused on **the means (motive) over ends (purpose)**.
    - **Actions are justified** by following moral law, not their results.
- **Moral actions stem from a sense of obligation**, not self-interest or achieving the greatest good.
- **Kantianism (Duty Over Consequences)**: It emphasizes **reason and moral responsibility** in ethical decision-making. It focuses on following universal moral principles rather than individual desires or outcomes.

Concepts	Description	Relevance in India
Categorical Imperative	• Act according **to maxims (universal rules) that could be universal laws**, emphasizing the inherent rightness or wrongness of an action, independent of outcome.	• Aligns with the principle **of Satya (truth) in Sanatana Dharma,** guiding ethical behavior in Indian society.
Good Will	• The **only true good is a good will,** motivated by a sense of duty and a desire to do what's right, not by self-interest or external pressure.	• Resonates **with Seva (selfless service) in India**, where helping others is seen as a moral duty beyond personal gain.
Deontological Ethics	• Focuses on duty and moral obligation over consequences. • A **positive outcome** doesn't make an action moral if the motivation wasn't to do what is right.	• **Whistleblower Protection Act (2014)** encourages fulfilling the duty to expose wrongdoing despite consequences.
Kingdom of Ends	• **Humans are ends in themselves**, not means to an end. • We should treat each other with respect and dignity.	• **Indian Constitution guarantees** fundamental rights to all citizens, respecting everyone as an end in themselves.
Universalizability Test	• A **practical application of the Categorical Imperative**; consider if you'd be comfortable with everyone acting the way you're considering.	• Initiatives promoting academic integrity in schools and universities encourage considering the wider implications.

John Rawls

- **John Rawls'** ***A Theory of Justice*** **(1971)** proposes principles for creating a **well-ordered society**.
- **Aim:** To create a just society that balances individual liberty with social fairness, ensuring everyone has the opportunity to thrive.
- **Two Key Elements of Theory**
    1. **Benefits Members & Publicly Accepted Justice:** The society advances the good of its members and is governed by a **public conception of justice** that everyone accepts. This means everyone understands and agrees to the same principles of justice, and the basic social institutions uphold them.
    2. **Two types of circumstances that influence the need for justice:**

Circumstances	Description	Impact on Justice
Objective	Refers to general societal conditions.	**Moderate Scarcity:** Resources are not overly abundant or scarce, creating a need for fair distribution and cooperation.
Subjective	Refers to individual motivations.	**Conflicting Interests:** When individual interests regarding resources clash, the need for justice arises to ensure fair allocation.

- **Principles of Justice:** Through a thought experiment called the "original position," Rawls argues that rational people would agree to these two principles of justice:

Principle	Description	Key Points
Equal Liberty	• All individuals have basic liberties essential for human existence.	• These liberties are non-negotiable, even for potential greater good. • **Ex**: Freedom of speech, religion, and assembly.
Difference & Fair Equality of Opportunity	• Social and economic inequalities are arranged to benefit the least advantaged and promote equal opportunity.	• **Difference Principle:** Inequality is acceptable only if it improves the situation of the worst-off (**maximin principle**). • **Fair Equality of Opportunity:** Everyone has a fair shot at competing for positions and achieving success, requiring investments in education and healthcare.

PYQs Corner

(Write the Answer and Get Free Evaluation)

1. What do each of these quotations convey to you in the present context?
"Ethics is knowing the difference between what you have the right to do and what is right to do." – Potter Stewart (2022, 10 Marks)

2. What do each of these quotations convey to you in the present context?
Life doesn't make any sense without interdependence. We need each other, and the sooner we learn that it is better for us all." -Erik Erikson word (2021, 10 Marks)

3. What do each of these quotations convey to you in the present context?
"A system of morality which is based on relative emotional values is a mere illusion. A thoroughly vulgar conception which has nothing sound in it and nothing true." – Socrates (2020, 10 Marks)

4. What do each of these quotations convey to you in the present context?
"An unexamined life is not worth living." – Socrates (2019, 10 Marks)

5. "In looking for people to hire, you look for three qualities: integrity, intelligence, and energy. And if they do not have the first, the other two will kill you." – Warren Buffett
What do you understand by this statement in the present-day scenario? Explain. (2018, 10 Marks)

6. "Great ambition is the passion of a great character. Those endowed with it may perform very good or very bad acts. All depends on the principles which direct them." – Napoleon Bonaparte. Stating examples mention the rulers (i) who have harmed society and country, (ii) who worked for the development of society and country. (2017, 10 Marks)

7. Analyse John Rawls's concept of social justice in the Indian context. (2016, 10 Marks)

18 Indian Moral Thinkers, Philosophers and Reformers

Buddhist Ethics

Moral Judgment (Intention Matters): Actions are good or bad based on motivation behind them.		
Bad Actions (Akusal Kamma)	• Stem from greed, hatred, or selfishness.	• **Ex:** Lying to cheat someone out of money (driven by greed)
Good Actions (Kusala Kamma)	• Rooted in generosity, love, and wisdom	• **Ex:** Volunteering at Langar (driven by compassion).
Three Essentials for Life (→ Conditions for Enlightenment)		
Wisdom (Prajna)	• Right understanding leads to right intention.	• **Ex:** Studying Buddhist teachings to understand karma and suffering.
Ethical Conduct (Sila)	Right behaviour guided by right intention: • **Right Speech:** Speaking truthfully and kindly. • **Right Action:** Acting with non-violence and compassion. • **Right Livelihood:** Earning a living ethically. • **Right Effort:** Putting effort into good thoughts and actions.	• **Ex: Right Speech →** Avoiding gossip or using hurtful language. • **Ex: Right Action →** Choosing a career that doesn't harm others (e.g., healthcare). • **Ex: Right Livelihood →** Avoiding jobs that involve harming others (e.g., selling weapons). • **Ex: Right Effort→** : Practicing meditation to cultivate positive emotions.
Concentration (Samadhi)	Focused mental state for mindfulness and meditation.	
Pancasila (Five Precepts): Voluntary guidelines for a moral life		
No Killing	• Respecting all living beings	• **Ex:** Choosing a vegetarian diet to avoid harming animals.
No Stealing	• Taking only what is freely given	• **Ex:** Returning borrowed items on time.
No Lying	• Speaking truthfully and avoiding deception	• **Ex:** Being honest with friends and family.
No Sexual Misconduct	• Acting with respect and responsibility in relationships	• **Ex:** Maintaining fidelity in a committed relationship.
No Intoxicants	• Avoiding substances that cloud the mind and hinder clear thinking	• **Ex:** Avoiding excessive alcohol consumption.

Ten Demeritorious Deeds: Actions to avoid due to their negative consequences	
Bodily Actions	• Killing, stealing, and sexual misconduct (covered in Pancasila).
Verbal Actions	• Lying, slander, harsh speech and meaningless talk. **Ex:** Avoiding gossiping about others or using abusive language.
Mental Actions	• Covetousness, ill-will and wrong views. ○ **Ex:** Wishing harm on someone who wronged you (ill-will).

Madhyam Marg (Middle Way) in Buddhist Ethics

- **Madhyam Marg, meaning "middle way" in Sanskrit,** is a central concept in Buddhist ethics. It emphasizes avoiding extremes in pursuit of a balanced and enlightened life.

Avoiding Extremes:

- **Self-Indulgence vs. Asceticism:** Buddha rejected both lives of excessive pleasure and extreme self-denial.
  - He **advocated a moderate approach** that fulfils basic needs without attachment to desires.
- **Eternalism vs. Annihilationism:** These are philosophical views on the nature of the self.
  - **Eternalism believes in a permanent self, while** annihilationism denies any lasting self.
  - **Madhyam Marg avoids these extremes**, acknowledging impermanence without denying the possibility of liberation from suffering.

Relevance of Buddhist Principles for Civil Services in the 21st Century

Principles	Relevance for Civil Services
Right Intention	• Prioritize public good over personal gain; make decisions based on fairness and justice.
Compassion	• Consider the impact of policies on all citizens, especially the most vulnerable.
Right Action	• Ensure integrity and avoid corruption through ethical conduct, transparency, and accountability.
Right Livelihood	• View work as a way to contribute positively to society, increasing motivation and effectiveness.
Right Speech	• Promote trust and cooperation through effective communication and avoiding inflammatory language.
Non-Violence	• Emphasize peaceful conflict resolution and social justice to build a harmonious society.
Mindfulness	• Enhance ability to stay calm under pressure, make clear-headed decisions, and avoid impulsive reactions.
Concentration	• Improve task prioritization, time management, and focus by developing mental concentration.
Sustainability	• Promote eco-friendly policies and resource conservation, reflecting Buddhist non-harming principles.
Income Equality	• Address social and economic inequalities to reduce suffering and promote equitable opportunities for all.

Jainism Ethics

Jainism offers a three-fold path (Ratnatraya) to achieve liberation (Moksha):

Path	Description	Examples
Right Faith (Samyag Darsana)	Belief in Jain principles and their effectiveness for liberation.	Faith in the teachings of Mahavira.
Right Knowledge (Samyag Jnana)	Understanding the nature of reality and the soul's journey.	To learn about karma and rebirth cycle.
Right Conduct (Samyag Charitra)	Living a moral life based on principles.	**Observance of five महाव्रत (Mahavrata) - great vows.**

Mahavrata		
Ahimsa (Non-Violence)	Avoiding harm to all living beings, moving or stationary.	Practicing vegetarianism; speaking kindly and avoiding hurtful language.
Satya (Truthfulness)	Speaking truthfully and avoiding falsehood.	Being honest in business dealings; withholding truth cautiously if it would cause harm.
Aparigraha (Non-Possession)	Abstaining from stealing and acquiring possessions unlawfully.	Refusing to take office supplies for personal use; returning borrowed items promptly.
Asteya (Non-stealing)	Living a moral and disciplined life, especially regarding sexual conduct.	Remaining faithful in a committed relationship; avoiding inappropriate physical contact.
Right Conduct (Samyog Charitra)	Detachment from material possessions and avoiding greed.	Living simply and avoiding unnecessary accumulation of wealth; donating to charity.

Relevance of Jainism Principles for Civil Services in the 21st Century

Principle	Relevance for Civil Services	Examples
Ahimsa (Non-Violence)	Prioritize peaceful conflict resolution and promote social justice.	Seeking harm-minimizing solutions; promoting sustainable practices and environmental protection.
Satya (Truthfulness)	Transparency and honesty are essential for effective governance.	Building public trust; reducing susceptibility to corruption.
Aparigraha (Non-Possession)	Foster impartiality and reduce temptation for personal gain.	Making decisions based on merit and public good; promoting equitable distribution of resources.
Asteya (Non-stealing)	Ensure fair use of public resources.	Preventing misuse of funds; ensuring efficient allocation of resources for public benefit.
Right Conduct (Samyog Charitra)	Set a high standard for ethical conduct.	Inspiring public trust and cooperation; leading to a more cohesive society.
Right Knowledge (Samyog Jnana)	Encourage continuous learning and improvement.	Better addressing complex challenges; adapting to evolving situations.

Hindu Philosophy

Principle	Description	Relevance for Civil Services
Satya (Truthfulness)	• Speaking truth with kindness and compassion.	• Fosters public confidence and ethical governance through transparency and honesty.
Ahimsa (Non-Violence)	• Compassion and respect for all living beings, including a vegetarian lifestyle.	• Prioritizes peaceful conflict resolution, social justice, and environmental protection.
Asteya (Non-stealing)	• Avoiding theft and using resources responsibly.	• Ensures fair use of public resources, reduces susceptibility to corruption, and promotes efficient fund allocation.
Karuna (Compassion)	• Developing genuine empathy and helping others selflessly.	• Attuned to public needs, promotes social welfare policies, and alleviates suffering.
Kshama (Forgiveness)	• Emphasizing tolerance, patience, and moving beyond resentment.	• Fosters collaboration, reduces conflicts, and builds stronger public relationships.
Dana (Generosity)	• Selflessly giving back to society without expecting returns.	• Promotes equitable distribution of resources and supports social welfare programs.
Aparigraha (Sin-free actions)	• Avoiding immoral and harmful actions.	• Upholds ethical conduct, inspires public trust, and strengthens governance.

Samata (Acceptance)	• Performing selfless actions and accepting outcomes with equanimity.	• Focuses on public good, maintains dedication regardless of personal success or failure.
Vasudhaiva Kutumbakam (Oneness of Humanity)	• Recognizing the unity of all beings.	• Treats all citizens with dignity and respect, fostering social harmony and community.
Atmavicharana (Listen to your conscience)	• Emphasizing introspection and following one's conscience.	• Makes ethical decisions benefiting the greater good, guided by a strong moral compass.
Moksha (Enlightenment)	• Achieving self-realization and continuous learning.	• Pursues knowledge and self-improvement, becoming better equipped to serve the public effectively.

Bhagvad Gita

When I started reading our old scriptures, like the Bhagavad Gita, I found it very useful for day-to-day life. I consider it an administrative gospel, one that will help you in doing things like running an organization.

- E. Sreedharan

Principle	Description	Application for Civil Servants
Dharma	• Fulfilling one's duty or following the right path, encompassing social, moral, and spiritual duties.	• Act in accordance with duty, even in difficult situations, ensuring moral and ethical governance.
Swadharma	• Specific duties and responsibilities related to one's social class, occupation, and life stage.	• Perform duties specific to their role, such as a leader guiding ethically and responsibly.
Nishkama Karma	• Performing actions without attachment to outcomes, focusing on the greater good.	• Act with integrity, avoiding actions motivated by personal gain, resolving dilemmas ethically.
Gunas	• Three qualities: Sattva (goodness), Rajas (passion), and Tamas (ignorance).	• Strive for honesty and compassion (Sattva), use energy for positive action (Rajas), overcome inertia (Tamas).
Yogas	• Path for spiritual liberation through practices like meditation and selfless action.	• Cultivate self-awareness and inner peace, promoting ethical conduct and effective decision-making.
Equanimity	• Maintaining emotional balance amidst pleasure and pain, success and failure.	• Make reasoned decisions based on stability, not fleeting emotions, ensuring consistent governance.
Universal Applicability	• Transcends social class, gender, or background, applicable to everyone.	• Implement inclusive policies, treating all citizens fairly regardless of their background.
Integrity	• Promotes selfless action over action for personal gain.	• Act with integrity, avoiding attachments and egotism, focusing on public benefit.
Svadharma	• Fulfilling one's duty righteously to set a positive example.	• Leaders performing duties righteously encourage ethical actions among subordinates.
Motivation and Emotional Intelligence	• Focuses on mind, cultivating Sattva (purity) and emotional intelligence (Sthitaprajna).	• Develop emotional intelligence and motivation, promoting clear, jealousy-free decision-making.

Compassionate Governance	• Emphasis on Sattva (purity) and Karuna (compassion).	• Make decisions with a compassionate mindset, free from prejudice, ensuring fairness and clarity.

Chanakya's Philosophy

Principle	Description	Application for Civil Servants
Ethical Leadership & Public Service	• King as "Rajrishi," combining the **qualities of a ruler and a sage (philosopher).** • Dharma (duty) guides decisions. • Rule by example, embody state values • Just rule & avoid wasteful spending.	• Uphold ethical principles. • Citizen-centric approach • Be a role model & leader. • Promote social justice & fair treatment.
Balanced & Sustainable Development	• Economic growth with social justice & sustainability. • Responsible resource management. • Focus on agriculture	• Balanced development plans. • Promote sustainable practices & food security
Effective Governance & Public Administration	• Acknowledge limitations & use evidence for policy. • Streamlined bureaucracy with minimized red tape. • Combat corruption	• Continuous learning & data-driven policies. • Efficient processes & accountability. • Champion transparency & fight corruption
Social Harmony & Security	• Equality and inclusion. • Ensure security and public safety. • Respect for diversity	• Promote social justice & eliminate discrimination. • Effective security measures. • Foster social harmony through inclusivity
Chanakya on Bureaucracy and Corruption	• Acknowledge limitations & continuously learn. • Well-functioning bureaucracy with defined roles. • Supervision & monitoring for efficiency & prevent corruption. • Utilize spies & whistleblowers to combat corruption	• Implement effective policies & adapt to new knowledge. • Clear division of responsibilities & accountability. Streamline processes & minimize red tape. • Promote transparency & encourage reporting of corruption
Strategic Alliances	• Forming beneficial partnerships and maintaining diplomatic relations.	• Alliances to strengthen position and achieve common goals (Ex: QUAD).
Intelligence and Espionage	• Essential for national security, involves gathering intelligence.	• Effective intelligence networks for proactive decision-making.
Law and Order	• Cornerstone of a stable society, involves fair enforcement of laws.	• Enforce laws justly to ensure social stability and public safety.

Mahatma Gandhi

Principle	Description	Application for Civil Servants
Dharma	• Duty, religion, and ethics as the foundation for moral conduct.	• Fulfill duties while adhering to ethical and religious principles.
Non-Violence (Ahimsa)	• Extends beyond physical actions to thoughts and intentions.	• Practice peaceful resistance and avoid all forms of violence.
Truth (Satyagraha)	• Pursuit of truth is essential.	• Uphold transparency and integrity in all actions.
Responsibility	• Accountability for actions and decisions.	• Be accountable to the people they serve.

Rejection of Modern ills	• Caution against materialism and excessive technology.	• Prioritize moral progress alongside material progress.
Non-violent Political Dissent	• Express disagreement with policies or laws through non-violent means, such as civil disobedience.	• Follow non-violent principles when dissenting against policies.
Economic Governance	• Balance economic development with social welfare and ethical considerations.	• Avoid corruption and prioritize the needs of the people.
Ethical Public Service	• Devotion to public service with humility and responsibility.	• Act with humility and take responsibility for actions.
Leadership	• Ministership as an opportunity for service, not personal gain.	• Earn public trust through genuine service to the people.

Swami Vivekananda

Principle	Description	Application for Civil Servants
Ethics & Inner Purity	• Act ethically not from fear, but from recognizing one's inherent goodness and duty to serve.	• Strong moral compass, prioritize service and integrity over societal pressures.
Universal Religion	• Respect all religions as paths to the same ultimate reality.	• Foster tolerance and understanding in a diverse society, treat all citizens equally.
Education & Character Building	• Education should empower individuals and build strong character.	• Promote education and development initiatives, lead with self-reliance and face challenges head-on.
Rationality & Progress	• Embrace reason and data for informed decision-making alongside intuition.	• Make data-driven and well-reasoned decisions to address complex societal issues.
Service & Nationalism (Karmayoga)	• Achieve national progress through selfless service.	• Dedicate service to national well-being, prioritize public good over personal gain.
Youth Empowerment	• Believe in the immense potential of youth and their power to contribute.	• Create opportunities for youth development, inspire young people to serve society.

Raja Ram Mohan Roy

Principle	Description	Application for Civil Servants
Monotheism & Cosmopolitanism	• Promote interfaith dialogue and global cooperation for social harmony.	• Foster peaceful coexistence in diverse communities. • Build trust through interfaith programs.
Rationalism & Modernity	• Base decisions on reason, evidence, and critical thinking.	• Develop effective policies using data and research. • Approach challenges with a scientific mindset.
Balancing Modernity & Tradition	• Embrace progress while respecting cultural sensitivities.	• Implement reforms considering local customs. Promote digital literacy while preserving heritage.
Social Reform & Humanism	• Champion social justice and empower marginalized communities.	• Advocate for women's rights and inclusion. • Design programs to uplift disadvantaged groups.
Education & Freedom of Press	• Promote education for an informed citizenry and safeguard press freedom.	• Increase budgetary allocation for quality education. • Defend journalists' right to report freely.

Separation of Powers & Individual Rights	• Uphold the rule of law, ensure a just government, and respect fundamental rights.	• Strive for impartial and swift justice delivery. • Protect the rights of all citizens.
Indigenous Industry & Sustainable Development	• Support domestic industries and promote sustainable economic growth.	• Encourage eco-friendly practices in businesses. • Formulate policies for responsible resource management.

Rabindranath Tagore

Principle	Description	Application for Civil Servants
Humanism & Empathy	• Prioritize love, fellowship, and public well-being.	• Cultivate a spirit of service and work for the benefit of all citizens.
Harmony & Coexistence	• Promote peace between humans, cultures, and nature.	• Bridge societal divides, advocate for environmental sustainability.
Synthesis over Division	• Embrace diversity and collaboration across cultures.	• Foster unity, understanding, and mutual respect in a polarized world.
Social Responsibility & Equity	• Challenge social hierarchy and work for an equitable society.	• Address social inequalities and ensure inclusive development programs.
Individual Rights & Empowerment	• Uphold democratic values and empower citizens.	• Promote access to education, opportunities, and encourage citizen participation.

Adi Shankaracharya

Principle	Description	Application for Civil Servants
Non-Duality (Advaita)	• Adi Shankaracharya advocated the existence of the individual self (Atman) and the ultimate reality (Brahman), emphasizing their indivisible unity.	• Civil servants should recognize the interconnectedness of all beings and work selflessly for the welfare of society.
Self-Realization	• Attaining knowledge of the non-dual truth (Atman = Brahman) is the ultimate goal.	• Civil servants should seek self-awareness, understanding their role in governance and service to the public.
Ethical Conduct	• Upholding dharma (righteousness) and avoiding adharma (unrighteousness).	• Civil servants must act ethically, ensuring fairness, honesty, and justice in their decisions.
Detachment	• Not being overly attached to material possessions or outcomes.	• Civil servants should focus on duty without personal bias or attachment.
Compassion	• Showing empathy and kindness toward all.	• Civil servants should serve with compassion, considering the needs of marginalized communities.
Knowledge	• Continuous learning and wisdom acquisition.	• Civil servants must stay informed, adapting to changing circumstances and making informed decisions.
Service to Humanity	• Serving others selflessly.	• Civil servants should prioritize public welfare over personal gain.
Humility	• Remaining humble despite accomplishments.	• Civil servants should avoid arrogance and treat everyone with respect.

Important Administrators

Principle	Description	Application for Civil Servants
S. R. Shankaran, IAS	• Land reforms and anti-poverty programs in A.P.; temple entry for SC/ST communities	• Empowerment of vulnerable communities, dedication to social justice
Omprakash Choudhary, IAS	• Educational initiatives in naxal-affected Dantewada; established "Education City"	• Innovation in education and community resilience
Amit Gupta, IAS	• "Daliya Jalao" campaign to end manual scavenging in Budaun district	• Commitment to human dignity and public health
J. K. Tripathy, IPS	• Community policing in Trichy; Beat Officers System, WAN connectivity, helplines for women	• Building trust and engagement between police and community
Upendra Tripathy, IAS	• Transformed BMTC in Bangalore; improved urban transport service quality	• Strategic management and improvement of public services
M. P. Vijaya Kumar, IAS	• Developed Activity Based Learning (ABL) methodology in Tamil Nadu schools	• Innovation in education and child-centred learning approaches.
Amarjit Singh, IAS	• Chiranjeevi Yojana for maternal health care in Gujarat	• Enhancing healthcare accessibility and maternal health
Samit Sharma, IAS	• Established fair price medical shops in Rajasthan; promoted generic medicines	• Making healthcare affordable and accessible
Pranjal Patil, IAS	• First blind woman IAS officer; innovative programs for women's self-help groups in Nashik	• Breaking barriers and empowering marginalized groups
Smitha Sabharwal, IAS	• Improved public administration and citizen engagement in Hyderabad	• Citizen-centric governance and public service improvements
Aruna Sundararajan, IAS	• Digital inclusion and sustainable mining policies	• Strategic policy-making and advocacy for environmental protection
Durga Shakti Nagpal, IAS	• Stood against corruption; took action against land mafia	• Integrity and ethical governance
Sanjukta Parashar, IPS	• Fighting human trafficking and child exploitation	• Courage and dedication in protecting vulnerable populations
Ashok Khemka, IAS	• Exposed corruption in land deals; stood against irregularities	• Upholding honesty and transparency despite challenges
Tukaram Mundhe, IAS	• Transformed Nagpur's waste management system	• Efficiency and eco-friendly governance
Rohini Sindhuri, IAS	• Conserved Hampi monuments and improved tourism infrastructure	• Heritage conservation and tourism development
K. Vijayakarthikeyan, IAS	• Improved public spaces, cleanliness, and citizen participation in Coimbatore	• Urban development and community engagement
D. Roopa, IAS	• Exposed corruption in Karnataka Prisons Department	• Integrity in public service and institutional reform
Dr. Raju Narayana Swamy, IAS	• Stood against corruption; demolished unauthorized resorts in Munnar	• Integrity, use of technology for transparency, and public engagement
Armstrong Pame, IAS	• Built 100-km road to connect Tousem, Manipur; community development initiatives	• Innovation and dedication to community development

S. R. Shankaran, IAS	• Land reforms and anti-poverty programs in A.P.; temple entry for SC/ST communities	• Empowerment of vulnerable communities, dedication to social justice
Kundan Kumar, IAS	• Addressed malpractices in RSBY in Bihar; medico-legal investigation of hysterectomies	• Importance of vigilance and reform in public health systems
Omprakash Choudhary, IAS	• Educational initiatives in naxal-affected Dantewada; established "Education City"	• Innovation in education and community resilience

PYQs Corner

(Write the Answer and Get Free Evaluation)

1 What do each of these quotations convey to you in the present context?
"The simplest acts of kindness are by far more powerful than a thousand heads bowing in prayer". –Mahatma Gandhi (2023, 10 Marks)
"To awaken the people, it is the women who must be awakened. Once she is on the move, the family moves, the village moves, the nation moves." –Jawharlal Nahru (2023, 10 Marks)
"Do not hate anybody, because that hatred that comes out from you must, in the long run, come back to you. If you love, that love will come back to you, completing the circle." Swami Vivekananda (2023, 10 Marks)

2 What were the major teachings of Guru Nanak? Explain their relevance in the contemporary world. (2023, 10 Marks)

3 What do each of these quotations convey to you in the present context?
"If a country is to be corruption free and become a nation of beautiful minds, I strongly feel that there are three key societal members who can make a difference. They are father, mother and teacher." – A.P.J. Abdul Kalam (2022, 10 Marks)
'Judge your success by what you had to give up in order to get it." – Dalai Lama (2022, 10 Marks)

4 What do each of these quotations convey to you in the present context?
"Every work has got to pass through hundreds of difficulties before succeeding. Those that persevere will see the light, sooner or later" - Swami Vivekananda (2021, 10 Marks)
"We can never obtain peace in the outer world until and unless we obtain peace within ourselves." – Dalai Lama (2021, 10 Marks)

5 What teachings of Buddha are most relevant today and why? Discuss. (2020, 10 Marks)

6 What are the main factors responsible for gender inequality in India? Discuss the contribution of Savitribai Phule in this regard. (2020, 10 Marks)

7 What do each of these quotations convey to you in the present context?
"Condemn none: if you can stretch out a helping hand, do so. If not, fold your hands, bless your brothers, and let them go their own way." – Swami Vivekanand (2020, 10 Marks)
"The best way to find yourself is to lose yourself in the service of others." – Mahatma Gandhi (2020, 10 Marks)

8 What do each of these quotations convey to you in the present context?
"A man is but the product of his thoughts. What he thinks, he becomes." – M.K. Gandhi (2019, 10 Marks)
"Where there is righteousness in the heart, there is beauty in the character. When there is beauty in the character, there is harmony in the home. When there is harmony in the home, there is order in the nation. When there is order in the nation, there is peace in the world." – A.P.J. Abdul Kalam (2019, 10 Marks)

9 What do each of the following quotations mean to you in the present context?
"The true rule, in determining to embrace, or reject anything, is not whether it has any evil in it; but whether it has more evil than good. There are few things wholly evil or wholly good. Almost everything, especially governmental policy, is an inseparable compound of the two; so our best judgment of the preponderance between them is continually demanded. " Abraham Lincoln (2018, 10 Marks)
"Anger and intolerance are the enemies of correct understanding. " - Mahatma Gandhi (2018, 10 Marks)
"Falsehood takes the place of truth when it results in unblemished common good." - Tirukkural (2018, 10 Marks)

10 What do each of these quotations convey to you in the present context?
"If a country is to be corruption free and become a nation of beautiful minds, I strongly feel there are three key societal members who can make a difference. they are father, the mother and the teacher." – A. P. J. Abdul Kalam. Analyse (2017, 10 Marks)

11 Discuss Mahatma Gandhi's concept of seven sins. (2016, 10 Marks)

19 Applied Ethics

66

"We do not inherit the Earth from our ancestors; we borrow it from our ancestors; we borrow it from our children." (Focus on inter-generational justice).

– Chief Seattle, Native American Leader

"The greatness of a nation and its moral progress can be judged by the way its animals are treated." (Connects animal treatment to a nation's moral standing)

– Mahatma Gandhi

"No experiment should be conducted where there is an a priori reason to believe that death or disabling injury will occur" (Emphasizes the importance of informed consent in research)

– Nuremberg Code (1947)

"The future of intelligence is not human vs machine, but human + machine." (Focuses on the potential for humans and AI to work together)

– Gary Kasparov, Chess Grandmaster

"Artificial Intelligence should be a tool to help us, not to replace us." (Expresses a concern about AI surpassing human control)

– Elon Musk (Entrepreneur)

Environmental Ethics

The environmental crisis demands a fundamental shift in our relationship with the planet. Environmental Ethics provides a moral framework for navigating complex challenges, promoting responsible action and ensuring a sustainable future.

Need of Environmental Ethics

1. **Looming Shadow of Climate Change**: Extreme weather events like heatwaves, flood and droughts are becoming more frequent and intense, displacing millions worldwide and in India too.
   - A 2023 World Bank report suggests that by 2030, water scarcity could affect 40% of India's population.

2. **Sixth Mass Extinction**: The UN estimates that we're currently experiencing the fastest rate of species extinction in human history.
   - There is decline in the populations of several endangered species including the Great One-Horned Rhino and the Asiatic Lion.

3. **Resource Depletion** According to 2023 UN report, one in three people globally already live under water stress.
   - Environmental ethics compels us to re-evaluate our resource use patterns and prioritize sustainable resource management strategies.

4. **Environmental Pollution** Air pollution is a major health concern in India, with a 2020 Lancet study linking it to over 1.6 million deaths annually.
   - Environmental ethics demands a focus on responsible waste management, pollution control strategies, and promoting cleaner production processes.

5. **Human Wildlife Conflict** Environmental ethics compels us to seek solutions that address the needs of both humans and wildlife. This can involve creating wildlife corridors, promoting coexistence strategies etc.

6. **Guiding Responsible Action** Example: The Namami Gange Program promotes responsible waste management and pollution control efforts, ensuring a cleaner river for generations to come.

7. Intrinsic value of the nature: the Philosophy of Vasudhaiva kutumbakam emphasizes our inter-connectedness with nature, inspiring individuals to act as guardians of the environment.

8. Safeguarding the environment for future generations

Case Studies on Environmental Ethics

1. Debate over large dams.

- Ethical dilemma: Development (Hydropower, Irrigation and flood control) vs Displacement of communities and environmental degradation.
- Example: Narmada Dam Project displaced over 250,000 people, primarily tribal communities dependent on the forest and rivers for livelihood. Construction submerged fertile land and disrupted fish migration patterns.
- Solution: Balancing energy needs with community well-being and ecosystem integrity. Exploring alternative energy sources and prioritizing sustainable dam construction practices that minimize social and environmental impacts.

2. Debate over felling of trees

- Ethical Dilemma: Urban Development vs Green spaces.
- Example: In 2020, there was a public outcry following the planned felling of trees in the Aarey forest for a metro car shed project. The Aarey forest is a crucial green lung for the city and provides habitat for diverse wildlife.
- Solution. Exploring alternative locations for development projects and prioritizing sustainable urban planning strategies that integrate nature into the cityscape

3. Rights of Indigenous communities

- Ethical Dilemma: Environmental conservation vs Traditional practices of community and livelihood.
- Example: The Gadgil committee Report proposed stricter environmental regulations to protect the Western Ghats (a biodiversity hotspot). However, some local communities felt the report restricted their traditional practices and livelihoods.
- Solution: Balancing environmental protection while respecting traditional practices and promoting sustainable livelihoods for local communities who have lived in harmony with these ecosystems for generations.

Philosophical Approach on Environmental Ethics

Approach	Core Belief	Example.
Anthropo-centrism (Human centred)	• Humans are the center of moral concern and the environment has value only in so far as it benefits humanity. • This approach might support deforestation if it creates short term economic gains for a community even if it harms biodiversity in long run	Construction of large dams in India, like Sardar Sarovar Dam on Narmada river displaces communities and disrupts ecosystem
Eco-centrism (Intrinsic value of all living things)	• Intrinsic value is inherent in all living things and ecosystems, independent of their usefulness to humans. • This philosophy emphasizes the inter-connectedness of nature & importance of preserving biodiversity	• Chipko movement in India exemplifies ecocentrism in action which highlighted the intrinsic value of forests beyond their economic benefits.
Deep Ecology (Radical change and bio-centric equality)	• It promotes biocentric equality, recognising the inherent value of all living beings and need for radical social and political change to achieve Sustainability.	• The fight against whaling by organisations like Greenpeace argues for the intrinsic value of whales inspite of its commercial benefits to some community
Land Ethics (Respecting the land community)	• Humans are seen as members of a land community, not conquerors. The health of land and people are inseparable. • Decisions must benefit and respect "integrity stability and beauty" of ecological system	The fight against desertification in Thar Desert of India, focuses on restoring ecological balance and promoting Sustainable management practices.
Eco-feminism	• Links environmental degradation to the oppression of women, advocating for a more holistic and inclusive approach to environmental protection	• Movements against the resource extraction projects led by indigenous women in Latin America.
Social Ecology	• Highlights the connection between environmental issues and social justice. It argues that Environmental problems often stem from social inequalities and power imbalances.	• Environmental justice movements fighting against pollution in low-income communities.

Philosophical Approach of Mahatma Gandhi on Environmental Ethics
1. Earth provides enough to satisfy every man's needs, but not every man's greeds 2. He advocated for sustainable living and respect for all living beings. 3. His concept of "Trusteeship" emphasizes humans as caretakers of the environment, not owners. 4. This approach highlights the moral obligation to protect the environment for future generations. 

Sustainable Development: Balance of Economy and Environment

- The pursuit of economic prosperity often collides with the need to protect our environment, creating a complex global challenge.
  - Studies estimates that environmental damage costs in India can be as high as 5-7% of GDP annually. This highlights the under-estimated economic value of a healthy environment
- This requires the approach of Sustainable Development. Described as development that "meet the needs of the present without compromising the ability of future generations to meet their own needs." (Our Common future 1987)
- Sustainable Development rests on three interconnected pillars.

Economic Sustainability	Social Sustainability	Environmental Sustainability
• Focuses on equal economic growth that generates wealth for all without harming the environment • Eradicating poverty in all forms and dimensions	• Foster gender equality, development of people, communities and cultures to help achieve a reasonable and fairly distributed quality of life, healthcare and education across the globe.	• Prevents nature from being used as an inexhaustible source of resources and ensure its protection and rational use

Integration of Environmental Ethics for Sustainable Development

Integrating environmental ethics into decision-making is crucial for achieving Sustainable development. Here are some key principles to be incorporated in the sustainable Development.

Inter-generational equity Fair distribution of resources. This means using resources responsibly today so future generations have access to what they need.

Green GDP This approach factors in environmental costs and benefits when calculating economic growth, providing a more accurate picture of nation's well-being. Eg: Uttarakhand GEP (Gross Environment Product) that measures and values environmental factors like forest cover and air quality alongside traditional economic indicators.

Environment Impact assessment (EIA) Assessing the environmental consequences before implementing any development project which allows for mitigation strategies to minimize negative impacts.

- EIA was made mandatory in India under Environmental (Protection) Act, 1986

Polluter Pays Principle (PPP) This principle holds that the polluter should be the the one to bear the cost of pollution control and environmental remediation. This incentivizes companies to adopt cleaner practices.

Example: Carbon Taxes implemented in the countries across the World.

Common But Differentiated Responsibilities It establishes that all states have shared obligation to address global environmental destruction, but are not equally responsible. Developed countries which have been historical polluters have greater responsibility in addressing the climate change problem.

- CBDR was first introduced in the Earth Summit, 1992. It has evolved into CBDR-RC with the addition of respective capacities in the Paris Accord 2015. The Principle considers the varying capacities of countries to deal with environmental challenges.

Precautionary Principle Where there are threats of serious or irreversible damage, lack of full scientific certainty shall not be used as a reason for postponing cost effective measures to prevent such environmental degradation.

Example: Ban on the sale and use of firecrackers in the National Capital Region (NCR) during the Diwali festival due to concerns over air pollution.

Public Participation Encouraging community involvement in decision making processes related to environment empowers individuals and fosters a sense of ownership.

Example. National Clean Air Programme (NCAP) launched in 2019 was developed through a participatory approach, involving stakeholders from various sectors, including government, Civil Society and academia.

Sustainable Development Goals (SDGs) Set of 17 goals adopted by UN in 2015, aimed at promoting Sustainable Development and addressing global challenges, including climate change and environmental degradation.

Indigenous knowledge Indigenous communities have a rich history of living off the land without depleting its resources. Their traditional knowledge and practices often embody sustainable resource management principles.
Example: The Sentinelese tribe of North Sentinel Island practice Sustainable fishing technique.

Climate Justice Acknowledges Climate change can have differing Social, economic, public health and other adverse impacts on underprivileged populations and addressing social, gender, economic, intergenerational and environmental injustice

Extended Producer Responsibility Responsibility of a producer for the environmentally sound management of the product (Plastic, electronic and electrical equipment) until the end of its life.

- India had first introduced EPR in 2011 under the Plastic Waste (Management and Handling) Rules, 2011 and E-waste Management and Handling rules 2011.

Mission LiFE India led global mass movement that aims to nudge individuals and communities to practice an environmentally conscious lifestyle that is Synchronous in nature.

- Launched by PM of India at COP26, Glasgow in 2021
- Emboldens the spirit of the P3 model i.e. Pro Planet People.

Principle of Net zero emissions Also referred to as carbon neutrality, it is a state in which a country's emissions are compensated by the absorption and removal of greenhouse gases from the atmosphere.

- India aims to achieve net-zero emissions by 2070.

"Balancing economic development and environmental protection requires a refocusing of economic activity - not towards producing less, but producing differently".

ETHICS AND ANIMALS

Ethical and philosophical foundation of Animal Rights and Welfare

The debate on animal rights and welfare hinges on a fundamental question: Do animals have intrinsic value, or are they valuable only in relation to humans (extrinsic value)?

Intrinsic Value	Extrinsic Value
• Animal Sentience: Animals, like humans are sentient beings capable of experiencing pain, suffering and emotions this inherent capacity for subjective experience grants them intrinsic value, independent of their usefulness to humans.	• Defining "Sentience": Drawing a clear line between sentient and non-sentient beings can be challenging
• Rights based Approach: Extends ethical rights to animals, similar to human rights, demanding respect and protection from unnecessary suffering. • Example: Philosophers like Tom Regan and Peter Singer advocate for animal rights, based on their inherent value	• Utilitarianism: This theory emphasizes maximising overall happiness and minimising suffering while animals may experience suffering, their value is weighed against human needs. • This approach can support animal testing if it leads to medical advancements that alleviate the suffering for many humans and animals.
• Animal liberation Movements: Animals are not simply resources for humans but deserve freedom from exploitation and oppression. • These movements advocate for abolishing practices that exploit animals, such as factory farming for trade, and some forms of animal testing • Speciesism: Discriminating against animals based solely on their species is seen as arbitrary and biased	• Anthropocentrism: This view places humans at the center of moral concern, valuing animals primarily for meeting the human needs (food, research, labour) • Examples: factory farming practices and traditional practices involving animal use often reflect an extrinsic value perspective.

The question of intrinsic vs extrinsic value shapes the ethical treatment of animals. Recognizing animal sentience and prioritizing their well-being, within or beyond human-centric frameworks, is crucial for moving towards a more ethical future for all living beings

Animal Rights in India

Constitution	
• Article 48 A	Makes it the state's responsibility to protect wildlife and the environment
• Article 51A(g)	Casts a duty on citizens to protect animals, promote compassion, and prevent cruelty.
Legislation	
• Central legislation	→ Prevention of Cruelty to Animals (PCA) Act, 1960: Prohibits cruelty to Animals → Wildlife Protection Act (WPA), 1972: focuses on wildlife conservation.
• State legislation	States can enact their own laws (e.g., Assam cattle preservation Act, 2021)
Institutions	
Animal welfare Board of India (AWBI)	Advises on legislation, investigates cruelty complaints, and sets guideline for animal transport.
NGOs	Raise awareness, lobby for stricter laws, and provide animal rescue and care. (Example: People for animals, Wildlife Trust of India).
Court Judgements	
Animal Welfare Board of India vs Nagaraja (2014).	Extended the right to life under the Indian constitution to animals, albiet not explicitly granting Personhood. • Supreme court banned Jallikattu on the grounds of cruelty to animals.
High courts of Uttarakhand and Haryana (2018 & 2019)	Conferred legal personhood on all animals within their respective states. (Decision overturned later)
Indian Penal code (IPC)	Section 428 and 429 penalize cruelty to animals.

Issues Under Animal Rights

1. Culture vs Animal Rights

- The clash between cultural practices involving animal use and animal rights presents a complex ethical dilemma.
- Some of these practices are: Bullfighting (Spain); Koshor slaughter (Judaism) Elephant festivals (South East Asia); Jallikattu (Tamil Nadu) and more.

Ethical consideration

- **Severity of Harm**: Is the animal suffering minimal, or is it a matter of extreme cruelty? This plays a major role in ethical evaluation
- **Alternatives Available**: Are these feasible alternatives that achieve the cultural purpose without animal use.
- **Gradual change**: Can a gradual shift towards less harmful practices be a more realistic approach compared to outright ban

Arguments regarding cultural practices

Arguments for cultural practices	Arguments against cultural practices
• **Respecting Tradition**: Cultural practices are often deeply ingrained and hold significant meaning for communities. Banning them outright can be seen as disrespectful and dismissive of cultural heritage • **Preserving identity**: These practices can be a way for communities to connect with their past, express their beliefs, and maintain a sense of identity.	• **Animal Sentience**: Ethical Considerations demand to minimise animal pain and suffering. • **Speciesism**: Discriminating against animals based solely on their species raises ethical concerns. • **Potential for Abuse**: Some cultural practices can be cruel and barbaric

2. Animal Research

Use of Animals in Scientific studies while ensuring their humane treatment and welfare. It involves a conflict between the following Principles.

Benefits of research: The potential for medical advancements and improved understanding of disease

Potential harm to animals: Minimising the suffering, pain and distress caused by research procedures.

4R's of Animal Research.

4R's of Animal Research

Rehabilitation: Providing appropriate care after experiments to improve animal well-being

Replacement: Developing alternative methods that avoid using animals together.

Reduction: Using the minimum number of animals necessary for valid results

Refinement: Minimising pain and distress through improved procedures and better housing conditions

3. Human wildlife conflict

Human-wildlife conflict (HWC) is a growing concern in India, posing threat to both human safety and wildlife populations. It presents a complex ethical dilemma.

Ethical Dilemma

Intrinsic value of wildlife: This perspective emphasizes upon the ethical obligation to protect wildlife populations and their habitat

Right to life and Safety and mitigating threats from wild animals is a valid concern.

Anthropocentrism vs Ecocentrism: Traditional approaches prioritize human needs (anthropocentrism) while an ecocentric view emphasizes the intrinsic value of all living beings & importance of ecosystem health

Addressing HWC ethically requires a holistic approach that considers the rights of both humans and wildlife.

Minimally Invasive Solutions: Prioritize non-lethal and humane methods for managing HWC

Ethical Research: Research solutions that minimise harm to animals and contribute to understanding wildlife behaviour.

Ethical Path forward

Community Involvement: Engage local communities in solutions that respect their needs and traditional knowledge.

Education and Awareness: Educate the public about the wildlife behaviour and ways to coexist peacefully.

Long Term Sustainability: focus on long term solutions like habitat restoration and Sustainable development practices.

5. One Health Approach.

One Health is an approach that recognizes that the health of people is closely connected to the health of animals and our shared environment. The concept has gained importance because of following reasons:

1. Increased Human-Animal interaction:
   a. Expanding populations encroach on new areas and come into closer contact with wild animals and their environments which creates more opportunities for diseases to jump from animals to humans (Zoonotic)
   b. Over 65% of infectious diseases that affect humans are zoonotic, highlighting the critical link between animal and human health.
2. Environmental disruption due to human activities can facilitate the spread of diseases to animals, potentially creating new reservoirs for zoonotic transmission.
3. International travel and trade: The rise in international trade and travel of animals and animal products allow diseases to spread quickly across borders, posing a global threat.
4. Viral Reservoir: Scientists estimate over 1.7 million viruses exist in wildlife, many with zoonotic potential. This unseen threat underscores the need for proactive surveillance and prevention

By embracing one Health Approach, India can better prepare for future pandemic and safeguard the health of its citizens, animals and the environment.

Investing in this collaborative, holistic strategy is key to building a more resilient future for all.

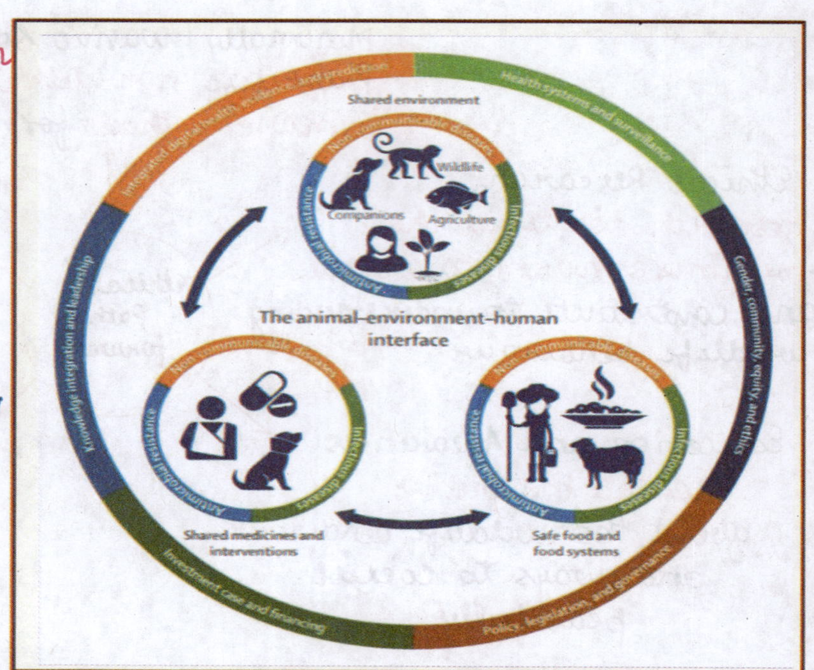

India's principles with respect to Animal Ethics.

India's principles with respect to Animal Ethics.

1. Respecting cultural practices while minimising animal suffering. This may involve modifying practices or incorporating animal welfare considerations

2. Emphasis on Non-Violence (ahimsa) present in many Indian religions to encourage a more compassionate approach towards animals.

3. Community based animal welfare: Supporting local initiatives for stray animal management, fostering responsible pet ownership and promoting ethical sourcing of animal products

4. Strengthening enforcement: Increasing resources for animal welfare agencies and strengthening legal frameworks with clear definitions of cruelty & harsher punishment for violations

5. Investing in animal welfare science: Conducting research on best practices for animal husbandary transportation, and slaughter methods tailored to Indian context.

Biothics

- Biothics is an interdisciplinary field that addresses the ethical, legal, and social implications of advances in biology, medicine, and biotechnology.
- It involves the examination of values and moral principles in medical and biological research and the application of these principles in clinical practice and public policy.

Four core principles of Bio-ethics

Autonomy: Respecting the decision making capacities of autonomous persons, enabling individuals to make reasoned informed choices

Non-Maleficence - Commitment to avoid harm to patients. Summarised by "first, do no harm". (Underlying tenet of professional mission statement - Hippocratic Oath.

Beneficence: the principle of doing good; ensuring that the benefits of research and medical practice overweigh risk and harms

Justice: Promoting equitable access to new technologies and avoiding widening existing disparities.

Other important principles in Bio-ethics:

- Transparency: Maintaining transparency about research results, ethical conflicts and funding sources.
- Respect: Upholding the rights of humans, animals and ecosystems in bio-engineering practices.
- Education: fostering learning and empowering communities to engage with the public responsibly.
- Open Science: Balancing open data access with data security for collaboration

Philosophical lenses on Bioethics

Philosophy	Focus	Bioethics Examples.
Utilitarianism	Maximising Overall Societal well-being	Supporting genetically modified crops for increased food production, reduced hunger, with some environmental concerns.
Deontology	Duty and moral principles (truthfulness, fairness, respect human dignity	Objecting to human germline editing on principle, regardless of potential benefits, due to issue of playing God and violating human potential
Virtue Ethics	Developing virtuous character traits (courage, honesty, compassion)	Emphasizing the importance of honesty and transparency in biotechnology research, valuing open communication with public.

Scope of Bioethics in India

Medical Ethics • **Informed consent** : Ensuring patients understand their treatment options and provide voluntary consent.

• **End-of-life care**: Addressing ethical considerations surrounding withdrawal or withholding of life support (Autonomy, quality of life and the nature of suffering).

• **Organ Transplantation** : Addressing ethical concerns related to organ donation, allocation and transplantation (Fairness in access)

Reproductive Ethics Issues such as In-vitro fertilization (IVF), Surrogacy and pre-implantation genetic diagnosis (PGD) raise questions about the commodifications of life, the rights of children and the definition of family.

Genetic Engineering and CRISPR The ethical implications of gene editing, including concerns about eugenics, genetic privacy, non-discrimination and the potential for unintended consequences in the human genome.

Clinical Trials and Research Ethics The Ethical Conduct of research, especially in vulnerable populations, involves ensuring informed consent, privacy, balancing risks and benefits and addressing issues of exploitation and justice.

Public Health Ethics Addressing Ethical issues related to healthcare access, resource allocation, and public health policies.

GENETIC MODIFICATION AND ENGINEERING

Genetic modification (GM) and engineering offer immense potential for advancement in medicine (Gene therapy), agriculture (GM crops) and environmental sustainability. However, these powerful tools also raise significant ethical concerns.

Concerns

• **Unintended consequences**: Manipulating the genetic makeup of organisms can have unforeseen consequences on the organism itself, other species in the ecosystem and even human health.

Example: Introduction of genetically modified crops might disrupt the food chain or create new allergens.

- Ethics of interference with natural selection and evolution: Human cloning challenges the concept of free will, individuality and the very essence of what it means to be human.
- Human germline editing: Changes made to the reproductive cells would be passed on to future generations, potentially creating unintended consequences and limiting individual choice.
- Accessibility and Equity concerns particularly for low and middle-income countries because of expensive technologies.

Ethical Considerations

- Balancing benefits and risks: A careful assessment of potential benefits (Example: Disease cures, improved food security) must be weighed against potential risks (Example: Environmental damage, unintended mutations) before widespread application.
- Transparency and public engagement: People should be informed about the potential risks, benefits and uncertainities from this technology so that people can take autonomous decisions.
- Regulation and oversight: Robust regulatory frameworks are necessary to ensure the safe and ethical development and application of GM technologies. Clear guidelines and independent oversight are essential.
- Global Collaborations: Ensure responsible development, equitable access to benefits, sharing of best practices and addressing ethical concerns in a unified manner.
- Long term Impacts: thorough research is essential to evaluate the long term impacts of GM technologies on ecosystems, biodiversity and human health.

India's Initiatives to address ethical concerns in biotechnology

Principles	India's solution.
Risk assessment and Regulation	GEAC assesses risks and approves applications for GMO research and development in India
Transparency and accountability	Clinical Trials Registry of India (CTRI) provides public information about ongoing clinical trials, promoting transparency and research accountability
International Collaboration	India's membership in international biothics organisations like UNESCO's International Biothics Committee (IBC) fosters collaboration on global ethical framework for biotechnology
fair share of benefits.	National Biodiversity Authority (NBA) of India implements the Nagoya Protocol, ensuring fair sharing of benefits arising from genetic resource utilization.

Privacy and Genetic Information

The rapid advancement of genetic testing has unlocked a wealth of information about our individual makeup. However, this newfound knowledge comes with significant privacy concerns:

Concerns	Ethical Considerations
1. Loss of Privacy - Data breaches, unauthorised access and potential misuse by insurance companies, employers or even governments.	1. Robust privacy safeguards - Strong legal framework to protect the privacy of genetic information 2. Informed consent before undergoing genetic testing. 3. Raising public awareness about genetic privacy rights. 4. International collaboration to develop harmonized regulations and best practices for protecting genetic privacy.
2. Genetic discrimination based on their genetic pre-dispositions to certain diseases which could limit employment opportunities, insurance coverage or access to certain services.	5. Preventing genetic discrimination through anti-discrimination laws
3. Data ownership concerns	6. Transparency about data ownership.

Bioethics Case Studies

Aspect	Indian Example
Designer babies and Germline editing.	India currently bans human germline editing.
Right to Die and family consent	The living will and Advance Directives framework in India allows individuals to express their wishes regarding end of life care.
Xenotransplantation and Animal Welfare	Currently not practiced in India
Exploitation and Right in Surrogacy	India banned commercial surgery and allows only altruistic surrogacy under the Surrogacy (Regulation) Act, 2021.
Healthcare data	Aarogya Setu App used for COVID-19 contact tracing, exposed data privacy and security concerns in India. This highlighted the need for robust data protection regulations.
Adoption of GMOs	The contentious issue of GM Mustard in India highlights the need for rigorous safety assessments and public awareness regarding GMOs.
Human Enhancement and Gene Doping	As with germline editing, India currently bans gene doping in athletics.

ABORTION

Abortion: Meaning and facts

- Abortion is the termination of a pregnancy resulting in the death of the embryo or the foetus.
- It can occur spontaneously (miscarriage) or be induced, either medically or surgically.
- Maternal Mortality Rate (MMR): According to UNICEF India and World Bank data, India counts among the highest number of maternal deaths worldwide and unsafe abortions are the third leading cause of maternal deaths in India.
- Unintended pregnancies with an estimated 15 million occurring annually.
- Scale of Abortion in India: It is estimated that 6.7 million abortions occur annually in India, with a concerningly high number (around 5.7 million) being illegal

Laws of Abortion in India

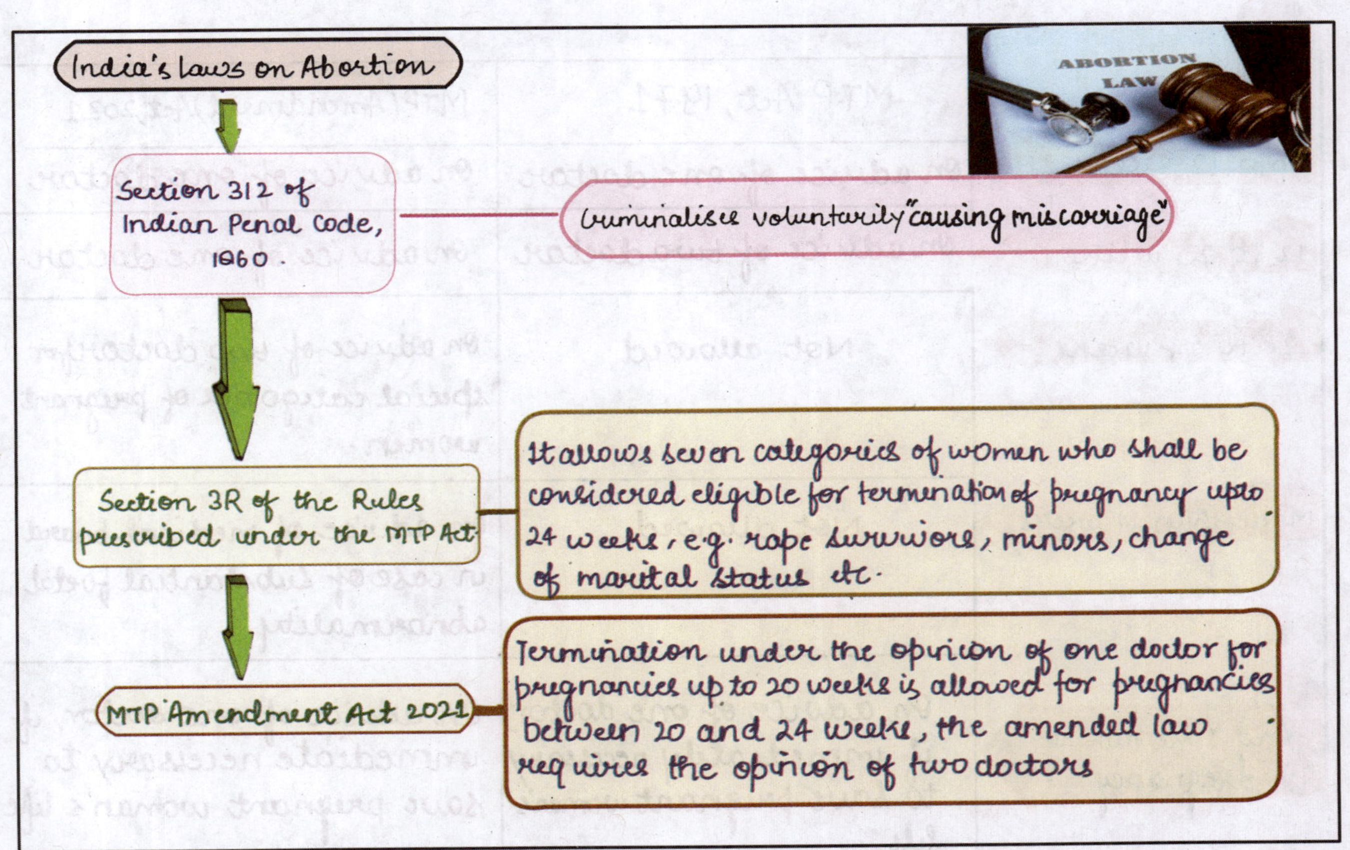

About the MTP Act

- Purpose: To Provide a legal framework for terminating pregnancies and reduce the health risks associated with unsafe abortions.
- key provisions:
- legal abortion under specific conditions up to 20 weeks of pregnancy.
- Permit termination of pregnancy in the following circumstances:
  - The pregnancy poses a risk to mother's life or physical/mental health.
  - Foetus abnormalities are detected.
  - The pregnancy is a result of rape or contraceptive failures.
- The law does not accomodate non-medical concerns in a case of an unwanted pregnancy beyond 20 weeks over the economic cost of raising a child, effects on career decisions, or any other personal considerations.
- Requires termination to be performed by a registered medical practitioner makes termination by an unregistered practitioner a punishable offense.
- Unmarried women: The MTP Act, 1971 prohibit unmarried women who are between 20 weeks to 24 weeks pregnant to abort with the help of registered medical practitioners.

	MTP Act, 1971	MTP (Amendment) Act, 2021.
Upto 12 weeks	On advice of one doctor	On advice of one doctor
12 to 20 weeks	On advice of two doctor	On advice of one doctor
20 to 24 weeks	Not allowed	On advice of two doctor for special categories of pregnant women.
More than 24 weeks	Not allowed	On advice of medical board in case of substantial foetal abnormality.
Any time during pregnancy	On advice of one doctor, if immediately necessary to save pregnant woman's life.	On advice of one doctor, if immediate necessary to save pregnant woman's life

- Supreme court in 2022 allowed all women in the country, regardless of marital status, can undergo an abortion up to 24 weeks into pregnancy to access safe and legal abortion care.
- It has ruled over a 51 year old abortion law (The Medical Termination of Pregnancy Act of 1971) which bars unmarried women from terminating pregnancies which are up to 24 weeks old.

Ethical issues of Abortion

Pro-Choice
- Support abortion rights of women
- Right of women to 'bodily autonomy' is paramount

Pro-life
- Oppose abortion rights of women
- 'Right to life' of foetus is paramount

ETHICAL ISSUES

1) With respect to women
- fundamental Right: Bodily Autonomy + Reproductive choices + Gender Equality.
- Navtej Singh Johar case (2018) and Puttaswamy Judgement (2017): Recognised right to Sexual Autonomy as a part of personal liberty (Art. 21)
- Reproductive Rights: Safe and legal Abortion + Proper Maternal health.

2. With respect to family.
- Emotionally complex decision to terminate a pregnancy.
- Conservative vs liberal values: families hold diverse values regarding abortion.
- Emotional and psychological implication for families.

3. With respect to foetus
- foetal rights: This is a core ethical question. When does life begin, and does the foetus have rights? There are differing beliefs on this.
- Motherly bond between Mother and foetus is acknowledged

4. With respect to society.
- Responsibility of state to value life
- Inclusion of all: without discrimination against differences
- female foeticide: favouring male offspring.
- Coerced abortion driven by socio-economic factors.

India's approach to abortion is reflected in the Medical Termination of Pregnancy (MTP) Act, 1971, and its subsequent amendments. This legislation attempts to strike a balance between:

- Women's Rights: Right to bodily autonomy and decision making regarding reproduction.
- Ethical concerns: The ethical concern surrounding abortion, including the potential impact on the foetus and societal values.

EUTHANASIA

Origin: The word "Euthanasia" comes from Greek and literally translates to "good death".

Meaning: It refers to the intentional ending of a person's life to relieve their suffering. This suffering is usually caused by an incurable or terminal illness.

- As Euthanasia aims to alleviate pain and misery, it's also known as "Mercy Killing".

Types of Euthanasia

1. Active vs Passive Euthanasia.

Active Euthanasia	Passive Euthanasia.
• Also known as assisted suicide, It is the act of deliberately and actively doing something to end a person's life • It is done through steps such as administering a lethal injection or overdose of medication. • Active Euthanasia involves directly causing the patient's death. • This type of Euthanasia is illegal in most countries, including India.	• It is defined as intentionally letting a patient die by withholding artificial life support such as ventilator or a feeding tube. • This can include removing a patient from life support or not providing treatment for terminal illness. • Passive Euthanasia is legal in some countries, including India, under certain circumstances with proper consent.

2. Voluntary vs Non-voluntary vs Involuntary.

Voluntary Euthanasia	Non-Voluntary Euthanasia	Involuntary Euthanasia.
• Performed with the patient's full consent. • Legal in some countries like Belgium and the Netherlands.	• Performed when the Patient cannot consent (e.g. coma), • Often based on previous wishes expressed by the patient.	• Euthanasia conducted against the patient's will is considered murder

Euthanasia in India: Evolution of legal status.

Concept of living Will.

- A "living will" grants individuals an authority to provide advance directives regarding their medical treatment, including the option to withdraw life support if necessary.
- A living will provision cannot be made entirely fool proof, as it may still require input from medical professionals or immediate decision makers involved in individual care.

1994 P. Rathinam vs Union of India: The court did not explicitly legalise Euthanasia but recognised the right to die with dignity as an inherent part of Article 21 (Right to life)

1996 Gian Kaur vs State of Punjab: The court ruled that Article 21 of the Indian constitution does not include the right to die. The court also observed that Euthanasia could only be made lawful by legislation.

2006 Law commission in its 196th report: A patient's decision to not receive medical treatment did not constitute an attempt to commit Suicide under Section 309 IPC.

- Also, a doctor who obeys the instructions of a competent patient to withdraw / withhold medical treatment does not commit a breach of professional duty.

2011 Aruna Shanbaug versus Union of India: Supreme court allowed passive Euthanasia for the nurse lying in vegetative state at a hospital in Mumbai establishing a crucial precedent for passive Euthanasia.

- Introduced the concept of "Living Will" as a way for terminally ill patients to express their wishes regarding end-of-life care.

2018

Common cause vs Union of India: Building upon Aruna Shanbaug case, this judgement legalised passive Euthanasia in India under specific conditions:

- Recognised the validity of living will made by terminally ill or permanently vegetative patients, allowing them to refuse life support.
- Establishment of medical boards to review such requests.

Note:
Active Euthanasia, where legal medication is administered to end a life, remains illegal in India

2020

Chandrakant Narayanrao Tandale vs State of Maharashtra: Active Euthanasia is a form of Euthanasia that is illegal.

Critical Analysis for the adoption of Euthanasia

Arguments for Euthanasia	Argument against Euthanasia.
Individual	Perspective
• Right to Die with Dignity: Emphasizes individual autonomy and the right to control one's body and healthcare decisions.	• Not necessarily autonomous: Terminally ill patients may be under duress from pain, depression or external pressures. Their decision making capacity could be compromised
• End of unbearable pain and mental distress providing a path towards emotional relief and dignified death.	• Palliative care advancements can effectively manage pain and suffering in many cases, making Euthanasia unnecessary.
Societal	Perspective
• Frees up resource allocation which could then be directed towards preventive care or treatment of other illness could benefit a larger population.	• Putting vulnerable population such as disabled or the elderly at the risk of coerced euthanasia. • Respect for the drug: Allowing Euthanasia will send a message that their lives are less worthy of protection
• No negative impact on healthcare system based on the studies in countries with legalised euthanasia	• Incentivise ending the lives of terminally ill patients to save healthcare costs. • Discouraging research into new treatment and cures for terminal illness, limiting medical innovation.

Moral Perspective	
• Act of compassion or mercy by allowing medical professionals to alleviate a patient's unbearable suffering. • Respect for family by alleviating the emotional and moral distress of a family members who witness their loved one endure unbearable suffering • Prevents from futile treatment and minimising the financial burden on family.	• Sanctity of life and taking it is morally wrong even with consent. Only a higher power has the right to end a life. • Slippery slope: Legalising euthanasia could lead to a gradual erosion of the value placed on human life. • Could potentially lead to situations where euthanasia is practiced on vulnerable population without their true consent. • Undermining of the trust in Doctor-Patient Relationship: Doctors traditionally focus on saving lives, and euthanasia could introduce a conflict in their professional duties.

Euthanasia laws across the World

- Netherlands, Luxembourg, Belgium: these countries permit both Euthanasia (doctor administered lethal medication) and physician assisted suicide (providing the means for self-administration) for terminally ill patients with unbearable suffering and no hope for improvements.
- Canada: Euthanasia and assisted dying are legal for terminally ill and mentally competent adults experiencing unbearable sufferings with no chance of improvements.

Conclusion

While some see it as a compassionate option to alleviate sufferings, others fear abuse and a devaluation of life. As medical care advances, the line between life-prolonging treatments and ending suffering blurs.

The Supreme court has recognised that a person with Persistent Vegetative state (PVS), with no scope of improvement has a right to end her/his life with dignity. Thus, passive euthanasia has been recognised in India as a facet of the Right to life under Article 21 of the Indian Constitution

MEDIA ETHICS

Media act as the fourth pillar of the democracy by playing a pivotal role in shaping public discourse and informing citizens. To fulfill this responsibility ethically, media professionals and organisations adhere to a set of guiding principles known as Media Ethics.

These principles ensure responsible journalism, fostering public trust and safeguarding individual rights.

Acts and Agencies in India

Acts and Agencies in India.

- **News Broadcasting Standards Authority (NBSA):** Regulates content on private television channels.
- **Advertising Standards council of India (ASCI)** is a self-regulatory voluntary organisation to ensure the protection of the interest of consumers by maintaining and promoting ethical standards in advertising.
- **Press council of India (PCI):** Self-Regulatory body on promoting ethical journalism and handling complaints against media outlets.
- **Cable Television Networks (Regulation) Act, 1995:** Regulates content on cable television networks.

Six Pillars of Media Ethics

6 Pillars

- **Veracity (Truthfulness):** Verified through credible sources to prevent the spread of misinformation
- **Objectivity (fairness and Impartiality):** Avoid personal bias and ensure a fair representation of all sides
- **Privacy:** Blurring faces in sensitive situations, avoiding intrusive questioning and obtaining informed consent for use of personal data.
- **Responsibility (Minimizing harm):** Appropriate language, voiding inflammatory rhetoric and upholding the human rights principles
- **Accountability:** Answerable to the people for their work is the hallmark of ethical journalism
- **Independence:** Freedom from influence to safeguard the journalistic integrity and prevent compromised reporting

Ethical Issues

1. Individual Level:

- Exposure to inaccurate or biased news reports can lead to confusion, manipulation of beliefs and difficulty in discerning truth.
  Example: Supreme court in 2021 criticised heavily on biased reporting by some media outlets in the Tablighi Jamaat gathering case during the first wave of the COVID-19 pandemic.
- Privacy intrusion: Aggressive paparazzi culture and insensitive reporting on personal lives can cause emotional distress and mental harassment
- Sensationalism: Letting personal ideology or the pursuit of TRP cloud journalistic objectivity.
  Example: Coverage of a political power shift in Maharashtra, focusing on drama and conflict rather than a nuanced analysis of the situation.
- Psychological impact: Sensationalized news coverage of crime, violence and tragedies can contribute to anxiety, fear and a distorted perception of risk.

2. Societal level

- Erosion of Trust: Ethical lapses in media can lead to a decline in public trust towards news outlets and journalists, hindering informed citizenship.
- Social Division: Inflammatory language and biased reporting can exacerbate social divisions, fuelling prejudice and hindering social cohesion.
- Manipulation of public opinion through paid news, fake news and agenda driven journalism, hindering democratic processes.

3. National Level:

- National Security threats: Sensationalized reporting on sensitive issues like terrorism or military operations can compromise national security by revealing crucial information.
  Example: News coverage of 26/11 Mumbai terror attacks.
- Disruption of Public order: Biased or inflammatory reporting can incite violence, riots or social unrest, jeopardising national stability.

  Example: In 2013, the Muzaffarnagar riots were triggered by a fake video circulating on social media, which was rumoured to depict a muslim mob brutally murdering a hindu youth.

- Undermining Public Institutions: Trial by media and biased reporting can erode public trust in institutions like the judiciary or the law enforcement, hindering their effectiveness.
  Example: Extensive media coverage of Aryan Khan (Celebrity Son) in drug related case or Sushant Singh Rajput Murder case.

4. Global Level

- Spread of misinformation: The interconnectedness of global media allows for the rapid dissemination of fake news and misinformation, impacting international relations.
  - Media outlets in authoritarian regimes like China and North Korea often rely on unverified confessions or accusations from government sources.
- Erosion of global norms: Unethical media practices like hate speech or cultural insensitivity can undermine international cooperation and understanding.
- Challenges to International peace and security: Media manipulation can be used to fuel conflicts between nations or justify military actions.

Ethical Concerns in the Social Media

- Speed vs Accuracy: The pressure to be first with breaking news online often leads to the dissemination of unverified information or incomplete stories that get retracted later.
- Invasion of privacy: The vast amount of personal data individuals leave online raises new questions about privacy and consent in reporting. Striking a balance between informing the public and protecting individual privacy is crucial.
  Example: Facebook-Cambridge Analytica Scandal, recent data leak of Zomato users or boat users etc.
- Data Ownership: The vast amount of data collected by social media platform raises questions about ownership and access.
- Fake news and Mis-information: Significant threat to public discourse and trust in media, hindering its role as 4th pillar of democracy.
- Spamming and unverified Content: Constant bombardment with irrelevant promotional messages or unsolicited content can be frustrating and intrusive.
- Public Shaming and Cyber bullying: Hampers the mental and emotional well-being of an individual.

Examples of Ethical Case Studies of Media in India

TRP Scam (2020): Manipulation of television viewership data to attract advertisers. This case highlighted the need for transparency and accountability in media practices	Cobrapost Sting operation (2018): Exposed the vulnerability of Indian media to political and corporate influence, raising concerns about media independence.
Sushant Singh Rajput Death Case Coverage (2020): Speculative reporting intrusion into privacy and sensationalism by some media outlets raised ethical concerns.	Nirbhaya Case Coverage (2012): Highlighted social injustice and led to changes in rape laws, demonstrating the positive impact of ethical journalism.

Cross Ownership of the Media

- Cross media ownership in India refers to a situation where a single entity owns or controls businesses across different media platforms.
- This can include print media (newspaper, magazines), TV channels, radio stations and increasingly, digital media platforms (websites, social media).
- India has no overarching policy on cross media restrictions unlike many developed nations with limitations on media ownership concentration.

Examples:
- Reliance owns interest in TV (Network 18), Newspaper (Hindustan Times, Deccan Herald) and digital platforms (Jio News)
- Times Group controls newspapers like The Times of India and Economic Times, also have a presence in digital news with Times Internet limited

Ethical Concerns:

- Reduced Plurality of voices: Concentration of power can limit the range of viewpoints available to the public (Homogenisation of news and information)
- Threat to Editorial independence: Media outlets might be pressured to promote the business interest of the conglomerate which can lead to self-censorship, pushing a specific agenda, etc resulting into compromised journalistic objectivity.
- Erosion of public trust if the public perceives media to be biased and therefore weakens its ability to hold powerful institutions accountable.
- Reinforcing social bias by catering to the dominant social and political narratives which can lead to the marginalization of minority voices and perspectives.
- Data privacy concerns: Lack of transparency and potential misuse of this data for targeted advertising.

ETHICAL ARTIFICIAL INTELLIGENCE

The rise of Artificial Intelligence (AI) has ushered in a new era of remarkable potential. From self-driving cars to medical diagnosis, AI promises to revolutionize many aspects of our lives.

Ethical AI or Moral AI or Responsible AI focuses on developing and deploying AI systems in a way that aligns with human values and human principles.

- It emphasizes the responsible use of AI technology to ensure that it benefits individuals, communities and society as a whole, while limiting potential harms and biases.

PILLARS OF ETHICAL ARTIFICIAL INTELLIGENCE

- Transparency Fostering trust
- Fairness mitigating biasness & preventing discrimination
- Robustness & Reliability with safeguard against manipulation
- Benefits to humanity by focusing on solving societal challenges
- Privacy and data protection
- Accountability and Responsibility

Challenges in AI usage

Individual level

- Loss of livelihood leading to unemployment and economic hardship. Mainly impacting those jobs which involve routing information processing, data entry and filling out forms.
- Privacy concerns and potential misuse of the data.
- Impact on mental health by the over-reliance on AI assistants and social media algorithms. Example. Addiction, loneliness.
- AI as a long term threat as some experts worry about super intelligence that can surpass human control.

Societal level

- Societal unrest and economic instability due to widespread job displacement
- Algorithmic bias can perpetuate discrimination in areas like loan approvals, hirings and criminal justice which can result in skewed or unfair outcomes

National level

- National Security risks as malicious actors could potentially use AI for cyberattacks or autonomous weapon development.
  - According to Capgemini report, 85% of the surveyed organisations in India have encountered concerns with AI.
- Lack of regulation by the governments has raised certain ethical issues such as metaverse sexual assaults in Jan 2024, Deepfake of Rashmika Mandana (Film Actress)
- India's limitations in the AI race.
  - Lack of comprehensive and composite AI strategy that connects governments, industry, academia and society
  - India doesnot have large corporations that invest heavily in inhouse AI research and chip hardware designs.
  - Absence of audited data sets for training and fine tuning models.
  - Brain drain from India to destinations like US and China.

Global level

- Economic Disruption: Automation powered by AI is predicted to displace millions of jobs across various sectors worldwide
  - A 2017 study by McKinsey Global Institute estimated that upto 800 million jobs globally could be automated by 2030.
- Widening Inequalities between rich and poor nations: Wealthier nations may have the resources to adapt and develop new industries, while poorer nations might struggle.
- Reduction of incentives for human creativity and innovation

India's three pronged Approach to Responsible AI

Global cooperation

- Global partnership on Artificial Intelligence (GPAI), of which India is a founding member, is an international and multi-stakeholder initiative to guide the responsible development and use of AI, grounded in human rights, inclusion, diversity, innovation and economic growth.
- US India Artificial Intelligence (USIAI) Initiative strengthens India's partnership with the US in AI research and development.

Institutional level (NITI Aayog)

- National strategy on Artificial Intelligence (2018) launched by NITI Aayog outlines the potential of AI for social good and economic growth
- #AI for All campaign focuses on leveraging AI for inclusive development
- National AI portal of India, launched in 2020, one stop digital platform for AI related development in the country.
  - Showcases AI initiatives, resources, events, research and innovation by various stakeholders from academia, industry and government.
- Collaboration with Private sector to adopt responsible AI development strategies.

Legislative and Regulatory Route

- Digital India Bill 2023: this proposed bill aims to categorize online platforms, including AI-based ones, and established tailored regulations for each category.
  - It seeks to address modern challenges like cybercrime, data protection, deepfakes and online safety.
- Proposal for the establishment of Artificial Intelligence and Data Authority of India (AIDAI) to oversee data governance, define responsible AI principles and enforces them throughout AI lifecycle.

Best practices in Ethical AI

Criteria	Global Example	Indian Example.
Clear ethical guidelines	• IEEE Global Initiative on Ethics of Autonomous and Intelligent Systems.	• National AI strategy.
Transparency and Accountability.	• US Department of Defence requires AI system developers to explain decision making processes.	• IIT Madras developing "Explainable AI" framework
fairness and Non-discrimination	• IBM's "AI fairness 360" toolkit can be used by developers to detect and mitigate bias in their machine learning models	• TISS mitigates bias in AI-based recruitment tools.

Privacy and Security.	• EU's General Data Protection Regulation (GDPR) gives individuals control over their personal information.	• Digital Personal Data Protection (DPDP) Act, 2023 regulates the collection, storage, use and protection of personal data in India.
Accountability and Human oversight.	• Partnership on AI emphasizes human oversight for accountable AI development.	• NITI Aayog's discussion paper highlights the need for human oversight boards in AI applications
Human Rights and Values.	• Council of Europe recommends AI development respecting children's rights and well-being.	• Indian National AI strategy aligns AI development with fundamental rights in the constitution.

Conclusion: India's ambitious efforts in responsible AI are making waves globally. From the visionary #AIFORALL campaign to the proposed establishment of a dedicated AI regulatory body, India is demonstrating strong leadership in this critical field.

However, ensuring ethical AI requires a global village. Collaboration across nations, industries, stakeholders is essential. The World must work together to develop a "Whole of Society" and "Whole of Globe" approach.

20 Case Studies

Work Culture

Q. At 9 pm on Saturday evening, Rashika, a Joint Secretary, was still engrossed in her work in her office. Her husband, Vikram, is an executive in an MNC and frequently out of town in connection with his work. Their two children aged 5 and 3 are looked after by their domestic helper. At 9:30 pm her superior, Mr. Suresh calls her and asks her to prepare a detailed note on an important matter to be discussed in a meeting in the Ministry. She realises that she will have to work on Sunday to finish the additional task given by her superior. She reflects on how she had looked forward to this posting and had worked long hours for months to achieve it. She had kept the welfare of people uppermost in discharging her duties. She feels that she has not done enough justice to her family and she has not fulfilled her duties in discharging essential social obligations. Even as recently as last month she had to leave her sick child in the nanny's care as she had to work in the office. Now, she feels that she must draw a line, beyond which her personal life should take precedence over her professional responsibilities. She thinks that there should be reasonable limits to the work ethics such as punctuality, hard work, dedication to duty and selfless service.

(a) Discuss the ethical issues involved in the case.

(b) Briefly describe at least four laws that have been enacted by the government with respect to providing a healthy, safe and equitable working environment for women.

(c) Imagine you are in a similar situation. What suggestions would you make to mitigate such working conditions? (UPSC 2023)

Context:

Rashika, a dedicated Joint Secretary, grapples with the ethical tension between professional commitment and personal responsibilities. This case study underscores the recurring challenge many professionals face in balancing work demands with familial and personal duties.

Major Stakeholders:

- **Rashika:** The Joint Secretary facing a work-life balance dilemma.
- **Vikram:** Rashika's husband, who is frequently away for work.
- **Children:** Rashika's two young children requiring parental attention.
- **Domestic Helper:** The person entrusted with childcare responsibilities.
- **Mr. Suresh:** Rashika's superior who assigns additional work tasks.
- **Government**: The entity responsible for enacting laws and regulations ensuring fair labor practices.

Values Associated:

- **Work Ethics:** Rashika embodies strong work ethic through dedication and commitment to duty.
- **Family Values:** The case underscores the importance of prioritizing family well-being.

- **Gender Equality:** The case subtly highlights potential societal expectations for women regarding domestic responsibilities.
- **Work-Life Balance:** Finding a healthy balance between professional and personal life is a key value.
- **Fairness and Equity:** Rashika's situation raises questions about workplace fairness and the right to manage personal time effectively.

(a) Major ethical issues involved in this case:

- **Work-Life Equilibrium:** Balancing professional obligations with personal commitments and well-being.
- **Work Culture & Gender Sensitivity:** Promoting a culture that respects personal boundaries and values inclusivity for all employees.
- **Shared Familial Responsibilities:** Encouraging all family members to equally participate in household and familial duties, ensuring collective well-being.
- **Rational work protocols:** Ensuring humane working conditions that consider both hours and the nature of tasks, avoiding unnecessary last-minute demands.
- **Personal Health and Well-being:** Prioritizing policies that allow for personal health needs without professional backlash.
- **Employee Autonomy and Voice:** Empowering employees to communicate boundaries and concerns, fostering open two-way communication.

(b) Laws that have been enacted by the government to ensure professional welfare of women

Laws	Description
Maternity Benefit (Amendment) Act, 2017	**Goal:** Guarantees extended paid maternity leave and access to childcare facilities for working mothers. **Key Points:** • Increased paid maternity leave from 12 weeks to 26 weeks, providing greater support for new mothers. • Option for work-from-home arrangements based on mutual agreement between employer and employee, promoting flexibility. • Mandatory crèche facilities established for companies with 50 or more employees, addressing childcare needs during working hours. • Allowance for women to work night shifts, provided proper safety measures are implemented to ensure their well-being.
Sexual Harassment of Women at Workplace (POSH Act) 2013	**Objective:** Shifts the responsibility of preventing and addressing sexual harassment to institutions, prioritizing prevention and offering a clear complaint redressal mechanism. **Key Provisions:** • Requires employers with 10 or more employees to establish an Internal Complaints Committee (ICC) to handle complaints efficiently. • Mandates adherence to "principles of natural justice" during inquiries, ensuring fairness and due process. • Provides a timeframe of three to six months for filing complaints after an incident occurs. • Offers options for resolving complaints through conciliation (mutual agreement) or a formal inquiry initiated by the ICC.
Code on Wages, 2019	**Objective:** Combines and strengthens existing legislation like The Equal Remuneration Act, 1976, prohibiting wage discrimination based on gender. **Key Points:** • Explicitly prohibits discrimination in wages based on gender for the same or similar work performed. • Prevents gender bias during recruitment processes for the same or similar positions, unless specific restrictions are outlined in existing laws.
Factories Act, 1948	**Objective:** Ensures the occupational safety, health, and well-being of all workers, including women, employed in factories. **Provision:** Ensures the welfare of workers in factories registered under the Act, especially emphasizing the safety and well-being of women workers

(c) Suggestion to mitigate such working conditions:

1. Ensuring Mental Resilience for Peak Performance:

- **Navigating Complexities:** Civil servants occupy positions that demand unwavering dedication to public service and the ability to navigate complex situations with composure.
- **Maintaining Composure for Effective Decision-Making:** Developing strong emotional intelligence and maintaining composure under pressure are crucial for making sound and effective decisions during critical situations.
- **Sustaining Motivation Through Self-Reflection:**
- **Encountering Ethical Dilemmas:** Civil service careers are not without ethical dilemmas that can test commitment and dedication.
- **Reinvigorating Core Values:** Regular self-reflection and revisiting the core values that inspired public service pursuits can serve as a powerful motivator during challenging times.
- **The Importance of a Supportive Work-Life Ecosystem:**
- **The Role of Family in Well-being:** A strong support system at home is essential for civil servants, especially those facing demanding work environments.
- **Balancing Public Service and Personal Life:** Family members can provide crucial emotional and moral support, enabling civil servants to maintain a healthy work-life balance and fulfill professional commitments with renewed energy.

2. Promoting Shared Parental Responsibilities:

- **Shared Responsibility for Child Rearing:** Raising children is a rewarding but demanding responsibility that should not solely fall upon one parent.
- **Equality and Shared Joys of Parenthood:** Involving both partners in childcare responsibilities, as in Rashika's case with Vikram, promotes gender equality and allows both parents to experience the joys of raising a family together.

Recommendations for Employer-Initiated Work-Life Balance Strategies:

- **Implementing Reasonable Work Hours:** Establishing reasonable working hours prevents employee burnout and ensures adequate time for rejuvenation and personal well-being.
- **Promoting Mental Health and Productivity:** Encouraging breaks and creating a culture that supports leisure activities can significantly enhance employee mental health and overall organizational productivity.
- **Acknowledging Unique Challenges of Female Employees:** Recognizing the specific challenges faced by female employees and providing support systems like on-site childcare facilities (crèches) can make a substantial difference in their work-life balance and career satisfaction.

By fostering a work environment that prioritizes mental well-being, offers strong support systems, and promotes a healthy work-life balance, employers can empower civil servants to deliver exceptional public service while maintaining their personal well-being.

Q. You have just been appointed as Additional Director General of Central Public Works Department. The Chief Architect of your division, who is to retire in six months, is passionately working on a very important project, the successful completion of which would earn him a lasting reputation for the rest of his life. A new lady architect. Seema, trained at Manchester School of Architecture, UK joined as Senior Architect in your division. During the briefing about the project, Seema made some suggestions which would not only add value to the project, but would also reduce completion time. This has made the Chief Architect insecure and he is constantly worried that all the credit will go to her. Subsequently, he adopted a passive and aggressive behaviour towards her and has become disrespectful to her. Seema felt it embarrassing as the Chief Architect left no chance of humiliating her. He would very often correct her in front of other colleagues and raise his voice while speaking to her. This continuous harassment has resulted in her losing confidence and self- esteem. She felt perpetually tensed, anxious and stressed. She appeared to be in awe of him since he has had a long tenure in the office and has vast experience in the area of her work. You are aware of her outstanding academi c credentials and career record in her previous organisations. However, you fear that this harassment-may result in compromising her much needed contribution in this important project and may adversely impact her emotional well-being. You have also come to know from her peers that she is contemplating tendering her resignation.

(a) What are the ethical issues involved in the above case?
(b) What are the options available to you in order to complete the project as well as to retain Seema in the organization?
(c) What would be your response to Seema's predicament? What measures would you institute to prevent such occurrences from happening in your organization? (UPSC 2023)

Context

The case presents an ethical dilemma regarding workplace harassment and a hostile work environment faced by Seema, a competent new employee, from the retiring Chief Architect who feels threatened by her talent. As the senior authority, I must uphold ethics, ensure project delivery and protect my subordinate's interests.

Mahatma Gandhi said, *"The true measure of any society can be found in how it treats its most vulnerable members." This applies to organisational culture as well.*

Stakeholders

- **Seema:** The architect being harassed, whose well-being and contribution are at stake.
- **Chief Architect:** The harasser, whose behavior needs correction.
- **You (Additional Director General):** Responsible for addressing the situation and creating a positive work environment.
- **Project Team:** Their productivity and project success can be impacted by the conflict.
- **Central Public Works Department:** The organization's reputation and ethical conduct are on the line.

Values involved

- **Respect:** All employees deserve a workplace free from harassment and intimidation.
- **Fairness:** Everyone should have equal opportunities to contribute and be recognized for their work.
- **Integrity:** Leadership must uphold ethical standards and address misconduct.
- **Collaboration:** A team environment fosters better project outcomes.
- **Well-being:** The organization should prioritize the mental and emotional health of its employees.

(a) Key Ethical Issues:

- **Hostile Work Environment:** The Chief Architect's behavior creates a hostile work environment for Seema through constant humiliation, insults, and disrespect. This not only violates ethical standards but potentially breaks the law.
- **Power Imbalance and Abuse:** The Chief Architect, in a position of authority, is misusing his power to harass a junior colleague (Seema) due to insecurity about her talent. This abuse of power is unethical.
- **Project at Risk:** The Chief Architect's actions risk jeopardizing project completion if Seema leaves due to harassment. Prioritizing personal insecurities over organizational goals demonstrates a lack of integrity.
- **Psychological Harm and Disrespect:** The constant harassment has caused Seema to lose confidence and experience mental stress. This behavior disregards human dignity and lacks empathy.

(b) To complete the project and retain Seema:

I can take the following steps:

- **Mentorship for Chief Architect:** Meet with the Chief Architect, emphasizing his valuable experience. Advise him to adjust his approach and collaborate effectively with Seema, highlighting how her ideas contribute to a successful project.
- **Anti-Harassment Training:** Partner with HR to conduct mandatory anti-harassment and gender sensitivity workshops for all employees. This promotes a respectful workplace for everyone.
- **Collaborative Workflow:** Establish clear roles and responsibilities for both architects, ensuring their work complements each other. Track progress transparently to minimize conflict.
- **Public Recognition:** Acknowledge Seema's skills, qualifications, and dedication publicly. This boosts her confidence and overall team morale.
- **Zero-Tolerance Policy:** Reaffirm the organization's strong stance against harassment. Emphasize discreet but firm action based on company policy. If necessary, consider project reassignments to address persistent issues.
- **Empower Seema:** Encourage Seema to maintain a professional demeanor and document any inappropriate interactions. This strengthens her position if needed.
- **Highlight Growth Opportunities:** Showcase Seema's critical role in the project and her future career prospects within the organization. This can help dissuade her from leaving.

Recommended course of action:

Immediate Actions

- **Address the Chief Architect:** Privately counsel him about the unprofessional behavior and emphasize the importance of ethical leadership. Clearly state that such conduct is unacceptable and continued violations will lead to disciplinary action.
- **Support Seema:** Offer Seema confidential support and counseling to help her regain confidence. Provide professional mentoring and opportunities to showcase her talent through independent tasks.
- **Long-Term Solutions:**
- **Workplace Sensitivity:** Implement mandatory ethics training for all employees, focusing on preventing harassment and promoting equal opportunity. Encourage bystanders to intervene or report inappropriate behavior.
- **Strengthen Redressal Mechanisms:** Review and strengthen the Internal Complaints Committee (ICC) and its processes to ensure prompt and fair investigation of harassment claims. Guarantee protection against retaliation for reporting misconduct.

Preventive Measures

- **Leadership Training:** Prioritize ethics and gender sensitivity training, especially for senior management, to foster understanding and responsible leadership.
- **Empowered ICC:** Ensure the ICC has adequate resources and diverse representation to effectively address complaints.
- **Zero-Tolerance Culture:** Publicly communicate a zero-tolerance policy for harassment from leadership, and reinforce it with consistent enforcement. This can involve positive messaging highlighting role models for appropriate behavior, alongside discouraging casual sexism in the workplace.
- **Diversity and Inclusion:** Actively promote diversity and inclusion initiatives throughout the organization. This creates a safe and respectful work environment where everyone feels valued and has the opportunity to thrive.
- **Leadership Role:**
  - **Moral Leadership:** As the head of the organization, demonstrate strong moral leadership by taking decisive action in this case. This sets the tone for the entire organization.
  - **Ethical Culture:** Promote the highest standards of ethics and empathy throughout the organization. Achieve this through a combination of training, counseling, open communication, and strict policy enforcement.

The Chief Architect's harassment towards Seema creates a hostile work environment, risks project success, and violates ethical and potentially legal boundaries. By addressing the Chief Architect, supporting Seema, and implementing anti-harassment training and robust reporting systems, the Additional Director General can foster a respectful workplace, retain talent, and ensure project completion. This commitment to ethics and a positive work environment strengthens the organization's reputation and overall productivity.

Corruption

Q. Vinod is an honest and sincere IAS officer. Recently, he has taken over as Managing Director of the State Road Transport Corporation, his sixth transfer in the past three years. His peers acknowledge his vast knowledge, affability and uprightness. The Chairman of the State Road Transport Corporation is a powerful politician and is very close to the Chief Minister. Vinod comes to know about many alleged irregularities of the Corporation and the high-handedness of the Chairman in financial Matters. A Board Member of the Corporation belonging to the Opposition Party meets Vinod and hands over a few documents along with a video recording in which the Chairman appears to be demanding bribe for placing a huge order for the supply of QMR tyres. Vinod recollects the Chairman expediting clearing of pending bills of QMR tyres. Vinod confronts the Board Member as to why he is shying away from exposing the Chairman with the so-called solid proof he has with him. The member informs him that the Chairman refuses to yield to his threats. He adds that Vinod may earn recognition and public support if he himself exposes the Chairman. Further, he tells Vinod that once his party comes to power, Vinod's professional growth would be assured. Vinod is aware that he may be penaliz ed if he exposes the Chairman and may further be transferred to a distant place. He knows that the Opposition Party

stands a better chance of coming to power in the forthcoming elections. However, he also realizes that the Board Member is trying to use him for his own political gains.

(a) As a conscientious civil servant, evaluate the options available to Vinod.

(b) In the light of the above case, comment upon the ethical issues that may arise due to the politicisation of bureaucracy. (UPSC 2023)

Context

The case presents an ethical dilemma for Vinod, an honest IAS officer, regarding exposing potential misconduct and corruption by the politically influential Chairman of the State Road Transport Corporation where Vinod is posted. It highlights issues of abuse of power, probity, whistleblowing, prudent conduct and politicisation of bureaucracy

Stakeholders

- **Vinod:** The honest and sincere IAS officer facing the ethical dilemma.
- **Chairman:** The powerful politician and head of the State Road Transport Corporation, suspected of corruption.
- **Board Member:** The Opposition Party representative who possesses evidence of the Chairman's wrongdoing.
- **State Road Transport Corporation:** The public entity entrusted to Vinod's care.
- **Citizens:** The public who rely on efficient and corruption-free public transportation.
- **Chief Minister:** The leader of the state government, with close ties to the Chairman.
- **Opposition Party:** The political party aiming to expose corruption and potentially come to power.

Values Associated with the Case

- **Honesty and Integrity:** Vinod's core value of being upright and truthful is central to the dilemma.
- **Accountability and Transparency:** The need for responsible leadership and open financial practices within the Corporation.
- **Courage and Moral Conviction:** Vinod must decide whether to prioritize personal safety or stand up for what's right.
- **Public Service and Duty:** Vinod's obligation to serve the public interest and uphold the law.
- **Political Interests:** The potential influence of political affiliations on decision-making.
- **Loyalty:** Balancing loyalty to superiors with the higher duty to expose corruption.
- **Professional Growth:** The potential impact of Vinod's decision on his career advancement.
- **Efficiency and Public Trust:** The importance of a well-functioning public transport system built on trust.

Potential Legislation Violated in Vinod's Case

Based on the information provided in the case study, Vinod, the Chairman, and potentially the Board Member could be in violation of several laws:

1. The Prevention of Corruption Act, 1988:

- **Section 7:** Bribery - If the Chairman demanded a bribe for placing the tire order, he would be in violation of this section.
- **Section 13(2):** Abetment by public servant - If Vinod knew about the bribery and didn't report it, he could be seen as an abettor under this section.

2. Indian Penal Code (IPC):

- **Section 161:** Abetment with illegal gratification by public servant - Similar to the Prevention of Corruption Act, Vinod could be charged under this section for not reporting the bribery.
- **Section 165:** Taking or obtaining undue advantage for oneself or for another person by public servant - This section could apply to the Chairman if he used his position to gain an unfair advantage through the bribe.
- **Section 409:** Criminal breach of trust by public servant - Both Vinod (for not reporting) and the Chairman (for potential misappropriation) could be liable under this section for violating the trust placed in them by their positions.

3. Whistleblower Protection Act, 2014:

- **This Act aims to protect whistleblowers who report corruption or wrongdoing within organizations.**
- If Vinod exposes the Chairman's actions, he could potentially seek protection under this act if he faces retaliation.

(a) Courses of Action for Vinod:

1. **Public Exposure:**
    - **Pros:** Upholds Vinod's duty to fight corruption and serve the public good. Aligns with the principle of speaking truth to power.

- **Cons:** Lack of concrete evidence beyond accusations could lead to dismissal as political maneuvering. The Chairman might retaliate with impunity.

2. **Private Confrontation:**
   - **Pros:** Provides an opportunity for the Chairman to rectify his actions before escalation.
   - **Cons:** Given the Chairman's past dismissive behavior, success seems unlikely. The misconduct might continue unabated.
3. **Internal Reporting:**
   - **Pros:** Follows established procedures and allows for a formal investigation.
   - **Cons:** The Chairman's political connections could influence officials to bury the case. Vinod might face a punitive transfer without a resolution.
4. **Remaining Silent:**
   - **Pros:** Avoids immediate retaliation and protects Vinod's family from potential harassment.
   - **Cons:** Dereliction of duty towards the public and the Constitution. Staying silent makes him complicit in wrongdoing.
5. **Seeking Guidance/Reporting Upward:**
   - **Pros:** Maintains Vinod's ethical stance while potentially bringing irregularities to light without antagonizing the Chairman directly.
   - **Cons:** The hierarchical system might be biased due to the Chairman's connections. Reporting might not lead to concrete action.
6. **Resignation:**
   - **Pros:** Demonstrates a strong personal stand against corruption and unwavering ethics.
   - **Cons:** Vinod loses his platform to influence change from within. This could be seen as giving up the fight against corruption

Recommended Course of Action:

- **Document Everything:** Maintain a detailed record of evidence and related interactions.
- **Internal Reporting:** Begin by reporting the matter through official channels to higher authorities.
- **Seek Legal Counsel:** Consult a legal expert for guidance on potential ramifications.
- **Diplomatic Engagement:** Engage privately with the Chairman to gauge the possibility of reforms.
- **Prepare for Repercussions:** Be ready for potential retaliations, considering the Chairman's political influence.
- **Act in Public Interest:** Only expose the matter publicly if internal measures fail and it's in the larger public good.
- **Avoid Political Manipulations:** Steer clear of becoming a pawn in political rivalries. This balances moral courage with prudence, giving the system a chance to remedy the situation first before external escalation.

Ethical Issues of Politicization

1. Unfair Personnel Practices:

- **Rewarding Favored Bureaucrats:** Political connections are used to promote or transfer bureaucrats who are loyal to politicians, not necessarily the most qualified.
- **Punishing Honest Officers:** Those who act impartially or disagree with political agendas are penalized with transfers or missed promotions.

2. Corruption and Abuse:

- **Bypassing Procedures:** Politicians or special interests pressure bureaucrats to ignore regulations for personal gain.

3. Weakened Bureaucracy:

- **Loss of Integrity:** Bureaucrats prioritize political interests over their duty to uphold the constitution and serve the public.
- **Devaluing Merit:** Promotions and appointments are based on political connections, not competence, leading to a less effective bureaucracy.

4. Unequal Governance:

- **Skewed Policies:** Political agendas distort how resources are allocated, policies are implemented, and regulations are enforced. This creates an unfair system.

Addressing Politicization

- **Enforce Civil Service Rules:** Strict adherence to established guidelines for postings, promotions, and performance evaluations minimizes political influence.
- **Protect Whistleblowers:** Strong legal protections and consequences for retaliation encourage reporting of misconduct.
- **Merit-Based System:** Transparent selection processes based on qualifications and experience ensure the best people get the job.
- **Streamlined Regulations:** Simplifying bureaucratic procedures reduces opportunities for manipulation and improves efficiency.
- **Electoral Reform:** Increasing public accountability of politicians helps reduce the power they hold over the bureaucracy.

Vinod should act with courage tempered by wisdom to uphold probity while avoiding futility. The case highlights the deep despair of politicisation that requires systemic reforms to safeguard bureaucratic autonomy and integrity essential for just and efficient governance

Compassion vs Proper Utilisation of Public Funds

Q. You are working as an executive in a nationalised bank for several years. One day one of your close colleagues tells you that her father is suffering from heart disease and needs surgery immediately to survive. She also tells you that she has no insurance and the operation will cost about Rs. 10 lakh. You are also aware of the fact that her husband is no more and that she is from a lower middle class family. You are empathetic about her situation. However, apart from expressing your sympathy, you do not have the resources to fund her. A few weeks later, you ask her about the well-being of her father and she informs you about his successful surgery and that he is recovering. She then confides in you that the bank manager was kind enough to facilitate the release of Rs. 10 lakh from a dormant account of someone to pay for the operation with a promise that it should be confidential and be repaid at the earliest. She has already started paying it back and will continue to do so until it is all returned.
(a) What are the ethical issues involved?
(b) Evaluate the behaviour of the bank manager from an ethical point of view.
(c) How would you react to the situation? (UPSC 2023)

Stakeholders Involved:

- Executive of national bank
- Bank
- Colleague
- Bank Manager
- Father of colleague

Violation of Legislations

- **Banking Regulation Act, 1949:** This Act outlines regulations for the safekeeping of customer deposits. Improper access to dormant accounts could be seen as a violation of these regulations.
- **Indian Penal Code (IPC):** Sections 405 (criminal breach of trust) and 409 (criminal breach of trust by public servant) could potentially apply if the manager's actions are deemed a misappropriation of funds entrusted to their care.

Values in Conflict

- **Compassion and Empathy:** The bank manager's action stemmed from a desire to help a colleague in a critical situation, demonstrating compassion and empathy.
- **Honesty and Integrity:** The method used, accessing a dormant account for personal reasons, contravenes the principles of honesty and integrity expected from a bank employee entrusted with safeguarding customer funds.
- **Accountability and Responsibility:** The bank manager, entrusted with a position of financial responsibility, failed to follow proper procedures and potentially exposed themselves and the bank to legal consequences.
- **Transparency and Fairness:** The lack of transparency surrounding the transaction raises questions about fairness and creates a precedent for potential favoritism in the future.

- **Confidentiality and Trust:** The bank manager promised confidentiality, but the situation creates a potential breach of trust with the bank and the dormant account holder.
- **Following the Law:** The bank manager's actions potentially violated banking regulations and the Indian Penal Code, highlighting the importance of adhering to legal principles.
- **Whistle-Blowing:** While you cannot condone the act, you might consider the value of whistle-blowing if you believe the situation poses a significant risk or ongoing misuse of funds. This requires balancing loyalty with the need to uphold ethical standards and potentially protect the bank and its customers.

(a) Ethical issues involved:

- **Transparency:** In this situation the bank manager as well as colleagues are not transparent about their actions.
- **Accountability:** The bank manager does not seem to be accountable to higher authorities as well as to rules and regulations of the bank. The bank manager has flouted obligations of his/her position.
- **Integrity and Probity:** Bank manager and colleague are not showing integrity as well as probity towards the bank. It is directed towards keeping self-interest over organisation's interest.
- **Empathy:** The executive and bank manager has shown empathy towards colleague.
- **Compassion:** Showing compassion, bank manager has shown compassion of giving large sum of money through unauthorised means.
- **Objectivity:** Making decisions with objectivity means relying on data and statistics rather than one's own bias or opinion. Here the bank manager's action can be seen as right or wrong regardless of the consequences.

(b) Behaviour of the bank manager from an ethical point of view.

- **Benevolence:** The act by the manager can be seen as an act of benevolence.
- **Unjust act:** The behaviour of manager has done injustice to the dormant account holder against his/her will, or without getting informed.
- **Misuse of authority:** In this situation there has been misuse of authority by the bank manager.
- **Ends justifying means:** The father of a colleague has done surgery, which shows that though the means are wrong, its end has justified it
- **Against the rule:** The behaviour of the bank manager is against the rules and regulations of the organisation.

(c) My reaction to the situation

1. **Promoting Transparency and Accountability:**
   - **Board-Level Advocacy:** Raise awareness at board meetings regarding the critical importance of strict transparency and accountability measures within the bank.
   - **Reputation Management:** Emphasize how maintaining the trust of customers and stakeholders hinges on adherence to established protocols and ethical practices.
2. **Combating Secrecy:**
   - **Policy Proposal:** Advocate for the implementation of a clear policy within the bank that explicitly prohibits the secretive authorization of funds to employees, regardless of their position.
   - **Fairness and Consistency:** Highlight how a transparent and standardized approach to financial matters ensures fairness and consistency for all employees.
3. **Employee Well-Being and Security:**
   - **Health Insurance Initiative:** Propose the introduction of comprehensive health insurance plans sponsored by the bank, covering employees and their immediate families.
   - **Dual Benefit:** This program would not only provide essential financial safeguards for employees during health crises but also reduce the likelihood of resorting to unethical means in personal emergencies.
4. **Compassionate yet Accountable Approach:**
   - **Acknowledge Motivations:** Recognize that the desperate circumstances of both your colleague and the manager may have driven their actions.
   - **Accountability with Compassion:** While holding them accountable for their actions is necessary, advocate for internal measures to ensure repayment and prevent future occurrences, potentially avoiding legal repercussions.
5. **Long-Term Preventive Measures:**
   - **Emergency Fund Creation:** Push for the establishment of a dedicated medical emergency fund accessible to all employees during critical situations.
   - **Ethical Alternatives:** This fund would provide employees with a reliable and ethical resource to address personal medical emergencies, preventing the need to consider potentially unethical solutions.

Conclusion

By implementing these proactive measures, promotion of a more ethical and transparent work environment within the bank can take place. While the manager's intent was positive, highlighting the importance of following established rules and regulations is crucial.

Development vs Environment

Q. You are appointed as an officer heading the section in the Environment Pollution Control Board to ensure compliance and its follow-up. In that region, there were a large number of small and medium industries which had been granted clearance. You learnt that these industries provide employment to many migrant workers. Most of the industrial units have got environmental clearance certificates in their possession. The environmental clearance seeks to curb industries and projects that supposedly hamper the environment and living species in the region. But in practice most of these units remain to be polluting units in several ways like air, water and soil pollution. As such, local people encountered persistent health problems. It was confirmed that the majority of the industries were violating environmental compliance. You issued notice to all the industrial units to apply for a fresh environmental clearance certificate from the competent authority. However, your action met with hostile response from a section of the industrial units, other vested interest persons and a section of the local politicians. The workers also became very hostile to you as they felt that your action would lead to the closure of these industrial units, and the resultant unemployment will lead to insecurity and uncertainty in their livelihood. Many owners of the industries approached you with the plea that you should not initiate harsh action as it would compel them to sell their units, and cause huge financial loss, or shortage of their products in the market. These would obviously add to the sufferings of the laborers and the consumer alike. The labor union also sent you a representation requesting against the closure of the units. You simultaneously started receiving threats from unknown corners. You however received support from some of your colleagues, who advised you to act freely to ensure environmental compliance. Local NGOs also came to your support and they demanded the closure of the polluting units immediately.

(a) What are the options available to you under the given situation?

(b) Critically examine the options listed by you.

(c) What type of mechanism would you suggest to ensure environmental compliance?

(d) What are the ethical dilemmas you faced in exercising your option? (UPSC 2022)

Context

The situation involves the enforcement of environmental compliance in a region with numerous small and medium industries. The industries are found to be **violating environmental regulations, leading to health issues for the local population**. The officer in charge is facing opposition from industrial units, vested interest groups, and politicians, while receiving support from colleagues and NGOs.

Stakeholders:

- **You (Officer):** Responsible for enforcing environmental regulations and ensuring compliance.
- **Industrial Units:** Businesses that might need to upgrade or face consequences for non-compliance.
- **Migrant Workers:** Employed by the industries and potentially impacted by closures.
- **Local People:** Affected by pollution and seeking a healthy environment.
- **Local Politicians:** Balancing economic activity with environmental concerns in their constituency.
- **NGOs:** Advocating for environmental protection and potentially stricter regulations.

Violated Legislations:

- **Water (Prevention and Control of Pollution) Act, 1974:** This act regulates the prevention and control of water pollution and maintains the wholesomeness of water.
- **Air (Prevention and Control of Pollution) Act, 1981:** This act aims to prevent, control, and abate air pollution.
- **Environment (Protection) Act, 1986:** This act is an umbrella legislation for the protection and improvement of the environment.

Values Involved:

- **Environmental Sustainability:** Protecting the environment for future generations.

- **Public Health:** Ensuring the well-being of citizens by minimizing pollution and its health effects.
- **Economic stability:** Maintaining a healthy economy that provides jobs and supports livelihoods.
- **Social Justice:** Ensuring the fair treatment of all stakeholders, including workers, community members, and industry owners.
- **Professional Integrity:** Upholding environmental regulations and fulfilling your professional duty to enforce compliance.

(a) Options available under the given situation:

- **Enhanced Enforcement:** Implement stricter enforcement measures with increased penalties for non-compliant industrial units.
- **Collaborative Engagement:** Foster dialogue and negotiation with industrial units to encourage the adoption of environmentally sustainable practices.
- **Strategic Escalation:** Seek the involvement of relevant government agencies or higher authorities for a more comprehensive approach to achieving compliance.
- **Community Stakeholder Collaboration:** Partner with local environmental NGOs and community members to raise awareness about the environmental impact of non-compliance and secure their cooperation in ensuring adherence to regulations.
- **Phased Compliance Plan:** Develop and implement a phased compliance plan, providing industrial units with a defined timeframe to progressively improve their practices.

Critical Examination of Options:

Pros	Cons
Option 1: Enhanced Enforcement	
• **Swift Compliance:** Can deter future violations and achieve immediate results. • **Deterrence:** Sends a strong message about environmental protection. • **Public Health:** Protects local communities from environmental harm.	• **Economic Impact:** May lead to job losses and financial hardship. • **Resistance:** Can create hostility and resistance from industry. • **Market Shortage:** Sudden closures might create product shortages.
Option 2: Collaborative Engagement	
• **Long-Term Change:** Provides opportunities for cooperation and lasting improvements. • **Education:** Allows for raising awareness about environmental impact. • **Trust Building:** Can foster trust and collaboration with industry.	• **Slow Progress:** Negotiations may not guarantee immediate compliance. • **Resistance:** Some industries might resist adopting eco-friendly practices. • **Commitment:** Requires industry willingness and commitment.
Option 3: Strategic Escalation	
• **Increased Resources:** Provides leverage and additional resources for tackling non-compliance. • **Stricter Measures:** Higher authorities can enforce stricter regulations and penalties. • **Bureaucracy:** Helps overcome bureaucratic hurdles and delays.	• **Bureaucracy:** May involve bureaucratic delays in acquiring support. • **Limited Control:** Reliance on higher authorities limits individual decision-making. • **Competing Priorities:** Higher authorities might have competing interests and limited resources.
Option 4: Community Stakeholder Collaboration	
• **Community Involvement:** Strengthens community engagement in environmental issues. • **NGO Expertise:** NGOs can offer expertise, resources, and advocacy. • **Collective Effort:** Creates a shared effort towards environmental sustainability.	• **Time Commitment:** Building consensus and cooperation requires time and effort. • **Reliance:** Effectiveness depends on NGO availability and capacity. • **Sustainability:** Maintaining collaboration over time can be challenging.
Option 5: Phased Compliance Plan	

• **Economic Balance:** Allows for gradual change without immediate economic disruptions. • **Adaptation:** Provides time for workers and owners to adjust to new practices. • **Monitoring:** Allows for progress tracking and evaluation during implementation.	• **Slow Pace:** Compliance may not be achieved within the desired timeframe. • **Enforcement:** Requires continuous monitoring and enforcement to ensure progress. • **Adequacy:** Critics may argue it doesn't address immediate environmental concerns.

Mechanism to ensure environmental compliance:

- Establish a robust monitoring system to regularly assess the industrial units' compliance with environmental regulations.
- Conduct regular inspections and audits to identify violations and non-compliant practices.
- Provide necessary training and awareness programs to industrial unit owners and workers regarding the importance of environmental compliance.
- Implement strict penalties and fines for non-compliance to create a deterrent effect.
- Encourage the adoption of sustainable and eco-friendly technologies and practices through incentives and rewards.
- Foster collaboration between the Environment Pollution Control Board, industry associations, NGOs, and other stakeholders to collectively work towards environmental protection.

Ethical Dilemmas in Ensuring Environmental Compliance:

1. **Balancing Act:** Striking a balance between protecting the environment and potential economic consequences. This involves weighing the costs of stricter regulations on jobs, businesses, and the overall economy against the long-term costs of environmental degradation.
2. **Navigating Resistance:** Dealing with opposition, hostility, and even threats from industries and powerful interest groups who may prioritize short-term profits over environmental responsibility. This requires courage and resilience in enforcing regulations.
3. **Ensuring Fairness:** Upholding environmental regulations fairly and consistently for all stakeholders, regardless of size, influence, or political connections. This can be challenging, especially when dealing with powerful industries.
4. **Long-Term vs. Short-Term:** Focusing on long-term environmental sustainability, even when faced with immediate pressures to prioritize economic growth or job creation. This requires a commitment to long-term planning and responsible decision-making.

Conclusion

This case exemplifies **John Stuart Mill's** utilitarian dilemma. Protecting the environment maximizes long-term societal well-being, but short-term economic hardship can decrease happiness. Collaborative solutions, incorporating industry incentives and community engagement, can promote environmental sustainability while minimizing economic disruption. This utilitarian approach fosters a future where environmental protection and economic prosperity coexist.

Illegal Migrants

Q. Ramesh is a State Civil Services Officer who got the opportunity of getting posted to the capital of a border State after rendering 20 years of service. Ramesh's mother has recently been diagnosed with cancer and has been admitted in the leading cancer hospital of the city. His two adolescent children have also got admission in one of the best public schools of the town. After settling down in his appointment as Director in the Home Department of the State, Ramesh got a confidential report through intelligence sources that illegal migrants are infiltrating in the State from the neighboring country. He decided to personally carry out surprise checks of the border posts along with his Home Department team. To his surprise, he caught red-handed two families of 12 members infiltrated with the connivance of the security personnel at the border posts. On further inquiry and investigation, it was found that after the migrants from neighboring countries infiltrate, their documentation like Aadhaar Card, Ration Card and Voter Card are also forged and they are made to settle down in a particular area of the State. Ramesh prepared the detailed and comprehensive report and submitted it to the Additional Secretary of the State. However, he was summoned by the Additional Home Secretary after a week and was instructed to withdraw the report. The Additional Home Secretary informed Ramesh that the report submitted by him has not been appreciated by the higher authorities. He further cautioned him that if he fails to withdraw the confidential report, he will not only be posted

out from the prestigious appointment from the State capital but his further promotion which is due in near future will also get in jeopardy.

a. **What are the Department options available to Ramesh as the Director of the Home Department of the bordering State?**
b. **What option should Ramesh adopt and why?**
c. **Critically evaluate each of the options.**
d. **What are the ethical dilemmas being faced by Ramesh?**
e. **What policy measures would you suggest to combat the menace of infiltration of illegal migrants from the neighboring country? (UPSC 2022)**

Context

The case study revolves around Ramesh, the Director of the Home Department in a bordering state, who uncovers the **infiltration of illegal migrants with the connivance of security personnel**. However, he faces pressure from the Additional Home Secretary to withdraw his comprehensive report on the matter.

Violation of Laws:

- **Foreigners Act, 1946:** This act regulates the entry and stay of foreigners in India. The illegal migrants entering the country and those aiding their infiltration violate this act.
- **Prevention of Corruption Act, 1988:** The security personnel at the border posts who connived with the migrants might be guilty of bribery and corruption under this act.
- **The Citizenship Act, 1955:** Forging documents like Aadhaar cards, ration cards and voter cards for the migrants violates this act, which governs Indian citizenship.
- **Representation of the People Act, 1950 (RP Act):** Issuing fake voter cards to ineligible individuals is a violation of this act that governs elections in India.

Major Stakeholders

- **Ramesh:** The State Civil Services Officer facing a moral and professional dilemma.
- **Illegal Migrants:** Individuals entering the country illegally.
- **Security Personnel:** Those stationed at the border posts who allegedly aided the infiltration.
- **State Government:** The authorities to whom Ramesh reports and who are potentially aware of the issue.
- **Citizens of the Border State:** Potentially impacted by the infiltration.
- **Central Government:** Responsible for national security and border control policies. Ramesh's Family: His mother and children who might be affected by his decisions.

Values Involved

- **Integrity vs. Obedience:** Upholding his findings (integrity) clashes with following orders from a superior (obedience).
- **Duty vs. Self-Interest:** Ramesh's duty to report illegal immigration conflicts with his desire to be near his family (self-interest).
- **Transparency vs. Expediency:** Transparency in addressing the issue may be inconvenient or create difficulties for his superiors (expediency).
- **National Security:** Unchecked illegal immigration can pose security threats. Addressing it prioritizes national security.
- **Accountability:** The government needs to be held accountable for border security and preventing illegal activities.
- **Rule of Law:** The law applies to everyone, and ignoring illegal immigration undermines the rule of law.
- **Courage:** Standing up for his principles and duty despite potential consequences requires courage.
- **Public Service:** Ramesh's actions reflect on his commitment to public service and the well-being of the citizens.

Ramesh's Options as Director (Home Department)

1. **Withdraw the Report (Compliance):** Follow the Additional Secretary's instructions and retract the report. This avoids career repercussions but allows illegal immigration to continue.
2. **Forward the report directly to the Union Home Ministry** and highlight (a) the issue of illegal immigration and (b) the non-cooperative attitude of his superiors at the state level.
3. **Whistleblowing:** He can share the report with the media for compelling the higher authorities to address the issue.

Evaluating each option:

1. Withdrawal of the report:

- **Pros:** Respect for bureaucratic hierarchy, Goodwill of his superior(s), Smooth career growth and progress.
- **Cons:** Compromises his integrity, allows illegal immigration to continue and potentially harms national security in the long run.

2. Forwarding the report to the Union Home Ministry

- **Pros:** Display of moral courage, ability to take a stand, aligns with the ethical principles.
- **Cons:** Display a lack of emotional quotient, Against the Code of Conduct.

3. Involving the Media

- **Pros:** Compel the authorities to act due to the resultant pressure.
- **Cons:** Against the service rules and Code of Conduct, Possibility of misuse due to the critical nature of the information.

Recommended Option: Continuing with the Report and forwarding it to Union Home Ministry

Ramesh should maintain the report for the following reasons:

- **Upholding Ethical Principles:** Transparency, accountability, and integrity are crucial for his role as Director. Withdrawing the report undermines these values.
- **Addressing National Security:** Illegal immigration can pose security threats. Addressing it is vital for the state's well-being.
- **Long-Term Impact:** Ignoring the issue might worsen the situation later, potentially causing more significant problems.
- **Whistleblowing should be used as last resort.**

Ethical Dilemmas Faced by Ramesh:

1. **Duty vs. Career:** Ramesh is caught between his duty to report illegal immigration and protect national security, and the potential consequences for his career if he disobeys his superior's instructions.
2. **Code of Conduct and Service Rules vs Dedication towards Duty:** Choice between doing his duty or not do his duty in favour of adhering to the codes of conduct and service rules
3. **Moral courage vs Adherence to Hierarchy:** Choice between taking a stand for the correct action vs adhering to hierarchy and earn the superior(s)' goodwill.
4. **Whistle-blowing vs. Career Progression:** Reporting the issue could be seen as whistle-blowing, potentially leading to retaliation or hindering his career advancement.
5. **Short-Term Benefit vs. Long-Term Consequences:** Withdrawing the report might provide temporary career security, but the long-term consequences of unchecked illegal immigration could be severe.
6. **Personal Interest vs. National Interest:** Ramesh's desire to be closer to his family due to his mother's illness conflicts with his responsibility to protect the public good by addressing illegal border crossings.
7. **Accountability towards the Seniors vs Accountability towards the people :** While following orders from a superior is generally expected, Ramesh must decide if those orders conflict with his moral responsibility to act in the best interest of the state.

Policy Measures to Combat Illegal Migration:

- Improvement of critical border infrastructure (roads, fences, lights etc.).
- Deployment of additional personnel for border guarding and monitoring duties.
- Zero-tolerance towards corruption in matters of illegal immigration.
- Use of technology (drones, satellite imagery, etc.) for efficient border management and surveillance.
- Effective implementation of Comprehensive Integrated Border Management System (CIBMS) and Border Electronically Dominated QRT Interception Technique (BOLD-QIT) projects.

Conclusion

Vasudev Kutumbakam, a Sanskrit phrase meaning "the world is one family," embodies the idea of global unity. **A balanced immigration policy** upholds national security while supporting those in need, reflecting this spirit. By implementing coordinated measures, governments can address illegal immigration and ensure stability, all while extending a hand to those truly deserving.

Cheating in Educational Institutions

Q. You are Vice Principal of a degree college in one of the middle-class towns. Principal has recently retired and management is looking for his replacement. There are also feelers that the management may promote you as principal. In the meantime, during the annual examination the flying squad which came from the university caught two students red-handed involved in unfair means. A senior lecturer of the college was personally helping these students in this act. This senior lecturer also happens to be close to the management. One of the students was the son of a local politician who was responsible for getting the college affiliated to the present reputed university. The second student was the son of a local businessman who has donated maximum funds for running the college. You immediately informed the management regarding this unfortunate incident. The management told you to resolve the issue with the flying squad at any cost. They further said that such incidents will not only tarnish the image of the college but also the politicians and businessmen are very important personalities for the functioning of the college. You were also given a hint that your further promotion to Principal depends on your capability in resolving this issue with the flying squad. In the meantime, you were intimidated by your administrative officer that certain members of the student union are protesting outside the college gate against the senior lecturer and the students involved in this incident and demanding strict action against defaulters.

a. **Discuss the ethical issues involved in the case.**
b. **Critically examine the options available with you as Vice Principal. What option will you adopt and why? (UPSC 2021)**

In the given case study, the Vice Principal of a college is faced with an ethical dilemma involving unfair means during examinations and the involvement of a senior lecturer who has close connections with influential individuals.

Stakeholders

- **College Management:** Concerned about reputation and maintaining good relations with influential figures.
- **Vice-Principal:** Caught between upholding ethics and potential career advancement.
- **Flying Squad:** Responsible for ensuring fair examinations and academic integrity.
- **Students:** Two students involved in cheating, the student body demanding fair action.
- **Senior Lecturer:** Engaged in unethical conduct and facing potential consequences.
- **Politician & Businessman:** Their sons are involved and they hold influence over the college.

Values Involved

- **Academic Integrity:** Ensuring fair examinations and ethical learning environment.
- **Fairness and Equity:** Treating all students equally based on merit.
- **Transparency and Accountability:** Open communication and consequences for wrongdoing.
- **Courage and Integrity:** Standing up for what's right despite pressure.
- **Due Process:** Following established procedures for handling disciplinary cases.

Ethical issues:

1. **Academic Dishonesty:** Cheating by students and a lecturer enabling it undermines academic integrity, a core value built on honesty and fairness.
2. **Potential Favoritism:** The students' backgrounds (politician's son and businessman's son) raise concerns about favoritism based on connections rather than merit.
3. **Abuse of Authority:** Management's pressure to resolve the issue at any cost, prioritizing influential figures, suggests a misuse of power and compromising ethical principles for personal gain.
4. **Conflict of Interest:** The lecturer's close relationship with management and the potential impact on the Vice Principal's promotion create a conflict of interest, hindering objective decision-making.

Options Available

Pros	Cons
Option-1: Cover up and Suppression	
• Short-term protection of the college's reputation. • Possible promotion for the Vice Principal. • Maintains positive relationships with influential people.	• Sacrifices academic integrity and ethics. • Breeds dishonesty and unfairness. • Erodes trust with students, faculty, and the community.

	• Sets a bad example for future misconduct. • Risks exposure and long-term damage.
Option-2: Transparent Investigation and Action	
• Upholds academic integrity and ethical principles. • Demonstrates fairness and justice. • Protects the college's reputation in the long run. • Fosters a culture of honesty. • Builds trust with stakeholders.	• Potential conflict with management or backlash from influential people. • May affect the Vice Principal's promotion. • Risk of negative publicity. • Requires time and resources for a thorough investigation.

Preferred Option:

- The Vice Principal should opt for a transparent investigation and take appropriate action based on the evidence.
- Upholding academic integrity and fairness is crucial for the reputation of the college in the long run.
- By demonstrating a commitment to ethical principles, the Vice Principal can establish trust among students, faculty, and the community.

Conclusion:

Choosing transparency might be challenging, but it aligns with professional ethics and fosters a culture of integrity.

Business Ethics

Q. A reputed food product company based in India developed a food product for the international market and started exporting the same after getting necessary approvals. The company announced this achievement and also indicated that soon the product will be made available for the domestic consumers with almost the same quality and health benefits. Accordingly, the company got its product approved by the domestic competent authority and launched the product in the Indian market. The company could increase its market share over a period of time and earn substantial profit both domestically and internationally. However, the random sample test conducted by the inspection team found the product being sold domestically in variance with the approval obtained from the competent authority. On further investigation, it was also discovered that the food company was not only selling products which were not meeting the health standard of the country but also selling the rejected export products in the domestic market. This episode adversely affected the reputation and profitability of the food company.

(a) What action do you visualize should be taken by the competent authority against the food company for violating the laid down domestic food standard and selling rejected export products in domestic market?

(b) What course of action is available with the food company to resolve the crisis and bring back its lost reputation?

(c) Examine the ethical dilemma involved in the case. (UPSC 2021)

The food company's violation of domestic food standards and selling rejected export products in the domestic market has resulted in damage to its reputation and profitability.

Stakeholders

- **Food Company:** Responsible for product quality and safety.
- **Competent Authority:** Ensures food safety through regulations and inspections.
- **Consumers:** Rely on safe and healthy food products.
- **Retailers:** Sell food products and are accountable for their quality.
- **International Market: Impacted** by the company's reputation and potential trade restrictions.

Violation of Legislations

The food product company's actions in this case study potentially contravened several key legislative provisions in India:

1. Food Safety and Standards Act, 2006 (FSS Act):

- **Section 2(1)(ad): Adulteration:** This section defines "adulteration" as the addition or subtraction of any substance to a food product that alters its nature, substance, or quality, making it detrimental to health. Selling a domestic product that does not meet the approved standards could be construed as adulteration under this provision.
- **Section 2(1)(fa): Misbranding:** The Act defines "misbranding" as labeling or presenting a food product in a way that is false, misleading, or deceptive. If the domestic product's labeling or marketing claims mirrored the export product's benefits while not meeting the same quality standards, this section could be invoked.
- **Section 26 & 27(2): Sale of Prohibited or Banned Food:** These sections specifically prohibit the sale of food products containing ingredients banned in India or deemed unfit for human consumption. If the rejected export products contained such ingredients or were otherwise unfit for consumption, selling them domestically would be a clear violation. Section 27(2) empowers authorities to seize and dispose of such products to protect public health.
- **Section 54:** This section provides the competent authority with the power to order the recall of food products if they are found to be unsafe or violate the FSS Act provisions. In this scenario, the substandard domestic product would likely be subject to a mandatory recall.

2. The Consumer Protection Act, 2019:

- **Section 2(1)(d): Unfair Trade Practice:** This section defines unfair trade practices as acts that mislead or exploit consumers. Selling a product significantly different from its advertised quality or failing to disclose its limitations constitutes an unfair trade practice. The significant discrepancy between the advertised and actual quality of the domestic product falls under this category.
- **Section 12:** This section empowers the Consumer Protection Authority to issue orders for product recall, refund, and compensation to consumers who have been affected by unfair trade practices. The affected consumers could potentially seek redressal under this provision.:
- Criminal charges could be pursued under the Indian Penal Code (IPC) for endangering public health (Sections 270 - 276).

Values compromised by the company

- **Public Health and Safety:** The company's actions prioritized profit over the well-being of consumers by knowingly distributing a product that did not meet safety standards.
- **Consumer Trust and Confidence:** Deliberately misleading consumers about the quality and safety of the domestic product eroded trust in the brand and the marketplace as a whole.
- **Transparency and Accountability:** The company failed to disclose the discrepancies between the export and domestic products, demonstrating a lack of transparency and accountability to stakeholders.
- **Business Ethics and Fairness:** The company's actions violated ethical business principles by prioritizing short-term gains over long-term brand sustainability and fair treatment of consumers.

Values Upheld by Regulatory Bodies:

- **Consumer Protection:** The primary function of regulatory bodies in this case is to ensure consumer safety and fair market practices by enforcing food safety regulations.
- **Public Health Responsibility:** Taking action against the company safeguards public health by prioritizing the well-being of citizens and preventing the circulation of potentially harmful products.
- **Enforcement and Accountability:** Enforcing food safety regulations ensures that businesses are held accountable for the quality and safety of their products, promoting responsible manufacturing practices.

Consumer Expectations of Businesses:

- **Product Quality and Safety:** Consumers have a fundamental right to expect safe and high-quality products that meet advertised standards and regulatory requirements.
- **Ethical Business Practices:** Consumers value companies that operate with integrity, transparency, and a commitment to responsible production and consumer well-being.
- **Transparency and Honesty:** Open communication regarding product information, potential risks, and production processes fosters trust and builds stronger relationships between consumers and businesses.

(a) Actions by the competent authority against the food company:

- Imposing fines, penalties, or legal consequences for violating domestic food standards.
- Conducting a thorough investigation to ensure consumer safety and prevent future incidents.
- Potential product recall or suspension of the company's license.

(b) Actions by the food company to resolve the crisis and regain reputation:

- Recall and replace non-compliant and rejected products from the market.

- Apologize to consumers and stakeholders for the quality control lapse.
- Conduct an internal review to identify and rectify quality control issues.
- Improve communication and transparency with consumers.
- Implement stricter quality control measures to comply with standards and regain trust

(c) Ethical dilemmas:

- **Prioritizing Profit over Consumer Safety:** The company's decision to sell substandard products compromised the health and well-being of consumers, creating a conflict between profit maximization and ethical responsibility towards public safety.
- **Deception vs. Transparency:** The company's actions involved misrepresenting the quality of the domestic product through labeling and marketing, reflecting a lack of transparency and honesty in their dealings with consumers.
- **Short-Term Gains vs. Long-Term Sustainability:** The company's focus on short-term profit by selling non-compliant products undermined the long-term sustainability of their business model, which relies on consumer trust and brand reputation. This dilemma highlights the need to balance immediate gains with ethical practices for long-term success.
- **Protecting Public Interest vs. Corporate Interests:** The company prioritized its own interests over the public interest by disregarding consumer well-being. This raises questions about the ethical responsibility of corporations to prioritize the safety and well-being of the communities they serve.
- **Restoring Trust vs. Accountability:** Regaining consumer trust requires the company to demonstrate accountability for its actions. This involves taking corrective measures, rebuilding trust through transparency, and prioritizing responsible business practices.

Reclaiming Trust: A Path Forward for the Food Product Company

The food product company's recent actions have resulted in a significant breach of consumer trust and a potential public health risk. To navigate this crisis and ensure long-term sustainability, a multi-pronged approach is necessary.

Immediate Damage Control:

- **Product Recall and Public Apology:** A comprehensive recall of all non-compliant products from the domestic market must be initiated promptly. This should synchronize with a sincere public apology acknowledging the lapse in judgment and expressing a firm commitment to regaining consumer confidence.
- **Internal Investigation and Regulatory Compliance Review:** A comprehensive internal investigation is crucial to identify the root causes of the violation and prevent future occurrences. Additionally, a thorough review of all product lines, both domestic and international, is necessary to ensure strict adherence to regulatory requirements and quality standards.
- **Enhanced Quality Control Measures:** Implementing robust and independent quality control measures throughout the production process is essential. This includes strengthening internal protocols and potentially engaging third-party auditors for verification.

Restoring Public Trust and Brand Reputation:

- **Transparency and Communication:** Open and honest communication with consumers is paramount. Detailed information regarding the product recall, corrective actions being taken, and changes in quality control procedures should be readily available.
- **Improved Product Labeling:** Consumers rely on accurate labeling for informed purchasing decisions. A complete review and revision of product labels to ensure they precisely reflect the contents and comply with all regulatory requirements is essential.
- **Customer Service and Engagement:** Building trust necessitates a strengthened customer service infrastructure. Dedicated channels for addressing consumer concerns and providing timely feedback mechanisms are crucial.
- **Building Brand Loyalty:** Rebuilding brand loyalty takes time and commitment. The company must focus on offering genuine value to consumers through high-quality products, ethical sourcing practices, and exceptional customer service.

Long-Term Sustainability and Ethical Practices:

- **Embedding Ethical Values:** Ethical considerations must become core tenets of the company's value system and decision-making processes. Developing a robust corporate social responsibility (CSR) program that prioritizes consumer well-being and ethical sourcing demonstrates genuine commitment.
- **Supply Chain Management:** Strengthening supply chain management practices ensures the quality and safety of ingredients throughout the production chain. Implementing rigorous supplier selection processes, quality control checks, and transparent traceability mechanisms are essential.

- **Employee Training and Education:** Ongoing training for employees on food safety regulations, ethical conduct, and responsible manufacturing practices fosters a culture of accountability and compliance within the organization.

Regulatory Action

- **Fines and Penalties:** The competent authority should impose appropriate financial penalties on the company to deter future violations and serve as a deterrent to others in the industry.
- **Enhanced Regulatory Framework:** A comprehensive review of existing food safety regulations and enforcement mechanisms may be necessary to address any identified weaknesses and prevent similar incidents in the future.

Conclusion

By taking these steps and demonstrating a sustained commitment to ethical business practices and consumer safety, the company can navigate this crisis and rebuild trust with stakeholders. Regulatory bodies also play a crucial role in enforcing food safety regulations and holding companies accountable for their actions. Ultimately, this case serves as a stark reminder of the importance of prioritizing ethical behavior and consumer well-being for long-term business success.

Negligence

Q. An elevated corridor is being constructed to reduce traffic congestion in the capital of a particular State. You have been selected as project manager of this prestigious project on your professional competence and experience. The deadline is to complete the project in the next two years by 30 June 2021, since this project is to be inaugurated by the Chief Minister before the elections are announced in the second week of July 2021. While carrying out the surprise inspection by the inspection team, a minor crack was noticed in one of the piers of the elevated corridor possibly due to poor material used. You immediately informed the chief engineer and stopped further work. It was assessed by you that a minimum three piers of the elevated corridor have to be demolished and reconstructed. But this process will delay the project minimum by four to six months. But the chief engineer overruled the observation of the inspection team on the ground that it was a minor crack which will not in any way impact the strength and durability of the bridge. He ordered you to overlook the observation of the inspecting team and continue working with the same speed and tempo. He informed you that the minister does not want any delay as he wants the Chief Minister to inaugurate the elevated corridor before the elections are declared. Also informed you that the contractor is a distant relative of the minister and he wants him to finish the project. He also gave you a hint that your further promotion as additional chief engineer is under consideration with the ministry. However, you strongly felt that the minor crack in the pier of the elevated corridor will adversely affect the health and life of the bridge and therefore it will be very dangerous not to repair the elevated corridor.

(a) Under the given conditions, what are the options available to you as a project manager?

(b) What are the ethical dilemmas being faced by the project manager?

(c) What are the professional challenges likely to be faced by the project manager and his response to overcome such challenges?

(d) What can be the consequences of overlooking the observation raised by the inspecting team? (UPSC 2021)

Context

In this case study, the project manager faces an ethical dilemma when a minor crack is noticed in one of the piers of an elevated corridor under construction. The chief engineer, driven by political pressure and personal interests, orders the manager to overlook the crack and continue working at the same speed. The project manager strongly believes that the crack will adversely affect the bridge's health and safety.

Stakeholders

- **Project Manager:** You, the professional responsible for overseeing the project's successful completion.
- **Chief Engineer:** Your superior who oversees the project's overall engineering aspects.
- **Inspection Team:** The team responsible for identifying any construction flaws or safety concerns.
- **Minister:** A government official with political influence over the project.
- **Contractor:** The company responsible for building the elevated corridor, potentially related to the minister.

- **Chief Minister:** The leader of the state government who is expected to inaugurate the project.
- **Public:** The citizens who will ultimately benefit from the reduced traffic congestion

Values Involved

- **Public Safety:** Ensuring the well-being of citizens by prioritizing bridge safety.
- **Professional Integrity:** Upholding ethical standards and prioritizing safety over personal gain.
- **Accountability:** Taking responsibility for project decisions and potential consequences.
- **Transparency:** Communicating safety concerns openly and honestly.
- **Sustainability:** Building infrastructure for long-term use and public benefit.

Violation of the Legislations

- **Construction Safety Standards:** Public Works Contract Acts or National Building Codes may be breached by neglecting the crack.
- **Negligence:** Indian Penal Code (IPC) Section 287 could apply if bridge failure due to the ignored crack causes harm.
- **Engineering Ethics:** Professional codes emphasizing public safety might be violated.
- **Environmental Impact:** Depending on the project, EIA regulations could be a concern.

(a) Options available to the project manager:

- **Adhere to Superior's Directive:** Proceed with construction as instructed by the Chief Engineer, ensuring clear documentation of the identified crack and any concerns raised.
- **Emphasize Structural Integrity:** Advocate for proper repair or reconstruction of the piers to guarantee the long-term safety and durability of the elevated corridor.
- **Solicit External Review:** Seek guidance from higher authorities within the engineering department or engage an independent engineering body to conduct a thorough evaluation of the situation.
- **Escalate to Highest Authority:** If necessary, communicate the identified crack and potential risks directly to the Chief Minister, seeking their approval for essential repairs before continuing construction.
- **Explore Expedited Repair Solutions:** Collaborate with the inspection team and other technical experts to identify and implement alternative repair methods that minimize project delays while adequately addressing the structural concerns.

(B) Ethical dilemmas faced by the project manager:

- **Safety vs. Expediency:** Prioritizing the safety of future users of the bridge over achieving a politically motivated deadline and potential career advancement.
- **Integrity vs. Pressure:** Making decisions based on objective safety concerns rather than succumbing to the influence of the minister and contractor with vested interests.
- **Public Interest vs. Authority:** Upholding the well-being of the public, even if it requires challenging the directives of a superior who prioritizes political agendas.
- **Accountability vs. Personal Risk:** Taking responsibility for decisions that ensure safety and avoiding potential legal and personal consequences associated with negligence.
- **Short-Term Goals vs. Long-Term Impact:** Weighing the short-term gain of completing the project on time against the long-term risk of a bridge failure due to a compromised structure.

(C) Professional Challenges and Responses for the Project Manager:

1. **Conveying Safety Concerns:**

- **Challenge:** Persuading the Chief Engineer and higher authorities to prioritize safety over deadlines.
- **Response:** Clearly articulate the potential risks associated with the crack, using data from the inspection report and potentially engaging additional experts for a stronger technical argument.

2. **Building a Strong Case:**

- **Challenge:** Demonstrating the necessity of repairs while addressing concerns about delays.
- **Response:** Gather additional evidence through further inspections, collect technical data, and consult with independent engineers to solidify the case for reconstruction.

3. **Negotiating with Stakeholders:**

- **Challenge:** Finding solutions that address safety without jeopardizing the minister and contractor's interests.
- **Response:** Explore alternative repair methods that minimize delay, demonstrate the long-term cost implications of neglecting the crack, and propose a revised timeline that balances safety and efficiency.

4. **Seeking External Support:**

- **Challenge:** Finding allies and resources beyond the immediate project team.

- **Response:** Reach out to professional engineering associations, regulatory bodies, or independent experts who can lend credibility and pressure to uphold safety standards.

5. Maintaining Transparency:

- **Challenge:** Documenting actions to protect yourself from potential accusations of negligence.
- **Response:** Maintain thorough records of all communications, decisions, inspections, and consultations to demonstrate due diligence and commitment to professional integrity.

(d) **Consequences of overlooking the observation raised by the inspecting team:**

- **Elevated Safety Risks:** Failure to address the identified crack significantly increases the likelihood of structural failure or accidents, posing a direct threat to the safety of future users.
- **Potential Reputational Harm:** Overlooking such a critical observation could lead to significant reputational damage for the project manager, the college, and the government, jeopardizing their commitment to upholding safety standards.
- **Legal and Financial Exposure:** Ignoring the inspection team's findings exposes all parties involved to potential legal repercussions and financial liabilities if structural issues arise due to the neglected crack.
- **Erosion of Public Trust:** Prioritizing expediency over safety can erode public confidence in the project and the responsible authorities. Transparency and addressing safety concerns are paramount in maintaining public trust.
- **Increased Long-Term Costs:** Addressing the crack during construction allows for a more cost-effective and less disruptive repair. Postponing the necessary work may necessitate resorting to expensive retrofitting solutions later.

In this ethically fraught situation, the project manager faces a stark choice: prioritize a potentially unsafe bridge for political gain or uphold public safety. Choosing the latter, though challenging, ensures quality public service delivery. By prioritizing long-term structural integrity over short-term deadlines, the project manager safeguards future users and exemplifies ethical infrastructure development. This commitment to quality fosters public trust and strengthens the foundation for reliable public services.

Sexual Harassment at Workplace

Q. An apparel manufacturing company having a large number of women employees was losing sales due to various factors. The company hired a reputed marketing executive, who increased the volume of sales within a short span of time. However, some unconfirmed reports came up regarding his indulgence in sexual harassment at the work place. After sometime, a woman employee lodged a formal complaint to the management against the marketing executive about sexually harassing her. Faced with the company's indifference in not taking cognizance of her grievance, she lodged an FIR with the Police. Realizing the sensitivity and gravity of the situation, the company called the women employee to negotiate. In that she was offered a hefty sum of money to withdraw the complaint and the FIR and also give in writing that the marketing executive is not involved in this case.
Identify the ethical issues involved in this case. What options are available to the women employee? (UPSC 2019)

Context

The case study involves an apparel manufacturing company that hired a marketing executive **who increased sales (boost revenue and higher performance) but was later accused of sexual harassment**. The ethical issues involved include sexual harassment in the workplace, failure of the company to address the complaint, offering a bribe to the victim, and attempting to cover up the incident.

Violation of Laws

- **The Sexual Harassment of Women at Workplace (Prevention, Prohibition and Redressal) Act, 2013:** This act defines sexual harassment and mandates every workplace to have an ICC for addressing complaints. The company's inaction violates this act.
- **Indian Penal Code (IPC):** Sections like 354 (outraging modesty), 506 (criminal intimidation) or even 376 (rape) might be applicable.

Major Stakeholders Involved

- **Employee:** Female employee who experienced sexual harassment.
- **Marketer:** Marketing executive accused of sexual harassment.
- **Company:** Apparel manufacturing company itself.

- **Other Employees:** The remaining female employees potentially working in an unsafe environment.

Ethical Issues in the Apparel Company Case:

1. **Sexual Harassment:** The core ethical violation lies in the marketing executive's alleged sexual harassment of the female employee, creating a **hostile work environment**.
2. **Power Imbalance:** The company's initial indifference to the employee's complaint highlights a **power imbalance**. This could lead to intimidation and discourage other employees from reporting harassment.
3. **Silencing the Victim:** The proposed settlement with a non-disclosure clause attempts to silence the victim and potentially prevent future complaints from occurring.
4. **Prioritizing profits over safety:** The company prioritizes **sales figures over employee's rights and safety** by initially ignoring the reports and later offering a hefty sum to hush up the issue.
5. **Lack of due diligence:** The company fails to conduct proper investigations into the unconfirmed reports before hiring the marketing executive.
6. **Obstruction of Justice:** The company's attempt to negotiate a settlement that involves the withdrawal of the FIR suggests **potential obstruction of justice**.
7. **Neglect of Internal Mechanisms:** The company doesn't appear to have used or promoted the mandated Internal Complaints Committee (ICC) for addressing sexual harassment complaints within the organization.
8. **Hostile Work Environment:** The company's inaction fosters a work environment where sexual harassment might be tolerated, impacting the morale and safety of all female employees.

Values Involved:

- **Safety:** All employees have the right to a safe and healthy work environment free from harassment and intimidation.
- **Respect:** Every employee deserves to be treated with dignity and respect, regardless of gender.
- **Equality:** All employees should have equal opportunities and be protected from discrimination or harassment.
- **Transparency:** Companies should be transparent in their handling of complaints and investigations.
- **Accountability:** Both the perpetrator and the company should be held accountable for their actions.
- **Justice:** The woman employee deserves a fair and impartial investigation and appropriate legal recourse.
- **Integrity:** Companies should act ethically and prioritize employee well-being over financial gain.

Options for the Woman Employee:

- **Pursue Legal Action:** Continue with the FIR and legal proceedings to hold the perpetrator accountable.
- **Seek External Support:** Reach out to advocacy groups specializing in sexual harassment cases for guidance, resources, and legal assistance.
- **Report to Higher Authorities:** Escalate the situation to labor commissions or government agencies responsible for workplace safety and gender equality.
- **Consult an Attorney:** Seek legal advice from an employment law specialist to understand her rights, options, and potential legal recourse.
- **Document Evidence:** Gather evidence like emails, messages, or witness testimonies to support her claims and strengthen her case.
- **Seek Emotional Support:** Connect with friends, family, or support groups for emotional well-being throughout the process.
- **Consider Alternative Resolutions:** Depending on her preferences, explore alternative methods like mediation or arbitration to address the issue outside of court.
- **Internal Complaint Mechanism:** (Optional) If comfortable, utilize the company's Internal Complaints Committee (ICC) for an internal investigation, following the SHARP Act guidelines.

Way forward for the Company:

1. **Prioritize the Complaint:** Acknowledge the severity of the issue and treat the woman's complaint with the utmost seriousness.
2. **Conduct a Fair Investigation:** Launch a thorough and impartial investigation into the alleged harassment, involving qualified and unbiased individuals.
3. **Support and Protect the Employee:** Ensure the employee's safety and well-being throughout the process. Maintain confidentiality, offer access to counseling, and provide any necessary support.
4. **Legal Compliance:** Adhere to all legal requirements concerning sexual harassment cases. This includes following reporting protocols, conducting investigations according to the law, and providing appropriate remedies.

Conclusion

Gandhiji said that **"commerce without morality"** was one of the seven deadly sins. So, it's not just an individual's fault, but also a company's fault if they lack values like respect for women, ethical work practices and equal opportunities for everyone.

NOTES

NOTES

NOTES